CW01203181

Harmonizing Global Efforts in Meeting Sustainable Development Goals

Ali Gökhan Gölçek
Niğde Ömer Halisdemir University, Turkey

Şeyda Güdek-Gölçek
Niğde Ömer Halisdemir University, Turkey

IGI Global
PUBLISHER of TIMELY KNOWLEDGE

A volume in the Advances in Human Services and Public Health (AHSPH) Book Series

Published in the United States of America by
IGI Global
Information Science Reference (an imprint of IGI Global)
701 E. Chocolate Avenue
Hershey PA, USA 17033
Tel: 717-533-8845
Fax: 717-533-8661
E-mail: cust@igi-global.com
Web site: http://www.igi-global.com

Copyright © 2024 by IGI Global. All rights reserved. No part of this publication may be reproduced, stored or distributed in any form or by any means, electronic or mechanical, including photocopying, without written permission from the publisher. Product or company names used in this set are for identification purposes only. Inclusion of the names of the products or companies does not indicate a claim of ownership by IGI Global of the trademark or registered trademark.
Library of Congress Cataloging-in-Publication Data

CIP Pending

Harmonizing Global Efforts in Meeting Sustainable Development Goals
Ali Gökhan Gölçek, Şeyda Güdek-Gölçek
2024 Information Science Reference

ISBN: 979-8-3693-2758-6
eISBN: 979-8-3693-2759-3

This book is published in the IGI Global book series Advances in Human Services and Public Health (AHSPH) (ISSN: 2475-6571; eISSN: 2475-658X)

British Cataloguing in Publication Data
A Cataloguing in Publication record for this book is available from the British Library.

All work contributed to this book is new, previously-unpublished material. The views expressed in this book are those of the authors, but not necessarily of the publisher.

For electronic access to this publication, please contact: eresources@igi-global.com.

Advances in Human Services and Public Health (AHSPH) Book Series

Jennifer Martin
RMIT University, Australia

ISSN:2475-6571
EISSN:2475-658X

Mission

The well-being of the general public should be a primary concern for any modern civilization. Ongoing research in the field of human services and public healthcare is necessary to evaluate, manage, and respond to the health and social needs of the global population.

The **Advances in Human Services and Public Health (AHSPH)** book series aims to publish high-quality reference publications focused on the latest methodologies, tools, issues, and strategies for managing the health and social welfare of the public. The AHSPH book series will be especially relevant for healthcare professionals, policy makers, government officials, and students seeking the latest research in this field.

Coverage

- Medicare and Medicaid
- Health Policy
- Domestic Violence
- Public Welfare
- Public Funding
- Youth Development
- Healthcare Reform
- Social Work
- Access to Healthcare Services
- Poverty

IGI Global is currently accepting manuscripts for publication within this series. To submit a proposal for a volume in this series, please contact our Acquisition Editors at Acquisitions@igi-global.com or visit: http://www.igi-global.com/publish/.

The Advances in Human Services and Public Health (AHSPH) Book Series (ISSN 2475-6571) is published by IGI Global, 701 E. Chocolate Avenue, Hershey, PA 17033-1240, USA, www.igi-global.com. This series is composed of titles available for purchase individually; each title is edited to be contextually exclusive from any other title within the series. For pricing and ordering information please visit http://www.igi-global.com/book-series/advances-human-services-public-health/102256. Postmaster: Send all address changes to above address. Copyright © 2024 IGI Global. All rights, including translation in other languages reserved by the publisher. No part of this series may be reproduced or used in any form or by any means – graphics, electronic, or mechanical, including photocopying, recording, taping, or information and retrieval systems – without written permission from the publisher, except for non commercial, educational use, including classroom teaching purposes. The views expressed in this series are those of the authors, but not necessarily of IGI Global.

Titles in this Series

For a list of additional titles in this series, please visit: http://www.igi-global.com/book-series/advances-human-services-public-health/102256

Challenges, Strategies, and Resiliency in Disaster and Risk Management
Zamokuhle Mbandlwa (Durban University of Technology, South Africa)
Information Science Reference • copyright 2024 • 361pp • H/C (ISBN: 9798369327210) • US $255.00 (our price)

Examining Corruption and the Sustainable Development Goals
Ibrahim Nandom Yakubu (University for Development Studies, Ghana)
Business Science Reference • copyright 2024 • 334pp • H/C (ISBN: 9798369321010) • US $255.00 (our price)

Analyzing Global Responses to Contemporary Regional Conflicts
Piotr Pietrzak (Sofia University, Bulgaria)
Information Science Reference • copyright 2024 • 395pp • H/C (ISBN: 9798369328378) • US $245.00 (our price)

Dealing With Regional Conflicts of Global Importance
Piotr Pietrzak (Sofia University, Bulgaria)
Information Science Reference • copyright 2024 • 411pp • H/C (ISBN: 9781668494677) • US $215.00 (our price)

The Role of Health Literacy in Major Healthcare Crises
Vassilios Papalois (Royal Berkshire Hospital NHS Foundation Trust, UK) and Kyriaki Papalois (Royal Berkshire Hospital NHS Foundation Trust, UK)
Information Science Reference • copyright 2024 • 326pp • H/C (ISBN: 9781799896524) • US $235.00 (our price)

Ecological and Evolutionary Perspectives on Infections and Morbidity
P.A. Azeez (Salim Ali Centre for Ornithology and Natural History, Coimbatore, India) P.P. Nikhil Raj (Amrita School of Engineering, Amrita Vishwa Vidyapeetham, India) and R. Mohanraj (Bharathidasan University, India)
Medical Information Science Reference • copyright 2023 • 331pp • H/C (ISBN: 9781799894148) • US $325.00 (our price)

Transformation and Efficiency Enhancement of Public Utilities Systems Multidimensional Aspects and Perspectives
Jordan Gjorchev (International Slavic University, North Macedonia) Samoil Malcheski (International Slavic University, North Macedonia) Tamara Rađenović (University of Niš, Serbia) Dejan Vasović (University of Niš, Serbia) and Snežana Živković (University of Niš, Serbia)
Information Science Reference • copyright 2023 • 457pp • H/C (ISBN: 9781668477304) • US $215.00 (our price)

IGI Global
PUBLISHER of TIMELY KNOWLEDGE

701 East Chocolate Avenue, Hershey, PA 17033, USA
Tel: 717-533-8845 x100 • Fax: 717-533-8661
E-Mail: cust@igi-global.com • www.igi-global.com

Table of Contents

Preface xii

Acknowledgment xv

Chapter 1
Orchestrating Change: The United Nations' Role in Harmonizing Sustainable Development With
Global Governance 1
    Şeyda Güdek-Gölçek, Niğde Ömer Halisdemir University, Turkey

Chapter 2
Sisyphean Goal: Sustainable Development 17
    Sureyya Yigit, New Vision University, Georgia

Chapter 3
The Other Face of Those Left Behind in the Silence of the Sustainable Development Goals
(SDGs): A Global Analysis of SDG Discontent Geography 39
    Isidore E. Agbokou, Centre d'Etudes Diplomatiques et Stratégiques de Paris (CEDS), France

Chapter 4
Sustainable Development: An Unhappy Consciousness... 75
    Parimal Kumar Roy, Bangladesh Public Administration Training Centre, Bangladesh

Chapter 5
Taxing Tomorrow: Eco-Fiscal Dynamics for Sustainable Development.................................. 92
    Ali Gökhan Gölçek, Niğde Ömer Halisdemir University, Turkey

Chapter 6
Advancing Sustainable Development Goals (SDGs) Through Public-Private Partnerships (PPPs) .. 119
    Siriyama Kanthi Herath, Clark Atlanta University, USA
    Laksitha Maheshi Herath, New York University, USA
    Marlissa Jones Phillips, Clark Atlanta University, USA

Chapter 7
Role of Public-Private Partnership Under China's BRI Framework of Sustainable Development in
Central and Eastern Europe 146
    Mukesh Shankar Bharti, Amity University, India
    Yogendra Singh, Amity University, India

Chapter 8
Assessment of Critical Raw Materials by Addressing Sustainable Development Goals Using
Fuzzy MCDM Approach 164
    Elifcan Göçmen-Polat, Munzur University, Turkey

Chapter 9
Analysing the Role and Contribution of Tourism in Achieving Sustainable Development Goals 182
    Pramendra Singh, Lovely Professional University, India
    Manisha Seal, Jyoti Nivas College (Autonomous), India
    Disha Sharma, Amity University, Raipur, India

Chapter 10
Moving Sustainable Development Goals (SDG-5) Forward: Challenges, Enablers, and Policy
Implications for Mumpreneurs in Developing Countries 196
    Nurul Hidayana Mohd Noor, Faculty of Administrative Science and Policy Studies,
        Universiti Teknologi MARA, Malaysia
    Noralina Omar, Department of Social Justice and Administration, Universiti Malaya,
        Malaysia

Chapter 11
Harnessing Competition Law and Policy for Achieving Sustainable Development Goals: The
Chinese Experience 223
    Mohamad Zreik, Sun Yat-sen University, China

Compilation of References 240

About the Contributors 273

Index 276

Detailed Table of Contents

Preface xii

Acknowledgment xv

Chapter 1
Orchestrating Change: The United Nations' Role in Harmonizing Sustainable Development With
Global Governance 1
   Şeyda Güdek-Gölçek, Niğde Ömer Halisdemir University, Turkey

This chapter delves into the UN's orchestrating role in aligning sustainable development with global governance via the SDGs. It traces the evolution from Agenda 21 to the SDGs' 2015 adoption, showcasing the inclusive process and wide stakeholder consensus. The analysis covers the UN's success in mobilizing stakeholders, promoting partnerships, and embedding the SDGs in policy frameworks, while addressing the challenges like their non-binding nature, state disparities, and complex actor coordination. Recommendations include enhancing SDGs' legal frameworks, boosting support for developing nations, and strengthening monitoring and accountability. Highlighting the need to tackle inequalities, raise awareness, and adapt to new challenges, the chapter affirms the UN's essential role in steering global governance towards sustainable development, offering strategies to navigate the SDGs' complexities and enhance their implementation.

Chapter 2
Sisyphean Goal: Sustainable Development 17
   Sureyya Yigit, New Vision University, Georgia

Intact and functional ecosystems are habitats for people, animals, and plants form the natural basis of humanity's existence. Ecosystems provide food, building materials, energy sources, and active ingredients for medicines. They regulate the climate, form humus in the soil, and are important for nutrient cycles and clean drinking water. Therefore, preserving biodiversity is important for the nutrition and economic, social, and cultural development of current and future generations. This chapter investigates the planet's challenges in maintaining an environmental balance.

Chapter 3
The Other Face of Those Left Behind in the Silence of the Sustainable Development Goals
(SDGs): A Global Analysis of SDG Discontent Geography 39
Isidore E. Agbokou, Centre d'Etudes Diplomatiques et Stratégiques de Paris (CEDS), France

This chapter identified the factors that could justify the growing social inequalities and reduce possible threats of discontent that may arise among disadvantaged groups across the world. The research has been conducted based on data provided by the VNR reported by the HLPF from 2016 to 2021. The number of actions implemented to comply with the principle of LNOB and the number of SDGs affected by the actions implemented at the country and regional levels are the two parameters that support the analysis which led to the conclusion of the potential pockets of discontent. Since 2016, a total of 143 countries have committed, with 605 actions for the implementation of the LNOB principle. The chapter revealed that people from all around the world have expressed a desire to move towards a more equal world of sustainable development. Nevertheless, some regions of the globe have shown more commitment and determination than others since the movement of LNOB was born. The risk of delay is that the need for managing conflicts will only grow from frustration and discontent.

Chapter 4
Sustainable Development: An Unhappy Consciousness.. 75
Parimal Kumar Roy, Bangladesh Public Administration Training Centre, Bangladesh

This chapter discusses sustainable development as an unhappy consciousness and suggests ratifying the development process in Bangladesh. To the author, sustainable development has been an imperfect coupling word in the context of the ethnic groups of Bangladesh; now, this chapter analysed sustainable development through customs, income disparity, and social justice, availing Amartya Sen's 'capability approach' to propose a framework for the inclusion community. Customary law is a sound and sustainable way to maintain social justice to ensure a sustainable community. Human behaviour, culture, attitudes, nature, supernatural power, values, norms, and traditions are all interlinked with growth and development in a country. Methodologically, it followed the ethnographic design and qualitative approach aligned with the post-positivism paradigm. This chapter suggests a sustainable community development framework as a policy recommendation and contextualizes global documents such as the SDGs, ILO 169, and UNDRIP to prioritize the lifeworld instead of the worldview.

Chapter 5
Taxing Tomorrow: Eco-Fiscal Dynamics for Sustainable Development... 92
Ali Gökhan Gölçek, Niğde Ömer Halisdemir University, Turkey

This chapter explores the role of ecological taxation in sustainable development, focusing on Uruguay and Chile's strategies. It discusses "taxing tomorrow," a concept that emphasizes using fiscal policies to preemptively address sustainability challenges by internalizing environmental costs. The analysis covers eco-fiscal policies like carbon taxes and congestion charges, demonstrating their impact on reducing environmental degradation and promoting sustainable behaviors. By comparing Uruguay and Chile, the chapter highlights how different approaches can reflect specific national contexts and contribute to achieving the United Nations' sustainable development goals (SDGs). This comparative insight underlines the importance of adaptable ecological taxes in global sustainability efforts, offering lessons on integrating these policies into broader economic and environmental strategies.

Chapter 6
Advancing Sustainable Development Goals (SDGs) Through Public-Private Partnerships (PPPs) .. 119
    Siriyama Kanthi Herath, Clark Atlanta University, USA
    Laksitha Maheshi Herath, New York University, USA
    Marlissa Jones Phillips, Clark Atlanta University, USA

This chapter discusses public-private partnerships (PPPs) and the role they play in sustainability development. It emphasizes the PPP's role in speeding up sustainable development using good governance, active participation across all stakeholder groups, and fulfilling legal and sector-specific standards and requirements. It offers a viewpoint on PPPs as crucial collaborative tools that promote sustainable development while encouraging the preservation of good governance, active stakeholder engagement, and adherence to ethical standards to guarantee their success. The contributions of PPPs to SDGs fulfillment are analyzed by secondary literature review and real case examples.

Chapter 7
Role of Public-Private Partnership Under China's BRI Framework of Sustainable Development in
Central and Eastern Europe 146
    Mukesh Shankar Bharti, Amity University, India
    Yogendra Singh, Amity University, India

This chapter aims to discuss the role of public-private partnership (PPP) under China's Belt and Road Initiative (BRI) in Central and Eastern European countries (CEECs) in the achievement of sustainable development goals. The purpose of this chapter is to explain more broadly major BRI-related sustainable development programs in CEE countries under the PPP model. Moreover, the neo-realist approach of study involved describing China's deeper trade and economic connectivity in this region under the BRI framework of the '17+1' cooperation. This chapter relies on a theoretical discussion of the soft power politics of China's successful connectivity in the CEE countries under the BRI projects. The role of the '17+1' framework of economic cooperation and PPP model in the infrastructural development under China's flagship economic project BRI relies on the qualitative approach to scientific study.

Chapter 8
Assessment of Critical Raw Materials by Addressing Sustainable Development Goals Using
Fuzzy MCDM Approach 164
    Elifcan Göçmen-Polat, Munzur University, Turkey

Critical raw materials (CRMs), constituting the first step of the industry, are vital to meet sustainable development. With increasing digital technology and green transition efforts under the scope of twin transformation, demand for CRMs has increased, and supply interruption is expected in the future. All countries should plan the supply chain of CRMs in the context of the green and digital transition. The sustainable development goals (SDGs) have presented a reference based on sustainability metrics. In the chapter, hesitant-fuzzy analytical hierarchy process-based order preference technique based on similarity to ideal solutions (HF-AHP based TOPSIS) has been developed to evaluate the critical raw materials in the context of sustainability. Most relevant goals with the CRMs are obtained as SDG 1, SDG 3, SDG 5, SDG 6, SDG 7, SDG 8, SDG 9, SDG 11, SDG 17. The findings show how raw materials have important strengths and weaknesses in sustainable development. Policies recommended for the most important CRMs are effective road maps in the context of twin transformation.

Chapter 9
Analysing the Role and Contribution of Tourism in Achieving Sustainable Development Goals..... 182
 Pramendra Singh, Lovely Professional University, India
 Manisha Seal, Jyoti Nivas College (Autonomous), India
 Disha Sharma, Amity University, Raipur, India

This chapter examines tourism's role in achieving sustainable development goals (SDGs), analyzing its contributions across all seventeen goals. Through extensive literature review and report analysis, it explores how tourism catalyzes economic growth, job creation, poverty alleviation, and uplifts marginalized communities. The chapter highlights responsible tourism's potential for environmental sustainability, cultural understanding, peace, and tourism's impact on critical issues like gender equality, education, and health. It also investigates the role different stakeholders play to achieving these SDGs. By recognizing and maximizing tourism's contributions, stakeholders can collectively build a more equitable, resilient, and sustainable future. The descriptive chapter, based on secondary data and literature review, aims to deepen understanding of the tourism-SDG relationship, offering insights for researchers, academics, and industry professionals to maximize their interrelationship's benefits.

Chapter 10
Moving Sustainable Development Goals (SDG-5) Forward: Challenges, Enablers, and Policy Implications for Mumpreneurs in Developing Countries 196
 Nurul Hidayana Mohd Noor, Faculty of Administrative Science and Policy Studies,
  Universiti Teknologi MARA, Malaysia
 Noralina Omar, Department of Social Justice and Administration, Universiti Malaya,
  Malaysia

Sustainable entrepreneurship positively impacts the 2030 United Nations (UN) Agenda and Goal 5. The chapter aims to discover mumpreneurs' entrepreneurial challenges and enablers. Mumpreneurs are the key to economic growth, and without attention to the gender dimension in economic development, Malaysia is unlikely to achieve its growth targets. This chapter employed a qualitative research approach under the interpretive research paradigm. Using purposive sampling, 20 mumpreneurs were selected as key informants. The chapter found various entrepreneurial challenges, including lack of financial assistance, poor business location, poor customer management, weak marketing strategy, product delivery issues, poor management, and shift competition. The enablers identified are capital and aid, motivation, business skills, innovation, network, technology absorption, and business support. This chapter contributes to the literature on entrepreneurship in general and specifically to the literature on female entrepreneurs from the perspective of developing country economies.

Chapter 11
Harnessing Competition Law and Policy for Achieving Sustainable Development Goals: The Chinese Experience.. 223
 Mohamad Zreik, Sun Yat-sen University, China

This research focuses on China, exploring the relationship between competition law and sustainable development within the context of rapid economic growth. It specifically examines how China's competition law and policies interact with selected SDGs - SDG 8, 12, 13, and 16. The study employs a qualitative approach, incorporating a systematic review of literature, legislative actions, and empirical data. Key case studies were chosen based on their relevance to SDGs, impact on competition laws, and data availability. These cases provide insights into the successes and challenges of China's approach, highlighting the tension between fostering national industries and maintaining healthy competition. The study also examines how competition laws can contribute to societal objectives beyond economic growth. It connects China's legislative framework with real-world outcomes, identifying areas of alignment and disparity.

Compilation of References 240

About the Contributors 273

Index 276

Preface

Since the 1990s, sustainable development has become a central focus of the international policy agenda. Environmental issues such as the depletion of natural resources, loss of biodiversity, environmental pollution, and global warming have emerged as urgent problems that transcend national borders in terms of their consequences and the strategies needed to combat them. Economic globalization can turn national economic issues into international crises. Problems such as poverty, development challenges, international migration, and political instabilities affect the entire world. The distinction between high and low politics in international relations, the components of power, and the state's role as the primary actor are changing. Consequently, all these issues and the actors in international relations converge within the international sustainable development agenda.

International economic and social inequalities, environmental damages, and climate change necessitate embedding development within a sustainability vision. Combating poverty, ensuring access to basic needs, economic growth, social inclusion, reducing international inequalities, resolving political instabilities, and maintaining international peace are among the goals of sustainable development. While achieving these goals—meeting today's societal needs—we must also ensure we do not endanger the lives of future generations and our planet. This necessity makes sustainable development a global overarching goal.

The overarching goal of sustainable development is translated into specific objectives under the leadership of the United Nations. Institutionalized as the Sustainable Development Goals (SDGs), these objectives bring together international actors for a common future vision. This global alignment is not only a path for mutual benefit but also a necessity. All actors in international relations, from individuals to local actors, states to regional and international organizations, develop international partnerships for the SDGs. Public sector and private sector relations are structured and organized for the SDGs. Within the framework of global governance, the United Nations organizes cooperation areas, plans, and actions of actors to harmonize sustainable development efforts.

This book addresses the organization and harmonization of global efforts to achieve the SDGs. Aiming to provide a comprehensive approach that aligns with the content of the SDGs, this book sheds light on the evolving international policy agenda on sustainable development. It aims to present a framework for sustainable development through examples, cases, and areas from different regions. This framework encompasses best practices, contentious areas, strategies, actors, and challenges. Each chapter of the book contributes va"luably to the harmonization of global efforts.

Preface

ORGANIZATION OF THE BOOK

The first chapter discusses the United Nations' integration of sustainable development into global governance. It examines the UN's role as an orchestrator in aligning the actions, strategies, and activities of various actors to achieve the SDGs. This chapter covers the UN's success in mobilizing stakeholders, promoting partnerships, and embedding the SDGs into policy frameworks, while also addressing challenges such as the non-binding nature of the SDGs, differences among states, and the complexity of coordinating diverse actors. By highlighting the need to address inequalities, raise international awareness, and adapt to new challenges, this chapter demonstrates the UN's crucial role in steering global governance towards sustainable development. It also provides strategies to overcome the complexity of the SDGs and improve their implementation.

The second chapter focuses on environmental issues, one of the foremost global challenges today. It examines the difficulties the planet faces in maintaining environmental balance. The importance of preserving biodiversity for the nutrition, economic, social, and cultural development of current and future generations is emphasized. This chapter also highlights the challenges of combating environmental issues through a metaphorical narrative. Therefore, it calls for urgent political determination, international cooperation, institutionalized measures, and sustainable economies to protect our shared planet.

The third chapter examines inequalities among states and regions in achieving the SDGs. It analyzes the threats posed by increasing social inequalities and the potential dissatisfaction among disadvantaged groups worldwide. The focus is on the Leaves No One Behind initiative, adopted by 143 states, to prevent such threats in regions lagging behind in achieving the SDGs. The initiative is crucial for mitigating the risk of delay in disadvantaged regions, with some areas showing greater commitment and determination than others. This chapter reveals the global desire for progress towards a more equitable world of sustainable development.

The fourth chapter examines the interaction of sustainable development built on a global framework with the specific conditions of states, using Bangladesh as an example. It focuses on the impact of elements that construct a society's particular characteristics, such as ethnic structure, culture, values, and norms, on sustainable development. This chapter has shown that sustainable development has created an unhappy consciousness in Bangladesh. Utilizing Amartya Sen's "capability approach" through a post-positivist perspective, a framework for an inclusive community is proposed. As a policy recommendation, this chapter suggests a sustainable social development framework and contextualizes global documents such as the SDGs, ILO 169, and UNDRIP to contextualize the lifeworld over worldview.

The fifth chapter focuses on ecological taxation, which lies at the intersection of states' national borders and the globally impactful nature of environmental issues. The role of ecological taxes in sustainable development is examined through the strategies of Uruguay and Chile. Comparing Uruguay and Chile, this chapter highlights how different approaches can reflect specific national contexts and contribute to achieving the United Nations' SDGs. This comparative perspective underscores the importance of adaptable ecological taxes in global sustainability efforts and offers lessons to national and international actors on integrating these policies into broader economic and environmental strategies.

The sixth chapter addresses the role of public-private partnerships in sustainable development. Due to their cross-border economic activities and influence, private sector actors have become significant stakeholders in the sustainable development agenda. Public-private collaboration, promoted within the framework of global governance, plays a role in accelerating sustainable development through good governance, active participation of all stakeholder groups, and adherence to legal standards and requirements. While presenting public-private cooperation as crucial collaborative tools for promoting sustainable development, this chapter emphasizes the importance of maintaining good governance, active stakeholder participation, and commitment to ethical standards to ensure their success.

The seventh chapter discusses the role of public-private partnerships in achieving sustainable development goals in Central and Eastern European countries under China's Belt and Road Initiative (BRI). It examines the BRI-related sustainable development programs in these countries through the public-private partnership model, highlighting China's rising power and deeper commercial and economic connectivity in the region within the BRI framework. The study's neo-realist approach assesses China's success in creating connections in Central and Eastern European countries, grounding the discussion in theoretical perspectives on soft power policies.

The eighth chapter focuses on the vital importance of critical raw materials (CRMs) in meeting sustainable development goals. The sustainability vision has redirected the international agenda and state priorities to areas like raw materials that could pose future risks. The demand for CRMs has increased with the rise of digital technology and green transformation efforts within the scope of the twin transition, and supply disruptions are expected in the future. All countries must plan the supply chain of CRMs in the context of green and digital transitions. This chapter illustrates how CRMs, directly related to many SDGs, hold significant strengths and weaknesses in sustainable development. The policies proposed for the most crucial CRMs provide effective roadmaps in the context of the twin transition.

The ninth chapter examines the role of tourism, a part of international mobility influenced by economic, social, and political factors, in achieving all SDGs. It investigates how tourism catalyzes economic growth, job creation, poverty reduction, and revitalizes marginalized communities. This chapter emphasizes responsible tourism's impact on environmental sustainability, cultural understanding, peace, and critical issues such as gender equality, education, and health. It also discusses the roles of various stakeholders in achieving these SDGs, demonstrating how stakeholders can build a more equitable, resilient, and sustainable future by recognizing and maximizing tourism's contributions.

The tenth chapter addresses sustainable entrepreneurship, an important aspect of the United Nations' sustainable development agenda, from a gender perspective. The role of women in sustainable entrepreneurship is included in the UN's SDGs and the World Bank's poverty alleviation strategies through microcredit programs. This chapter examines the contributions of women entrepreneurs to development in developing countries, using Malaysia as a case study. It explores the challenges and facilitators faced by women entrepreneurs, influenced by gender norms. Thus, it provides national and international actors with a sustainable and inclusive development perspective from a gender standpoint.

The eleventh chapter focuses on China, which has attracted international attention with its development initiatives and rapid economic growth. The relationship between competition law and sustainable development is examined through relevant SDGs. This chapter provides insights into the successes and challenges of China's approach, highlighting the tension between promoting national industries and maintaining healthy international competition. By linking China's legal framework with real-world outcomes, it identifies areas of alignment and misalignment. Thus, it offers valuable insights into the global governance framework for sustainable development through a significant example.

Şeyda Güdek-Gölçek
Niğde Ömer Halisdemir University, Turkey

Ali Gökhan Gölçek
Niğde Ömer Halisdemir University, Turkey

Acknowledgment

We extend our deepest gratitude to all the authors whose contributions form the core of this book, *Harmonizing Global Efforts in Meeting Sustainable Development Goals*. Your insightful research and dedicated efforts have made this publication not only possible but profoundly impactful. Each chapter reflects a commitment to understanding and addressing the complex issues surrounding sustainable development, and for this, we are profoundly thankful.

Our sincere appreciation also goes to the referees who have played a crucial role in the editorial process. Your expertise, meticulous attention to detail, and constructive feedback have been indispensable in enhancing the quality and integrity of each contribution.

We are also grateful to the IGI Global team for their support throughout the publication process. Their professionalism and dedication have been crucial in bringing this project to fruition.

Lastly, we wish to acknowledge the collaborative spirit of everyone involved, which has been the cornerstone of this endeavor. This book is a testament to what can be achieved when diverse minds come together in a shared pursuit of knowledge and progress.

Thank you to everyone involved for your commitment and hard work, which have greatly contributed to the development of *Harmonizing Global Efforts in Meeting Sustainable Development Goals*.

Ali Gökhan Gölçek
Niğde Ömer Halisdemir University, Türkiye

Şeyda Güdek-Gölçek
Niğde Ömer Halisdemir University, Türkiye

Chapter 1
Orchestrating Change:
The United Nations' Role in Harmonizing Sustainable Development With Global Governance

Şeyda Güdek-Gölçek
https://orcid.org/0000-0001-8753-2998
Niğde Ömer Halisdemir University, Turkey

ABSTRACT

This chapter delves into the UN's orchestrating role in aligning sustainable development with global governance via the SDGs. It traces the evolution from Agenda 21 to the SDGs' 2015 adoption, showcasing the inclusive process and wide stakeholder consensus. The analysis covers the UN's success in mobilizing stakeholders, promoting partnerships, and embedding the SDGs in policy frameworks, while addressing the challenges like their non-binding nature, state disparities, and complex actor coordination. Recommendations include enhancing SDGs' legal frameworks, boosting support for developing nations, and strengthening monitoring and accountability. Highlighting the need to tackle inequalities, raise awareness, and adapt to new challenges, the chapter affirms the UN's essential role in steering global governance towards sustainable development, offering strategies to navigate the SDGs' complexities and enhance their implementation.

INTRODUCTION

Global governance separates the tools, content, and actors of governance, organizing them into areas of cooperation among national and international actors. In this respect, global governance demonstrates that governance beyond the nation-state is possible even without a supranational authority. It helps to regulate and justify norms and rules for the common good or global public goods in the international arena (Mulley, 2008; Green, 2012; Zürn, 2013). It paves the way for forming conventions in theory and solving problems and opening up areas of cooperation in practice for the common issues of the international community. Global governance constructs a field based on the coordination and partnership of actors to achieve common interests and goals.

Globalization and increasing environmental issues have made global governance a mandatory strategy for tackling international problems. The expansion and deepening of economic interdependence due to globalization are causing global economic crises (Odén, 2002). The permeability of national borders results in migration becoming a transnational issue, while environmental problems, especially the climate crisis, are inherently global in nature. Therefore, many socioeconomic and environmental issues have international connections in their solution strategies. For these reasons, global governance has increasingly occupied the international policy agenda since the 1990s to address and combat these transboundary issues (Weiss, 2000; Väyrynen, 2002). Under the leadership of international organizations, a global governance framework is being incorporated into international politics and strategies.

In theory and practice, the UN plays a significant role in global governance (Weiss, 2000). The UN transforms the field of global governance into a target-based mechanism within the framework of specific global goals. It sets these goals and sub-goals to direct the policies of actors towards these specific areas, organizing and coordinating efforts (Biermann, et al., 2017). In this regard, the UN takes on the role of an orchestrator in global governance studies. The primary theme of this role is international development. The UN began its orchestrating work in target-based global governance with the Millennium Development Goals (MDGs) adopted in 2000. It has further developed these goals with the Sustainable Development Goals (SDGs) adopted in 2015. The UN conducts activities to align the efforts of actors ranging from local to national, and regional to international, to achieve these goals.

This section focuses on the UN's target-based global governance efforts through the Sustainable Development Goals (SDGs). It examines the areas, actors, and strategies where these efforts are concentrated. The successes of the UN's orchestrator role in target-based global governance aimed at achieving the SDGs and the challenges encountered in fulfilling this role are assessed. Initially, the section provides a brief background on the process of incorporating the SDGs into global governance. Subsequently, the placement of target-based governance that has gained visibility with the SDGs and strategies for leveraging it are analyzed. This part is followed by a section evaluating the challenges the UN faces in target-based global governance. The importance of this chapter lies in shedding light on the function of the SDGs in combating global issues, especially environmental issues, which are becoming increasingly significant. Ultimately, the aim is to present policy recommendations related to the UN's efforts in combating global issues and achieving the SDGs.

BACKGROUND

The UN's target-based global governance initiatives began in 1992 with Agenda 21, adopted at the Earth Summit, also known as the United Nations Conference on Environment and Development (UNCED). Agenda 21 is a comprehensive action plan involving organizations within the UN system, governments, and major groups, addressing all areas affected by human interaction with the environment. It was adopted by more than 178 governments at the United Nations Conference on Environment and Development held in Rio de Janeiro, Brazil, from June 3-14, 1992, along with the Rio Declaration on Environment and Development and the Statement of Principles for the Sustainable Management of Forests (UN, 1992a).

Agenda 21 emphasizes the integration of environment and development, aiming for sustainable development. Combating poverty is a top priority, while protecting the environment and biodiversity, regulating production processes accordingly, and implementing environmentally sensitive technology are fundamental issues. The UN highlights global governance, which it will organize to achieve these goals, with a special focus on major groups. The actors of global governance extend from women, children, and youths, emphasizing their roles in sustainable development, to local communities, including indigenous peoples, civil society organizations, regional formations, expert institutions, and companies (UN, 1992b).

The Commission on Sustainable Development (CSD) was established to monitor and report on the implementation of UNCED at local, national, regional, and international levels. A United Nations General Assembly special session was planned in 1997 to follow up on the progress recorded in 1992. The Program for the Further Implementation of Agenda 21 underscored the principles agreed upon in Rio, ensuring the effective implementation of Agenda 21 (UN, 1992b).

In 2000, the UN Millennium Conference held in New York City adopted the Millennium Development Goals (MDGs). The MDGs reflect a summary of the principles agreed upon during the summits and conferences of the 1990s, including Agenda 21 (Norman & Carr, 2009). Adopted with the aim of achieving them by 2015, the MDGs include eight goals ranging from combating poverty and hunger to ensuring environmental sustainability. Global governance was highlighted as the primary strategy to achieve the MDGs, with the ultimate goal of targeting global governance for direct development (UN, 2015). The MDGs have grounded the UN's global governance strategy on a target-based foundation, specifying development objectives (Fukuda-Parr et al., 2013).

In 2015, the UN General Assembly reviewed the MDGs and adopted 17 Sustainable Development Goals (SDGs). The ultimate goal of the SDGs, which have increased targets in sustainability, environment, and climate issues, remains the strengthening of global partnerships for sustainable development. Moreover, the SDGs emphasize the importance of sustainability, climate, and environmental targets, necessitating global governance. The SDGs also demonstrate the expanded scope of goals that the UN aims to achieve through global governance (Kumar et al., 2016). Poverty, health, and environmental sustainability, previously prominent in the sustainable development agenda, continue to be included in the SDGs. Additionally, more specific areas such as gender equality, clean energy, decent work, and sustainable cities have been added to these goals, thus strengthening the UN's target-based global governance approach with the SDGs.

THE UNITED NATIONS' ROLE IN HARMONIZING SUSTAINABLE DEVELOPMENT WITH GLOBAL GOVERNANCE

In this section, the mechanisms, strategies, and frameworks used by the UN to integrate the Sustainable Development Goals (SDGs) into global governance are explained and evaluated. Initially, the processes through which the UN has integrated the SDGs into global governance are examined. This part explores the foundations on which the relationship between global governance and the SDGs is constructed. Subsequently, the strategies developed on these foundations are analyzed. The strategies utilized by the UN within the framework of global if governance and the general framework of these strategies are detailed.

UN Strategies for Incorporating Sustainable Development into Global Governance

The SDGs represent a combination of economic and social development with environmental sustainability created by the UN. The multidimensional nature of development and the intersecting areas in development necessitate a comprehensive framework. The relationship between education, health, employment, gender inequality, and poverty; the relationship between economic growth, industry, innovation, and infrastructure; and all their links to environmental issues have resulted in the construction of the global development goals with an inclusive character. Each goal not only facilitates achieving the other goals but also carries the risk of reversing gains in other goals if one fails. Therefore, the process of integrating the SDGs into global governance by the UN is based on constructing an integrated area representing sustainable development, focusing on specific objectives.

While sustainable development is divided into specific goals within the SDGs framework, partnerships are also formed within the constructed integrated area. This facilitates the shaping of collaborative processes among actors in practice. Specific goals enable the development of regional and international cooperation areas where relevant actors come together. The integrated structure of the goals emphasizes the plurality of both the issues and the actors involved in the SDGs. The SDGs ensure that the economic, social, and political dimensions of development are addressed in relation. They also promote global cooperation in areas with global implications like the environment.

In this context, the integration of the SDGs into global governance by the UN has been based on two interrelated pillars: (1) International Cooperation and Global Partnership and (2) Science and Policy Collaboration.

International Cooperation and Global Partnership

Another significant aspect of the UN's global governance process is the shift from a state-centric approach to one centered on the international community. Multi-stakeholder partnerships are considered crucial tools for mobilizing and sharing knowledge, expertise, technology, and financial resources to achieve sustainable development goals across all countries, especially in developing ones. SDG 17 also seeks to promote and support effective public, public-private, and civil society partnerships based on strategies for sharing experience and resources (UNDESA 2020). The UN involves all members of the international community in the policy and action areas necessary to achieve the goals.

The UN invites all local, national, regional, and international actors to collaborate on the SDGs. Under its role as an orchestrator, the UN is constructing a common international development agenda that transcends all levels and sectors. Non-state actors are included in many stages of governance, from decision-making to policy implementation, due to their influence on transnational activities. International corporations, international and national NGOs, women's and agricultural cooperatives are involved in supporting implementations. Artists are engaged in representing and disseminating SDGs goals widely, while academics incorporate them into their research, supporting the internalization and implementation process of the SDGs from macro to micro levels.

Though the global governance shaped within the SDGs framework is based on actor plurality, the role of international organizations is particularly prominent. The influence of member states' policies and their roles in international policymaking make these organizations key actors in achieving global goals. Particularly, the European Union (EU), the World Bank, and the Organization for Economic Cooperation and Development (OECD) stand out in SDG implementations due to their membership composition and policymaking power. The EU is taking steps to shape member states' policies to achieve the SDGs, significantly aiding in achieving these goals. Additionally, the EU and the UN collaborate on initiatives for the SDGs (European Commission, 2024). The World Bank expands the reach of SDG priorities by shaping its development support according to the SDGs, assisting the targeted countries to focus on these areas. It supports countries in achieving the SDGs through project support, financing, knowledge, and implementation processes (World Bank, 2024). The OECD provides data, policy tools, and a dialogue platform that states developing national strategies for the SDGs can benefit from. It integrates its efforts within the SDG framework and adopts an action plan targeted at the SDGs (OECD, 2024). The participation of specialized organizations in this process involves numerous international organizations in the global governance emerging around the SDGs agenda, solidifying the role of international organizations in international relations.

Science and Policy Collaboration

The final component of the UN's integration of the SDGs into global governance is the relationship between science and policy. The UN views the science-policy-society relationship as a crucial network for achieving the SDGs. Sustainable transformations and social development are anticipated to benefit from the production of scientific knowledge. Scientifically based information is utilized to reduce uncertainties, identify tipping points, accelerate the adoption of innovations, and lay the foundations for the next frontier of ideas. Science also provides evidence that helps eliminate barriers or paradigms that hinder the rapid acceleration of new technologies and other solutions. Scientists, policymakers, and social actors are included in global governance to build trust, establish a scientific basis for progress toward the SDGs, present findings, and communicate these findings to the broader society (UN, 2024).

The UN supports an interdisciplinary knowledge production process in tandem with policymaking. Conferences, workshops, webinars, and academic projects are encouraged during the SDG achievement process to promote the production of knowledge for a better world vision. The development of knowledge production technologies is utilized to support the knowledge production process, generate data, and share information. By leveraging such science-policy interactions, expertise and stakeholder collaboration are being merged. The goal is to integrate different sectors and actors by pooling financial resources, knowledge, and expertise (UNDESA, 2024a). A common ground is being constructed by bridging the gap between political pragmatism and scientists working on the world's life support systems (Kanie, 2016).

Strategies for Using Global Governance to Achieve the SDGs

The UN employs two fundamental strategies at theoretical and practical levels to achieve the SDGs. Theoretically, the UN adopts an agenda-setting strategy to keep the SDGs lively and enriched, steer the international agenda, and deepen intellectual activities concerning the SDGs. This involves utilizing platforms that bring together both UN bodies and stakeholders for agenda-setting. Practically, the UN's strategies encompass the implementations, initiatives, and activities aimed at achieving these goals. At this stage, the UN focuses on facilitating partnerships among actors for specific missions and projects.

International Agenda Setting

At the forefront of reaching the SDGs, the UN maintains a lively international agenda focused on the SDGs. Establishing governance within a target-based framework is the initial step in agenda-setting. This target-oriented approach directs short-term decisions and desires toward long-term objectives (Young et al., 2014), thus initiating a process where the SDGs will be monitored and tracked until the projected achievement date. Agenda 2030 represents a successful initiative in shaping the international agenda. It has been agreed upon as a collective action by all countries and stakeholders for people, planet, and prosperity (UNDESA, 2024b). The UN builds a global governance platform for Agenda 2030 by bringing together members of the international community in many scientific and operational studies. The UN World Development Report evaluates SDGs achievements by comparing them with poverty and inequality indices. Summits and multilateral discussions keep stakeholders within the framework of Agenda 2030. At the 2019 SDG Summit, the urgent need for harmonized and accelerated actions by all stakeholders was emphasized, leading to the adoption of SDG Acceleration Actions (UNDESA, 2024c).

As both an aspect and a result of the UN's international agenda-setting strategy, intergovernmental processes and multilateral agreements follow (Underdal & Kim, 2017). The strongest implementation within the SDGs framework is the Paris Agreement, signed in 2015 and entered into force in 2016 (United Nations Framework Convention on Climate Change). The Agreement, adopted by 196 states at the UN Climate Change Conference (COP21), aims to combat global warming and the climate crisis. Its implementation is realized through the transfer to national policies and legal regulations, supported by science-based transformations of member states' economies and societies. Starting in 2020, states have been developing national climate action plans to support this process (UNFCCC, 2024). A binding international process accelerates the journey towards achieving the SDGs.

The UN's strategy for building intergovernmental processes assumes a significant function in the international realm where there is no supreme authority. However, due to the limitation on economic and social policies, it is not easy for states to agree on binding mechanisms, especially regarding sustainability and development. Therefore, the UN tends to adopt more flexible, voluntary-based intergovernmental processes. The High-Level Political Forum (HLPF) on Sustainable Development holds a central role in the UN's agenda-setting strategy. Established at The United Nations Conference on Sustainable Development (Rio+20) in 2012, the HLPF, as a result of "The Future We Want," directly aims to monitor and review Agenda 2030. Thus, the HLPF is equipped with extensive authorities, such as monitoring the sustainable development agenda, coordinating actors, and tracking goals and commitments (UN, 2012). While setting the agenda, the HLPF is also tasked with orchestrating global governance, serving as a common platform to support the relationships, works, and actions of actors (Abbot & Berstein, 2015). The regularly convened HLPF guides major groups and other stakeholders within the framework of Agenda 2030 (HLPF, 2024).

The UN also utilizes smaller intergovernmental processes created by the HLPF to set the agenda. Thematic UN Conferences and High-Level Events Related to Sustainable Development bring important issues related to one aspect of the SDGs to the international agenda. The Multi-stakeholder Forum on Science, Technology, and Innovation for the SDGs, established by General Assembly Resolution 70/1 on Agenda 2030 for Sustainable Development, gathers stakeholders to utilize science and technology in achieving the goals. The UN coordinates efforts to achieve these goals, creates a vision for the future, and promotes innovative thinking through the ECOSOC Partnership Forum using the Economic and Social Council. The Second Committee of the General Assembly and the SAMOA Pathway perform a similar function in setting the agenda (UNDESA, 2024d). Through these processes, the UN influences the actions of member states and other stakeholders on the SDGs and strives to keep activities active. Thus, a continuous focus on the SDGs and an effective achievement process are maintained.

Target-Based Governance Practices

The UN organizes a network of global governance by concurrently maintaining numerous activities within the framework of goals. It encourages academic studies for the SDGs and supports the scientific knowledge production process aimed at the goals. Consequently, activities that will achieve the goals are accompanied by knowledge production and sharing processes. Figure 1 demonstrates the activities conducted by the UN to achieve the SDGs. Publications and events shown in Figure 1 represent the knowledge production process related to the SDGs. The knowledge production and sharing process is carried out through webinars, workshops, conferences, forums, and publications.

As seen in Figure 1, the number of events significantly surpasses publications, especially regarding SDG 6 (Clean Water and Sanitation) and SDG 7 (Partnership for the Goals). Actions encompass programs, initiatives, applications, and activities conducted to achieve the goals. The progress for each goal has been much faster than the knowledge production and sharing process. Actions for SDG 14 (Life below Water) have surpassed other goals. However, it is generally understood that practices related to SDG 1 (No Poverty), SDG 2 (Zero Hunger), SDG 3 (Good Health and Well-Being), SDG 4 (Quality Education), and SDG 6 focus on basic needs. Similar attention is also given to climate and environmental issues.

The UN implements activities targeted at the SDGs by facilitating collaboration among actors through projects. These projects are carried out under the overarching theme of laying the foundations for peace and sustainable development. Figure 2 shows ongoing projects aimed at achieving the SDGs.

According to Figure 2, ongoing projects are concentrated on SDG 3 (Good Health and Well-Being) and SDG 16 (Peace, Justice, and Strong Institutions), followed by SDG 10 (Reduced Inequalities) and SDG 13 (Climate Action). The objectives of global governance under a global theme are determined according to regional conditions. The UN builds target-based global governance networks focused on specific objectives related to SDGs activities, suitable for the unique conditions of countries through regional approaches. The UN implements its programs targeting countries in five regions: Africa, Asia, Europe, Latin America and the Caribbean, and the Middle East. Humanitarian aid, access to basic services in vulnerable communities, infrastructure and sanitation services, as well as tackling the impacts of climate change and poverty, are concentrated in Africa and Asia. In Europe, the focus of global governance spans a broad area due to the diversity of issues in different countries. European projects, including Eastern Europe, the Western Balkans, the South Caucasus, and Central Asia, vary from peacebuilding to emergency response in humanitarian crises, from climate change to healthcare provision. In Latin America and the Caribbean and the Middle East, humanitarian crises, longstanding security issues, and peacebuilding are prominent. Innovative solutions to development problems, local capacity building, transparency, and efficiency are other focal areas of projects in these regions. Environmental protection and climate actions are priority areas for projects across all regions. When looking at the distribution of projects, it is observed that the number of projects implemented in Sub-Saharan Africa, South Asia, and Latin America and the Caribbean is higher compared to other regions (UNOPS, 2024).

The UN also conducts projects under the multi-country program for shared sustainable solutions. The multi-country program is based on three main themes: (1) Peace and Security Cluster, (2) Water and Energy Cluster, and (3) Sustainable Development Cluster. The Peace and Security Cluster covers

Figure 1. UN's SDGs practice
(UNDESA, 2024d)

[Bar chart – Actions by SDG:
SDGs 1: 1433; SDGs 2: 1371; SDGs 3: 1287; SDGs 4: 1816; SDGs 5: 1655; SDGs 6: 1820; SDGs 7: 1045; SDGs 8: 1921; SDGs 9: 1044; SDGs 10: 990; SDGs 11: 1237; SDGs 12: 1604; SDGs 13: 2133; SDGs 14: 2855; SDGs 15: 1316; SDGs 16: 1037; SDGs 17: 2198]

[Bar chart – Publications and Events by SDG:
Publications: SDGs 1: 49; SDGs 2: 17; SDGs 3: 47; SDGs 4: 11; SDGs 5: 46; SDGs 6: 16; SDGs 7: 45; SDGs 8: 48; SDGs 9: 17; SDGs 10: 14; SDGs 11: 20; SDGs 12: 16; SDGs 13: 36; SDGs 14: 42; SDGs 15: 34; SDGs 16: 104; SDGs 17: 76]

a wide area including post-conflict peacebuilding and rehabilitation, humanitarian aid, development, innovation, and risk management. The Water and Energy Cluster supports the management of water resources, environmental protection, and climate actions. The Sustainable Development Cluster provides services for global programs, supporting development and private ventures with technology and grant management services (UNOPS, 2024).

These projects are built as multi-stakeholder processes, primarily involving national authorities and local organizations. In projects conducted for countries, collaboration with local governments and communities is prominent. Moreover, the UN extends its partnerships from supporting states to international NGOs. The role and impact of UN specialized agencies vary according to the content of the projects.

Figure 2. UN's SDGs ongoing projects
(UNOPS, 2024)

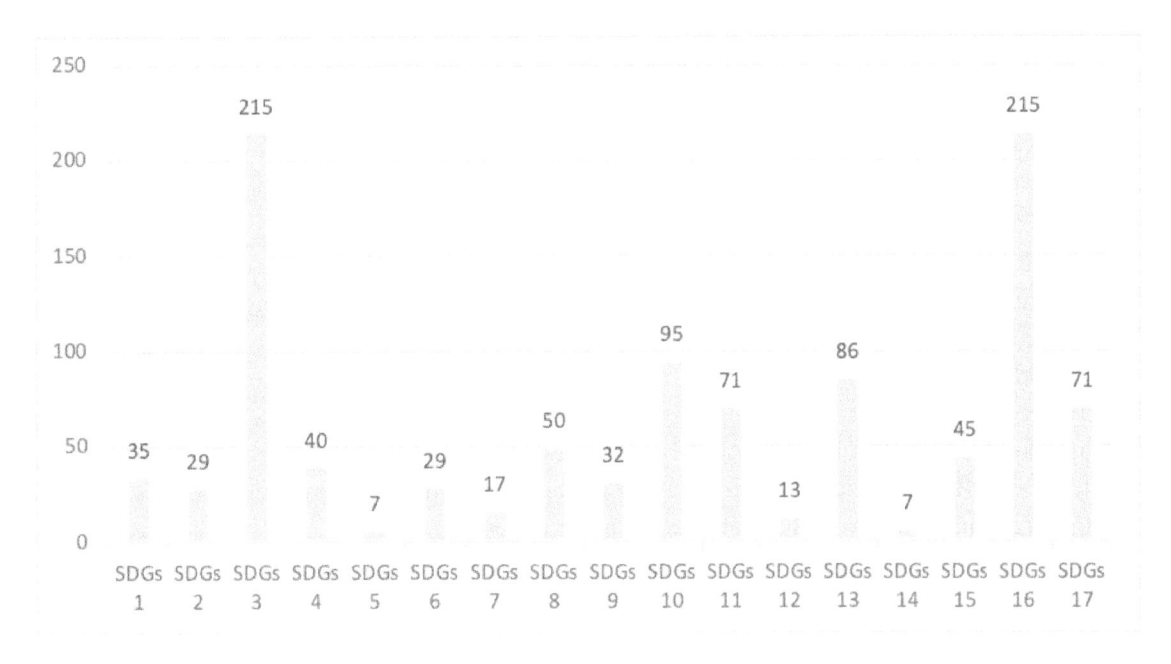

SDGs 1	35
SDGs 2	29
SDGs 3	215
SDGs 4	40
SDGs 5	7
SDGs 6	29
SDGs 7	17
SDGs 8	50
SDGs 9	32
SDGs 10	95
SDGs 11	71
SDGs 12	13
SDGs 13	86
SDGs 14	7
SDGs 15	45
SDGs 16	215
SDGs 17	71

In the multi-country program, stakeholders vary widely depending on the countries involved (UNOPS, 2024). The multi-country program provides a more global outlook in terms of stakeholder qualities, more clearly demonstrating the UN's orchestrator role in target-based global governance. These programs involve numerous target states and local actors. Additionally, the WB, WHO, many of UN's specialized agencies, international companies, national development agencies from various regions, and civil society organizations are involved in the process.

CHALLENGES OF GLOBAL GOVERNANCE IN ACHIEVING THE SDGs

The first challenge in achieving the SDGs arises from the structure of the international system. The structural characteristic of the international system, which is not regulated by a supreme authority, presents two significant challenges. The first challenge stems from the legal nature of the SDGs. Since the SDGs are adopted by a UN General Assembly resolution, they do not constitute a legally binding document. They merely create a normative obligation for states to transpose the necessary legal regulations into their domestic law (Biermann & Kanie, 2017). The absence of a binding international treaty slows down the process of integrating the SDGs into domestic law.

Another issue related to the legal aspect and stemming from the international system is that the necessary policies and practices for achieving the SDGs are left to the initiative of the actors. The international agenda formed over the SDGs influences the policy agendas of various actors such as states, civil society organizations, and international companies. However, the lack of a supreme authority to regulate and coordinate these actors' practices, and the limitation of the UN's effectiveness by states' sovereignty areas, complicates implementation (Joshi et al., 2015). States and international companies can focus on targets that align with their policy priorities. Conversely, the specializations of civil society organizations inevitably direct their activities towards specific targets (Borgers et al., 2023). This situation adversely affects the implementation and harmonization of all SDG targets. Particularly in areas with global linkages like environment and climate, strong coordination is essential for success.

Another challenge hindering the harmonization of the SDGs is the socioeconomic differences among states. The implementation of the goals is directly affected by the socioeconomic structures of the states in two ways: (1) policy dynamics, and (2) consolidation of democracy and strengthening of institutions. The levels of development, societal issues, and geographical locations of states shape their policy dynamics and ultimately their practices. In a state where wealth is not widespread, combating poverty is a fundamental area, while environmental priorities are critical for a state directly facing drought and climate crises. This situation inevitably makes state policy dynamics a determining factor in SDG preferences.

Another related issue is the challenge of financing. Especially in the areas of environment and sustainability, the implementations requiring high technology are costly (Vortiguez et al., 2014). Although institutions like the World Bank offer project-based financial support to include the SDGs in this process, these efforts are often insufficient. Therefore, economic development differentiates states' success in achieving targets, particularly those related to the environment.

The second fundamental problem arising from states' socioeconomic differences is the consolidation of democracy and strengthening of institutions. This issue significantly affects the achievement of the SDGs. Firstly, weak institutions cause failures in objectivity and combating corruption, jeopardizing the effectiveness of policy implementation. From directing resources to the right channels to merit-based appointments, many stages in the implementation process of SDG policies face the threat of failure (Rothstein, 2011). A second risk associated with this problem arises from governments' tendencies towards populist policies. The lack of consolidated democracy, weak institutions, and non-enforcement of the rule of law allow governments to arbitrarily shape their priorities, especially during election periods, prioritizing their power retention over SDG goals and priorities (Acemoglu & Robinson, 2012).

In addition to issues related to the international system and state-based problems, issues stemming from the nature and content of the SDGs also negatively affect the process. Firstly, the nature of the SDGs constructs a series of integrated and inclusive targets for sustainable development. However, the scope of activities of actors who are to coordinate efforts to achieve these targets does not exhibit the same inclusivity. The work of international and regional organizations and civil society organizations focuses on areas where they specialize (Borgers et al., 2023). These actors, by their nature, cannot be involved in every SDG target. A problem arising from the content of the SDGs is that the targets are mostly qualitative, which allows for interpretation. Actors may interpret the targets differently based on their priorities or expertise. This situation hinders global alignment and the establishment of standards for achieving the targets.

The last hurdle in achieving the SDGs is the difficulties encountered in measurement, monitoring, and evaluation. This task is attempted to be carried out by the High-Level Political Forum on Sustainable Development. However, the lack of a comparable and inclusive data set in practice prevents success (Bernstein, 2017). While international actors fall short in creating a data set, national statistical offices show variations in maintaining data standards. As a result, a comprehensive measurement of the successes and shortcomings of SDG implementations cannot be made. This situation prevents the understanding of differences between states, negatively affecting the creation of targeted policies.

CONCLUSION

The UN's strategy for integrating the Sustainable Development Goals (SDGs) into global governance theoretically offers a framework that is both inclusive and pluralistic in terms of content and actors. This strategy represents a significant effort to orchestrate change towards a sustainable future. The SDGs present a comprehensive and ambitious agenda covering a wide range of issues from reducing poverty to protecting the environment and climate action. These goals and the strategies used to achieve them have been supported by an interdisciplinary knowledge structure. This process has ensured that the goals reflect a broad consensus and respond to the diverse needs and priorities of the global community.

The adoption of the SDGs has created a universal agenda for a sustainable future vision, marking a significant turning point in the history of global governance. The process founded on these goals demonstrates that the UN has developed an inclusive and participatory process, adopting a multilateral approach. The orchestrator role of the UN in this global effort is critical as it tries to harmonize the varied efforts of diverse actors across different governance levels. The UN's strategies for using global governance to achieve the SDGs form a valuable practical example. A wide range of actors including member states, civil society, the private sector, and international organizations have been mobilized to work towards the common goals of the SDGs. National and international actors have been included in global governance as part of the same community working towards the common good highlighted by the SDGs. The emphasis on partnerships (SDG 17) underscores the recognition that achieving these ambitious goals requires a collective effort.

The UN's efforts to integrate the SDGs into various policy frameworks and monitor progress through mechanisms like the High-Level Political Forum on Sustainable Development (HLPF) have helped maintain a global focus on these goals. The alignment of the SDGs with national development plans and strategies in many countries demonstrates the impact of the UN's advocacy and capacity-building efforts.

Despite these successes, the journey towards achieving the SDGs is filled with challenges. The non-binding nature of the SDGs, stemming from the structural features of the international system, poses a significant barrier. The elements of global governance focused on the SDGs mostly create a normative obligation. The structural features of the international system prevent such a comprehensive set of goals from being signed as a binding international treaty. Producing a legally binding document with clear and precise standards for implementation requires the consent of states with differing socioeconomic structures and policy priorities. The potential for such a document to intervene in states' economic, social, and environmental policies and practices makes it challenging for states to accept obligations related to the SDGs.

The reliance on voluntary national commitments and the absence of a legally binding enforcement mechanism limit the ability to hold actors accountable for their progress. Socio-economic differences between states further complicate the implementation of the SDGs. Particularly, developing countries face significant challenges in mobilizing the necessary resources and capacities to achieve the targets. The differing priorities and policy dynamics of states also lead to uneven progress across different targets and regions.

While the pluralistic nature of global governance is a strength, it also presents challenges in terms of coordination and consistency. The SDG agenda includes numerous actors, each with its own agenda and approach, which risks fragmentation and inefficiency. Ensuring that all efforts are harmonious and mutually reinforcing remains a challenging task for the UN, despite all its structural features and resources. Moreover, the SDGs' broad and ambitious set of goals, while comprehensive, can also be inhibitive. The interconnectedness of the goals means that progress in one area can affect others, potentially negatively impacting the efforts and motivations of the actors, as well as complicating the focus and measurement of progress. The qualitative nature of many goals and the lack of standardized indicators further complicate monitoring and evaluation.

Despite these challenges, the adoption of the SDGs is significant in terms of establishing an international precedent. Creating such a precedent is likely to pave the way for a binding international agreement in the future. Therefore, it is beneficial to focus on areas that need improvement despite limitations and challenges. Several recommendations can be made to overcome these challenges and strengthen the UN's role in harmonizing sustainable development with global governance. One key suggestion is to explore ways to increase the legal weight of the goals; for example, through international agreements or treaties that could enforce more binding commitments from states. Additionally, continuing to promote multi-stakeholder partnerships while emphasizing coordination and consistency more, and creating clear frameworks for cooperation that align the efforts of different actors towards common goals, is essential.

Mobilizing additional financial resources, particularly for developing countries, is essential to support the implementation of the SDGs. This could involve innovative financing mechanisms, increased aid, and support for capacity-building. Enhancing monitoring and accountability is also crucial, which could include strengthening the role of the High-level Political Forum on Sustainable Development, enhancing transparency and reporting, and promoting peer review processes.

Focusing on the interlinkages between different SDGs is necessary to ensure that progress in one area supports progress in others, requiring an integrated approach to policy-making and implementation. Addressing inequality is another important recommendation, prioritizing efforts to reduce inequalities both within and between countries, which includes addressing issues of access to resources, technology, and opportunities.

Enhancing public awareness and engagement is vital to increase efforts to raise public awareness about the SDGs and engage citizens in the implementation process, which can help build public support and foster a sense of shared responsibility. Strengthening the science-policy interface is also recommended, enhancing the integration of scientific knowledge into policy-making processes related to the SDGs, which involves strengthening the role of scientific advisory bodies and promoting interdisciplinary research.

Adapting to emerging challenges is necessary, being responsive to global challenges such as the COVID-19 pandemic and the climate crisis and adapting the SDG agenda accordingly. This requires flexibility and resilience in global governance structures. Finally, promoting regional cooperation is recommended, encouraging regional initiatives and cooperation as a means of addressing shared challenges and leveraging regional strengths in the pursuit of the SDGs.

REFERENCES

Abbot, K. W., & Bernstein, S. (2015). The High-Level Political Forum on Sustainable Development: Orchestration by default and design. *Global Policy, 6*(3), 222–233. doi:10.1111/1758-5899.12199

Acemoğlu, D., & Robinson, J. A. (2012). *Why nations fail: The origins of power, prosperity, and poverty*. Random House.

Bernstein, S. (2017). The United Nations and the governance of Sustainable Development Goals. In N. Kanie & F. Biermann (Eds.), *Governing Through Goals: Sustainable Development Goals as Governance Innovation* (pp. 213–240). MIT Press. doi:10.7551/mitpress/9780262035620.003.0009

Biermann, F., & Kanie, N. (2017). Conclusion: Key Challenges for Global Governance through Goals. In N. Kanie & F. Biermann (Eds.), *Governing Through Goals: Sustainable Development Goals as Governance Innovation* (pp. 295–310). MIT Press. doi:10.7551/mitpress/9780262035620.003.0013

Biermann, F., Kanie, N., & Kim, R. (2017). Global governance by goal-setting: The novel approach of the UN Sustainable Development Goals. *Current Opinion in Environmental Sustainability, 26-27,* 26–31. doi:10.1016/j.cosust.2017.01.010

Borgers, M., Biermann, B., Kalfagianni, A., & Kim, R. E. (2023). The SDGs as integrating force in global governance? Challenges and opportunities. *International Environmental Agreement: Politics, Law and Economics, 23*(2), 157–164. doi:10.1007/s10784-023-09607-9

European Commission. (2024). *Sustainable Development Goals.* EC. https://commission.europa.eu/strategy-and-policy/sustainable-development-goals_en#:~:text=Sustainable%20development%20is%20a%20core,Sustainable%20Development%20Goals%20(SDGs)

Fukuda-Parr, S., Yamin, A. E., & Greenstein, J. (2013). *The Power of Numbers: A Critical Review of MDG Targets for Human Development and Human Rights.* Working Paper Series. https://www.worldbank.org/content/dam/Worldbank/document/Gender/Synthesis%20paper%20PoN_Final.pdf

Green, D. (2012). *From poverty to power: How active citizens and effective states can change the world.* Practical Action Publishing and Oxfam International. doi:10.3362/9781780447407

HLPF. (2024). *High-Level Political Forum.* HLPF. https://hlpf.un.org/

Joshi, D. K., Hughes, B. B., & Sisk, T. D. (2015). Improving governance for the post-2015 Sustainable Development Goals: Scenario forecasting the next 50 years. *World Development, 70,* 286–302. doi:10.1016/j.worlddev.2015.01.013

Kanie, N. (2016). Governance through goal-setting: A new governance challenge for navigating sustainability in the 21st century. In N. Kanie (Ed.), *The WSPC reference on natural resources and environmental policy in the era of global change* (pp. 61–76). World Scientific. doi:10.1142/9789813208162_0003

Kumar, S., Kumar, N., & Vivekadhish, S. (2016). Millennium Development Goals (MDGs) to Sustainable Development Goals (SDGs): Addressing unfinished agenda and strengthening sustainable development and partnership. *Indian Journal of Community Medicine, 41*(1), 1–4. doi:10.4103/0970-0218.170955 PMID:26917865

Mulley, S. (2008). From *Poverty to Power: How Active Citizens and Effective States Can Change the World.* Oxfam International. https://oxfamilibrary.openrepository.com/bitstream/handle/10546/112422/fp2p-bp-global-governance-_1;jsessionid=28E506FF03D9E298EA44D2D56DA52435?sequence=1

Norman, E. S., & Carr, D. (2009). Rio Summit. In R. Kitchen & N. Thrift (Eds.), *International encyclopedia of human geography* (pp. 406–411). Elsevier Science. doi:10.1016/B978-008044910-4.00119-X

Odén, B. (2002). Implications for International Governance and Development Cooperation. In B. Hettne & B. Odén (Eds.), *Global Governance in the 21st Century: Alternative Perspectives on World Order* (pp. 184–202). Almkvist & Wiksell International.

OECD. (2024). *OECD and the Sustainable Development Goals*. OECD. https://www.oecd.org/sdgs/

Rothstein, B. (2011). *The quality of government: Corruption, social trust, and inequality in international perspective*. University of Chicago. doi:10.7208/chicago/9780226729589.001.0001

UN. (1992a). *United Nations Conference on Environment and Development*. UN. https://www.un.org/en/conferences/environment/rio1992

UN. (1992b). *United Nations Conference on Environment & Development*. UN. https://sdgs.un.org/sites/default/files/publications/Agenda21.pdf

UN. (2012). *The Future We Want: Outcome document of the United Nations Conference on Sustainable Development, RIO+20*. UN. https://sustainabledevelopment.un.org/content/documents/733FutureWeWant.pdf

UN. (2015). *We can end poverty: Millennium Development Goals and beyond 2015*. UN. https://www.un.org/millenniumgoals/bkgd.shtml

UN. (2024). *Times of crisis, times of change: Science for accelerating transformations to sustainable development*. Global Sustainable Development Report. https://sdgs.un.org/sites/default/files/2023-09/FINAL%20GSDR%202023-Digital%20-110923_1.pdf

Underdal, A., & Kim, R. E. (2017). The Sustainable Development Goals and multilateral agreements. In N. Kanie & F. Biermann (Eds.), *Governing Through Goals: Sustainable Development Goals as Governance Innovation* (pp. 241–258). MIT Press. doi:10.7551/mitpress/9780262035620.003.0010

UNDESA. (2020). *The SDG partnership guidebook: A practical guide to building high impact multi-stakeholder partnerships for the Sustainable Development Goals*. UNDESA. https://sdgs.un.org/sites/default/files/2022-02/SDG%20Partnership%20Guidebook%201.11.pdf

UNDESA. (2024a). *Multi-stakeholder partnerships*. UNDESA. https://sdgs.un.org/topics/multi-stakeholder-partnerships

UNDESA. (2024b). *Transforming our world: the 2030 Agenda for Sustainable Development*. UNDESA. https://sdgs.un.org/2030agenda

UNDESA. (2024c). *About the SDG accelerations*. UNDESA. https://sdgs.un.org/partnerships/action-networks/acceleration-actions/about

UNDESA. (2024d). *Sustainable Development*. UNDESA. https://sdgs.un.org/goals

UNFCCC. (2024). *The Paris Agreement: What is the Paris Agreement?* UNFCC. https://unfccc.int/process-and-meetings/the-paris-agreement

UNOPS. (2024). *Projects and locations*. UNOPS. https://www.unops.org/project-locations

Väyrynen, R. (2002). Reforming the World Order: Multi- and Plurilateral Approaches. In B. Hettne & B. Odén (Eds.), *Global Governance in the 21st Century: Alternative Perspectives on World Order* (pp. 106–146). Almkvist & Wiksell International.

Vortiguez, T., Giordano, T., Bakkour, N., & Boussichas, M. (2014). Financing the post-2015 sustainable development agenda. In R. K. Pachauri, A. Paugam, T. Ribera, L. Tubiana, P. G. D. Chakrabarti, R. Jozan, D. Kamelgarn & T. Voituriez (Eds.), Building the future we want (179-190). UNDESA.

Weiss, T. G. (2000). Governance, good governance and global governance: Conceptual and actual challenges. *Third World Quarterly, 21*(5), 795–814. doi:10.1080/713701075

World Bank. (2024). *World Bank Group and The 2030 Agenda*. World Bank. https://www.worldbank.org/en/programs/sdgs-2030-agenda

Young, O., Arild, U., Kanie, N., Andresen, S., Bernstein, S., Biermann, F., Gupta, J., Haas, P. M., Iguchi, M., Kok, M., Levy, M., Nilsson, M., Pintér, L., & Stevens, C. (2014). Earth System Challenges and a Multi-Layered Approach for the Sustainable Development Goals. *POST2015/UNU-IAS Policy Brief. United Nations University Institute for the Advanced Study of Sustainability*. UNU. https://i.unu.edu/media/ias.unu.edu-en/project/2218/Post2015_UNU-IAS_PolicyBrief1.pdf

Zürn, M. (2013). Globalization and global governance. In *Handbook of International Relations* (pp. 401–425). SAGE Publications. doi:10.4135/9781446247587.n16

ADDITIONAL READING

Bourmistrov, A., Mellemvik, F., & Mineev, A. (2022). International cooperation for global development: What can we learn from the Arctic? In A. Mineev, A. Bourmistrov, & F. Mellemvik (Eds.), *Global development in the arctic: International cooperation for the future* (pp. 267–278). Routledge. doi:10.4324/9781003246015-21

Bracho, G., Carey, R., Hynes, W., Klingebiel, S., & Trzeciak-Duval, A. (2021). *Origins, evolution and future of global development cooperation*, German Development Institute. https://www.idos-research.de/uploads/media/Study_104.pdf

Cruz, S. A. (2023). SDG 17 and global partnership for sustainable development: unraveling the rhetoric of collaboration. *Frontiers in Environmental Science, 11*, 01-011. doi:10.3389/fenvs.2023.1155828

Honcharenko, I., Berezina, O., Berezhna, L., & Zhuk, V. (2021). Global partnership for sustainable development: challenges and perspectives for Ukraine, *SHS Web of Conferences 92*(4), 2-12. doi: 10.1051/shsconf/20219209005 10.1051/shsconf/20219209005

Kirchner, S., & Koivurova, T. (2022). International governance facilitating sustainable development in the Arctic-The Arctic Council as a multi-role actor and forum. In A. Mineev, A. Bourmistrov & F. Mellemvik (Eds.), *Global development in the arctic: International cooperation for the future* (33-46). Routledge. 10.4324/9781003246015-3

Safonov, G. V., & Piskulova, N. (2018). Sustainable development and international cooperation. In V. I. Danilov-Danilyan & N. A. Piskulova (Eds.), *New challenges in sustainable development for Russia and the world* (pp. 150–175). Cambridge Scholars Publishing.

Vyas-Doorgapersad, S. (2011). The impact of global partnership for development (Goal Number 8) in achieving the Millennium Development Goals in Africa. *Africa Insight*, 2(40), 39–53. doi:10.4314/ai.v40i2.64374

KEY TERMS AND DEFINITIONS

Global Governance: Global governance refers to institutions that coordinate the behavior and actions of the international system's actors, help ensure cooperation, resolve disputes, and promote collective action. It requires the establishment, implementation, monitoring, and evaluation of rules and conventions on issues with global repercussions.

Global Partnership: For parts of the world, it involves organizing all actors in the international arena, from individuals to international organizations. In this context, an international partnership involving various actors including international organizations, governments, civil society organizations, and private companies is being constructed to achieve the SDGs.

Goal-setting Governance: This governance strategy involves integrating globally accepted goals into global governance, gathering, and coordinating actors around specific objectives. Goal-setting governance facilitates the development of multilateral solutions by leveraging the global governance structure to overcome challenges that arise in achieving these goals.

International Cooperation: International cooperation refers to collaboration based on division of labor and partnership among national and international actors to achieve a common goal. It encompasses the joint actions of actors from local, regional, and international levels. Therefore, international cooperation is a process based on coordinated policies, strategies, and plans among actors.

International Development: It represents an interdisciplinary field that aims to ameliorate international inequalities and redistribute prosperity in sociological, economic, and political terms. Within the framework of human development, it aims to tackle all inequalities and underdevelopment problems, especially the fight against poverty.

Sustainable Development: Sustainable development is built on three pillars: economic development, social inclusion, and environmental protection. It requires meeting the needs of today's societies without compromising the ability of future generations to meet their needs and without risking the planet's life. Sustainable development moves the fight against various problems such as economic inequality, social instability, and environmental destruction to the international policy agenda.

Chapter 2
Sisyphean Goal:
Sustainable Development

Sureyya Yigit
https://orcid.org/0000-0002-8025-5147
New Vision University, Georgia

ABSTRACT

Intact and functional ecosystems are habitats for people, animals, and plants form the natural basis of humanity's existence. Ecosystems provide food, building materials, energy sources, and active ingredients for medicines. They regulate the climate, form humus in the soil, and are important for nutrient cycles and clean drinking water. Therefore, preserving biodiversity is important for the nutrition and economic, social, and cultural development of current and future generations. This chapter investigates the planet's challenges in maintaining an environmental balance.

We owe today's young activists a huge debt for sounding the alarm. Now, we need to turn their enthusiasm into an institutionalized political force, and develop a blueprint for a potent, well-designed, and productive economic agenda.

DARON ACEMOĞLU

INTRODUCTION

The mythological tales of ancient Greece have had a profound impact on the way leaders made decisions during that time. The fear of punishment and retribution, along with the ominous uncertainty of the future, were vital instruments that guided the leaders of the polis. The oracles, with their prophetic vision, provided a glimpse into the future, warning the leaders of the consequences of their actions.

The plays written by famous playwrights, such as Euripides and Sophocles, were a reflection of these themes and provided an entertaining and thought-provoking experience for audiences in the amphitheatres of Athens and Ephesus. These plays continue to survive the test of time and still have a profound impact on modern audiences.

In today's world, political leaders are acutely aware of their responsibility for the future through their actions. This is especially true in democracies, where they know that their actions must lead to a better future, or they will face political consequences. While there is no oracle at Delphi that predicts this, the political system demands it. Despite the differences between the ancient and modern worlds, the tales of Greek mythology continue to inspire us to make decisions that lead to a better future.

One of the most famous concerns during the wedding of Peleus and Thetis, related to the three goddesses, namely Hera, Athena, and Aphrodite, argue over who was the most beautiful of them all. To settle the argument, they decided to ask Paris, the prince of Troy, to judge them. Each goddess offered him a bribe to sway his decision. Hera offered him power and wealth, Athena promised him wisdom and victory, and Aphrodite offered him the most beautiful mortal woman in the world, Helen of Sparta. Paris was swayed by Aphrodite's bribe and declared her as the fairest. However, this decision led to the abduction of Helen and brought about the Trojan War. Paris took Helen to Troy, and the Greeks, led by Agamemnon, invaded Troy to retrieve her. The war lasted for ten years and ended with the defeat of Troy. The very least one learns from this is that there are consequences for every choice made, which is apt for this piece of research.

Following this trail of thought perhaps the most appropriate ancient myth is also the story of Sisyphus. If Homer is to be believed, Sisyphus was the wisest and cleverest among all the mortals. If one recalls the myth of Sisyphus, the gods had condemned him to continually carry a boulder to the top of a mountain, from the summit of which the stone rolled back again of its own accord. The gods had decided on the worst punishment possible, which was useless and hopeless. What the world faces today regarding environmental protection is similarly an unenviable task.

Regardless of our beliefs about the ethical relationship that women and men should have with nature, the evidence is mounting that our collective actions are pushing earth's biogeochemical system further each day from the previously existing conditions. Nine bio-geochemical limits must not be transgressed to maintain an environment conducive to human societies. There is, therefore, a reason to question the relative carelessness and inertia that characterizes the current world in the face of these global problems (Pietrzak, 2024). The scientific diagnosis is clear: climate disruption, mass extinctions, overexploitation of natural resources, and widespread pollution are associated with the principle of precaution, which dictates prudence and forethought.

People still need to feel concerned. A distance still separates individuals from the social and environmental consequences of their daily actions (Yigit, 2024). Additionally, most people now live in large cities isolated from nature, work or study for many hours inside buildings with strictly controlled conditions, and travel in vehicles that also cut them off from the world. Such future threats, often conveyed in scientific knowledge imbued with margins of uncertainty, compete with the pressing reality of daily life, where providing for our needs (primary or derived) and those of our family leaves us with the feeling of having little room for maneuver.

People can invest in three ways in favor of an ecological transition: with their minds, hearts and bodies. This is because one must first understand the situation by documenting the problem, the risks and the uncertainties. It is then important that each person integrates this new knowledge within its value system and socio-economic context. New information is only considered valid and useful if it harmonizes with pre-existing beliefs - mental models - even if a solid argument supports it. Let us take an example. It has been documented that people recently exposed to a violent weather event are more concerned about a future dominated by climate change since they can better imagine the consequences of the risks to their lives - the distance is then reduced. The communication of climate change and the loss of biodiversity, to name only these two biogeochemical limits, would undoubtedly be more effective if we could discern and overcome these cultural blockages and consider them in speeches. Getting involved ultimately only becomes possible after understanding and integrating. Such a degree of adhesion then calls upon all dimensions of men and women: the cognitive, the emotional and the behavioral. Individual commitment leads to a concrete and generalized way of acting in favor of our common future, to borrow from the title of the Brundtland Report.

Hence, one must explore different avenues to analyze the current situation and propose actions to shape our future. This chapter will point out the footprints and trajectories alongside what formulas and concepts are proposed to measure human beings' pressure on the environment, what are the significant trends in human population since the second half of the 20th century, what are the main drivers of consumption, what were the main technological and industrial revolutions, what are the main principles of internalization of environmental costs, what are the main stages of the linear economy and what are the main stages of the circular economy? It will introduce the formula of $I = PCT$, of ecological footprints supporting capacity, the rivalry between basic and positional needs, the impact of the steam engine, rail transport, electricity, the petrochemical industry and information technology, the principle of polluter pays as well as the user pays, the notion of extract produce and discard, finally outlining the proposal of the 5 R's: Reduce Reuse Repair Refactor Recycle.

There is something quite moving about observing the biosphere, an appeal, perhaps the feeling of being a part of the grandiose. Firstly, because it has not always been there and could disappear, but above all, because humanity is still experiencing its place within it. The biosphere brings together the living fraction of nature, therefore, all the organisms occupying the earth, the air and the oceans.

In order to better understand the relationships between the components of the biosphere, we will focus on three pivotal moments in the earth's history: the appearance of water, that of vascular plants and that of humans. The earth was formed approximately 4.6 billion years ago. Since the oldest sedimentary rocks found in Greenland are 3.8 billion years old and water is required to form such rocks, one can safely say there has been water on earth since that time (Zimmer, 2014). The biosphere would have followed shortly, geologically speaking, 3.5 billion years ago, while Homo Sapiens only joined the biosphere 200,000 years ago.

The origin of water is still the subject of debate, but everyone agrees that it is closely linked to the birth of the earth. The main hypothesis is based on the particularly active volcanism which followed the initial formation of our planet. The earth's crust contains negligible amounts of water. On the other hand, we know that certain meteorites contain up to 20%. Therefore, celestial bodies of this type likely collided with the young earth and merged with it. The intense volcanic activity at the beginning would then release large quantities of water vapor and carbon dioxide, nitrogen, ammonia, and methane. These gases formed an atmosphere which, after slowly cooling, favored water accumulation on the surface through the condensation of steam. This atmosphere stabilized about 4.5 billion years ago, although the bombardment of the earth by meteorites continued until 3.8 billion years ago, and some meteorites could have brought water subsequently (Buckle & Mavtavish, 2013). The amount of water available on the earth's surface has been more or less constant since ancient times. Earth is reluctant to lose water to space because the thermal structure of its atmosphere is such that vapor is virtually non-existent beyond

15 km from its surface, taking into account condensation and precipitation. In return, the process of releasing water from the depths of the earth would now be negligible, at least on a human scale.

We know that water is the main agent in the incessant landscape remodeling. The location, size and shape of rivers were dictated by the competition between the processes that create mountains and those that tear them apart. The first rise is due to interactions between tectonic plates while the incessant circulation of water flattens them. The appearance of vascular plants - typical terrestrial plants made up of stems, leaves and roots - around 400 million years ago increased resistance to erosion. It slowed down the process of landscape remodeling: their leaves protect the soil from the impact of water drops, and their roots hold the loose soil on the slopes in place.

Over 3.5 billion years, the biosphere has thus become a planetary living tissue linking the lithosphere, the atmosphere, and the hydrosphere. Practically innumerable individuals who make it up and whose survival depends exclusively on themselves interact to form complex and resilient ecosystems. Remember that if ecosystems are resilient to small disturbances, larger reactions or even irreversible upheavals occur when the accumulation of disturbances exceeds a certain threshold.

However, human ingenuity has proven very effective in modifying the natural state of the territory: deforestation, draining of marshes, and alteration of the flow of water - to name just a few common interventions. What follows is a progressive takeover of the biosphere by the human species, which leads us towards overcoming some of its bigger limits, such as chemicals, particularly those relating to ocean acidification, the transformation of natural ecosystems and the loss of biodiversity.

OCEANS

What is curious about terrestrial biogeochemical limits is the relative carelessness of human beings about their existence. Take the case of carbon dioxide. Few people worried about the consequences of anthropogenic discharges since it was generally accepted, although not verified, that the mass of the oceans would soon destroy them, absorbing, thus ensuring the stability of concentrations of this greenhouse gas in the atmosphere. However, atmospheric carbon dioxide concentrations have increased substantially and continue to do so, demonstrating that the oceans need more than are insufficient. Indeed, it is estimated that the latter have only captured 155 of the 555 billion tons of carbon released since 1750 (Pawłowski & Cao, 2014).

Moreover, we have discovered a new biogeochemical limit. The absorption of carbon dioxide by the oceans increases their acidity and directly threatens certain species and possibly entire ecosystems (Sarma et al., 2015). Moreover, it was initially thought that the rate of absorption by the oceans was faster, which would have resulted in even more frantic acidification. The acidification mechanism by dissolving atmospheric carbon dioxide works in the oceans. We know how the ocean's acidity will change depending on the intensity of our carbon dioxide releases into the atmosphere. We also know that self-correcting mechanisms are slow: tens of thousands of years would be necessary for the oceans to return to their pre-industrial level of acidity.

However, the consequences of ocean acidification on marine life are less known. However, organisms that exploit calcification to build shells and external plates that protect them against predators are the most vulnerable in the short term. The problem for these organisms is that water has the potential to dissolve the calcium carbonate, returning it to an ion state, thereby depriving these organisms of their protection. Dissolution, however, is impossible as long as the water is saturated with carbonate, which was the case at the pre-industrial pH level. However, the increased presence of hydrogen ions following acidification had the effect of reducing the carbonate concentration (increased production of bicarbonate), stressful the organisms mentioned, which then have no other choice than to compensate for the dissolution of their shell or their plates by an increase in their calcification activity.

Calcium carbonate precipitates exist primarily in aragonite or calcite, two different crystalline structures. The first is more easily dissolved by water, which makes the animals that depend on it more immediately vulnerable to ocean acidification. This is particularly the case with corals, mollusks and algae. The experts who looked at terrestrial biogeochemical limits under the leadership of Rockström, therefore, targeted the saturation state of aragonite as an indicator of the consequences of ocean acidification (Rockström et al., 2023). The saturation state of a mineral has a value of 1 in equilibrium and a value greater than unity in the supersaturated state. Supersaturation with calcium carbonate is desired in order to avoid the dissolution of aragonite by seawater. However, the saturation state of aragonite has fallen, going from 3.44 to 2.90 since the beginning of industrialization. Although this value is still greater than unity, it hides local and seasonal variations that endanger the marine organisms that depend on it. Experts have established the lower limit of aragonite saturation state at 2.75, or 80% of its pre-industrial value.

The Intergovernmental Panel on Climate Change's (IPCC) work, reported in its fifth assessment report, reveals that for most carbon dioxide release scenarios, the upper layer of the oceans will become corrosive to aragonite within a decade in certain regions of the Arctic and some coastal areas known for their upwelling of deep water and within 10 to 30 years in several other parts of the oceans of the southern hemisphere (Werners et al., 2021). The situation would get worse later.

Therefore, anthropogenic carbon dioxide releases have two distinct and independent consequences: climate change and ocean acidification. While some can imagine living on a warmer planet, ocean acidification can also potentially generate socio-economic disorders. For example, damage to coral reefs will impact the fishing and tourism industries that depend on them, resulting in colossal economic losses for these sectors. One must remember that the oceans provide 17% of animal protein consumed worldwide and that six out of 10 marine animals are traded by developing countries.

Ultimately, several species, including some with commercial value, will gradually see their habitat and source of food and protection disappear, opening the door to their replacement by other species, often of lesser or even zero value. The stress imposed by ocean acidification on corals and mollusks is added to several others: asphyxiation, pollution, rising temperatures, and overfishing. It is, therefore, difficult to anticipate all the possible consequences on coral reefs and all organisms living at sea whose sensitivity to pH still needs to be discovered.

AGRICULTURAL EXPANSION

Feeding everyone on the planet remains a constant challenge today, as demonstrated by the third target of the first millennium development goal, which was intended to halve between 1990 and 2015, the proportion of people who suffer from hunger (Unterhalter, 2017). Given the increase in the human population, consumption, and waste, we must produce more and more, which puts pressure on soil and water resources. World agricultural production has thus increased on average by 2% to 4% per year over the last fifty years, while the cultivated area increased by only 1% per year. Forty per cent of production gains result from the partial transition from rain-fed agriculture to irrigated agriculture, the latter having doubled in surface area during this period. The use of increasingly productive varieties is another factor which ultimately means that we succeed in extracting more food from our overall agricultural activities. The cultivated area per capita consequently fell from 0.44 to 0.25 hectares in the same period. Rainfed production remains the dominant form of agriculture (80%), but as it is subject to the vagaries of the climate, it does not guarantee maximum yield. Under optimal climatic conditions and agricultural practices, the yield of this land could generally double. This is proof that the potential to feed future generations still exists. Water still needs to be available to irrigate everything as needed. However, 70% of global water collection is already used for agricultural irrigation. This use causes significant stress on several local resources, with varied consequences (drying of rivers, lowering groundwater levels, disagreement between riparian countries), which slow development potential.

Increasing the proportion of agricultural land has proven to be the preferred solution for increasing agricultural production. The undisturbed forests and grasslands of early civilization would not support the needs of human beings today. Covering the entire planet with fields interspersed with villages and towns is no longer feasible, as the upheavals in the earth's biogeochemical systems would be great. However, the world population is anticipated to increase from 7 to 9.7 billion individuals by 2050 (Gu, Andreev & Dupre, 2021). Generally richer than in the past, the demand for food exploded during this period; the Food and Agriculture Organization of the United Nations (FAO) predicts an increase of 60%. The demand for food for humans is already growing faster than the population due to new dietary habits relying more on the consumption of animals.

We have already significantly modified the natural occupation of the continents, mainly by converting land to agriculture. To give a better idea, the potential surface area of the fourteen terrestrial biomes – a biome is a set of ecosystems sharing common qualities – was evaluated and compared to that of 1990. It appears that, for two of these – the Mediterranean forests, woods and scrub, and temperate grasslands, savannahs, and scrub – more than two-thirds have already been converted to agriculture. Over half of four other biomes have been converted to agriculture: temperate deciduous and mixed forests, tropical and subtropical dry deciduous forests, flooded grasslands and savannahs, and tropical and tropical grasslands, savannahs, and scrub. If, before engaging in livestock farming, humans only accounted for 0.1% of the total mass of mammals, today it is estimated that humans and their livestock form 90% of this mass.

Forests today occupy only 30% of the territory and are under immense pressure, even though they play a central role in the biogeochemical balance of the earth. They also meet the direct needs of at least a billion people through uses other than wood extraction. They even offer solutions to the fight against climate change since it is possible to strengthen their role as a sink of carbon by countering their degradation and substituting forest products for concrete and steel, which result in high carbon dioxide emissions for their manufacture. Forests also regulate water flow by promoting rain infiltration into the ground, which helps control harmful effects such as flooding and soil erosion. They are also home to more than 80% of earth's biodiversity. However, the degradation and disappearance of forests continue despite the efforts invested to counter them (Hamunyela et al, 2020).

Changes to land use in support of agriculture can further disrupt the earth's biogeochemical functioning, particularly because of the strong interactions between agricultural activities and environmental cycles. Nitrogen and phosphorus (massive use of chemical fertilizers), but also between the climate (source and sink of carbon), the water cycle (overexploitation and pollution) and biodiversity (monoculture). 75% of the plant food consumed comes from seven species: wheat, rice, corn, potatoes, barley, sweet potatoes, and cassava.

The experts brought together by Rockström retained the area of land dedicated to plant production as an indicator of the proper biogeochemical functioning of the earth and proposed an area of 15% of the territory as a limit not to be violated (Rockström et al., 2009). However, at the current growth rate of 1% per year, this portion of land allocated to plant production will increase from 12% to 15% in just a few decades. It, therefore, becomes imperative to adequately feed everyone without expanding the areas devoted to this activity. This involves, among other things, curbing urban spillover onto the best land, making the best use of irrigation water, controlling the expansion of land use for non-food crops (such as those intended for ethanol production) and counter soil degradation. In the latter case, better agricultural practices must be adopted in order to prevent erosion of the topsoil by water and wind and to prevent any damage, whether of a natural chemical (decline in fertility, drop in organic matter levels, salinization), physical (compaction, sealing, crusting, asphyxiation), biological (loss of soil fauna, increase in pests, reduction in predators) or water (aridification, decline in surface and groundwater quality).

It should not be forgotten that agricultural practices are closely linked to land tenure systems and traditional knowledge and are often regulated by traditional practices. Improving the efficiency of production practices must consider the importance of these traditional practices and knowledge to ensure the food security of local populations and the maintenance of local food varieties, which constitute an essential element of biodiversity and preserve food security.

The colossal efforts invested in food production to ensure adequate access for all in the spirit of the third target of the first-millennium development goal are undermined by significant problems of conservation, distribution and development of the food produced. The FAO estimates that around a third of the food produced is not consumed because it is wasted before reaching markets or simply by end buyers (Chen, Chaudhary & Mathys, 2020). Considering intensive food production's social, energy and environmental costs, acting at this link in the food chain is imperative. We need to rethink distribution to avoid all this waste.

Objective 2 of the Sustainable Development Goals aims to increase small farmers' productivity and income and improve the functioning of food markets (Atukunda et al., 2021). It also limits the fight against hunger within the framework of adequate ecosystem management while preserving biodiversity.

BIODIVERSITY LOSS

The extent of biological diversity is striking and must have been just as striking in the eyes of the people who lived by hunting and gathering before the very concept of the city appeared. Biodiversity brings hope, notably conveyed during the Earth Summit in Rio de Janeiro in 1992, that the diversity of living things and the interactions between the elements of the biosphere go beyond the interest of the biologist and capture that of the whole society. States have also adopted the Convention on Biological Diversity, a determining element of their multilateral strategy in favor of sustainable development (Shin et al., 2022). This agreement is structured around three objectives concerning:

1. the conservation of biological diversity,
2. the sustainable use of its elements and
3. the fair and equitable sharing of the benefits from exploiting its genetic resources.

Each plant, animal, and human thus contributes to this diversity through its genetic background as a species and constituent of a particular ecosystem. These three facets are also at the heart of the definition included in the convention relating to diversity within species and between species and ecosystems.

Studying biodiversity means, first of all, listing it, but it is also considerably more than that. It is desirable to list and name each living organism, whether plant, mammal, insect or other – a task made colossal by the extent of the territory to be covered and the diversity of living things. It is a work that we have been busy with since the time of the gatherer-hunters, as it was essential to our survival to know the edibility or even the medicinal properties of plants and the characteristics and behaviors of the animals being hunted and eventually domesticated. Over time, this knowledge was recorded in documents, often illustrated with sketches, for the teaching profession but even more to consolidate the collective experience. Today, if it is easy to obtain an illustrated guide to mushrooms or native birds, it is because nearly two million species have been inventoried, mostly insects. However, there are many more; there would be between five million and thirty million. We will need a few more centuries to complete this planetary biological inventory at the rate things are going. Therefore, we can imagine that several species will disappear by then before even being listed and named.

This is because human activities (water diversion, agricultural expansion), as well as their numerous consequences (climate change, ocean acidification, eutrophication, pollution, depletion of the ozone layer, among others), have direct repercussions on the habitat of most species, as well as on how they interact with each other. An overview of the situation was compiled by experts commissioned by the United Nations during the Millennium Ecosystem Assessment (Dede et al., 2023). The conclusion reached is that man is radically, and to a certain degree irreversibly, changing the biological diversity on the planet. More precisely, they report that the extinction rate of species during the 20th century exceeded 50 to 500 times that had been established from the study of fossils; this reference rate is between 0.1 and 1 extinction per thousand species over a thousand years. If we include species for which extinction is probable but not yet demonstrated with certainty, the exceedance will reach a thousand times the reference rate. Using various models, these same experts estimate that this rate will increase further, possibly by a factor of 10. The main direct causes of extinction are the loss of habitats and their degradation, the introduction of competing species, overexploitation, diseases, pollution, and climate change. Extinction remains a natural phenomenon; every species is doomed to disappear. Palaeontologists have also estimated the average lifespan of species to be around eleven million years (Scheiner, 2024). On this basis, only 2% of the species that appeared on earth are still active today.

Let us take a closer look at how humans depend on the biosphere of which they are a part. Ecosystem services are the benefits humans derive from the healthy ecosystems around them. These services are divided into four groups:

1. supply services in food, materials, fibers, energy (wood and hydroelectricity) or genetic resources.
2. control services (resilience), climate, floods, erosion, populations and diseases.
3. cultural, spiritual, aesthetic, recreational and even creative services (source of inspiration);
4. Life support services include the water cycle, biogeochemical cycles, soil formation, self-purification (air and water), and pollination.

However, ecosystems exist first of all through the elements that constitute them. The loss of biodiversity has, therefore, been recognized as a concrete limit to the proper biogeochemical functioning of the earth. Although not all species have the same level of influence on ecosystem services, it seems imperative to conserve them as best as possible. The limit Rockström's team proposed is ten extinctions per thousand species over a thousand years, i.e. ten times more than the historical value but 100 times less than the current rate, which constitutes a colossal challenge for our society (Rockström et al, 2009).

The uncertainty associated with climate change and its repercussions will not simplify our efforts. It leads us to envisage increased biodiversity losses and increased disruption of ecosystems. Preventing the disappearance of endangered species is, of course, essential. However, it is, above all, the dynamics of relationships within ecosystems that must be ensured, which is an even greater challenge.

One then returns to the question of going beyond inventory. The list of the living resembles an album of passport photos. While this inventory is useful for identification, it provides little information about the history of the people in front of us or their interactions with others. We need information equivalent to videos to perceive the slow evolution of each ecosystem - we could go back some 3.5 billion years -but above all, we need to know the dynamics between species, including human beings, and which give life to ecosystems. There is nothing static about these. Each photo of an ecosystem describes a particular moment, a point along a trajectory among many possible ones. For some, in the spirit of sustainable development, it is up to us to specify the components or processes that must be preserved, strengthened, or modified so that the evolution of ecosystems is harmonious and beneficial to generations. In the future, this challenge will take on its full meaning in the ecoregions most subject to the human footprint, such as agrosystems, cities, and overexploited coastal areas.

We can also let nature work, for example, by designating protected areas to conserve biological diversity. Humans systematically favor producing three ecosystem services – crops, livestock and aquaculture – at the expense of other services. The concept of protected areas seeks to reduce, or even eliminate, this type of intervention to safeguard the diversity of life and natural resources, the health of all ecosystem services, and their cultural value. This last point is particularly important because eliminating all human presence from these areas is rarely possible (and probably undesirable). Certain peoples have inhabited these territories for a very long time and have the knowledge that allows them to manage them adequately. Moreover, studies show that certain traditional agricultural ecosystems have richer biodiversity, thanks to human intervention than when left fallow, in opposition to modern agriculture, favoring monoculture.

However, protected areas alone are not enough to maintain global biodiversity. We must also work to preserve the health of all major ecosystems. However, the indicators published by the experts of the Millennium Ecosystem Assessment are not encouraging (Solomon, 2023). Furthermore, the representation of nature as external and hostile to man, as nature to be subjugated, which characterizes Western culture and guides its activities, makes any ecological reconversion difficult to accept.

Goal 15 of the Sustainable Development Goals aims to curb all factors that affect biodiversity. Its targets concern the conservation of ecosystems, the sustainable management of forests, the fight against land degradation, and the prevention of species extinction, as well as other means of implementing the instruments that are part of the international biodiversity regime (Prip, 2022).

INTEGRATION OF LIMITS

Terrestrial biogeochemical limits are one of the six fundamental elements that UN Secretary-General Ban Ki-Moon identified in the development agenda for 2015-2030 (Jesenský & Jesenský, 2019): To respect our planetary boundaries, we must address climate change with equity, halt the loss of biological diversity, and address desertification and overexploitation of land. We must protect wildlife, preserve forests and mountains, and reduce disaster risks through resilience. We must protect our oceans, seas, rivers, and atmosphere, part of our global heritage, and ensure climate justice. We must keep in mind the imperative of sustainability in agriculture, fisheries and food systems; management of water resources and waste and chemicals; the use of renewable and more efficient energy sources; the need to decouple economic growth from environmental degradation; the promotion of industrialization and the establishment of resilient infrastructure; the adoption of new modes of consumption and production; and the management of marine and terrestrial ecosystems and land use.

The other five key elements are people, dignity, prosperity, justice, and partnerships, which are all integrated, interdependent, and indivisible dimensions that constitute this agenda. This proves that the synthesis of research and the communication tools developed by the Rockström team has widely penetrated UN spaces. It testifies to a notable improvement in mutual understanding between scientists, diplomats, and technocrats in international governance and to the strength of the scientific evidence that we currently have (Folke et al., 2021).

Rockström asserts that scientists have been moving out of their comfort zones for several years and becoming increasingly worried (Österblom et al., 2017). This is because the scientific evidence shows, in a potentially worrying, even catastrophic way, what can happen if the world does not make the transition to sustainable development. Global issues are no longer simply environmental issues. These are existential questions. It is a change in mentality and in this vein from an ecological point of view, sustainability requires that resources be exploited at a rate slower than their renewal and that waste be released into the environment at a rate lower than the self-purification capacity of nature. The ecological footprint measures human beings' pressure on the biosphere; it quantifies the territorial area required to support our lifestyles. This territory, land, air, and water, inhabited by living organisms, provides the resources humans consume and use during their activities. It absorbs waste or accumulates it once its self-purification capacity is exceeded and undergoes modifications resulting from human activities. Ecological footprint measurements consider current technologies and practices to establish the resources and services that can be obtained on average from a given territorial area. The ecological footprint specifically targets supply services (food, materials, fibers, energy) and self-purification; therefore, it does not consider all previously mentioned ecosystem services. It combines three factors: demography, the consumption rate per person and the technological level, which dictates the intensity of resource consumption and waste production.

The ecological footprint concept is thus part of the debates undertaken in the 1970s and mentioned in the first chapter on the consequences of economic and demographic trends. Paul Ehrlich, John Holdren, and Barry Commoner then agreed that population, consumption, and technology were the three factors that could be modulated to reduce the impact on nature. This paradigm became known under the formulation $I = PAT$, i.e., the human impact on the environment is the product of the population, its consumption, and available technologies ($I = PAT$, Impact = Population · Affluence · Technology) (DeHart & Soulé, 2000). These authors had divergent opinions on the weight to be attributed to each of these variables. However, it already seemed that technology constituted the most important solution to the crisis in our context of increasing population and consumption.

The ecological footprint is based on a type $I = PAT$ accounting structure. The concept behind the ecological footprint is the earth's carrying capacity, that is, the effective surface area available to produce resources and eliminate waste. The carrying capacity represents all the land and seas available to humanity for its activities, whether growing plants, livestock, forestry, fishing, aquaculture, and assimilating waste and support infrastructure.

Comparing the ecological footprint and the support capacity allows us to assess the ecological sustainability of our consumption and activities. Our global mode of operation could be more sustainable from an ecological point of view since it leads either to the exhaustion of resources or to dysfunctions of the earth system. For example, fishing beyond the renewal capacity of species leads to the fall of populations, and the release of carbon dioxide in the atmosphere beyond the fixation capacity of ecosystems leads to the intensification of the greenhouse effect and climate change.

This section addresses the main keys to interpreting the trajectories of our socio-economic system, within which multiple activities and dynamics specific to human populations are intertwined. These dynamics are open and changing and arise from all forms of social, political, economic, cultural and religious organization. They interact in diverse ways with natural systems. A better understanding of these trajectories makes it possible to distinguish the elements that take us further away from or closer to a desired future.

POPULATION

The first warning signals of the consequences of demographic growth on the future of the global environment in the 1970s were triggered by the United Nations Population Fund (UNFPA) analysis in 1969 (Bracke, 2022). Their approach aimed to promote active birth control in the Third World with a firm family planning policy. This conception, inspired by natural sciences, guided the demographic policies of the North towards the South. This approach put forward non-binding policies aimed at promoting access to information and family planning methods, and restrictive interventions, sometimes carried out without women's knowledge, were denounced. The dominant view of the problem then echoed the thinking of many biologists and ecologists. Among them, Paul Ehrlich described the repercussions of population growth as an explosion, even comparing them to a "bomb" (Ritchie & Roser, 2024). This reasoning, still widespread in the natural sciences and the public, was criticized since it needs to consider the human dimensions of the demographic question.

Analyses became more nuanced when technological innovations in agriculture, known as the "green revolution", favored the expansion of food production, particularly in developing countries where undernourishment was rife (Chand & Singh, 2023). However, contrary to what its name might suggest, this major technological and financial mobilization, carried out between 1960 and 1990, had no ecological aim. Some experts also denounced the negative consequences of this initiative: impoverishment of small farmers, loss of biodiversity and disappearance of traditional practices and knowledge.

The observation of a close link between the conditions of poverty and the high birth rates of the countries of the South emerged clearly at the time and was expressed in the Brundtland report. It then appears that any demographic policy with real social and economic development would be effective. The problem lies in the demographic numbers and how these numbers are distributed among the available resources. This is why the demographic problem must be partly solved by efforts to eliminate mass poverty, to ensure more equitable access to resources, and by educational action aimed at improving the human management capacities of these resources. This question is not, however, only a demographic one: providing people with the means and information to enable them to choose the size of their families is a way of guaranteeing them, particularly women, the enjoyment of the right to self-determination, which is a fundamental human right.

It is now known that improving health and hygiene conditions reduces child mortality, which, in the long term, encourages parents to have fewer children. Likewise, schooling for girls supports the diversification of women's societal roles and often reduces the birth rate. In 1994, the International Conference on Population and Development placed human rights at the center of this issue and outlined an action plan for the 21st century around recommendations on health and education and the definition of new demographic realities: the ageing of the population of industrialized countries, urbanization and migration (Kawwass et al., 2021). Data from the two decades following this conference reveal a substantial reduction in the birth rate for the entire population and an increase in life expectancy.

The world population exceeded seven billion people in 2011, and recent projections announce eight billion humans in 2025 and 9.7 billion in 2050. This is because people are also living longer since the Average life expectancy recently increased from 65 years (1990-1995) to 70 years (2010-2014). Overall, the share of people aged 65 and over increased from 9% in 1994 to 12% in 2014 and is expected to reach 21% in 2050. Population growth, however, varies considerably from one region to another: that of 49 least developed countries is expected to double while that of 40 other countries will decline - Eastern Europe, East, South-East and West Asia, Latin America and the Caribbean. Improving the life expectancy of the most vulnerable populations and reducing the birth rate in certain regions are challenges that still need to be addressed but are now being addressed through access to education, gender equity, and the reduction of maternal mortality.

International migration is a factor whose importance is now recognized. One hundred fifty-four million people lived outside their country of origin in 1990, compared to 281 million in 2020 (Gu, Andreev & Dupre, 2021). This migratory trend, considered by the United Nations as an important development factor, is expected to increase. Humans are also deserting rural areas in favor of cities: 13% of individuals were city dwellers in 1900, compared to 29% in 1950, 52% in 2010 and potentially 70% in 2050, a progression reminding us of the importance of planning a sustainable urban environment (Harris et al., 2020). Thus, the population is central in I = PCT models, such as the ecological footprint, since the beginning of the 1980s, humans' ecological footprint has exceeded the earth's supporting capacity.

CONSUMPTION

Our consumption of products and services has repercussions on the exploitation of resources and the creation of waste. In the case of renewable resources, their consumption can be sustainable to the extent that it does not exceed their renewal rate. For example, if wood consumption exceeds the renewal rate of a forest, it will disappear. Considering that, beyond the advances made possible by new technologies, environmental limits prevent us from indefinitely increasing the exploitation of resources, the question of consumption patterns necessarily arises, particularly that of the overconsumption of industrialized countries. The Brundtland report stated that a level higher than the subsistence minimum would be possible on the sole condition that consumption patterns take long-term possibilities into account. However, many of us live above the planet's ecological means, particularly in terms of energy consumption. The notion of needs is certainly socially and culturally determined. To ensure sustainable development, however, we must promote values that will facilitate consumption within the limits of ecological possibility and to which everyone can reasonably aspire.

With a population that continues to increase, knowing that sustainable development involves satisfying the minimum needs of all and that the technologies which underpin the current economy do not allow us to respect the limits of the planet, it becomes imperative to promote more sustainable modes of production and consumption. However, official responses to the questioning of consumption patterns have been coming for a long time. While numerous citizen initiatives have existed since the 1970s, only in 2012, during the Rio+20 Conference, a program targeting sustainable consumption and production patterns saw the light of day after nine years of negotiations (Adamowicz, 2022). This is the 10-year programming framework for sustainable consumption and production patterns, which aims to support regional and national policies and initiatives to accelerate the transition to sustainable consumption and production patterns6.

This delay could be explained by the difficulty in taking a step back from consumer behavior to the extent that it constitutes a strategic pivot of our modern society, which is rightly described as a consumer society. To analyze the phenomenon further, let us examine its different dimensions. Biologists Ehrlich and Commoner relied on an ecological definition of consumption (Wapner, 2021). In an ecosystem, living organisms consume the resources of their environment to ensure their survival and produce waste coveted by other living organisms. Resource availability and interactions between species, therefore, directly impact population size. In this spirit, Thomas Malthus wrote the Principle of Population in 1798, which evokes a nature pushed beyond its capacity to support a continuous increase in population and consumption (Kreager, 2022). Living at the dawn of the Industrial Revolution, Malthus could not anticipate the positive role of technology on environmental impact. However, this changes nothing in his reasoning since this positive effect is generally limited to a shift in time when the support capacity will be exceeded.

Individual behavior and collective consumption practices also depend on many social and cultural factors beyond technological transformations. In 1976, the economist Hirsch described the mechanisms of social differentiation as the main drivers of consumption (Hirsch, 1976). "Beyond the satisfaction of essential needs," said Hirsch, the individual in our industrial society directs his consumption towards "positional goods", that is to say, those which allow the owner to stand out from those who do not have them. Beyond a certain threshold, these goods no longer respond to natural needs but only to the need for distinction, and they are produced and recreated infinitely by industry. This characterizes the consumer society that Walt W. Rostow gave as a model and final stage of society (Willis, 2023). If sustainable development wants to lead us to formulate other consumption models, we must consider the complexity of the social and psychological mechanisms that underlie them.

The Brundtland Report included an analysis of issues related to resource consumption. The authors called on industrialized countries to produce products that consume less energy and materials and developing countries to meet the essential needs of all their inhabitants. They were concerned about the overconsumption of water and certain fisheries resources and noted the existence of a limit to the possibility of adequately feeding ever more people. They calculated that the earth's plant production capacity could provide sufficient food for between 7.5 and 9.7 billion people (Mhlanga, 2023). The authors specified that this would require changing eating habits and considerably improving the efficiency of traditional agriculture. More recent assessments show that the state of nutrition in the world has improved in recent years, which is expected to continue. However, given that food production responds to solvent demand, that is to say, purchasing capacity, responding to the needs of thousands of people who do not have the financial resources to obtain products in the market or to produce them themselves, will remain the main food security problem in the coming years.

Other recommendations from the WCED aimed to change the consumption model of manufactured products, encourage consumer awareness, and strengthen labelling measures for products containing ingredients potentially harmful to health or the environment. Concerning waste, the Brundtland report made numerous recommendations for controlling pollution and improving the management of solid residues, particularly concerning the fate of the oceans, the ultimate waste receptors. It also highlighted the fact that the value of waste was largely underestimated. By promoting the recovery, reuse or recycling of materials, we can reduce the problem of solid waste, stimulate employment and save on raw materials. Composting can be used for urban agriculture. If a municipality needs the necessary means to remove garbage households regularly, it can support systems set up by communities. In many cities, thousands earn their living by hand sorting waste in municipal landfills. Investing in an automatic recycling plant requiring greater capital could be doubly counterproductive if such a plant unnecessarily absorbs scarce capital and if it eliminates the means of living of many people.

These few examples show that the effectiveness of strategies depends on their ability to consider the many factors at play and their interrelationships. By 2010, it was noted that increasingly efficient technologies in resource and energy use had resulted in a notable reduction in the use of materials and energy per unit produced in industrialized countries. However, this improvement has yet to reduce total resource consumption since the other variables, population, and per capita consumption, continue growing.

Forecasts indicate that the world population will stabilize by the middle of this century at under 10 billion. This is called the demographic transition. Therefore, some increase in global production and consumption is necessary to meet the unmet needs of a large part of the world's population. We use the term convergence to illustrate this objective of increasing consumption by the most deprived sectors in order to meet needs that we consider socially legitimate. But what about other needs? If what Hirsch tells us is true, we should change the mechanisms that push us to consume "positional goods" if we want to direct the world population towards sustainable consumption patterns (Blosser, 2024). In short, the objective of sustainable development is to achieve this convergence while reducing the ecological footprint of all of humanity. This is called decoupling (Elahi et al., 2024). There are a variety of strategies to achieve this goal, and they are distinguished by their appreciation of the factors that influence population, consumption, and technology, as well as their interrelationships.

TECHNOLOGY

Much more than population growth, Commoner argued that technological change accompanying industrialization was the main cause of environmental degradation, especially since the Second World War (Commoner, 2020). This industrial revolution, which began in England around 1750, marked the parallel evolution of two inseparable phenomena: the exploitation of resources by new, ever more powerful technologies and the improvement in the living conditions of populations wishing to benefit from products resulting from the transformation of resources. Manufacturing techniques, as well as daily living conditions, had previously remained virtually unchanged for centuries.

Combining ingenuity, scientific knowledge, and social conditions enabled England to design an unprecedented production system based on capitalist economics intimately linked to machine power. Steam was invented at the beginning of the 18th century and then improved by James Watt in 1776. This new economy allowed England and the rest of Europe to escape the cycle of famines and wars that had marked its story so far. Also propelled by the steam engine, new transport systems, boats and railways were deployed. Strengthened by these technological developments and the vast coal deposits of the region Lancashire, England acquired the status of an empire, a dominion further consolidated by the exploitation of the resources of the entire empire, including the forests of Canada. Then came industrialization based on oil exploitation, first in the United States, followed by Canada, Poland, and Romania. Intended mainly for lighting but superseded by the electric light bulb in 1878, oil favored the expansion of the mass automobile industry, which Henry Ford started in 1905. Subsequently, the petrochemical industry was deployed.

According to Schumpeter, technological innovations marked different growth cycles: the steam engine, rail transport, electricity, the petrochemical industry and information technology and communication (Lianos & Sloev, 2024). Each of these cycles, which we also call "techno-economic revolutions", has had a major influence on society, organizing its economic production, modifying its consumption methods, and sometimes designing new rural and urban structures. However, the benefits of these transformations were only accessible to part of the population, while another part suffered the disadvantages. Modernization thus became an opportunity to improve productivity, commerce and comfort, simultaneously as a potential cause of the impoverishment of marginalized regions or sections of the population. Thus, what we call poverty today is, above all, the result of this divide deepened over the last two centuries.

Moreover, we must not believe that technology only has positive consequences for those with access to it. Suppose the flashiness of certain gadgets encourages positive results and confidence in the future. In that case, certain technological advances that are less polluting and harmful to the health of humans and ecosystems need to materialize faster.

Major technological innovations were motivated and made possible by the development of the economy, the exploitation of resources and the creation of markets worldwide. If the first three growth cycles defined by Schumpeter – steam engine, rail transport, electricity – were largely oriented by the interest of states, the last two resulted from an increasingly complex interweaving of multinational companies and the financial system. Technologies thus include an institutional dimension in addition to the technoscientific, social and environmental dimensions. Technoscientific innovations are closely linked to the exploitation of new markets and the behavior of wealthy consumers. The billion and a half people living below the poverty line and whose improved living conditions are integral to sustainable development often remain neglected. Hence, there is a need for public investments and the application of new technologies that meet the requirements of sustainable development.

To appreciate the limits of technoscientific solutions intended to resolve environmental problems, we must consider the irreversible consequences caused by industrialization, such as climate change and loss of biodiversity. Technical solutions make it possible to reduce the pressure on ecosystems and biogeochemical cycles without eliminating the negative effects. In certain cases, for example, the repercussions of atmospheric pollution or wastewater, solutions exist without all users being able to access them due to a lack of economic means. Thus, for sustainable development to take full advantage of technological development, it is imperative to learn lessons from the major technological transformations of the past.

LINEAR ECONOMY

The economic mode of production inherited from the Industrial Revolution developed in three linear stages: extract, produce and throw away. Resource providers extract and make available raw materials and energy; companies manufacture, and market products dedicated to consumption; users acquire these products and throw them away at the end of their useful life. This explains that many wastes contain reusable materials of identical quality to those sold by resource suppliers.

Take the case of metals. Their recovery and recycling potential is very high, as their degradation through wear and oxidation is slow. Although some are exploited in the form of more or less complex alloys and are sometimes expensive to recycle, others are mainly used in their elementary form, notably copper, gold, lead, platinum, palladium and rhodium. However, the linear economy has yet to be able to take advantage of the copper present in objects at the end of their life (Born & Ciftci, 2024). We can see that any system based on consumption rather than the best possible yield of raw materials leads to significant losses. Today, except for automobiles, few industries achieve a recovery rate of 25% (Abdullah, 2024).

Life cycle analysis or life cycle thinking is a method which takes into account all the relationships (environmental, economic and social) specific to a product or service throughout its life cycle, from the extraction of raw materials until their final disposal; this concept is also called from the cradle to the grave (Moresi & Cimini, 2024). Decisions based on the life cycle provide a global vision, thus avoiding transferring problems from one stage to another. The purpose of life cycle analysis is thus to reduce the negative socio-environmental effects associated with extraction, production, use and disposal that characterize the linear economy. This analysis subscribes to eco-efficiency, which consists of extracting maximum value from a minimum of resources while generating a minimum of pollution.

The principles of "polluter pays" and "user pays" are well recognized in economics. Accepted by the Organization for Economic Cooperation and Development countries since 1972, they provide that a natural or legal person who uses a natural resource or pollutes an environment should cover the costs of renewing this resource or restoring the environment (Steenge, 1997). Environmental economists have used the concept of externality to introduce pollution problems into economic calculations. Governments can resort to taxation or the creation of markets, such as carbon, to internalize the costs of certain activities, such as pollution, or to promote the goods and services provided by ecosystems.

More systematically and fundamentally, currents of thought offer a new vision of economic relationships. Several can be linked to ecological economics, a plural discipline interested in the relationships between natural, social, and economic systems to better human well-being and nature. Faced with the disciplinary specialization developed over the centuries, ecological economics establishes links between the knowledge necessary to resolve the problems arising from human and natural systems' interactions to respect their limits. Several trends can be associated with this multidiscipline, including the circular economy (industrial ecology), the economy and the steady state economy. Efforts to transform production systems and their measurement towards systems that are lower in emissions and more efficient in the use of resources and energy are encouraged by international organizations, which group them under the rubric "green economy", a theme which was on the agenda at the Rio+20 Conference in 2012 (Kuldoshev, 2024).

For example, the circular economy puts forward an economic model where resources already extracted are the raw materials of the future. This vision of the economy thus pushes life cycle analysis a step further towards the concept of "cradle to grave". Another basic principle of the circular economy is not to tax what is desired. This avoids taxing renewable resources, including human labor (wages). This favors the renewable energy, reuse, reuse and recycling sectors and social services (health care, elderly care, education). In a circular economy, goods travel in cycles, where we reuse what works, repair what is broken, remanufacture what cannot be repaired and recycle what cannot be remanufactured locally to avoid transport costs. This model is the antithesis of the current linear economy, based on the extraction and transformation of raw materials where recyclable materials are sent abroad to benefit from the lowest wages without regard to energy consumption. They consider that 75% of the energy used to produce a good is used to extract raw materials and 25% for its manufacture. In comparison, 25% of the human labor invested in a product is used for extraction and 75% for its manufacture; the circular economy effectively reduces emissions and creates jobs.

A durable product is designed to be used for as long as possible, then repaired, remanufactured, and eventually recycled. The functionality economy recommends renting or sharing durable products as much as possible, in particular, to discourage companies from marketing products whose end-of-use life is programmed to force their replacement as quickly as possible.

CONCLUSION

Given the challenges facing the world one solution put forward is the 5 Rs of the circular economy - reduce, reuse, repair, refurbish and recycle – though they do not all have the same weight (Dragan et al., 2024). Suppose the emphasis is often placed on recycling at the end of an object's useful life to maintain the use of these materials. In that case, recycling also has an environmental impact and does not resolve the increase in consumption. For example, if a contractor succeeds in recycling all the materials from a house, he can rebuild one of equivalent size, not two. However, in a context of population increase, although reuse, repair and remanufacturing make it possible to extend the lifespan of products, it is also necessary to reduce the rate of consumption in order to limit pressure on stocks and material flow.

One can thus gain insight into the complexity of the variables to consider in assessing our current impacts on the environment and the effect of these trends in the future. Technical choices, knowledge models, and representations of nature are factors to consider, as well as public policies and institutions that express collective choices. One could add the ethical variable and values to this equation too. These values are sometimes translated into standards and institutions which influence our choices and future trajectories and must, therefore, also be integrated. The ecological footprint of the linear economy requires innovative actions, particularly on the sustainable use of stocks and flows of materials.

According to Homer, Sisyphus was the most intelligent and shrewd among all humans. In the myth of Sisyphus, it is said that the gods had punished him by condemning him to carry a heavy boulder to the top of a mountain, only to watch it roll back to the bottom again and forcing him to repeat the task endlessly. This punishment was considered the cruelest and most futile, lacking purpose or hope. Similarly, the world is facing a daunting challenge today regarding environmental protection. All countries are required to make difficult decisions to address this issue. Although we have failed to prevent the damage so far, a solution is still available. Sustainable development provides a path to balance economic growth and environmental protection, thereby ensuring a better future for generations to come. Hence, it is something that needs to be addressed. Now.

REFERENCES

Abdullah, Z. T. (2024). Remanufacturing waste steel sheet from end-of-life vehicles into electrical installation wall junction boxes: Quantitative sustainability assessment. *Results in Engineering*, *21*, 101767. doi:10.1016/j.rineng.2024.101767

Adamowicz, M. (2022). Green deal, green growth and green economy as a means of support for attaining the sustainable development goals. *Sustainability (Basel)*, *14*(10), 5901. doi:10.3390/su14105901

Atukunda, P., Eide, W. B., Kardel, K. R., Iversen, P. O., & Westerberg, A. C. (2021). Unlocking the potential for achievement of the UN Sustainable Development Goal 2–'Zero Hunger'–in Africa: Targets, strategies, synergies and challenges. *Food & Nutrition Research*, *65*, 65. doi:10.29219/fnr.v65.7686 PMID:34262413

Blosser, A. (2024). *The Concept of Sacramental Goods: Addressing Veblen's Critique of Liturgy*. Studia Liturgica.

Born, K., & Ciftci, M. M. (2024). The limitations of end-of-life copper recycling and its implications for the circular economy of metals. *Resources, Conservation and Recycling*, *200*, 107318. doi:10.1016/j.resconrec.2023.107318

Bracke, M. A. (2022). Women's rights, family planning, and population control: The emergence of reproductive rights in the united nations (1960s–70s). *The International History Review*, *44*(4), 751–771. doi:10.1080/07075332.2021.1985585

Buckle, D. S., & Mactavish, D. F. (2013). *Grantham Briefing Note 4: The Earth's energy budget*.

Chand, R., & Singh, J. (2023). *From green revolution to amrit kaal*. National Institution for Transforming India. GoI.

Chen, C., Chaudhary, A., & Mathys, A. (2020). Nutritional and environmental losses embedded in global food waste. *Resources, Conservation and Recycling*, *160*, 104912. doi:10.1016/j.resconrec.2020.104912

Commoner, B. (2020). *The closing circle: nature, man, and technology*. Courier Dover Publications.

Dede, M., Sunardi, S., Lam, K. C., & Withaningsih, S. (2023). Relationship between landscape and river ecosystem services. *Global Journal of Environmental Science and Management*, *9*(3), 637–652.

DeHart, J. L., & Soulé, P. T. (2000). Does I= PAT work in local places? *The Professional Geographer*, *52*(1), 1–10. doi:10.1111/0033-0124.00200

Dragan, G. B., Arfi, W. B., Tiberius, V., Ammari, A., & Ferasso, M. (2024). Acceptance of circular entrepreneurship: Employees' perceptions on organizations' transition to the circular economy. *Journal of Business Research*, *173*, 114461. doi:10.1016/j.jbusres.2023.114461

Elahi, E., Li, G., Han, X., Zhu, W., Liu, Y., Cheng, A., & Yang, Y. (2024). Decoupling livestock and poultry pollution emissions from industrial development: A step towards reducing environmental emissions. *Journal of Environmental Management*, *350*, 119654. doi:10.1016/j.jenvman.2023.119654 PMID:38016232

Folke, C., Carpenter, S., Elmqvist, T., Gunderson, L., & Walker, B. (2021). Resilience: Now more than ever: This article belongs to Ambio's 50th Anniversary Collection. Theme: Anthropocene. *Ambio*, *50*(10), 1774–1777. doi:10.1007/s13280-020-01487-6 PMID:33721222

Gu, D., Andreev, K., & Dupre, M. E. (2021). Major trends in population growth around the world. *China CDC Weekly*, *3*(28), 604. doi:10.46234/ccdcw2021.160 PMID:34594946

Hamunyela, E., Brandt, P., Shirima, D., Do, H. T. T., Herold, M., & Roman-Cuesta, R. M. (2020). Space-time detection of deforestation, forest degradation and regeneration in montane forests of Eastern Tanzania. *International Journal of Applied Earth Observation and Geoinformation*, *88*, 102063. doi:10.1016/j.jag.2020.102063

Harris, S., Weinzettel, J., Bigano, A., & Källmén, A. (2020). Low carbon cities in 2050? GHG emissions of European cities using production-based and consumption-based emission accounting methods. *Journal of Cleaner Production*, *248*, 119206. doi:10.1016/j.jclepro.2019.119206

Hirsch, F. (1976). *Social limits to growth*. Harvard University Press. doi:10.4159/harvard.9780674497900

Jesenský, M., & Jesenský, M. (2019). Development for All: We Still Can. *The United Nations under Ban Ki-moon: Give Diplomacy a Chance*, 11-20.

Kawwass, J. F., Penzias, A. S., & Adashi, E. Y. (2021). Fertility—a human right worthy of mandated insurance coverage: The evolution, limitations, and future of access to care. *Fertility and Sterility*, *115*(1), 29–42. doi:10.1016/j.fertnstert.2020.09.155 PMID:33342534

Kreager, P. (2022). Smith or Malthus? A Sea-Change in the Concept of a Population. *Population and Development Review*, *48*(3), 645–688. doi:10.1111/padr.12488

Kuldoshev, A. T. (2024). THE NECESSITY OF DEVELOPING A" GREEN ECONOMY". Best Journal of Innovation in Science. *Research for Development*, *3*(2), 611–615.

Lianos, G., & Sloev, I. (2024). Investment and Innovation in Emerging Versus Advanced Market Economies: A Schumpeterian Approach. *Journal of the Knowledge Economy*, 1–24. doi:10.1007/s13132-023-01681-3

Mhlanga, D. (2023). The Role of FinTech and AI in Agriculture, Towards Eradicating Hunger and Ensuring Food Security. In *FinTech and Artificial Intelligence for Sustainable Development: The Role of Smart Technologies in Achieving Development Goals* (pp. 119–143). Springer Nature Switzerland. doi:10.1007/978-3-031-37776-1_6

Moresi, M., & Cimini, A. (2024). A Comprehensive Study from Cradle-to-Grave on the Environmental Profile of Malted Legumes. *Foods*, *13*(5), 655. doi:10.3390/foods13050655 PMID:38472768

Österblom, H., Jouffray, J. B., Folke, C., & Rockström, J. (2017). Emergence of a global science–business initiative for ocean stewardship. *Proceedings of the National Academy of Sciences of the United States of America*, *114*(34), 9038–9043. doi:10.1073/pnas.1704453114 PMID:28784792

Pawłowski, A., & Cao, Y. (2014). The role of CO_2 in the Earth's ecosystem and the possibility of controlling flows between subsystems. *Gospodarka Surowcami Mineralnymi*, *30*(4), 5–19. doi:10.2478/gospo-2014-0037

Pietrzak, P. (2024). The Sixth Great Debate in International Relations Theory Revolves Around Clarity: Ontology in Statu Nascendi as a Cutting-Edge Tool for Conflict Management. In Dealing With Regional Conflicts of Global Importance (pp. 1-27). IGI Global.

Prip, C. (2022). Arctic Ocean governance in light of an of an international legally binding instrument on the conservation and sustainable use of marine biodiversity of areas beyond national jurisdiction. *Marine Policy*, *142*, 103768. doi:10.1016/j.marpol.2019.103768

Ritchie, H., & Roser, M. (2024). *How many people does synthetic fertilizer feed?* Our World in Data.

Rockström, J., Gupta, J., Qin, D., Lade, S. J., Abrams, J. F., Andersen, L. S., Armstrong McKay, D. I., Bai, X., Bala, G., Bunn, S. E., Ciobanu, D., DeClerck, F., Ebi, K., Gifford, L., Gordon, C., Hasan, S., Kanie, N., Lenton, T. M., Loriani, S., & Zhang, X. (2023). Safe and just Earth system boundaries. *Nature*, *619*(7968), 102–111. doi:10.1038/s41586-023-06083-8 PMID:37258676

Rockström, J., Steffen, W., Noone, K., Persson, Å., Chapin, F. S. III, Lambin, E., Lenton, T. M., Scheffer, M., Folke, C., Schellnhuber, H. J., Nykvist, B., de Wit, C. A., Hughes, T., van der Leeuw, S., Rodhe, H., Sörlin, S., Snyder, P. K., Costanza, R., Svedin, U., & Foley, J. (2009). Planetary boundaries: Exploring the safe operating space for humanity. *Ecology and Society*, *14*(2), art32. doi:10.5751/ES-03180-140232

Sarma, V. V. S. S., Krishna, M. S., Paul, Y. S., & Murty, V. S. N. (2015). Observed changes in ocean acidity and carbon dioxide exchange in the coastal Bay of Bengal–a link to air pollution. Tellus B. *Tellus. Series B, Chemical and Physical Meteorology*, *67*(1), 24638. doi:10.3402/tellusb.v67.24638

Scheiner, S. M. (Ed.). (2024). *Encyclopedia of Biodiversity*. Elsevier, Academic Press.

Shin, Y. J., Midgley, G. F., Archer, E. R., Arneth, A., Barnes, D. K., Chan, L., Hashimoto, S., Hoegh-Guldberg, O., Insarov, G., Leadley, P., Levin, L. A., Ngo, H. T., Pandit, R., Pires, A. P. F., Pörtner, H.-O., Rogers, A. D., Scholes, R. J., Settele, J., & Smith, P. (2022). Actions to halt biodiversity loss generally benefit the climate. *Global Change Biology*, *28*(9), 2846–2874. doi:10.1111/gcb.16109 PMID:35098619

Solomon, B. D. (2023). Millennium Ecosystem Assessment. In Dictionary of Ecological Economics (pp. 352-353). Edward Elgar Publishing. doi:10.4337/9781788974912.M.48

Steenge, A. E. (1997). On background principles for environmental policy:"polluter pays","user pays" or "victim pays"? In *Public priority setting: Rules and costs* (pp. 121–137). Springer Netherlands. doi:10.1007/978-94-009-1487-2_7

Unterhalter, E. (2017). Measuring education for the Millennium Development Goals: reflections on targets, indicators, and a post-2015 framework. In The MDGs, Capabilities and Human Rights (pp. 80-91). Routledge.

Wapner, P. (2021). Thresholds of injustice: challenging the politics of environmental postponement. In *Our Extractive Age* (pp. 48–67). Routledge. doi:10.4324/9781003127611-5

Werners, S. E., Sparkes, E., Totin, E., Abel, N., Bhadwal, S., Butler, J. R., Douxchamps, S., James, H., Methner, N., Siebeneck, J., Stringer, L. C., Vincent, K., Wise, R. M., & Tebboth, M. G. (2021). Advancing climate resilient development pathways since the IPCC's fifth assessment report. *Environmental Science & Policy*, *126*, 168–176. doi:10.1016/j.envsci.2021.09.017

Willis, K. (2023). Development as modernisation: Rostow's the stages of economic growth. *Geography (Sheffield, England)*, *108*(1), 33–37. doi:10.1080/00167487.2023.2170073

Yigit, S. (2023). New Perspectives on Public Diplomacy. in Kavoğlu, S. & Köksoy, E. (Eds.). (2023). Global Perspectives on the Emerging Trends in Public Diplomacy. IGI Global. (pp.102-130). https://doi.org/ doi:10.4018/978-1-6684-9161-4

Yigit, S. (2024). States, Sustainable Development, and Multilateral Environmental Agreements. In P. Ordóñez de Pablos (Ed.), *Digital Technologies for a Resource Efficient Economy* (pp. 88–106). IGI Global., doi:10.4018/979-8-3693-2750-0.ch005

Zimmer, C. (2014). The Oldest Rocks on Earth. *Scientific American*, *310*(3), 58–63. doi:10.1038/scientificamerican0314-58 PMID:24660329

ADDITIONAL READING

Adisa, O., Ilugbusi, B. S., Adewunmi, O., Franca, O., & Ndubuisi, L. (2024). A comprehensive review of redefining agricultural economics for sustainable development: Overcoming challenges and seizing opportunities in a changing world. *World Journal of Advanced Research and Reviews*, *21*(1), 2329–2341. doi:10.30574/wjarr.2024.21.1.0322

Adshead, D., Paszkowski, A., Gall, S. S., Peard, A. M., Adnan, M. S. G., Verschuur, J., & Hall, J. W. (2024). Climate threats to coastal infrastructure and sustainable development outcomes. *Nature Climate Change*, *14*(4), 1–9. doi:10.1038/s41558-024-01950-2

Gayen, D., Chatterjee, R., & Roy, S. (2024). A review on environmental impacts of renewable energy for sustainable development. *International Journal of Environmental Science and Technology*, *21*(5), 5285–5310. doi:10.1007/s13762-023-05380-z

Sahoo, S., & Goswami, S. (2024). Theoretical framework for assessing the economic and environmental impact of water pollution: A detailed study on sustainable development of India. *Journal of Future Sustainability*, *4*(1), 23–34. doi:10.5267/j.jfs.2024.1.003

Stein, S. (2024). Universities confronting climate change: Beyond sustainable development and solutionism. *Higher Education*, *87*(1), 165–183. doi:10.1007/s10734-023-00999-w

KEY TERMS AND DEFINITIONS

Biosphere: The region on, above, and below the Earth's surface where life exists; a narrow zone where soil, water, and air combine to sustain life.

Carbon Footprint: The emissions of carbon equivalent greenhouse gases such as the amount of carbon dioxide and methane produced by individuals or organizations.

Carbon Neutral: A company offsetting the amount of carbon they produce by removing carbon emissions elsewhere or purchasing carbon credits, thereby achieving net-zero carbon emissions.

Circular Economy: A process whereby there are measures taken to the 'make' and 'dispose' and maximize 'use' in the economy, keeping products in circulation to the fullest extent possible by reducing material consumption, streamlining processes and collecting waste for reuse.

Climate Change: Refers to the periodic change in Earth's climate due to changes in the atmosphere but the Earth's climate is shifting at an unprecedented level given the short period. Climate change has come to mean the rise in global temperatures from heat-trapping gases resulting from mining and using oil, coal, and other fossil fuels. Climate change indicators include rising sea levels; increase and severity of extreme weather, such as hurricanes, droughts, and floods; and ice loss at the Earth's poles.

Corporate Social Responsibility: Profit maximizing companies use the CSR business model to gauge social and environmental benefits alongside organizational goals such as profitability.

Greenwashing: A marketing ploy that falsely, deceptively, misleadingly, or inaccurately portrays a "green" or "eco-friendly" product or service having a positive environmental effect to help increase sales.

Pollution: The introduction of harmful materials into the environment. Sustainable Development: Development is considered sustainable if it meets the needs of the present without compromising the ability of future generations to meet their own needs.

Sustainable Development Goals: Intergovernmental set of development goals to which all United Nations members have committed to work towards by 2030. They consist of 17 goals and 169 indicators.

Chapter 3
The Other Face of Those Left Behind in the Silence of the Sustainable Development Goals (SDGs):
A Global Analysis of SDG Discontent Geography

Isidore E. Agbokou
https://orcid.org/0000-0003-1225-9311
Centre d'Etudes Diplomatiques et Stratégiques de Paris (CEDS), France

ABSTRACT

This chapter identified the factors that could justify the growing social inequalities and reduce possible threats of discontent that may arise among disadvantaged groups across the world. The research has been conducted based on data provided by the VNR reported by the HLPF from 2016 to 2021. The number of actions implemented to comply with the principle of LNOB and the number of SDGs affected by the actions implemented at the country and regional levels are the two parameters that support the analysis which led to the conclusion of the potential pockets of discontent. Since 2016, a total of 143 countries have committed, with 605 actions for the implementation of the LNOB principle. The chapter revealed that people from all around the world have expressed a desire to move towards a more equal world of sustainable development. Nevertheless, some regions of the globe have shown more commitment and determination than others since the movement of LNOB was born. The risk of delay is that the need for managing conflicts will only grow from frustration and discontent.

DOI: 10.4018/979-8-3693-2758-6.ch003

INTRODUCTION

Humanity is increasingly tightened in the vice of inequalities, to the point of being suffocated by its weight that is gaining ground every day. There is reason to believe that the policies put in place by states, both national and international, condition the resurgence of the scourge. For example, the inequalities induced by the global coronavirus health crisis in recent years is sobering. From inequalities in economic recovery and access to vaccines, to worsening income losses and widening learning gaps, COVID-19 has disproportionately penalized poor and vulnerable populations in 2021 (Gopalakrishnan et al., 2021). What could be the fate of the disadvantaged victims left behind, whose numbers are increasing day by day? Is the international community acting for the reduction of the social disparities caused by emerging crises? What are the outputs of these actions, especially with the aim of building a world where access to well-being is equal for all? What should be done to avoid all attempts to self-justice discontents could generate and increase among the peoples, the social belonging felling? These are the concerns that deserve to be answered through the present work.

Rationales

Adopted on 25 September 2015 by all member states of the United Nations (UN), the 2030 Agenda defines a program of 17 goals set for the sustainable development of the planet and is planned to be implemented over a period of 15 years, by 2030. Broken down into 169 targets, these goals should respond to the common challenges of sustainable development, especially for the underserved, leaving no one behind (LNOB). LNOB represents the unequivocal commitment of all UN Member States to eradicate poverty in all its forms, end discrimination and exclusion, and reduce the inequalities and vulnerabilities that leave people behind and undermine the potential of individuals and of humanity. Fewer than ten years before the 2030 deadline, however, actions implemented do not to seem to be making much difference, a principle that can be viewed as an indicator in the achievement of the Sustainable Development Goals (SDGs). The SDGs have been adopted in 2015 by the international community to set the course for the future of our world. Indeed, at the UN General Assembly in September 2015, 193 countries have committed to ensuring that all people can live in dignity by 2030 while at the same time preserving the natural foundations of life in the long term, whether social, economic, or ecological. The 17 SDGs including their 169 targets adopted concern everyone: governments worldwide, indigenous peoples, grassroot communities, civil society, the private sector, academia, and individuals. Together they provide a holistic framework for achieving a sustainable society globally. The SDGs are a call to action for all countries worldwide to foster prosperity while protecting our planet. Therefore, the targets include tackling poverty and strategies that address people's social needs, such as health, education, social protection, employment opportunities etc. To assess the progress in the implementation of the SDGs, UN member states are encouraged to "conduct regular and inclusive reviews of progress at the national and sub-national levels, which are country-led and country-driven" (paragraph 79 of the 2030 Agenda). These national reviews are expected to serve as a basis for the regular reviews by the High-Level Political Forum (HLPF), meeting under the auspices of Economic and Social Council (ECOSOC) of UN. The HLPFs is therefore the central UN platform for the follow-up and review of the 2030 Agenda for Sustainable Development and the SDGs.

The Sustainable Development Report (SDR) released in 2023 reveals that for the third year in a row, global progress on the SDGs has been static, and there is a risk that the gap in SDG outcomes between high-income countries (HICs) and low-income countries (LICs) will be larger in 2030 than when the goals were universally agreed upon in 2015. The SDR shows that based on the current pace of progress since 2015, none of the goals will be achieved by 2030, and on average, less than 20% of the SDG targets are on track to be achieved. While from 2015 to 2019, the world was making some modest progress on the SDGs, since the outbreak of the COVID-19 pandemic and simultaneous global crises and setbacks, progress has stalled and is one full point below the projected level based on pre-pandemic trends. Furthermore, the report highlights that there is a risk that the gap in SDG outcomes between Hight-Income Countries (HICs) and Low-Income Countries (LICs) will be larger in 2030 (29 points) than it was in 2015 (28 points) – underscoring the danger of losing a decade of progress towards convergence globally (SDR, 2023). Some of the indicators that experienced the most significant reversals in progress include subjective well-being, access to vaccination, poverty, and unemployment rate. SDG goals related to hunger, sustainable diets, and health outcomes (SDG 2 and SDG 3) are particularly off-track, as well as terrestrial and marine biodiversity (SDGs 14 and 15), air and plastic pollution (SDG 11 and SDG 12), and strong institutions and peaceful societies (SDG 16). On average, since the adoption of the SDGs in 2015, the world made some progress in strengthening access to key infrastructure, covered notably under SDG 6 (Clean Water and Sanitation), SDG 7 (Affordable and Clean Energy), and SDG 9 (Industry, Innovation, and Infrastructure) (SDR, 2023).

Furthermore, the Report demonstrated that all countries, poorer and richer alike, should use the halfway momentum to self-critically review and revise their national SDG strategies and long-term investment frameworks by highlighting that government effort and commitment to the SDGs is too low, and no country is close to obtaining a perfect score. There is significant variation across countries, with some developing and emerging economies. At least, the Report among overall shows that despite most governments having signalled "soft" SDG integration into their public management practices and procedures, "hard" SDG integration is missing in most countries, including the use of the SDGs to support long-term budget and investment frameworks. In a survey of 74 countries and the European Union, only one-third of governments mention the SDGs or use related terms in their latest official budget document, with even fewer including the SDGs in a dedicated section, budget lines, or allocation.

With the current geopolitical context marked by political and health crises around the world, one should wonder if the global ambition called, "Transforming our world: the 2030 Agenda for Sustainable Development" remains faithful to its commitments. It is therefore necessary to evaluate the progress of the 2030 Agenda and consider the principle of LNOB. Addressing the weaknesses of the 2030 Agenda now, from its conception to its implementation, with a specific focus on populations left behind, seems legitimate. Such an upstream analysis could make it possible to identify new challenges that the international community might expect in terms of social inclusion. Downstream, measures can be defined in the light of the results of the diagnosis to reframe actions for social equity and thus prevent the 2030 Agenda from being treated as inadequate or poorly applied. The diagnostic analysis can be done based on the achievements made to promote social inclusion, without losing sight of the five pillars (5 Ps) of sustainable development: planet, people, prosperity, peace, and partnerships.

The outcomes of the 2023 SDR highlighted that promoting sustainable development requires analyzing challenges and identifying policy solutions both at an administrative and at a functional scale as well as at continental level. According to the OECD, effective policies, and strategies to achieve the SDGs should be coordinated across administrative boundaries to cover the entire functional area (OECD, 2019).

PROBLEM, SCOPE, ASSUMPTIONS, OBJECTIVES, AND METHOD

What is the problem? Why its matter? What should be a solution and how the current insight could contribute to solving it?

Problem

The world is no longer making progress on the SDGs and, at mid-point on the way to 2030, government commitments and efforts vary greatly.

While the SDGs are oriented towards 2030 and the Paris Climate Agreement towards 2050, achieving these objectives requires a major shift in public policies and government operations right now. Tomorrow will too late and risky for people, planet, prosperity, peace, and partnership.

At all levels, politicians should be aware that the world is at risk of discontent with its consequences and recognize the importance of closing without delay the gap between SDG rhetoric and action.

Scope

In the literature, authors generally center their analysis on disparities between in-countries territorial subdivisions and comparisons between counties. They also center their analysis on the disparities between HIC, LIC, poorest and richest countries. Their analysis targets a balance and synergy between broader social, environmental, and economic issues putting emphasis on the LNOB principle. The actions taken to comply with the LNOB and their subsequent impacts on the SDG's implementation are not usual in the literature.

In the current reflections, the regions refer particularly to: America, Europe, Africa, Oceania and Asia and not only in-countries territorial subdivisions and analysis are based on policy actions planned, taken and implemented to ensure that no citizen is left at the margin of development. Thematically, the 17 SDGs have been considered under the prism of the principle of LNOB.

Assumptions

The study lies on the assumptions that while significant works have been done to highlight (i) the potential of SDGs to serve as a tool for implementation a new local and regional development paradigm; (ii) how cities and regions are using the SDGs to develop new plans and strategies or adapt and assess existing ones; (iii) the level of awareness, actions and tools, sectoral priorities and main challenges of cities and regions addressing the SDGs and ; (iv) that, regardless of the level of decentralization across countries, cities and regions have core responsibilities in policies that are central to sustainable development and people's well-being now and in the future; few studies attempted to computed and analyzed locally and globally how the Governments are consistent with their political commitments and how to narrow or to close the gap between rhetoric and effective actions with regards to SDGs. According to our research, works based on the consistency of political willing and realities vis-à-vis the SDGs aiming at highlighting the needs of gap narrowing or closing may not exist, while such a gap leads to societal discontent and feeling of non-belonging in the countries and across the world. This is a truly LNOB analytical perspective that will complement the existing SDGs progress analysis and draw the decision-makers attention to the potential discontent across the world that needs regards in the future.

Study Objectives

We aim to draw the attention of the international community to consider the world's populations in the implementation of the agenda in achieving the SDGs by 2030. The state of play of compliance with the principle of LNOB will enable decision-makers at different levels to:

- redefine the target populations to benefit from actions aimed at transformation.
- Re-examine and review priorities in terms of actions for target populations for a more significant impact on sustainable development so desired.
- Suggest development of more inclusive strategies that consider all targets without exclusion. Greater than or equal to 6 and the number of SDGs achieved is strictly equal to 17.

Method

The observation period covers six (6) years starting from 2016 to 2021 and the study withdraws data on number of actions taken, proposed, and implemented to the benefit of marginalized populations directly from released by the governments at the HLPF. Intra and inter countries and regions comparisons are made in the purpose of sizing the scope of disparities in terms of policy commitments and political willing consistency of the Governments.

The various reports of the HLPFs on sustainable development serve as the basis of the analysis made here to create a more realistic overview of the LNOB. Specifically, the Voluntary National Reviews (VNRs) presented during these HLPFs are the elements that will feed into this reflection. The voluntary national reviews (VNRs) aim to facilitate the sharing of experiences, including successes, challenges and lessons learned, with a view to accelerating the implementation of the 2030 Agenda. Additionally, the VNRs seek to contribute to strengthen policies and institutions of governments and to mobilize multi-stakeholder support and partnerships for the implementation of the SDGs.

To better appreciate the level of commitment of the international community to LNOB, the information contained in the VNRs synthesis reports have indeed served as a support and has been used here with the greatest attention. This information has been provided in Appendices A-F in the present document, which allows for a better gauge to understand states' commitments to the principle. The tables show the measures taken during the VNR reports, as well as the results produced by the implementation of those measures, from 2016 to 2021. The analysis focused on the states mentioned in the reports, so as not to undermine the authenticity of the information and remain faithful to the idea that is shared in these documents. We understand that, although there are several countries involved at various levels, the synthesis reports highlight those that have been more determined in the cause to significantly reduce the harm done to vulnerable groups left behind.

In addition, a study on the SDGs helped to situate the general opinion on those that have been most affected by the implementation of measures taken to leave no one behind. In fact, all SDGs should be affected by these measures, particularly SDG 10, addressing reduced inequalities. But it is through the achievements of these measures that data on the SDGs could be determined. Indeed, the reading of the SDGs achieved was based on the analysis of the actions conducted.

To assess the adherence of the regions from a geostrategic point of view, the distribution of the countries involved in the analysis by continent was made, which made it possible to generate their arithmetic averages, to estimate the effort made by each region in terms of issuing decisions, attachment to decisions, and adopting the LNOB principle through the actions conducted.

To evaluate the commitment efforts of each region in the respect or adoption of the LNOB principle, we first proceeded to calculate the cumulative number of actions by all the states of a region during the six-year period. Then, an arithmetic average of the SDGs achieved by country in each region made it possible to estimate the average number of SDGs reached by the efforts of each continent determined to achieve the LNOB principle. It should be noted that Russia, since it shares parts of both Europe and Asia, should be considered on both continents. But to avoid duplication and allow for an objective analysis of the situation, it has been considered here as part of the Asian continent. Thus, based on these two criteria, a comparison of the engagement efforts of each region was conducted.

Finally, a grid for assessing the risks of discontent linked to the implementation of actions taken for groups suffering from social exclusion has been initiated. That has made possible the identifications of regions and countries that could be potential pockets of discontent because of the weak or non-adoption of the LNOB principle. According to the grid, the country or region will have to be rated "weak" to hope to be protected from sudden social crises linked to inequality. Otherwise, the risk of discontent is low or non-existent when the number of actions conducted is:

- greater than or equal to 6 and the number of SDGs achieved is strictly equal to 17.
- greater than or equal to 7 and the number of SDGs achieved is strictly greater than or equal to 16.
- greater than or equal to 8 and the number of SDGs achieved is strictly greater than or equal to 15.
- greater than or equal to 9 and the number of SDGs achieved is strictly greater than or equal to 14.
- greater than or equal to 10 and the number of SDGs achieved is strictly greater than or equal to 13.
- greater than or equal to 11 and the number of SDGs achieved is strictly greater than or equal to 12.
- greater than or equal to 12 and the number of SDGs achieved is strictly greater than or equal to 11.
- greater than or equal to 13 and the number of SDGs achieved is strictly greater than or equal to 10.
- greater than or equal to 14 and the number of SDGs achieved is strictly greater than or equal to 9.
- greater than or equal to 15 and the number of SDGs achieved is strictly greater than or equal to 8.
- greater than or equal to 16 and the number of SDGs achieved is strictly greater than or equal to 7.
- greater than or equal to 17 and the number of SDGs achieved is strictly greater than or equal to 6.

We used the Excel table for the statistical processing of the data and to produce the figures used for the interpretation of the results. The production of maps, for its part, allows us to better read the behavior of states regarding the adoption of the LNOB principle. And the risk of existence of discontent was clearly assessed through the maps.

RESULTS AND DISCUSSION ON GLOBAL ACHIEVEMENTS IN IMPLEMENTING THE PRINCIPLE

Learning Points From the HLPF

The creation of the UN HLPF on Sustainable Development was mandated in 2012 by the outcome document of the UN Conference on Sustainable Development (Rio+20), "The Future We Want". As a replacement for the Commission on Sustainable Development, the HLPF's role as stated previously, is to ensure the follow-up and review of the 2030 Agenda for Sustainable Development and the SDGs at the global level. Overall, this forum adopts political declarations negotiated at the intergovernmental level. Otherwise, this body would build on the resolutions of regular and inclusive reviews of progress at national and sub-national VNR levels to set directions for achieving the 2030 Agenda and the SDGs.

The Efforts of the International Community to Respect the LNOB Principle

Several states participated in the VNRs and intervened both on the part of the proposal of measures, the accession to the measures, and on the adoption of measures. The countries that have received attention in the reports on actions taken to implement the 2030 Agenda are those mentioned here. And it is on these countries which we focused since they have been the most involved in LNOB.

State Involvement in the Commitment to Respect the LNOB Principle

Figures 1-3 show the countries that made proposals at the VNRs for compliance with the LNOB principle and those that expressed interest in the measures, as well as those that have, through actions implemented within this framework, adopted the decisions.

The will to make the social environment an area of peace and security for minorities has been felt over the years by the progressive accession of the states constituting the international community. Although many countries have proposed or expressed their commitment to the measures, some have not been able to go beyond their promises. Despite this, more countries that withdrew or remained neutral or even hostile to the cause of the disenfranchised made a commendable effort towards a more egalitarian and just world.

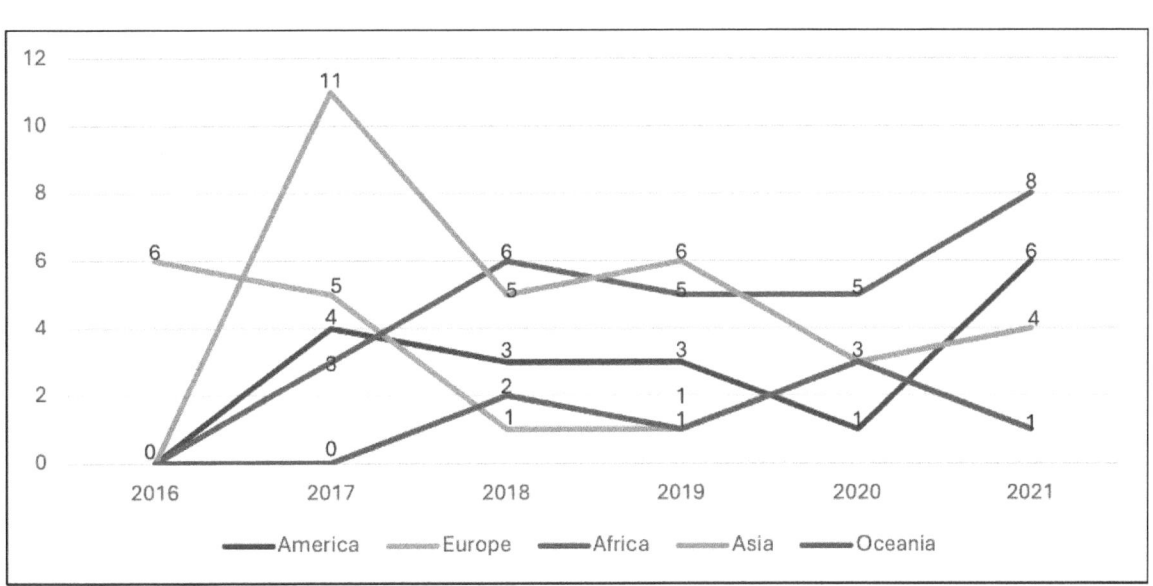

Figure 1. Evolution of the countries that have proposed measures by region
(Author, 2023. Excerpt from Appendix B)

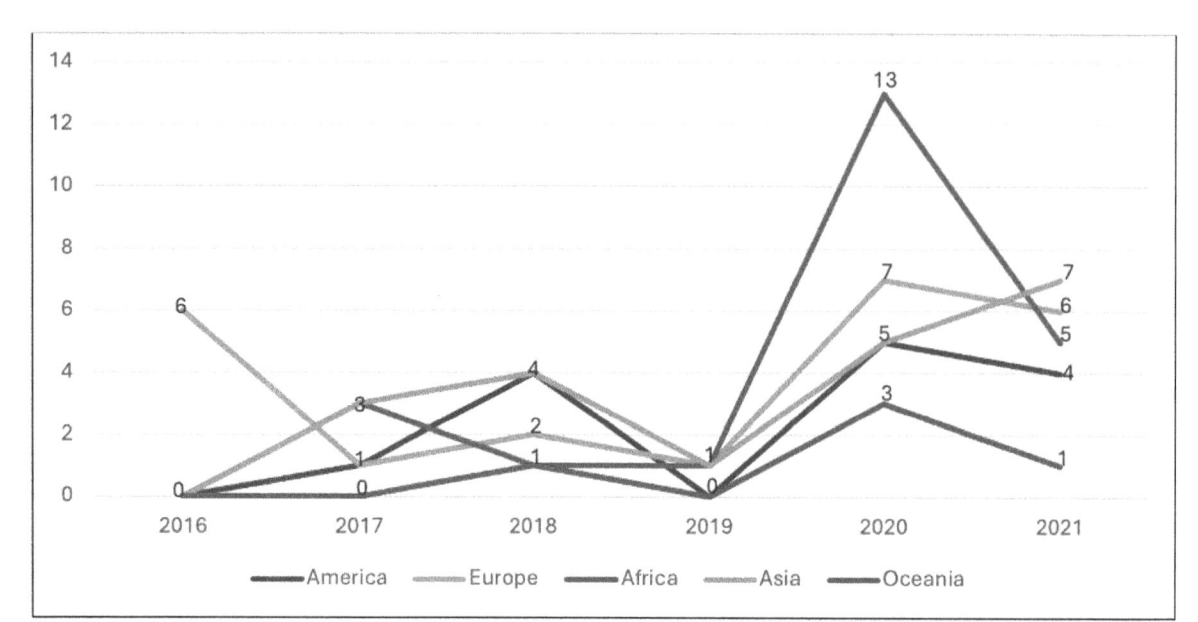

Figure 2. Evolution of the countries concerned by measures by region
(Author, 2023. Excerpt from Appendix C)

Figure 3. Evolution of countries that have adopted the measures by region
(Author, 2023. Excerpt from Appendix D)

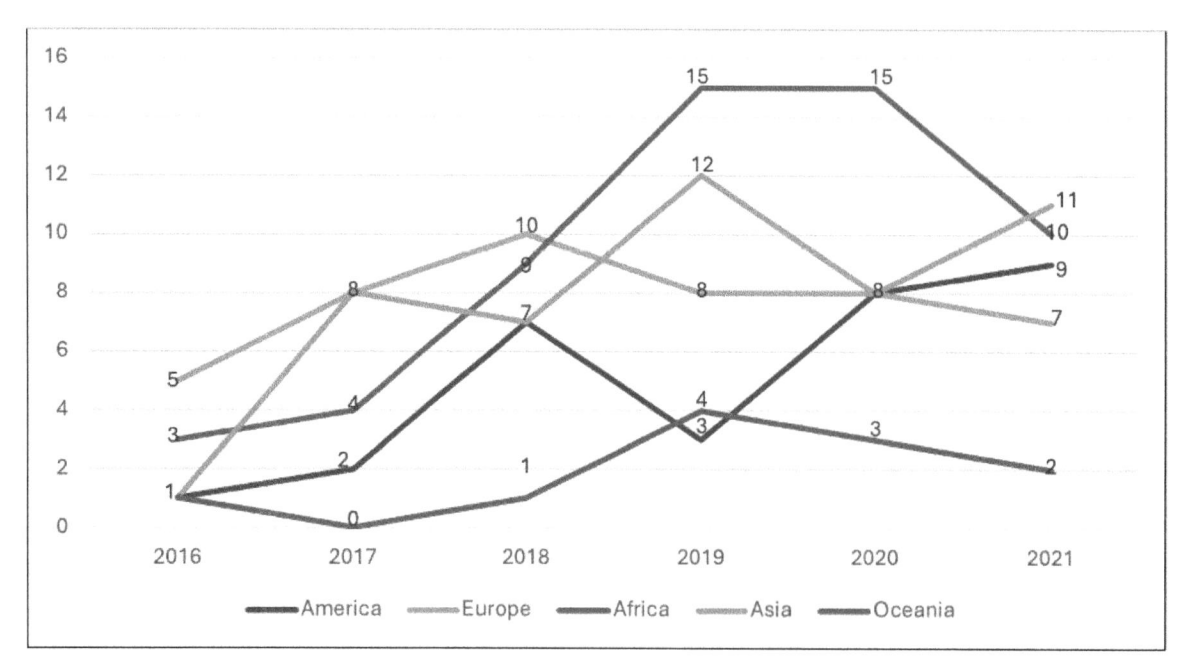

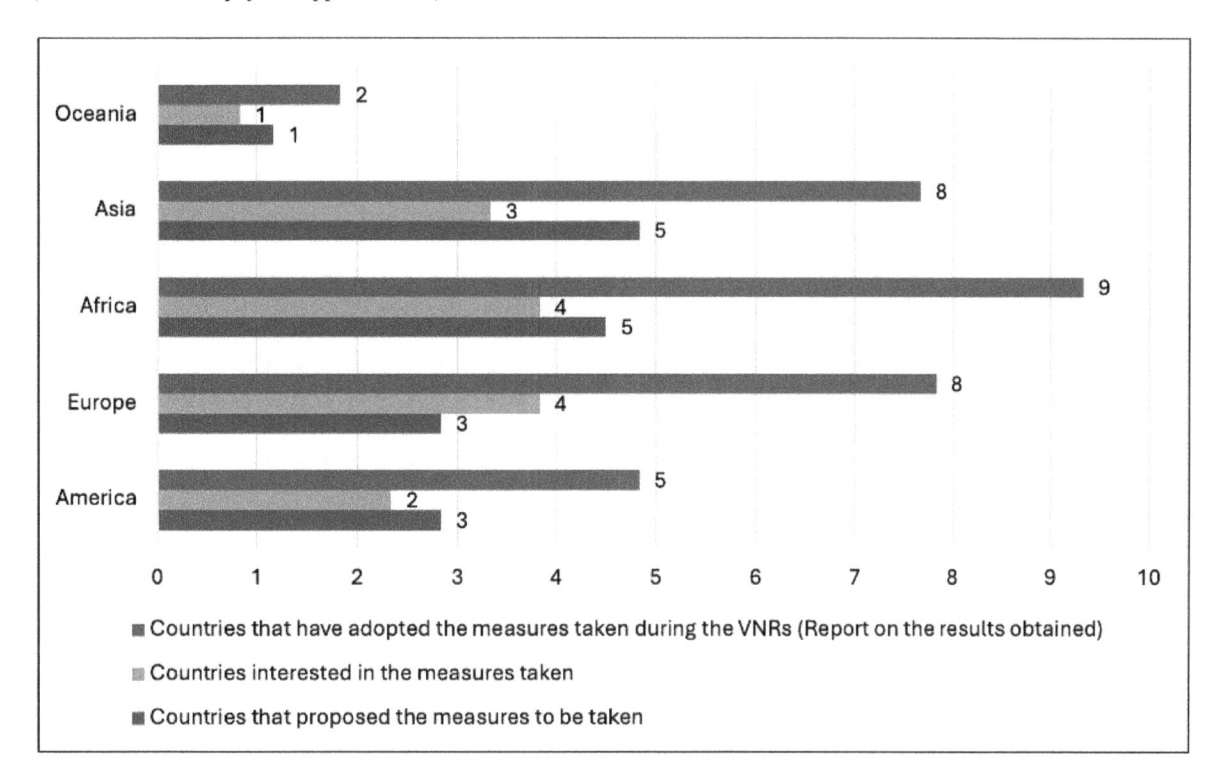

Figure 4. Regional commitment to the adoption of the LNOB principle
(Author, 2023. Excerpt from Appendix B-D)

```
Oceania:   proposed=2, interested=1, adopted=1
Asia:      proposed=8, interested=3, adopted=5
Africa:    proposed=9, interested=4, adopted=5
Europe:    proposed=8, interested=4, adopted=3
America:   proposed=5, interested=2, adopted=3
```

- Countries that have adopted the measures taken during the VNRs (Report on the results obtained)
- Countries interested in the measures taken
- Countries that proposed the measures to be taken

Figure 4 reflects the efforts made by each continent in terms of project or program achievements to respect the LNOB principle, from 2016 to 2021. The analysis is based on the average number of countries that have been able to take concrete action to reduce inequalities to marginalized groups, in terms of proposals, commitment, and adoption of measures taken.

In general, regardless of the continent, the number of countries that have adopted decisions taken within the framework of compliance with the LNOB principle is much higher than the number of countries that have made proposals for measures or are interested in the proposed measures. From promises to action, there is a trend in a positive direction. It can therefore be assumed that all continents have expressed the desire to move towards a more egalitarian world in terms of sustainable development. Nevertheless, in terms of commitment, some regions of the world have been more determined than others since this desire to leave no one on the margins of development was born.

Thus, in the light of the results, a determination that could be characterized as regional or geographical regarding commitment through the measures taken to reduce social inequalities emerges. Africa is more determined in terms of participation in discussions and the adoption of the decisions, ahead of Asia and Europe. America seems less committed to trade and to the resolution to adopt decisions; even less Oceania, whose engagement efforts are still timid. On the other hand, in terms of fidelity to the commitments made, Europe is clearly more advanced than the other continents.

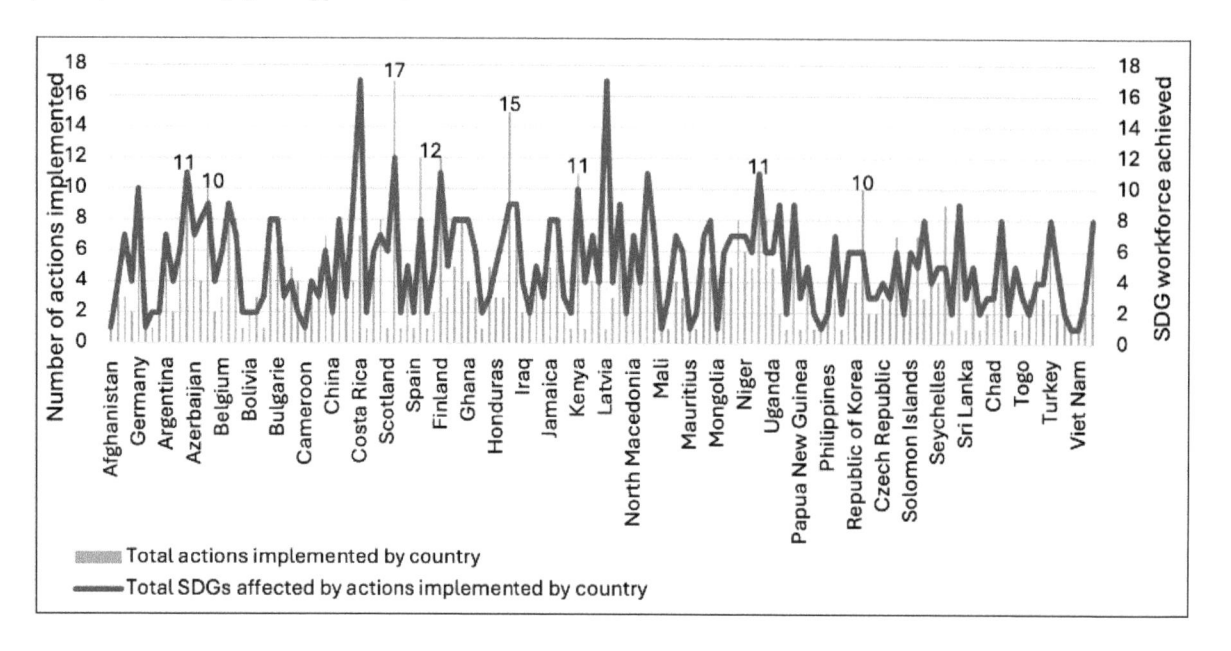

Figure 5. Actions implemented and effective of the SDGs achieved
(Author, 2023. Excerpt from Appendix 5)

Commitment of States in the Implementation of Actions for the Respect of the LNOB Principle

Figure 5 shows the actions taken by all states of the international community during the six years of implementation of the LNOB principle, in terms of cumulative numbers. This figure also refers to the total number of SDGs achieved by each country that has made achievements in this framework.

A total of 143 countries have committed themselves from 2016 to 2021, through 605 actions conducted for the implementation of the LNOB principle. Egypt appears have the most with 17 achievements to its credit, followed by India with 15 actions completed, Estonia and Finland each with 12. Austria, Kenya, and Norway are also on the chessboard of countries that have conducted the most actions with 11 projects or programs to their credit. They are followed by Bangladesh and the Democratic Republic of Congo (DRC) with 10 during the observation period. All the other countries, over six years, have conducted fewer than 10.

From a regional point of view, Africa stands out first with a total of 40 countries having conducted social inclusion actions, slightly ahead of Europe, which has 38 countries compared to 35 countries for Asia. America has 21 countries that have conducted actions within the framework of compliance with the LNOB principle, while Oceania has registered only 9 countries (Appendix E). In addition, an analysis of the parameter "number of actions carried out with a view to complying with the LNOB principle" reveals that the African continent holds the lead with 187 actions, ahead of Europe (170 actions), Asia (144 actions), America (71 actions), and Oceania (33 actions) (Figure 6; Appendix E).

A more refined look must be taken at the question of commitment of states or regions to assess whether, with this abundance of actions conducted, all the SDGs set are achieved and whether precisely the priority targets and, in this case, the marginalized groups are all met. The coming section removes the doubt on this concern.

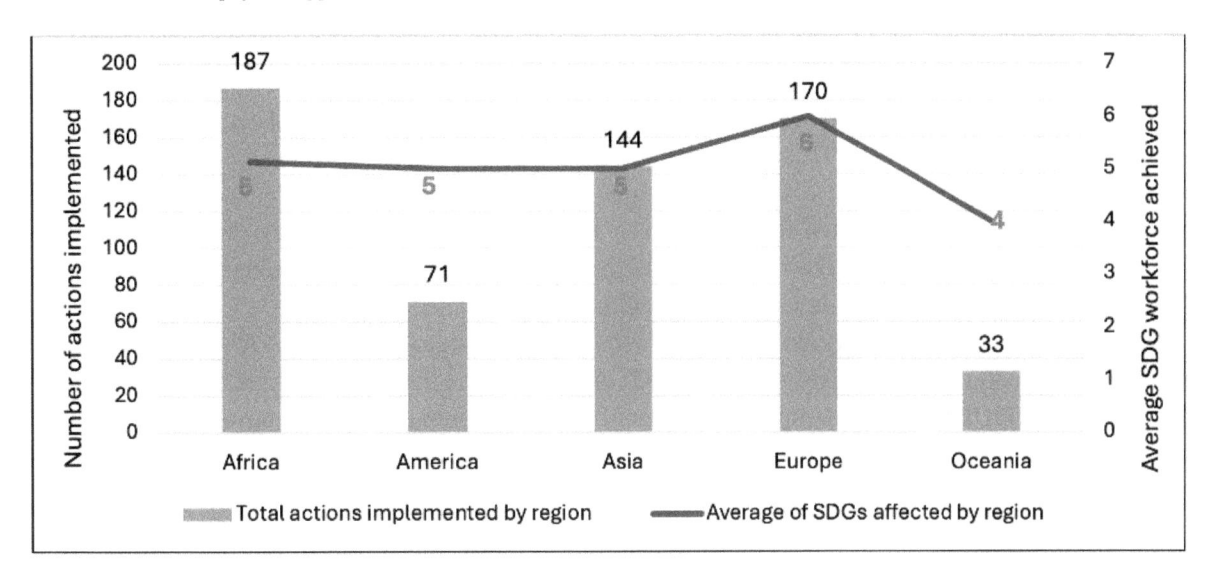

Figure 6. Actions implemented and average number of SDGs achieved
(Author, 2023. Excerpt from Appendix 5)

Commitment of States to Achieving the SDGs Through the Implementation of Actions for the Respect of the LNOB Principle

Figure 7 shows the frequency with which the SDGs are considered by achievements made since 2016 to 2021.

In general, the SDGs most affected by actions for marginalized groups concern SDGs 10, 16, 1, 8, 4, 3 and 17, respectively. SDG 10 is counted 605 times, equivalent to the total number of achievements made by the international community because of its cross-cutting nature.

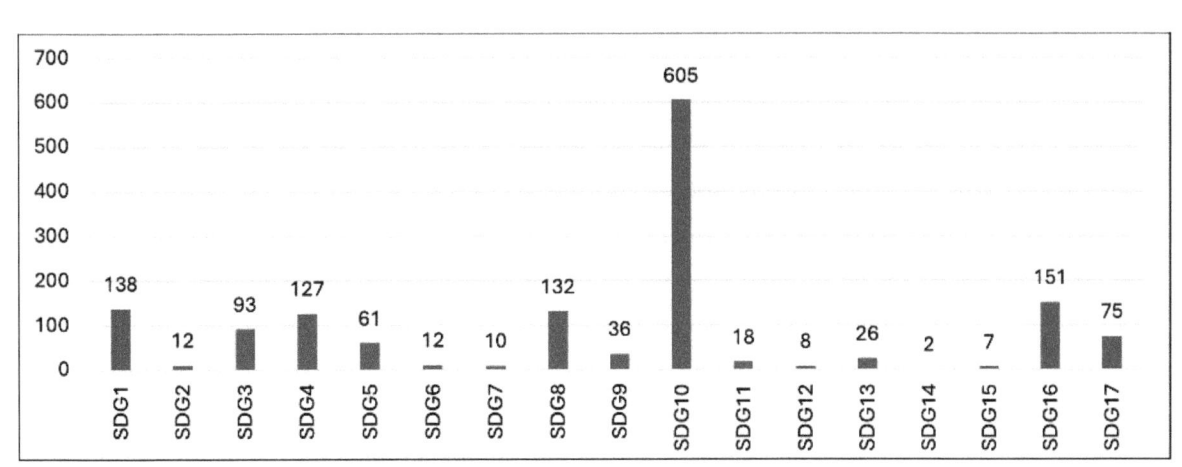

Figure 7. Frequency of consideration of an SDG by the actions implemented
(Author, 2023. Excerpt from Appendix 5)

At the level of the other SDGs affected by the actions, a very remarkable progression has been noted in reducing inequalities such as SDG 10. Indeed, many draft laws, 151 in total, have been initiated or are in the process of being initiated to improve the living conditions of certain categories of vulnerable people such as persons with disabilities, women and girls, the elderly, children, migrants or refugees, and others (SDG 16). At least 138 actions were conducted in the context of facilitation of basic services and social protection (SDG 1); 97 actions were recorded in the context of access to health (SDG 3), compared to 132 to make decent working conditions for people identified as vulnerable or victims of exclusion (SDG 8); not to mention the 127 projects for quality education for their children (SDG 4). There was also an average of 75 projects in the sense of fostering cooperation between private and public structures to provide services or assistance to marginalized people (SDG 17).

Very little action has been directed towards vulnerable people targeted by other SDGs that are vital for sustainable development. The analysis of the SDGs affected by the actions implemented in the context of compliance with the LNOB principle has only confirmed the doubt mentioned above. Figure 7 shows that SDG 14 was considered only two times out of the 605 projects or actions conducted in total. This may suggest that groups marginalized in this area have benefited from only two projects or actions that have addressed some of their concerns. SDGs 2, 5, 6, 7, 9, 11 and 13 are not to be neglected; they are among the ones that have received little action. Some of these SDGs are recognized by the World Social Report 2020 as factors further influencing inequality in the world. The report examines the impact of four megatrends affecting global inequality: technological innovation, climate change, urbanization, and international migration (UN News, 2020).

However, some countries have been able to raise the level of consideration of the SDGs through the implementation of a few actions for the benefit of marginalized groups. It is only Latvia and Costa Rica that have been able to achieve all the SDGs. Through a single action carried out by Latvia in the six years, it addressed the 17 SDGs selected. This is highly effective, since the country collaborated with both local and international NGOs on each SDG, to create the greatest impact. Costa Rica has also tried to address the concerns identified for the 17 SDGs through seven actions (Figure 5). These are feats that should inspire other countries that have achieved only 11 to 12 SDGs. Nevertheless, it would be advisable for the most successful countries to continue to multiply their actions, at the risk of being exposed to uprisings caused by frustration of certain categories of vulnerable people.

The trend is the same regionally, if not worse. Figure 6 reveals that despite the remarkable number of actions conducted by the different regions, namely Africa (187) and Asia (144 actions), on average, only five SDGs were reached by each of these regions. Europe (170 actions) is doing well with six SDGs to its credit. America (71 actions) was able to achieve, on average, five SDGs. Oceania (33 actions) only impacted vulnerable populations on four SDGs, on average (Figure 6; Appendix E). Figure 8 illustrates efforts made by each region of the globe affecting SDGs.

Geography of the Actions Implemented and the SDGs Achieved to Respect the LNOB Principle

We made a more disaggregated analysis of the commitment of states at the level of each region vis-à-vis the LNOB principle. The analysis made it possible to better highlight, from a geographical point of view, the efforts of each country in the fight for the left behind, both in terms of actions and SDGs.

The African countries that are more committed to the cause of those left behind are Egypt (17 actions and 12 SDGs achieved), followed by Kenya (11 actions and 10 SDGs) and Benin (9 actions and 9 SDGs

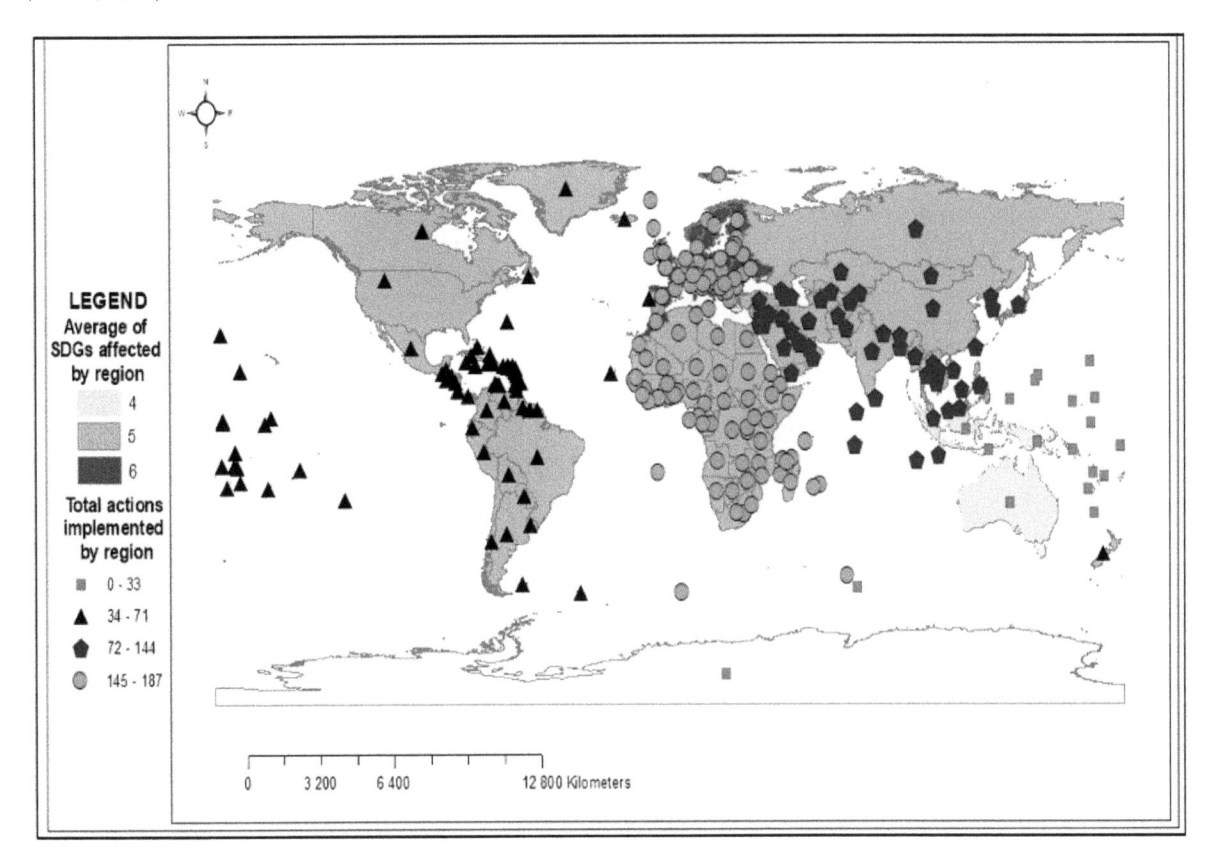

Figure 8. Geographical distribution of actions implemented worldwide
(Author, 2023)

achieved). On the other hand, Cameroon and Mali are the least committed to LNOB with each having one action implemented and one SDG achieved (Figure 9).

The American countries most committed to the cause are Costa Rica (7 actions with 17 SDGs achieved), followed by Panama (5 actions and 9 SDGs achieved), Jamaica (5 actions with 8 SDGs achieved), Argentina and Mexico tied (5 actions with 7 SDGs achieved). At the low end, Guatemala (1 action implemented and 2 SDGs achieved) and Peru (1 action with 1 SDG achieved) seem the least committed (Figure 10).

The Asian countries most committed to the cause of those left behind are India (15 actions affecting and 9 SDGs achieved) and Bangladesh (10 actions and 9 SDGs achieved). Malaysia (8 actions implemented and 11 SDGs achieved) and Indonesia (9 actions implemented with 9 SDGs achieved) are also committed. On the other hand, Afghanistan and Vietnam are the least committed to this noble cause of LNOB, each with one action implemented and one SDG achieved. Admittedly, other countries such as the United Arab Emirates, Kazakhstan, and Singapore are no better than the latter, with the only difference that they have each achieved two SDGs through the action taken (Figure 11).

Finland (12 with 11 SDGs achieved), Norway (11 and 11), and Austria (11 actions implemented and 11 SDGs achieved) appear to be the European countries most committed to the cause of those left behind. And, the countries of Belarus, Spain, the Netherlands, Portugal, and Switzerland are the least, with one action implemented and two SDGs achieved (Figure12).

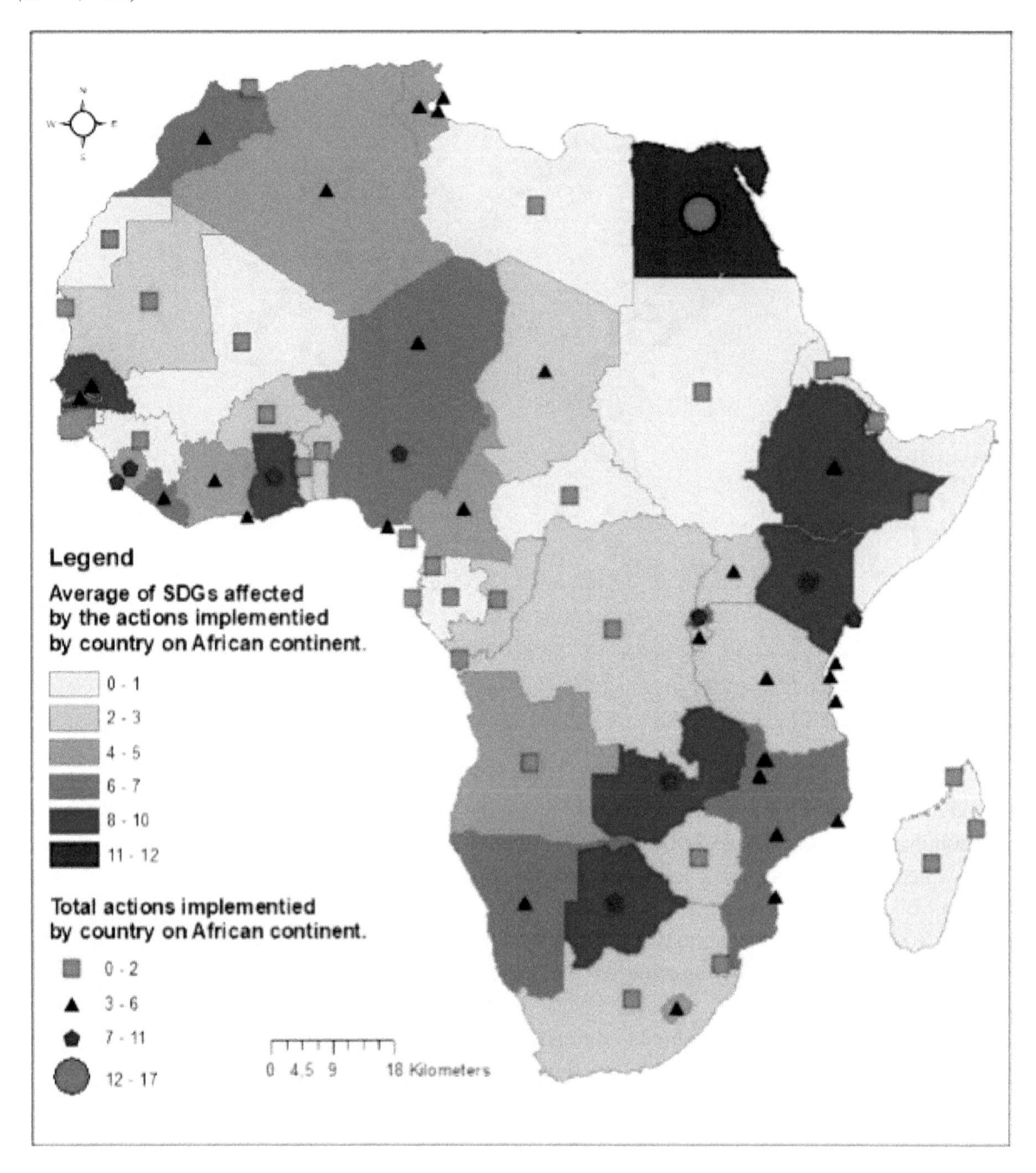

Figure 9. Geographical distribution of actions implemented in Africa
(Author, 2023)

New Zealand (8 actions implemented and 6 SDGs achieved) and Samoa (7 actions implemented and 5 SDGs achieved) are favorites on the continent. Palau and Vanuatu are lagging, each with one action implemented and only two SDGs achieved (Figure 13).

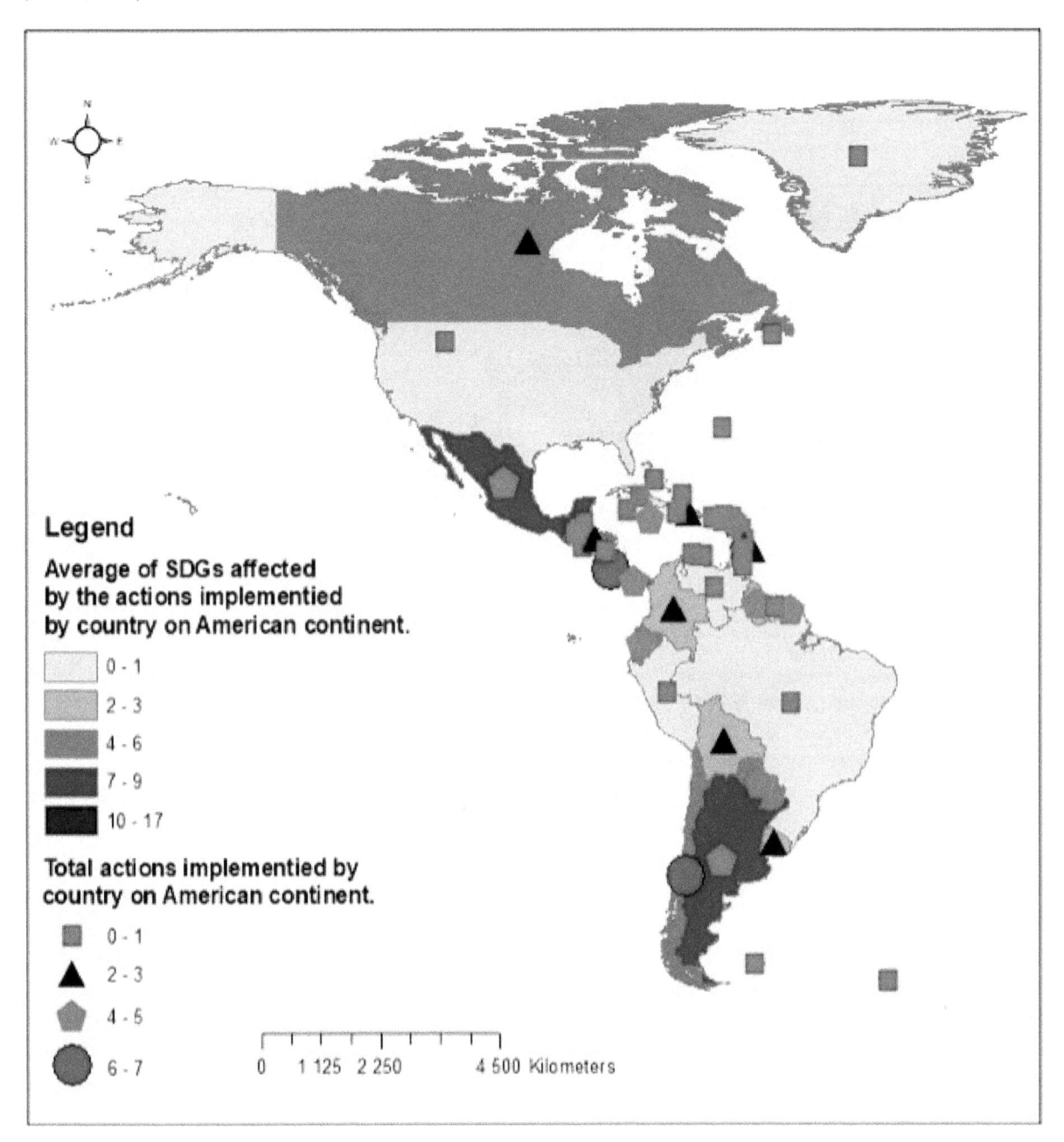

The Other Face of Those Left Behind in the Silence of the Sustainable Development Goals (SDGs)

Figure 10. Geographical distribution of actions implemented in America
(Author, 2023)

Much work remains to be done to create tolerance towards minority groups in society. The risk of not doing so widens the disparity between the haves and have-nots, creating more potential for conflicts because frustrations and discontent will continue to grow.

It should be noted that a region where no or few actions are implemented to reduce inequalities, and even less SDGs are set for the benefit of minorities, is a territory predisposed to revolts. And unfortunately, these two conditions are met in many countries today. This actively contributes to the upsurge of

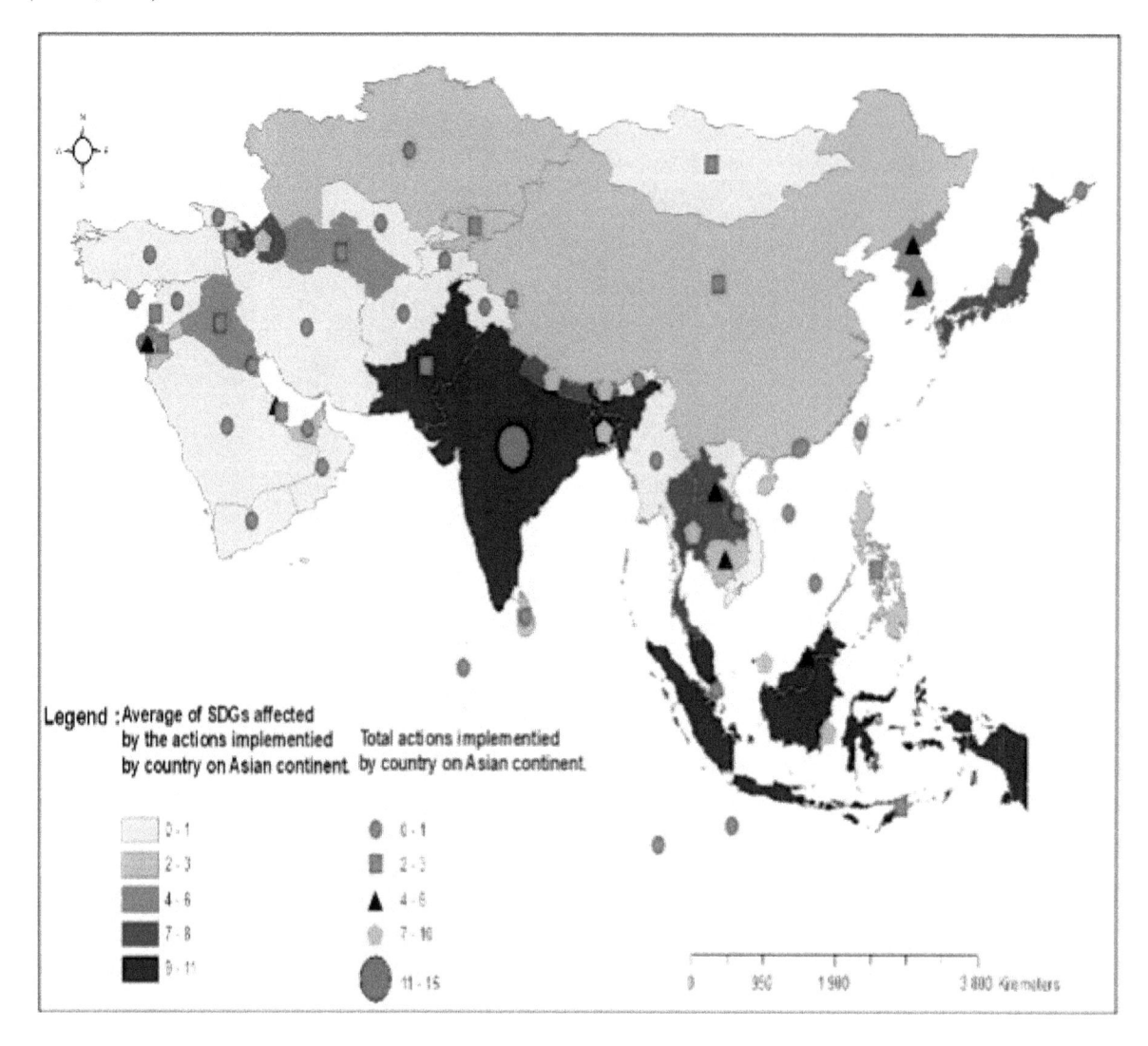

Figure 11. Geographical distribution of actions implemented in America
(Author, 2023)

inequalities, and therefore to the birth of possible conflicts. High inequality undermines development by hindering economic progress, weakening democratic life, and threatening social cohesion (United Nations Development Program [UNDP], 2013).

In analyzing these results, it seems important to map where potential pockets of discontent could increase the most if LNOB principles were not considered and SDGs were not focused the most vulnerable groups. We looked at the regions where inequalities are worsening due to non-compliance or weak adoption of the LNOB principle.

Geography of Areas of Discontent Around the World

The geography of discontent is a social phenomenon that refers to the feeling of grievance or dissatisfaction perceived by a good part of the population living in those territories that feel abandoned by

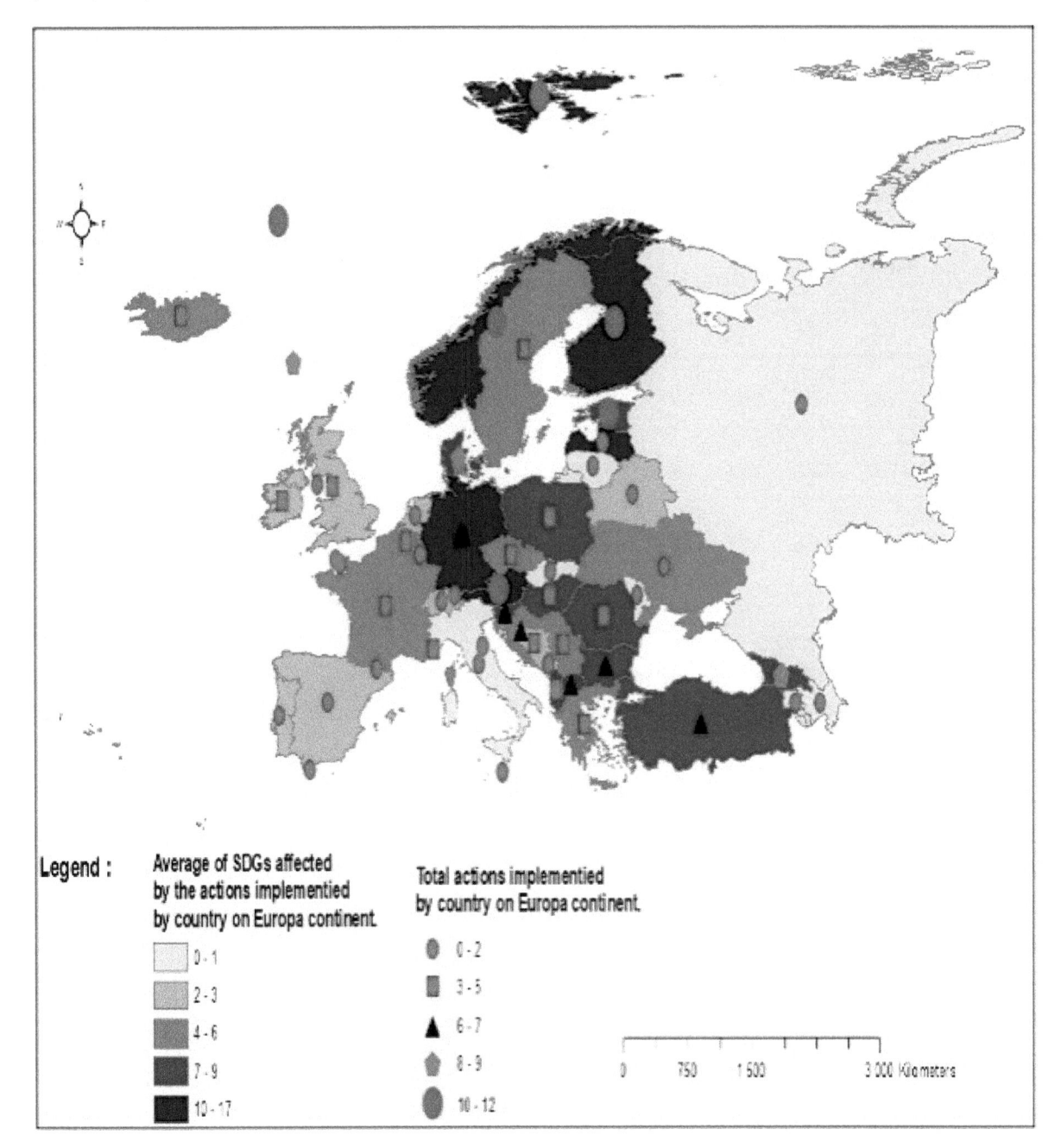

Figure 12. Geographical distribution of actions implemented in Europe
(Author, 2023)

governments and policy makers. This phenomenon appears as a factor that can make the SDGs a valuable tool for more inclusive and people-centred policymaking. Indeed, high unemployment, low wage growth and other symptoms of poor socioeconomic performance have led to growing public discontent with the political and economic status quo. The geography of discontent stresses on a growing mistrust from citizens about the capacity of their governments to ensure well-being now and in the future. This

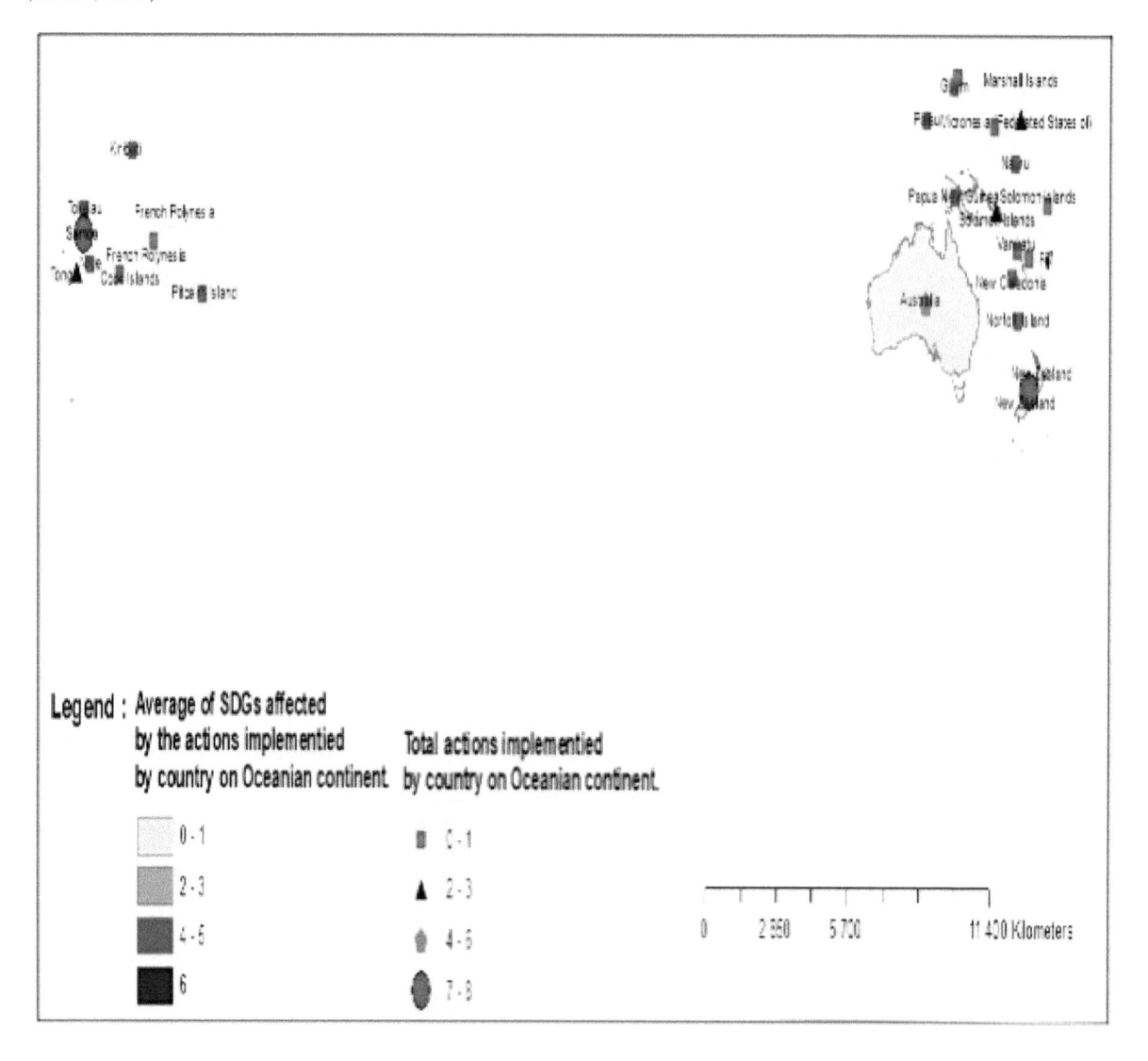

Figure 13. Geographical distribution of actions implemented in Oceania
(Author, 2023)

mistrust has generated a pattern in which the degree of discontent reflects the economic performance of a region relative to others in the country, inside country disparities depending of levels decentralization. The geography of discontent is a symptom of an underlying policy failure. Too many regions struggle because public policy has not responded adequately to their problems. A focus on aggregate performance at the national level has obscured that struggling regions require distinct solutions. Only if policymakers address this fundamental issue will they be able to deal with the cause behind the geography of discontent (OECD, 2019a).

As a result of the current study, at regional level, assessing the risks of dissatisfaction associated with the implementation of actions for groups suffering from social exclusion (Appendix F) and looking again at Figure 6, it can be deduced that all regions of the world are potentially pockets of discontent. Only a few countries seem to be reasonably free from this risk, as shown in Figure 14.

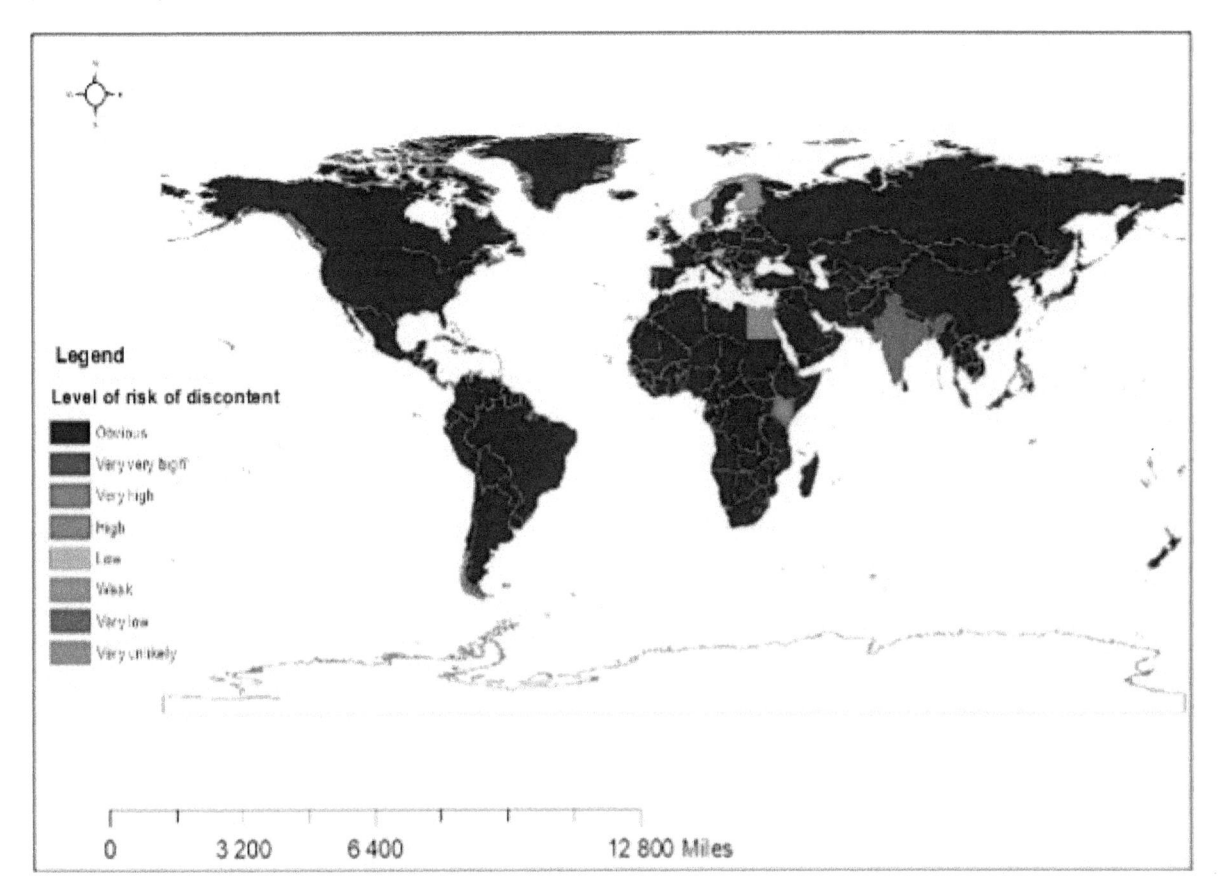

Figure 14. Risk levels of discontent through the world
(Author, 2023)

All regions of the world are exposed to discontent. Only a minority of countries on either side are exceptions to the rule (Figure 14). The trend is indisputable: over the past forty years, inequality has been increasing in almost every country in the world. In detail, if we divide the world population into geographical areas and no longer into income brackets, we see that the share that corresponds to the highest incomes has increased in almost all countries over the last decades (Damgé, 2017). Indeed, because of the low coverage of the areas to benefit from social inclusion actions assessed through the consideration of the SDGs in the actions implemented, Africa, Europe, Asia, and America are niches of uprising for vulnerable populations (Figures 8-12). With more than 17 actions implemented and an average of six SDGs achieved, the risk of possible discontent is low but not non-existent, at the level of the European continent. As for the African, Asian, and American continents, with more than 17 actions implemented and on average five SDGs affected, the risk of existence of discontent in these regions is low and therefore exists. Further confirmation of these results is the fact that at the level of these four regions, only one country per region can ensure that it is free from discontent.

Egypt in Africa presents a risk of "very unlikely" discontent (Figure 15 in Appendix G). Costa Rica in the Americas and India in Asia have the same level of risk described as "very low" (Figures 16 and 17 in Appendix G). Finland can rejoice a level of risk of discontent described as "low" (Figure 18 in Appendix G). The rest of the countries of these four continents are even more exposed to the risk of being confronted with discontent on the part of the populations left behind. Indeed, if the risk is found to be below the conditions previously stated, it can only be "low," "high," "very high," or even "obvious." Still, at this level, few countries pose a low or high risk. Austria and Norway (Europe) are low risk in terms of discontent, while the risk appears high in Kenya (Africa) (Figure 15), very high in Bangladesh and evident in Indonesia (Asia) (Figure 17). The other countries that do not appear at these low levels of risk listed above are outside the classification norm, and therefore constitute potential pockets of discontent or even imminent grounds of social conflict. It is very likely that Europe has the lowest proportion of pockets of discontent, ahead of Africa, Asia, and America, respectively, because of the performance achieved by the countries. Given the very small number of the actions in Oceania and the small number of SDGs achieved, it is more predisposed to the risk of existence of discontent than the aforementioned, since the risk at its level is considered "obvious" (Figure 19 in Appendix G). The proof is that New Zealand, which is the country that has made more efforts to comply with the LNOB principle, presents an extraordinary risk, more than obvious. Otherwise, all countries in this region should always expect conflicts due to weak or non-compliance with the LNOB principle since social inclusion seems to be very little observed.

This analysis shows that the rate of exposure to discontent is lower in Europe than in Africa, Asia, America, and Oceania, respectively. And the difference between these regions lies in the policies put in place to eliminate social disparities. This seems to be confirmed by the literature based on income inequality. Comparatively, Europe is doing well, and sees the share of the richest 10% increase from 34% to 37% of the Old Continent's wealth, a moderate increase in inequality compared to the situation in other areas (Damgé, 2017).

At the Country Level

The absence of some countries with strong economic power from the list that must contribute to the achievement of the LNOB principle through concrete actions could justify the low number of actions implemented and the low coverage of targets at the regional level. Even more so at the level of the last two most unequal regions, and especially at the level of the American continent, this observation seems to be verified. Thus, some countries such as the United States and Italy, which have been totally absent from the chessboard of supporters of respect for the LNOB principle and where regional disparities are still and increasingly observable, will be the subject of this analysis.

Non-LNOB Countries: Italy and the United States of America

In Europe, the richest 1% of society account for 12% of the continent's income, while their peers in the United States of America (USA) would have achieved double this performance, or more than 20% of the income of the American continent. While European policy forces the richest 1% to reduce their income share to the bottom 50%, USA policy encourages the richest 1% to increase their income share by more than 20% at the expense of the bottom 50%. The latter's income share began to fall from more than 20% in 1980 to about 13% in 2016; A trend diametrically opposed to that of the richest 1%.

In many other respects, the USA is failing to respect the rights of minority groups. On the security front, the crime rate continues to rise daily. Access to decent work, especially for certain racial groups, appears to be limited. According to US News and World Report (2020), blacks are the most affected by poverty, 21% compared to 18% for Hispanics, 10% for Asians, and 8% for whites. Blacks are overrepresented in prison. In 2018, 1501 blacks were incarcerated against 797 Hispanics and 268 whites. There is also a digital and racial divide: 25% of black teenagers have difficulty completing their homework because they do not have a computer or a reliable internet connection. All these facts could fuel frustration and create social tensions in the country.

Dealing with inequality in Italy is not just about the difference between a rich North and a poorer Mezzogiorno; it is also a question of talking about inequalities between men and women, and inequalities in terms of access to health, education, or employment (Joncoux, 2020). As for inequalities between regions of the country, a southern Italian earns only 57% of what a northern Italian earns for an equivalent job, and 11% of families seem to live below the poverty line. Women work proportionally more than men, 512 minutes, compared to 453 minutes. Added to this is a deplorable under-representation of women in politics: only 30% make up the Italian Parliament. In addition, only 45% of retired women receive pensions, compared to 70% of men (Kaval, 2023). Girls are less educated than boys and have less access to the Internet, which handicaps them for through their studies. Such inequalities are also noted in terms of access to health. The Italian healthcare system is decentralized, and therefore not all regions have equivalent resources. The South is once again neglected (trascurato in Italian) and many southern Italians therefore choose to seek treatment in the North, which generates even more costs (Joncoux, 2020).

Countries that have made no effort to respect the LNOB principle seem to be potentially susceptible to social conflicts that would be induced by the aggravation of the strong social disparities already permanent in their territories. These countries do not seem to have any social inclusion policies, especially for minorities. In these circumstances, it is obvious that at any time discontent is observed, even in the form of regular riots.

Universal Development Issues Not Considered When the SDGs Were Adopted in 2015

Some development issues had not been considered, or at least underestimated, when defining the 2030 Agenda. But today, like the dust emanating from gunpowder, they are returning to make invisible all the effort hitherto made by the United Nations towards sustainable development. Indeed, these minimized issues seem to be an obstacle to the vision of the United Nations, that of having a more just and inclusive world. These include local or international conflicts, natural disasters, instability of trade prices, to name a few.

These topics now seem to be gaining ground, blunting the progress made in the implementation of the 2030 Agenda. It would be logical to have an idea of the scale that these phenomena are taking, to deduce the left-behind created by these new global challenges. Such a diagnosis should serve as a basis for the elaboration of new SDGs or the reformulation of existing SDGs to readjust actions on the road to sustainable development.

A development topic not considered or drowned in the set of measures proposed to LNOB, and which could be distinctly taken in the category of the new SDGs, we present here is "The voice of the voiceless in all decisions taken for sustainable development." Indeed, the analysis made of the actions conducted reveals that measures are certainly being taken for the social inclusion of all categories of people. When these decisions are implemented, however, actions are conducted without considering the opinion of minority groups. This undoubtedly intensifies feelings of frustration, creates pockets of discontent, and worsens inequalities. It turns out that the strategies for implementing the measures do not otherwise define actions aimed, upstream, at considering the opinion of the "voiceless" in achievement. This is an example of consultation frameworks involving, or organized for the benefit of, vulnerable groups, to collect their ideas for solutions on sustainable development issues. These initiatives are almost nonexistent in many organizations; decisions are generally made ignoring minorities or substituting for them. This indicates an indignation or disdain developed by society vis-à-vis these social groups, and it is necessary to correct this behavior gradually and definitively to limit irresponsible decisions. Priority targets must be identified, and steps taken to encourage society to cultivate tolerance and respect for marginal groups. These priority targets could include:

X.1. By 2030, substantially increase the participation rate of minority groups in all community-based activities, with priority given to the actions of marginalized people.

X.2. By 2030, make the effective participation of all representatives of minority groups a reality, in decision-making bodies in all sectors of activity, even if these minorities are passive.

Otherwise, this proposal could be classified as one of the priority targets of SDG 10.

RECOMMENDATIONS

It would be interesting to see the conclusions of the next session of the HLPF to ensure that the issue of the disenfranchised is addressed by all participating nations. With the latest crises (i.e., geopolitical conflicts: Russo-Ukrainian armed conflict- Hamas -Israel armed conflict, pandemics, natural disasters etc.) falling on the planet like inevitable blows to dodge, it would be difficult to contain the new forms of social inequalities that could arise. In the current states of emergency, and given the scale of the crises, it seems unlikely to define, objectively and comprehensively, those left behind. As it stands, so far, the international community has struggled to match words with deeds, as not all members of the United Nations system have yet resolved to implement the decisions taken at the global level for a more sustainable and inclusive development. Therefore, it is the responsibility of this reflection to propose measures to be taken to improve the level of adoption of the LNOB principle by all states of the international community.

It will be necessary to require each member state of the international community to submit to the exercise of the reporting of their Voluntary National Evaluation, so that good guidelines are given to the policies to be put in place for a better adoption of the LNOB principle.

Sanctions must be upheld and enforced against countries that refuse to respect human rights and promote social exclusion through unorthodox development policies or strategies.

It is desirable that all countries, without exception, make efforts to multiply their actions with a focus on the inclusion of minorities, at the risk of creating hotbeds of discontent likely to degenerate into uncontrollable conflicts.

States will need to ensure that national policies or strategies define actions to address all the SDGs without excluding any category of minorities. This approach would be the best way to reduce the risk of discontent.

It is also advisable to review priorities in terms of actions for targeted populations for a more significant impact on sustainable development so desired.

International dialogue and leadership must now go further to put in place incentives and encouragement measures for states that initiate and implement measures for the effectiveness of the principle of leaving no one behind.

Beyond this, global mechanisms must be put in place to ensure the effectiveness of these measures and the assessment of their impact on peace, global social cohesion, and the reduction of inequalities around the world.

On the other hand, against timid states on the adoption or adherence to measures in favor of the left behind, the international community is called upon to set up a special agenda of advocacy and constructive and effective dialogue. Such an agenda must be accompanied by a roadmap to reverse their tendencies of timidity to the effectiveness and effectiveness of the implementation of the universal catalytic principle of peace, social cohesion and, by extension, security in the world.

At least, as stated by the United Nations Development Group (UNDG) in September 2023 in the "Six Transitions: Investment Pathways to Deliver the SDGs", the SDGs are deeply intertwined. Therefore, any action taken to achieve one may advance some others. This means and should lead to an -integrated policy approach is needed to achieve the SDGs – one that navigates the synergies and trade-offs in taking a certain line of action. This is akin to solving a Rubik's cube, where a solution is impossible with a focus only on one side at a time: all sides must be considered in relation to each other if the puzzle is to be solved. The UNDG rightly considers that, the most pressing priority for policymakers is to -ensure the integrated approach goes viral so that economic models and policy processes are revamped commensurate with ambitions, and investments are galvanized at scale for SDG acceleration-.

CONCLUSION

The desire to achieve an egalitarian world where minorities are no longer excluded is clear. Through the actions implemented by 143 countries determined to respect the LNOB principle, hope shows its glimmer. Already, it is significant to note that accountability has been achieved for this principle, during the HLPF, since 2016 where the implementation of the defined measures is made official. Indeed, several countries lend themselves from one year to the next to the accountability exercise about this crucial principle for sustainable and inclusive development. On the other hand, little effort has been made to reduce social disparities at both the country and regional levels. A situation that puts the whole planet on the ember of discontent and certainly leads it to successive conflicts that will require increased attention in years to come. If firmer measures are not taken now to reverse the trend, it will only be a matter of time before all humanity finds itself in chaos that will expose the complicity of everyone who remained silent in the face of social exclusion.

REFERENCES

Breuil, F. (2015a, June). BNT: High-level political forum on sustainable development: Highlights of 26 June. MediaEarth. https://www.mediaterre.org/actu,20150630095111,1.html

Damgé, M. (2017). Inequality in the world, which has been on the rise for forty years. *Le Monde*. https://www.lemonde.fr/les-decodeurs/article/2017/12/14/les-inegalites-dans-le-monde-en-hausse-depuis-quarante-ans_5229478_4355770.html

Gopalakrishnan, V., Wadhwa, D., & Hadd, S. (2021). *A look back at 2021 in 11 graphs: The inequality pandemic*. World Bank. https://www.banquemondiale.org/fr/news/feature/2021/12/20/year-2021-in-review-the-inequality-pandemic

IDRC. (2019). *Leaving no one behind: Principles of research in fragile contexts*. IDRC. https://www.idrc.ca/fr/perspectives/ne-laisser-personne-de-cote-principes-de-la-recherche-dans-les-contextes-fragiles

IISD. (2022, July 18). Summary of the 2022 session of the high-level political Forum on sustainable development: 5-15 July 2022. *Earth Negotiations Bulletin*. IISD. enb.iisd.org/high-level-political-forum-hlpf-2022

Joncoux, F. (2020). *Focus on inequalities in Italy*. Major-Prep. https://major-prepa.com/langues/italien/inegalites-italie/#Les%20In%C3%A9galit%C3%A9s%20Hommes/Femmes%20en%20Italie

Kaval, A. (2023). Pensions: In Italy persistent inequalities between women and men. *Le Monde*. https://www.lemonde.fr/economie/article/2023/01/18/retraites-en-italie-des-inegalites-persistantes-entre-les-femmes-et-les-hommes_6158374_3234.html

McCann, P. (2019). *Perceptions of regional inequality and the geography of discontent: insights from the UK*. Regional Studies.

Ministry for Europe and Foreign Affairs. (2019). *2030 Agenda for sustainable development: Where is France?* Diplomatie. https://www.diplomatie.gouv.fr/fr/politique-etrangere-de-la-france/developpement/l-agenda-2030-du-developpement/article/l-agenda-2030-et-les-objectifs-de-developpement-durable-odd

OECD. (2016). *Regional inequalities are worsening in many countries*. OECD. https://www.oecd.org/fr/social/les-inegalites-regionales-saggravent-dans-de-nombreux-pays.htm

Piketty, T. (2020). Global inequality: Where do we stand? *Le Monde*. https://www.lemonde.fr/blog/piketty/2020/11/17/inegalites-mondiales-ou-en-sommes-nous/

SachsJ. D.LafortuneG.FullerG.DrummE. (2023). Implementing the SDG Stimulus. Sustainable Development Report 2023. Paris: SDSN, Dublin: Dublin University Press, 2023. doi:10.25546/102924

UN. (2019). *The sustainable development agenda*. UN. https://www.un.org/sustainabledevelopment/fr/development-agenda/

UNDDG. (2019). *Leaving no one behind*. UNDDG. https://unsdg.un.org/fr/2030-agenda/universal-values/leave-no-one-behind

UNDDG. (2022). T*he high-level political forum on sustainable development calls for a renewed global commitment to save the SDGs and get the world back on track*. UNSDG. https://unsdg.un.org/fr/latest/stories/le-forum-politique-de-haut-niveau-pour-le-developpement-durable-appelle-un

United Nations. (2022, December). *High level political forum on sustainable development*. UN. https://sustainabledevelopment.un.org/hlpf

United Nations Development Programme. (2013). *Humanity divided: Tackling inequality in developing countries. UNDP, Bureau for Development Policy (BDP)*. UNDP. https://www.undp.org/sites/g/files/zskgke326/files/publications/French_web_low.pdf

United Nations Sustainable Development Group. (2023). *Six Transitions: Investment Pathways to Deliver the SDGs*. UN.

KEY TERMS AND DEFINITIONS

Commitment: An agreement or pledge to do something in the future; especially: an firm engagement to assume or achieve some development obligation at a future at the benefice of people. It is also a promise to do something or to behave in a particular way; a promise to support somebody/something.

Discontent: A feeling of wanting better treatments or an improved condition of life. It is an expression of unsatisfaction on the way things are going or managing. Discontent among the people contributes to pressure from many quarters to check the powers in force. General feeling of discontent and despair, stimulated mass demonstrations and the emergence of pro-democracy movements across a geographical sphere or entity (country or region).

Leaves No One Behind (LNOB): Leave no one behind (LNOB) is the central, transformative promise of the 2030 Agenda for Sustainable Development and its Sustainable Development Goals (SDGs). It represents the unequivocal commitment of all UN Member States to eradicate poverty in all its forms, end discrimination and exclusion, and reduce the inequalities and vulnerabilities that leave people behind and undermine the potential of individuals and of humanity as a whole. LNOB not only entails reaching the poorest of the poor, but requires combating discrimination and rising inequalities within and amongst countries, and their root causes. A major cause of people being left behind is persistent forms of discrimination, including gender discrimination, which leaves individuals, families and whole communities marginalized, and excluded. It is grounded in the UN's normative standards that are foundational principles of the Charter of the United Nations, international human rights law and national legal systems across the world.

Member States: The 193 United Nations countries and territories that adopted the Agenda 2030 and the 17 Sustainable Development Goals in 2015 and committed to achieve them. Through sustainable (economic, environmental, and social) development, their overall objective is to create a better world, and a better life for all, by 2030.

SDGs: Sustainable Development Goals (SDG's). In 2015, the United Nations drew up 17 Sustainable Development Goals to set the course for the future of our world. With the 2030 Agenda, 193 countries have committed to ensuring that all people can live in dignity by 2030 while at the same time preserving the natural foundations of life in the long term, whether social, economic, or ecological. The 17 SDGs concern everyone: governments worldwide, civil society, the private sector, academia, and individuals. The United Nations (UN) 2030 Agenda and its 17 SDGs include 169 targets. Together they provide a holistic framework for achieving a sustainable society globally. The SDGs are a call to action for all countries worldwide to foster prosperity while protecting our planet. Therefore, the targets include tackling poverty and strategies that address people's social needs, such as health, education, social protection, employment opportunities etc.

Social Inequalities: Social inequality is the condition of unequal access to the benefits and rights of society. Social inequality is usually the result of unfair inter-social treatment (biases and prejudices) and unjust government regulations. Social inequality can be further broken down into two types: direct and indirect. It is characterized by the existence of unequal opportunities and rewards for different social positions or statuses within a group or society. It contains structured and recurrent patterns of unequal distributions of goods, wealth, opportunities, rewards, and punishments. In a purely equal society, every citizen is equally able to contribute to the overall wellbeing of that society, and they are equally able to benefit from their membership within that society.

The Geography of Discontent: The geography of discontent is a social phenomenon that refers to the feeling of grievance or dissatisfaction perceived by a good part of the population living in those territories that feel abandoned by governments and policy makers. This phenomenon appears as a factor that can make the SDGs a valuable tool for more inclusive and people-centered policymaking. Indeed, high unemployment, low wage growth and other symptoms of poor socioeconomic performance have led to growing public discontent with the political and economic status quo. The geography of discontent stresses a growing mistrust from citizens about the capacity of their governments to ensure well-being now and in the future. This mistrust has generated a pattern in which the degree of discontent reflects the economic performance of a region relative to others in the country, inside country disparities depending on levels decentralization. The geography of discontent is a symptom of an underlying policy failure. Too many regions struggle because public policy has not responded adequately to their problems. A focus on aggregate performance at the national level has obscured that struggling regions require distinct solutions. Only if policymakers address this fundamental issue will they be able to deal with the cause behind the geography of discontent (OECD, 2019a). It is considered that SDGs can help to address some of the underlying causes of the discontents shown by the citizens through responsive and effective local and regional policies considering the principle of LNOB.

APPENDIX A

Table A1. List of countries involved in the proposal, attachment, and adoption of measures taken within the framework of compliance with the LNOB principle (Part 1)

	Countries That Proposed the Measures to be Taken	Countries Interested in the Measures Taken	Countries That Have Adopted the Measures Taken During the VNRs (Report on the Results Obtained)
2016	Finland, Germany, Norway, Estonia, France, and Switzerland	Finland, Germany, Norway, Estonia, France, and Switzerland	Egypt, Finland, Germany, Norway, Estonia, Madagascar, Mexico, Togo, Samoa, Republic of Korea, France
2017	Azerbaijan, Afghanistan, Bangladesh, Belgium, Botswana, India, Tajikistan, Maldives, Indonesia, Costa Rica, Chile, Denmark, Nepal, Malaysia, Cyprus, Japan, Sweden, Thailand, Zimbabwe, Nigeria, Portugal, Uruguay and Guatemala	Ethiopia, Kenya, Netherlands, Nigeria, Bangladesh, Japan, Thailand, Chile	Cyprus, Qatar, India, Bangladesh, Belgium, Ethiopia, Sweden, Nigeria, Belarus, Botswana, Costa Rica, Chile, Nepal, Malaysia, Slovenia, Netherlands, Japan, Thailand, Denmark, Jordan, Portugal, and Kenya
2018	Australia, Bahrain, Benin, Cape Verde, Canada, Mexico, Jamaica, Mali, Guinea, Kiribati, Lao People's Democratic Republic, Namibia, Spain, Viet Nam, Bhutan, State of Palestine and Senegal	Lao People's Democratic Republic, Bahamas, Bhutan, Benin, Jamaica, Australia, Ireland, Palestine, Qatar, Switzerland, Uruguay, Ecuador	Bahrain, Greece, Jamaica, Mali, Benin, Bhutan, Albania, Namibia, Singapore, Guinea, Senegal, Cape Verde, Andorra, Poland, Malta, Colombia, Lebanon, Ecuador, Latvia, Paraguay, Niger, Hungary, Azerbaijan, Canada, Egypt, Australia, Spain, Switzerland, Sri Lanka, Togo, Mexico, Ireland, United Arab Emirates and Uruguay
2019	Iraq, Azerbaijan, Ghana, Guyana, Pakistan, Serbia, Sierra Leone, Cambodia, Cameroon, Chile, Republic of the Congo, Guatemala, New Zealand, Philippines, South Africa and Timor-Leste	Lesotho, Indonesia, Bosnia and Herzegovina	Algeria, Rwanda, Lesotho, Serbia, Guyana, Bosnia and Herzegovina, Azerbaijan, Cameroon, Burkina Faso, Cambodia, Republic of Congo, Mauritius, Mongolia, Saint Lucia, South Africa, Sierra Leone, Indonesia, United Kingdom, Liechtenstein, Mauritania, Palau, Kuwait, New Zealand, Chile, Israel, Chad, Croatia, Iceland, Kazakhstan, Pakistan, Tonga, Philippines, Tunisia, Ghana, Côte d'Ivoire, Iraq, Turkmenistan, Scotland, Turkey, Timor-Leste, United Republic of Tanzania, and Vanuatu

Table A2. *List of countries involved in the proposal, attachment, and adoption of measures taken in accordance with the LNOB principle (Part 2)*

	Countries That Proposed the Measures to be Taken	Countries Interested in the Measures Taken	Countries That Have Adopted the Measures Taken During the VNRs (Report on the Results Obtained)
2020	Bangladesh, Kyrgyz Republic, Ecuador, Finland, Kenya, Kyrgyz Republic, Nigeria, Zambia, Burundi, India, Seychelles, Slovenia, Samoa, Solomon Islands, Ukraine,	Argentina, Austria, Bangladesh, Benin, Comoros, Costa Rica, Democratic Republic of the Congo, Finland, Gambia, India, Kenya, Kyrgyz Republic, Malawi, Morocco, Mozambique, Nepal, Niger, North Macedonia, Papua New Guinea, Moldova, Samoa, Seychelles, Solomon Islands, Ukraine, Ecuador, Uganda, Zambia, Panama, Libya, Trinidad and Tobago, Georgia, Bulgaria, Slovenia	Kyrgyz Republic, Gambia, India, Mozambique, Argentina, Costa Rica, Democratic Republic of the Congo, Nepal, Kenya, Ukraine, Finland, Liberia, Georgia, Comoros, Benin, Burundi, Bulgaria, Bangladesh, Austria, Malawi, Nigeria, Seychelles, Slovenia, Uganda, Zambia, Honduras, Moldova, Panama, Trinidad and Tobago, Brunei, Samoa, Armenia, Barbados, Estonia, Papua New Guinea, Morocco, Niger, Russian Federation, Ecuador, and Peru
2021	Egypt, Zimbabwe, Angola, Bolivia, China, Colombia, Denmark, Guatemala, Mexico, Sierra Leone, Cambodia, Cameroon, Chile, Republic of Congo, Ghana, Guyana, New Zealand, Philippines, South Africa, and Timor-Leste	Angola, Antigua and Barbuda, Bhutan, Bolivia, Chad, Colombia, Cuba, Cape Verde, Cyprus, Czech Republic, Denmark, Egypt, Indonesia, Japan, Lao People's Democratic Republic, Malaysia, Namibia, Norway, Qatar, San Marino, Germany, Iraq	Afghanistan, Antigua and Barbuda, Azerbaijan, China, Chad, Iraq, Cape Verde, Cyprus, Czech Republic, Dominican Republic, Egypt, Zimbabwe, Namibia, Colombia, Madagascar, Niger, Thailand, Japan, Norway, Sierra Leone, Denmark, New Zealand, Bolivia, Paraguay, Mexico, Germany, Tunisia, Lao People's Democratic Republic (Lao PDR), Malaysia, Indonesia, Sweden, Guatemala, Qatar, Bhutan, Nicaragua, Cuba, Angola, Lao People's Democratic Republic, United Kingdom and Marshall Islands

Source: Author, 2023. Excerpt from Appendix A.

APPENDIX B

Table B1. *Distribution by region of countries that have proposed measures to be taken in the context of compliance with the LNOB principle*

Year	America	Europe	Africa	Asia	Oceania
2016	0	6	0	0	0
2017	4	5	3	11	0
2018	3	1	6	5	2
2019	3	1	5	6	1
2020	1	3	5	3	3
2021	6	1	8	4	1
Average country workforce	3	3	5	5	1

Source: Author, 2023. Excerpt from Appendix A.

APPENDIX C

Table C1. Distribution by region of countries concerned by measures taken in the context of compliance with the LNOB principle

Year	America	Europe	Africa	Asia	Oceania
2016	0	6	0	0	0
2017	1	1	3	3	0
2018	4	2	1	4	1
2019	0	1	1	1	0
2020	5	7	13	5	3
2021	4	6	5	7	1
Average country workforce	2	4	4	3	1

Source: Author, 2023. Excerpt from Appendix A.

APPENDIX D

Table D1. Distribution by region of countries that have adopted measures taken in accordance with the LNOB principle

Year	America	Europe	Africa	Asia	Oceania
2016	0	6	0	0	0
2017	1	1	3	3	0
2018	4	2	1	4	1
2019	0	1	1	1	0
2020	5	7	13	5	3
2021	4	6	5	7	1
Average country workforce	2	4	4	3	1

Source: Author, 2023. Excerpt from Appendix A.

APPENDIX E

Table E1. Cumulative number of actions implemented and SDGs achieved in terms of compliance with the LNOB principle by states of the international community from 2016 to 2021 (Part 1)

	Total SDGs Affected by Actions Implemented by Country	Total Actions Implemented by Country		Total SDGs Affected by Actions Implemented by Country	Total Actions Implemented by Country		Total SDGs Affected by Actions Implemented by Country	Total Actions Implemented by Country
Afghanistan	1	1	Bulgaria	8	7	Finland	11	12
South Africa	4	3	Burkina Faso	3	5	France	5	3
Albania	7	3	Burundi	4	5	Gambia	8	5
Algeria	4	2	Cambodia	2	4	Georgia	8	8
Germany	10	7	Cameroon	1	1	Ghana	8	4
Andorra	1	2	Canada	4	3	Greece	6	3
Angola	2	1	Cape Verde	3	5	Guatemala	2	1
Antigua and Barbuda	2	2	Chile	6	7	Guyana	3	5
Argentina	7	5	China	2	2	Honduras	5	3
Armenia	4	2	Cyprus	8	6	Hungary	7	3
Australia	6	6	Colombia	3	3	India	9	15
Austria	11	11	Comoros	9	4	Indonesia	9	9
Azerbaijan	7	8	Costa Rica	17	7	Iraq	4	2
Bahrain	8	4	Ivory Coast	2	1	Ireland	2	3
Bangladesh	9	10	Croatia	6	6	Iceland	5	4
Barbados	4	2	Denmark	7	8	Israel	3	4
Belgium	6	3	Scotland	6	1	Jamaica	8	5
Benin	9	9	Egypt	12	17	Japan	8	7
Bhutan	7	8	United Arab Emirates	2	1	Jordan	3	2
Belarus	2	1	Ecuador	5	4	Kazakhstan	2	1
Bolivia	2	2	Spain	2	1	Kenya	10	11
Bosnia and Herzegovina	2	3	Estonia	8	12	Kuwait	4	1
Botswana	3	1	Ethiopia	2	1	Lao PDR	7	4
Brunei Darussalam	8	6	Russian Federation	5	2	Lesotho	4	5

Source: Author, 2023.

Table E2. Cumulative Number of actions implemented and sdgs achieved in terms of compliance with the LNOB principle by states of the international community from 2016 to 2021 (Part 2)

	Total SDGs Affected by Actions Implemented by Country	Total Actions Implemented by Country		Total SDGs Affected by Actions Implemented by Country	Total Actions Implemented by Country		Total SDGs Affected by Actions Implemented by Country	Total Actions Implemented by Country
Latvia	17	1	Uganda	6	5	Seychelles	5	4
Lebanon	4	3	Pakistan	9	2	Sierra Leone	5	9
Liberia	9	7	Palau	2	1	Singapore	2	1
Liechtenstein	2	2	Panama	9	5	Slovenia	9	7
North Macedonia	7	6	Papua New Guinea	3	1	Sri Lanka	3	1
Madagascar	4	4	Paraguay	5	4	Sweden	5	4
Malaysia	11	8	Netherlands	2	1	Switzerland	2	1
Malawi	7	5	Peru	1	1	Tanzania	3	2
Mali	1	1	Philippines	2	3	Chad	3	4
Malta	3	1	Poland	7	3	Thailand	8	8
Morocco	7	4	Portugal	2	1	Timor-Leste	2	2
Marshall Islands	6	3	Qatar	6	3	Trinidad and Tobago	5	1
Mauritius	1	2	Republic of Korea	6	4	Togo	3	2
Mauritania	2	1	DRC	6	10	Tonga	2	3
Mexico	7	5	Dominican Republic	3	2	Tunisia	4	5
Moldova	8	5	Kyrgyz Republic	3	2	Turkmenistan	4	3
Mongolia	1	2	Czech Republic	4	3	Turkey	8	7
Mozambique	6	6	United Kingdom	3	3	Ukraine	5	2
Namibia	7	5	Rwanda	6	7	Uruguay	2	2
Nepal	7	8	Saint Lucia	2	2	Vanuatu	1	1
Niger	7	6	Solomon Islands	6	3	Viet Nam	1	1
Nigeria	6	5	Samoa	5	7	Zambia	3	3
Norway	11	11	Senegal	8	3	Zimbabwe	8	7
New Zealand	6	8	Serbia	4	5			

Source: Author, 2023.

APPENDIX F

Figure 15. Grid for assessing the risks of dissatisfaction linked to the implementation of actions for groups suffering from social exclusion
(Author, 2023)

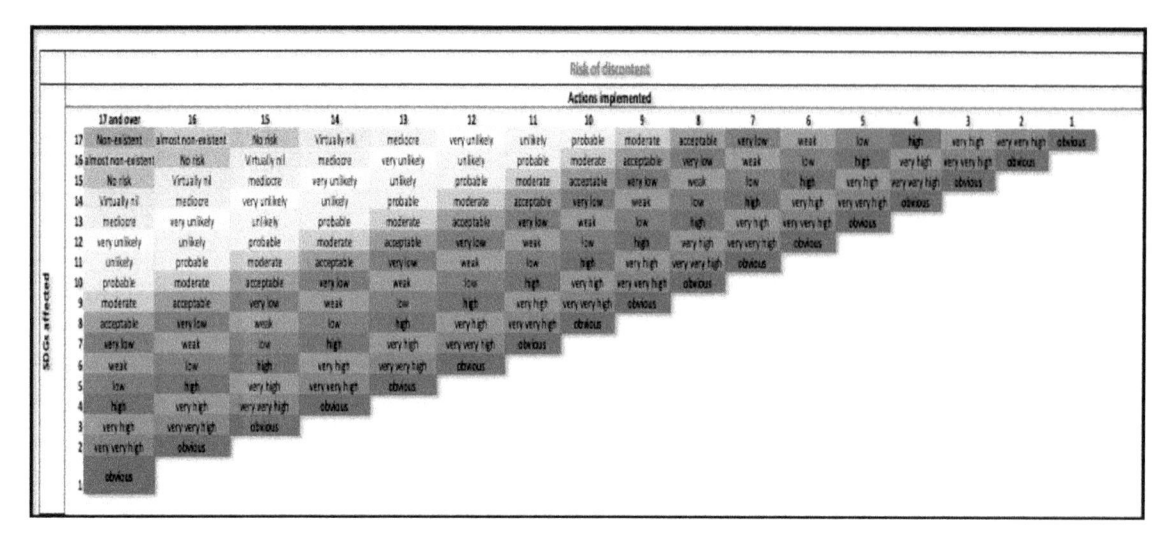

APPENDIX G

Figure 17. Status of risk levels of discontent in America
(Author, 2023)

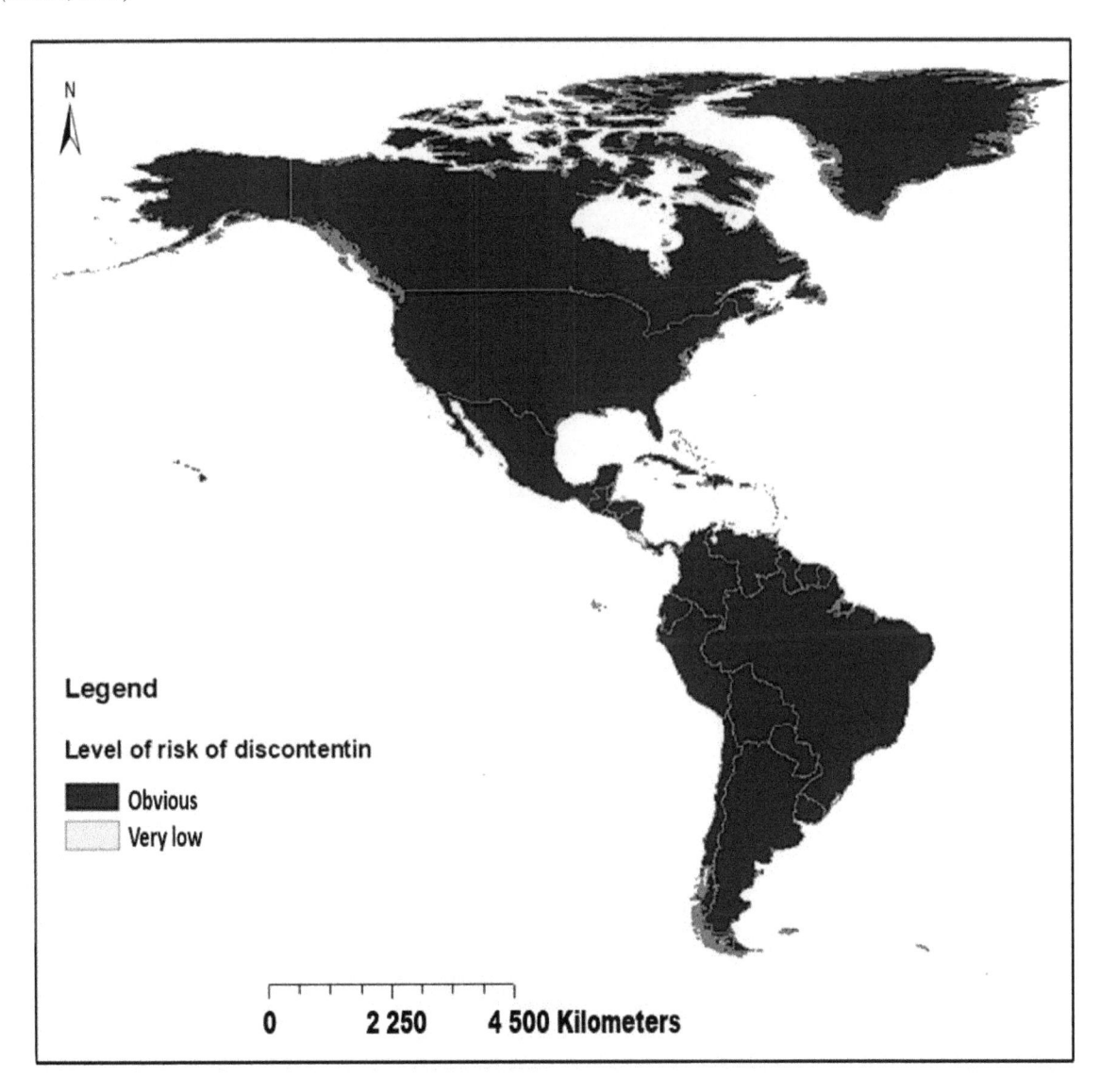

Figure 16. Status of risk levels of discontent in Africa
(Author, 2023)

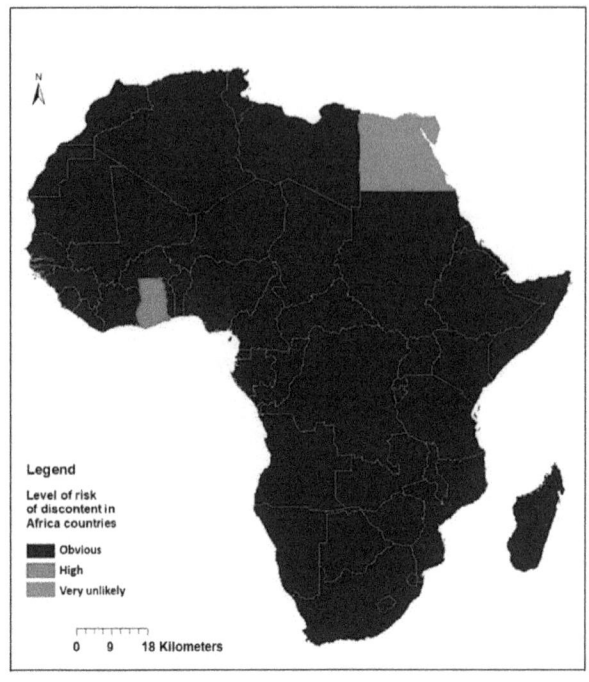

APPENDIX H

Figure 18. Status of risk levels of discontent in Asia
(Author, 2023)

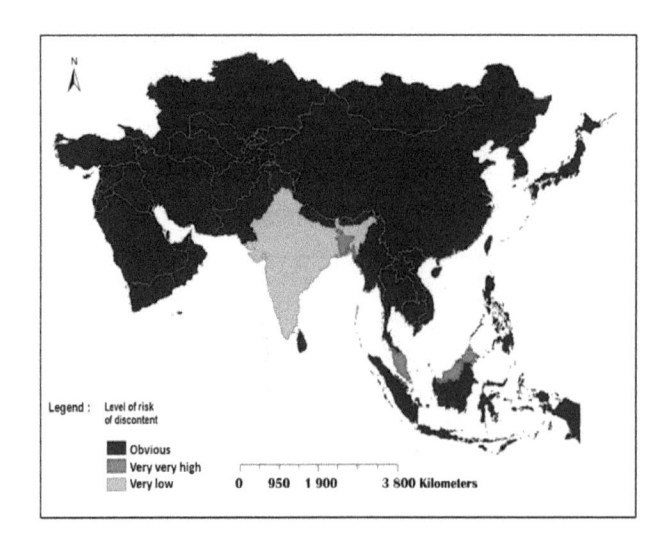

Figure 19. Status of risk levels of discontent in Europe
(Author, 2023)

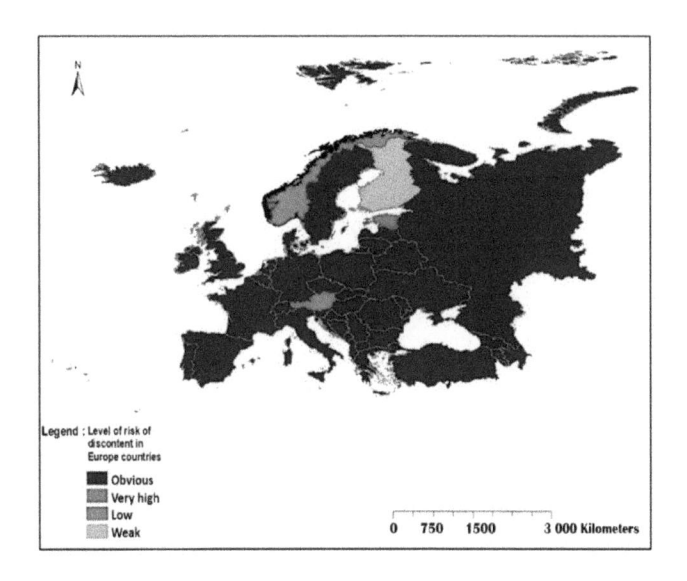

Figure 20. Status of risk levels of discontent in Africa Oceania
(Author, 2023)

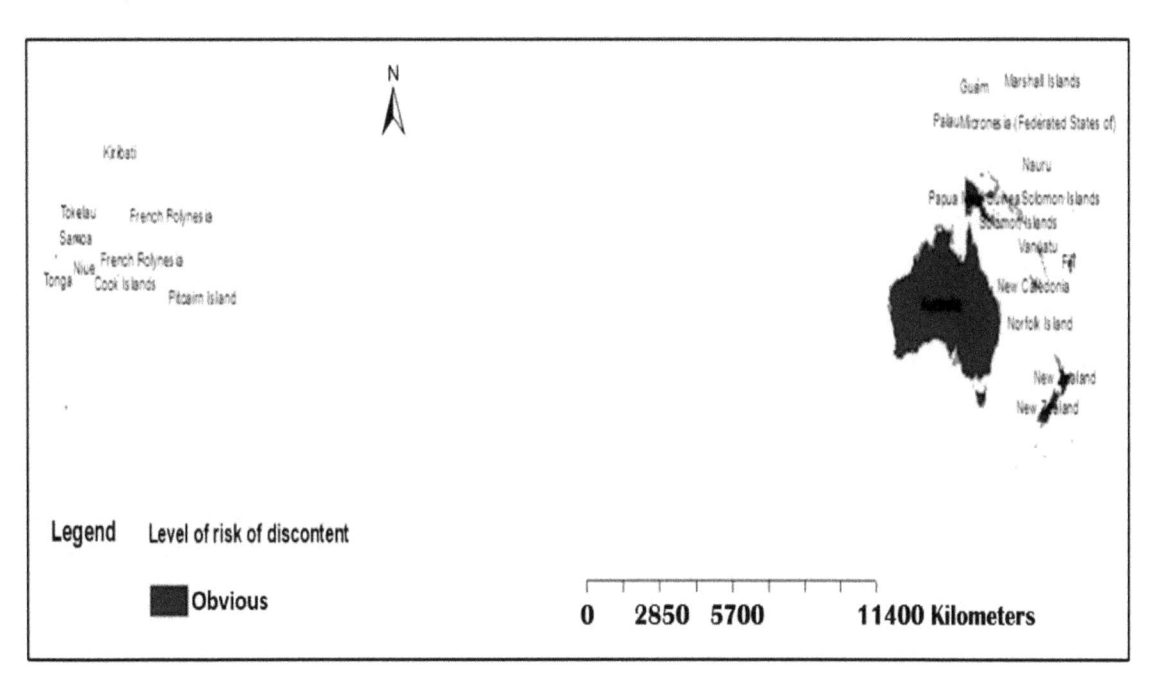

Figure 21. Share of income in the area or country held by the richest 1% compared to that held by the bottom 50%
(World Wealth and Income Database (WID))

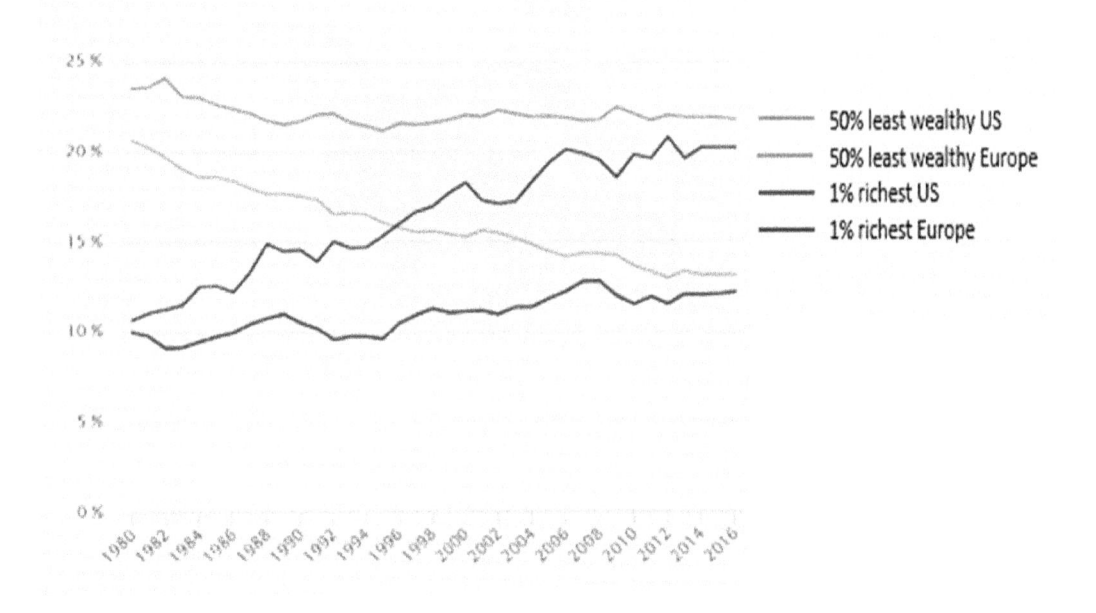

Chapter 4
Sustainable Development:
An Unhappy Consciousness

Parimal Kumar Roy
https://orcid.org/0000-0002-0461-2587
Bangladesh Public Administration Training Centre, Bangladesh

ABSTRACT

This chapter discusses sustainable development as an unhappy consciousness and suggests ratifying the development process in Bangladesh. To the author, sustainable development has been an imperfect coupling word in the context of the ethnic groups of Bangladesh; now, this chapter analysed sustainable development through customs, income disparity, and social justice, availing Amartya Sen's 'capability approach' to propose a framework for the inclusion community. Customary law is a sound and sustainable way to maintain social justice to ensure a sustainable community. Human behaviour, culture, attitudes, nature, supernatural power, values, norms, and traditions are all interlinked with growth and development in a country. Methodologically, it followed the ethnographic design and qualitative approach aligned with the post-positivism paradigm. This chapter suggests a sustainable community development framework as a policy recommendation and contextualizes global documents such as the SDGs, ILO 169, and UNDRIP to prioritize the lifeworld instead of the worldview.

INTRODUCTION

The discussion of this chapter intends to critique sustainable development occurring around the world, similar to positive economic change (Sen,2009) and sometimes includes environmental issues (Benjaminsen & Savarstad,2021; Mebratu,2017) in the community. However, apart from these, I intend to include the 'community' between the two words— sustainable and development in text and practice. Before proposing the Sustainable Community Development Framework (SCDF) as a prospective solution to development issues and appropriation of the comments, feelings, and suggestions of small ethnic groups (SEGs). Furthermore, the author intends to provide a concise and logical argument on the history of 'Sustainable Development,' and this combined term bears the meaning of 'unhappy consciousness' in the scholarly and academic realm (Paul,2008; Parris et al.,2003) along with the exclusive Communi-

DOI: 10.4018/979-8-3693-2758-6.ch004

ties. There is no way to avoid the relationship between customary law and community development, which have been connected for a long time. This deliberate action by the community of the area and local government policy connects with culture, customs, and customary law, helping to transform it into a modern community-based development alongside customary law and great traditions. As a case study, this chapter describes how customary law and culture are entrenched within sustainable community development, policy, programs, and goals at the local level (Amanda,2018). For example, scholars have also used logical connotations; examples from life have been taken to prove logical arguments regarding sustainable development (SD). Although there is a trending debate in academia, for instance, the conceptual lineage of 'Development' has yet to come directly from Western society and its generated philosophical root (Grober,2007; Pissani,2006; Rist,2014; Sen,2017. However, as per the paper's objective, this side-lined the debate, and the researcher believes it is only worth this scholarly argument constructively and sustainably for the community. However, a briefing is pertinent for establishing the core objective. Unfortunately, economic growth and development have been vitally linked to a society's bird's eye view instead of a community perspective. That is why I glimpse a development gap between the ethnic community and integrated development projects. SDGs 11 and 16 cannot relieve marginal communities' suffering; scholars or development practitioners must understand the causes of SDG gaps for ethnic development. I assert that SEGs cannot access political power and economic resources (Barkat,2016; Sarker et al.,2016) and cannot represent mainstream people. For that reason, I would like to draw a framework based on the SEGs lens—Customary law—for the inclusion of community development and representation skills among people of the mainstream.

SD is an imperfect coupling word that was subsequently discussed; this study analyses sustainable development through customary law to propose a framework for SEGs. Customary law is a sound and sustainable way to maintain security and human rights to ensure a sustainable community at the root level. Because human behavior, culture, attitudes, nature, supernatural power, values, norms, and traditions are all involved with customary systems, they are also interlinked with growth and development in India (Mahapatra,1986). Therefore, before ensuring sustainable community development, not sustainable development, the present research needs to comprehend the community's customary law. Why? For example, in Bangladesh, the Phulbari coal mine or Nawabganj Forest Authority—which evicted the minority people from their historical dwellings; the Gobindaganj clash between Santals and State Forces; and recently, all may appear to have been an accident or planned, but there was a root cause in those incidents—development occurred beyond and behind community guidelines.

Another example is the construction of a five-star hotel—Marriot—and an Amusement Park on Bandarban's hill through ruining the Mro community's culture, customs, ancestral housing, and traditional community guidelines—such development interventions drive the back side of development; Kaptai Lake in the 1960s already proved in that region (Mohsin,2022). These types of events for the SEGs brought endless suffering to the community. In this sense, this discussion tried to show a light at the end of the day and analyzed the field data [PhD Thesis] to ensure the development of a sustainable community. Therefore, the community has to add to the middle of the terms Sustainable and Development, such as Sustainable Community Development.

However, sustainable development has emerged as an evolutionary concept. The evolutionary conceptual process, for example, "simple to complex, is progress—economic growth—development—environmental protection—sustainable development" (Roy,2024); this paper now emphasizes sustainable community development. There is an established discourse on sustainable development worldwide. Moreover, European colonization spread differently according to the interests of metropolises and colonies. We can assume the following examples:

For its part, France had two groups of territories: (a) Guyana, Guadeloupe, and Martinique in the Americas; and the 'historic' colonies of St Pierre and Miquelon; St Louis and Gorey in Senegal, Reunion Island and trading stations in Gabon and India; (b) Algeria (1830), Marquesas Islands and Tahiti (1845), New Caledonia (1853), Cambodia (1865), the more recent possessions of Cochin-China (1867) and Senegal (1854–65) (cited from Paul, 2008, p. 48).

The Second World War paved the way for 'Development' in this sense, and the Brundtland Report of 1987 is the journey point of today's Sustainable Development discussion as a popular concept in sense-making to academic text. Before describing the Sustainable Development voyage, we should understand our 'Development' in light of the social position where the author's thoughts, consciousness, and actions are embedded. Sustainable, meaning is here to protect nature, in the sense of landscape that it is localizing through its journey started globally to impact society. When the sustainable concept is adopted with respect to corporate profit, it does not have any meaning for small ethnic groups, at least in Bangladesh. Instead, it pushed into a multifaceted crisis; the SEGs are in Bangladesh to understand exclusive development, and here, I am advocating for inclusion development.

GALLOPING SUSTAINABILITY: WHY INCLUSIVE DEVELOPMENT?

Bangladesh has a colonial legacy in the administration system and has been ruled over more than two hundred years by the EIC and Pakistan. (1757-1947; 1947-1971). Regarding GDP and per capita improvement, positive change-oriented interventions include sheltering the bird's eye strategy—'a core of course of beliefs for action that guide action before or after World War II, from Western countries. Postcolonial states [known as third-world countries] later became independent from the colony, generally during the 1950s, and adopted colonial acts and regulations (Biermann et al.,2022; Du Pisani,2006). As a result, the market shrunk, and the flow of goods became necessary.

On the other hand, profit maximization for progress was reshaping in industrialized countries. It became imperative to spread new strategies and concepts among underdeveloped countries—such as Bangladesh—for capital proliferation (Mamun, eds,2018). The industrialized developed countries divided the world mainly into two parts by GDP indicators. The GDP of these countries is lower—the third world—than that of industrialized or Western countries. When the honeymoon period did not finish, the prior colonized state was due to achieve independence, and then, people needed aid and loans to ensure their welfare. We can also refer to all these countries, including Bangladesh, that were lagging in the development journey.

Again, international organizations and industrialized countries came forward to help them, basically involving them in loan and aid traps (Muhammad,2006). Currently, studies are being conducted at sustainable development or international organizations, and concomitantly, studies show the glitch voice of trapped countries, such as Bangladesh.

As an upshot, this study undoubtedly articulates that sustainable development does not bear any meaning to SEGs such as the Santals people (Roy et al.,2023; Roy,2024). For example, the we can remember one of the key informant's extracts from the PhD journey, "What are the implications of

Sustainable Development to me when one of the ethnic girls got married before 18 years, then indeed, what candid bears the meaning of SDGs for us to transform our quality of life"? On the other hand, statistical indicators or government documents showed a more worrying position among the SEGs than among the national or mainstream people (Roy et al., 2022). Against this backdrop, whatever, it is a pertinent question to all concerned—whom problem is solved by whom? The answer is that 'Inclusive Development' is needed to continue.

SUSTAINABLE (COMMUNITY) DEVELOPMENT: POLITICS AND INCLUSIVENESS

Bangladesh achieved a flag and a constitution through a bloodshed war of nine months in 1971 against Pakistan. If the constitution is a mirror of a nation-state, roups are reflected from time rather to time; the Government of Bangladesh gives where the hopes and aspirations of all ethnic groups a circular reminder to all concerned people that there is one nation—— one country (Ministry of Information, PID, Circular number 2704). Earlier in 2011, the government sent a letter to the administration, and all were concerned about not using the word "indigenous" in official papers. Furthermore, in 2022, the same circular was circulated (Ref.15.00.0000.024.18.183.14.596/Dated 19 July 2022). Civil society delivered a press note to all newspapers. This regular circular will open a grappling ground instead of bridging the gaps between state and ethnic communities. To an extent, the constitution is the mother's womb, which provides shelter to all her citizens, from street children to LGBT people to far-reaching hill people. A debate, almost since the inception of the Constitution, started in the national assembly of Bangladesh on 31 October 1972, when all the small ethnic groups were advised to become 'Bengali' (Mohsin, 2002; Chakma & Maitrot, 2016). This debate gave birth to many bloodshed occurrences in this country and is currently a topic among civil society, academicians, politicians, and ethnic leaders, particularly Barrister Raja Debashis Roy, Sanjeeb Drang, Prashanta Tripura, Advocate Gonesh Shoren, and Rabindra Shoren. This debate is the point of the journey of the ethnic crisis in independent Bangladesh.

However, the mentioned statement is the core of the government's political decision on what they would do for ethnic people. A good number (17 times from 1972 to 2022) of constitutional amendments have occurred over the last fifty years. Not only the Santals but also all the ethnic people were ignored regarding their collective identity, respectful space, and recognition of the constitution. As stated, the Government of Bangladesh has not yet ratified the two treaties. Rather, the state was called by different names from time to time—for example, primitive, tribal, Adivasi, indigenous, and small ethnic groups. According to the Small Ethnic Groups Institutions Act of 2010, ethnic people have not been freed from the crisis of making their identity far from inclusive development. Even the 15th amendment of the constitution declared that the People of Bangladesh shall be as Bengali as a nation, and citizens of Bangladesh shall be known as Bangladeshi (the 15th Amendment of the Constitution, 2011). Nevertheless, the People's identity crisis has now turned into Bangladesh, which started almost fifty years ago in parliament (Tripura,2020; Chakma& Maitrot, 2016).

Now, UNDRIP 2007 is at the fore; ILO 169 (ilo.org; un.org) also guides the nation-states. With these changes in scope, formalism is seen in a new context without the need to modify its discourse; if anything, power is seen up by mutating. It now entails an ethnic title of its right before the State, precedent in the ordering by precedent in history. An example? Many Aboriginal Communities have represented the Education Curricula in Australia. The Maori community made their education system within and with the state's permission, even with government patronization. India has Tribal Universities. The Provincial Council of India is mandated to take 25% of them as a form of freedom, and the autonomous government is integrated into formal participatory democracy. In the context of States that exert more significant pressure with constitutions and codes, formalism essentially materializes in the ability to dispose of their ordering. This is how formal and participatory modernity can be generated in congruence with the SDGs and in times of constitutionalism in this new context. In current terminology, formality means, before and after constitutionalism, autonomy. What this study experienced is not on the fly that such a novelty put his collective existence at risk with a "legal-political personality." This study had just gone through a similar experience against the State and its attempt to integrate SEGs' customary law into the mainstream with the loss of its political entity.

A PACE OF SUSTAINABLE COLLABORATION: GLOBAL TREATIES WITH INCLUSIVE INTERVENTIONS

The UNDRIP and ILO are directive documents that work to protect and enhance the quality of the ethnic lifeworld. The Sustainable Development Goals (SDGs) are one of the steps the United Nations has taken to make the enduring endeavor of Sustainable Development Goals (2015-2030). Among the SDGs, 'Sustainable Communities' is the eleventh goal out of 17 in the sustainable initiatives by the UN, which, along with others, obviously address people's issues. While implementing sustainable development goals since 2015, as in other states, the government of Bangladesh needs to ensure sustainable communities (Goals11), which UNDRIP and ILO 169 have also advocated for a long time worldwide.

To sustain the SEG community, allowing them to go their way is wise. The rooted reason is that the SDGs, UNDRIP, and ILO are a few years old, but the sustainability mechanism practiced in these communities has been time-tested. To scholars, this is the key to a sustainable community or actual development without creating a predicament for future generations, such as the Brundtland Report 1987 or the Club of Rome (Meadows et al.,2018 [1972]), but the fact is denied local history and customs (Roy& Chakma,2010; Tobin,2014). The process of taking local customs into account for legal participation is seeded in the Community Resource Pool, Common Property Resources, and Political Participation. When customary leadership is involved in either decision-making at the community level or in the case of directing policies by the government of Bangladesh, then two direct outcomes are revealed in the excluded communities. Nevertheless, in light of UNDRIP 2007 and ILO 169, which are legal dimensions for incorporating peoples' knowledge, the community must continue to move towards political rights for sustainable community development.

All over the world, the ethnic community has a lifelong relationship with land and forests. While discussing the concept of sustainability, we need to look at the back of Western history. The New Science or the Society of the West significantly contributes to the flourishing of Sustainable Development; how advanced are developing countries such as Bangladesh to measure disadvantaged people by Western standards? The meaning of development, for example, is calculated on the scale of this new science or by determined indicators—GDP and per capita income—and how far will progress within the SDG strategy? For the meaning of this paragraph or against this backdrop, this section discusses international documents to protect human rights, security, and capability power as the principles of the neoliberalism paradigm. However, here is a question: when the treaties are still not ratified by the Government of Bangladesh, what are the benefits here to discuss? Policy recommendations and the proposal of an SCDF are the pillars of this discourse.

SUSTAINABLE (COMMUNITY) DEVELOPMENT FRAMEWORK FOR THE INCLUSIVE DEVELOPMENT

The core aim of this paper is to propose a sustainable community development framework that will focus on improving the capabilities, representation, and effectiveness of customary aspects of sustainable governance among the 50 ethnic groups in Bangladesh and how a state has absorbed an established system

Figure 1. A sustainable community development framework
(Roy, 2024)

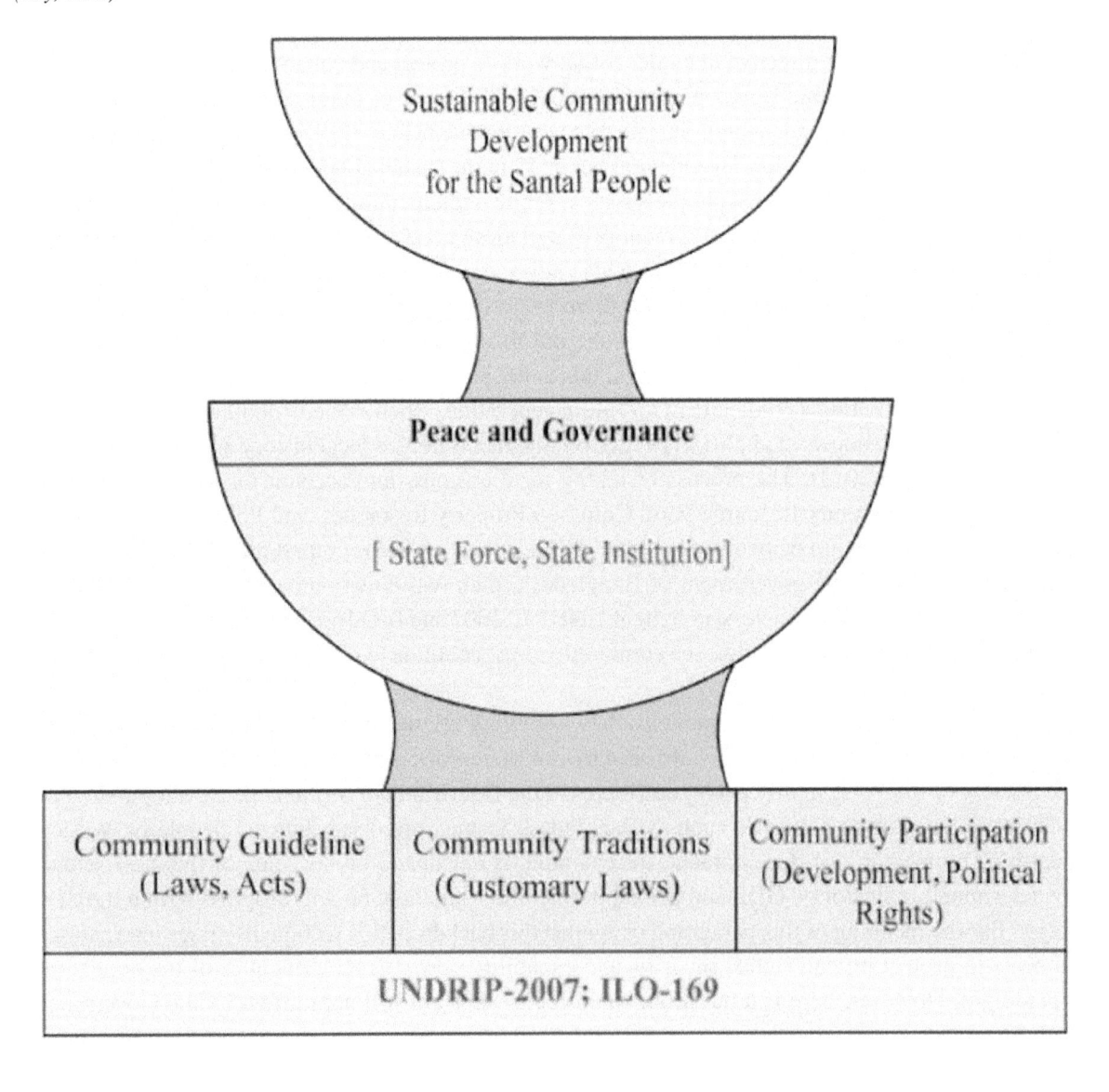

```
                    Sustainable Community
                         Development
                     for the Santal People

                      Peace and Governance

                   [ State Force, State Institution]

   Community Guideline   Community Traditions   Community Participation
       (Laws, Acts)        (Customary Laws)     (Development, Political
                                                        Rights)

                        UNDRIP-2007; ILO-169
```

trivially and introduced a new approach by taking the help of a decolonial strategy in the community. This framework presents salient features, a review of the existing frameworks, basic structures, and finally, the whole process, including input, output, and impact on the Santal community. Against this backdrop, this proposed framework is the first step in this process of the implementation and effectiveness of established principles for sustainable community development. Furthermore, the framework provides a disciplined basis for stimulating constructive discussion about reform while respecting others' proposed frameworks for the Santal people (Besra, 2014; Hasan, 2020), which are studied but lack the core issues—capabilities and presentation strategies—in mainstream society. This chapter's aims to stimulate customary practices under a framework to improve sustainable community governance as follows:

Governance is a system for shaping behavior to socially beneficial ends, involving many stakeholders serving diverse roles. This system includes government officials, legal authorities, customary organizations, and nongovernmental actors such as industry stakeholders and missionaries. The actors involved in developmental governance can also pursue objectives inconsistent with either environmental or community sustainability and social justice, such as advancing harmful economic developments or socially exploitative activities. However, governance systems contrast between communities, change over time, and intersect. Nation-state governance intersects with private sector approaches, such as voluntary commitments and traditional and ethnic norms and practices for conserving and using Santal's world. Considering the effect of complementary and competing governance arrangements and the result of the broader context is crucial. "The concept of sustainable development is multi-constructed—as a social construct, contested and highly political" (Jeje, 2006, p. 5).

Salient Features of Sustainable Community Development Framework

The researcher depicted the salient features of human rights instruments—the proposed framework is one of those instruments—how to effectively conquer the existing impediments to protect the rights of ethnic peoples. Additionally, to endorse the best practices for stepping on infringements of the human rights of small ethnic groups (SEGs) along with formulating recommendations to do ethnic capabilities by and for the ethnic peoples within the statute in Bangladesh.

Sustainable is a buzzword in development discourse (Pisani, 2006), especially after mentioning the UN and SDGs strategy to ensure global development (SDGs Declaration, 2005). However, the development of technology has changed human behavior over time. As a result, technology not only impacts the environment but also changes the course of action of society and culture (Benjaminsen & Svarsted, 2021; Meadows et al., 2018). Moreover, according to this logic, we must ensure a sustainable community before implementing sustainable development. Because development would not have been sustainable without making the community sustainable, we glimpse such a type of development in a philosophical reflection in the Brundtland Report in 1987. This report mentioned "sustainable development that meets the needs of the present without compromising the ability of future generations to meet their needs" (Du Pisani, 2006; Sen, 2009, p.248). Noble Laurette Amartya Sen (2009) reported that the "Brundtland committee's view of what to sustain is exactly right...they have generated that the value of the environment cannot be divorced from the lives of living creatures [community]" (Sen, 2009, p.,249). In addition, scholars (Benjaminsen & Svarsted, 2021; Meadows et al.,2018) mentioned a similar development philosophy in their writings—what good is sustainable development if communities do not survive? Amartya Sen (2009), therefore, advocated ensuring the preservation of community rights, which is social justice; indirectly, it is a sustainable community. This study, however, debriefs the salient features of the sustainable community development framework (see Figure 1) in the following—

Collaborating

Collaboration is a social accord that is an unwritten adhesive among the communities within the state apparatus. Although members of all communities generally hold different social, political, or spiritual viewpoints, they collaborate; they share responsibilities and resources to live in peace. All communities' stays include cohousing, residential land trust, ecovillage, communes, ashrams, and clubs. Therefore, the proposed framework should have these collaborative qualities to make the community sustainable under the statute. The framework is collaborative and has a collaborative relationship among three entities. These three entities are employees, governments, and workers (ILO-169). However, carrying over the proposed framework requires establishing this tripartite relationship.

Nonetheless, when someone talks about sustainable development but sidesteps the subject of the sustainable community if the community is sustainable, the development will carry over from there instantly or in the course of sustainability. Academicians and organizations have an avid interest (for example, Meadows, 2018; Pissani, 2006; Brudlandland,1987; IUCN, WWF), who are always looking for connections between development and sustainability in terms of the environment. However, they forget what the relationship between community and sustainability should be and whether sustainability and development are inversely related.

Skills and Training

Skills and training are essential parts of human development in society. To ensure a sustainable community and economic solvency, skilled human resources can contribute to leading families with dignity. This is why the SCDF has one of the traits for incorporating disadvantaged people—the Santal commonality. Without giving any sustainable priorities such as upholding skills and training to improve ethnic life patterns, the development of ethnic people burdens society. For that reason, the chapter has added or enlisted this feature of the SCDF to address social predicaments, restlessness in the community, and economic impoverishment in the community.

Common Practice

The country's legal system or customary rules control human behavior and are determined to be binding. However, the sources of law include customary laws, international conventions, constitutions, statutes, regulations, court decisions, administrative instruments, traditions, agreements, standards, customary norms, obligatory traditional practices, and religious decisions or texts. When the project articulates an SCDF, it should include all the mentioned common features in this framework to lead the community effectively. The community system for governing behavior involves interactions among structures, processes, customs, and traditions that determine how power and responsibilities are exercised, decisions are made, and how citizens or other stakeholders explain the belonging systems—customary or statutes.

Participation in Economic and Practical Activities

Although SEGs have different contexts and economic structures, the core element of all SEGs' traditions and beliefs, substantive economic participation, is living in communion with nature. The most important lesson to be drawn from ethnic traditions and beliefs is the "holistic vision" inherent in all beliefs and the importance of constant communication with nature. Against this backdrop, economic characteristics should be included in this framework.

Legal and Ethical Issues

Regardless of which environmental values are available in different reports (Brundtland, 1987; IUCN, 1980; Club of Rome, 1968; Stockholm, 1972; WCED, 1980), it would be reasonable to advocate any of these traditions as the basis for addressing the current environmental crisis. Nonetheless, traditional wisdom has much to offer regarding living in harmony with nature in the community. This is one of the fundamental tenets of the concept of sustainability (Mebratu,1998), and it has been endorsed in the SCDF as a characteristic of ethnic welfare.

A Framework to Make the Sustainable Community Development

The researcher used "sustainable" to describe the desired "state of global equilibrium." This chapter searches for a framework that represents a global system but acts locally to ensure that the community is "sustainable without sudden and uncontrolled collapse, and then capable of satisfying the basic material requirements of all of its people" (Graber, 2007, p. 6). Based on human rights and equity, both confirmed in the constitution, this research seeks the proposed framework to redress imbalances in governance initiatives by fully recognizing ethnic or minority peoples' contributions to society and culture, including development. However, first, some concepts must be addressed before discussing the proposed framework (PF) to provide the human rights of the Santal community to evade ethnic discrimination. PF is divided into three stages—

- *Stage 1*: The first stage is the input or base of the PF. The inputs are—two international treaties—the UNDRIP 2007 and the ILO Convention169—to implement the SCDF. The inputs generated the outcome in the second step of the SCDF as another result to maintain effective governance and peace in the Santal community.
- *Stage 2*: After completing the first stage's tasks, the results of the second stage will be effective after a minimum of 5 to 10 years, which is called the outcome; completing the second steps will bring another result—Impact.
- *Stage 3*: The impact is the third-level result of the SCDF that changes the community's in depth, sustainable community development.

These are intergenerational concepts honoring the historical struggles and knowledge of past generations, drawing on the experience and innovations of today's generations, and symbolizing the inheritance of hopes for future generations. The SCDF contributes to human rights to save our typical cultural traits (IWGIA, 2020. p.,666). The UN adopted the Declaration on the Rights of Indigenous Peoples (UNDRIP) in 2007 after illustrating 25 years of negotiations with states to respect and uphold the inherent human rights of ethnic Peoples. The International Labor Organization Convention 169 is also working to improve ethnic communities by building triparty relationships to make the community sustainable. In other words, this framework stands on these treaties for ensuring Santal's community development.

Structure of Sustainable Community Development Framework

The UNDRIP and ILO 169 are directive documents that protect and enhance Indigenous peoples' quality of life. The Sustainable Development Goals (SDGs) are one of the steps the United Nations has taken to make the enduring endeavor of sustainable development. Looking at the time frame, both are ongoing international programs for the capacity development of ethnic people worldwide. Denial of the fact is to deny the local history; it is the irony of the ethnic development of Bangladesh. The process of taking local customs into account for legal participation is seeded in the community resource pool, common property resources, and political participation. People of the minority community, imagine, are involved in decision-making at the community level when developing or directing policies taken by the government of Bangladesh for this community; then, the research explores two direct outcomes, 'no human rights violation' and 'no exclusion' in the state's development interventions. However, because the UNDRIP and ILO are legal dimensions for incorporating peoples' knowledge, the community must continue to move towards political rights for sustainable community development.

Now let us look at the elements of the proposed framework. The three elements are –

- Community Guidelines,
- Community Traditions,
- Community Participation.

Each element is composed of a few elements. First, community guidelines include laws, regulations, and acts to focus peoples' direction in society. The community tradition beholds customary law; finally, participation in development and politics are rights under community participation. Community peace and governance depend on these two inputs. The state will nurture these inputs under its purview with its institutions and forces. This is what the proposed structure wants to say to support the sustainable community development of people. The SCDF would not go astray conditionally if the input and outcome did not deviate in this structure, at least for the theoretical guidelines such as directions.

Community Guidelines

UNDRIP and ILO 169 suggest that a customary-based society cannot run or compete with the mainstream population. To meet the current crisis, this type of community worldwide feels social security and community guidelines would ensure that. Against this backdrop, the State will formulate acts and policies on governance to impact its land management and life settings positively. UNDRIP and ILO-169 are examples of grounding work to ensure Santal's lifeworld.

Community Traditions

The ILO 169 is an international agreement on indigenous development established in 1989 after a long process (www.ilo.org). Like the UNDRIP, Bangladesh has not signed this treaty. However, this approach is an effective strategy for the overall development of SEGs. Let us take a snapshot of what has been said in this strategy. For the first time, the ILO169 provides structural policy for ethnic people and states that if the following elements exist, then people should be treated as Indigenous (Ethnic is in Bangladesh, here, this chapter adopted them as Ethnic instead of Indigenous or Tribal, as per the current legal provisions) Peoples—

i. Traditional lifestyles.
ii. Culture and way of life differ from the other national population segments. e.g., in their ways of making a living. Language, customs, etc.
iii. Own social organization and political institution
iv. Living in historical continuity in a certain area or before Others "invaded" or came to the area (Convention 169 of the ILO).

Community Participation

Small ethnic groups, therefore, have become 'scapegoats' for development interventions in the country. For example, in Kaptai Lake, from 1957 to 1962 in Rangamati, as a result of the construction of a dam, 655 sq. km was submerged. The ethnic dwellers of the Kaptai area have lost their houses and cultivable land. Approximately 16,000 families and 1,00,000 ethnic people have been displaced. More than forty thousand Chakma people migrated to neighboring India. Land acquisition is one of the leading causes of conflict in that area (Hossain et al.,2021). Clash for Coalmine in Phulbari in 2006 is one of many examples across the country where the small minority are paying the cost of development; vividly, human rights are at stake (ADB,1998; Barkat,2016). On these mega-development projects, the people, their melodies, and their voices are not presented, heard, or reflected by any means. Ironically, their voices merge with mainstream trends to turn into a withering community from others. The Santal community is one of the ethnic groups that suffers from polarization in power, marginalization of economic conditions, and victimization of human rights to make collective or individual claims available. With an ethnographic lens, this chapter's aims to find a pathway to address the existing issues of the Santal community, shaded by two major international accords—the UNDRIP and the ILO. Community participation is one of the pillars of the Santal community's empowerment or the ability to make them capable of society.

Based on the diversified literature reviews, this chapter proposed a sustainable community development framework (see Figure 1) as the paramount objective, followed by the two international treaties. This proposed framework has been delineated; however, sustainable development is a disputable (Pisani,2006) global phenomenon that fails to make the appropriate solution at the community level (James Rosenau, 2003, p.16 cited in Sneddon et al.,2006, p.,257; Grober, 2007, p.6). In this context, Ulrich Grober (2007) suggested two solutions to sustainability at the local level to protect natural resources, such as the 'Club of Rome' in the 1920s (Meadows et al.,2018): "sustainable without sudden and unconditional collapse, two, capable of satisfying the basic requirements of all its people (Meadows et al.,2018[1972] cited in Grober,2007, p. 6)". In other words, sustainability will occur in communities that follow customary laws, followed by community sustainability, as presented in Figure 1 in this research project.

However, the UNDRIP and ILO 1989/169 are two major international legal instruments and pertinent treaties regarding the crisis of the existence of minorities and their human rights demands. Scholarly and policy aspects, these two are established, and yet to date, legal manifestations that both have taken human rights as core, particularly of ethnic groups. Both tools are towering tools, and people want to ensure their living standards with dignity, self-determination, and recognition in their respective society. This is why community participation in any intervention is one of the bases of this chapter's sustainable community development framework. The following statement shows the justification and sustainable development but does not mean this imperfect coupling word to the ethnic community. The researcher explored the following significance to indicate the current status of the Santals and the justifications in favour of the SCDF.

Significance of the Sustainable Community Development Framework

The outcome is the consequence of the outputs—which will lead to self-determination. The following results are discussed.

Law, Acts: Under this framework, the Sangathan practices rules and regulations concerning natural resources and the general conduct of village life. Those violating rules are liable to be punished. Additionally, the Santal people follow the statute and suggest that the authorities formulate laws and acts.

Minimizing Ethnic Clash: It is the duty of the Para Sangathan to address and dive into issues of intemperance and confrontations, drugs, gambling, and theft. The Sangathan also performs as a judiciary body for settling intra village land and property disputes, including Community Resources Pool or Community Resources Management.

Participation in Development Project: In the framework line-up, the Sangathan (traditional organization) can levy contributions and duties from householders within its jurisdiction to meet expenses such as constructing roads and bridges. Currently, the Sangathan is responsible for village development in terms of the structure of schools, community halls, and roads. Sangathan leaders liaise with different government departments and NGOs to implement rural development programs. The management of natural and common property resources such as land, forest, and water bodies is a key focus of this proposed model. In Santal village, where the study was conducted, there are significant forest areas, the government now owns the forest, and the village councils claim to belong like traditional proverbs—the land belongs to them because of Adivasi in this land. It is the responsibility of the customary parishad to look after the sustainable utilization of the forest and, at the same time, to meet the day-to-day livelihood needs of the community. Furthermore, the Sangathan's responsibility is to implement customary laws to stop indiscriminate and unnecessary hunting and fishing. Some customary laws discourage the use of chemical fertilizers and pesticides on agricultural lands. The natural resource base was degraded when traditional leaders were restricted from exercising their power through laws and acts. As this is the only grassroots-level governing body, these institutions need to be empowered to handle the indiscriminate use of resources within their jurisdiction area, even in private property.

Conservation of Customary Laws: This SCDF will expand academic knowledge practices not only in the case of the Santal community but also in other communities. This knowledge practice will produce many publications on their customary systems and development practices. The customary Sangathan had to function based on collective decision-making. However, respondents in the study area were mainly dissatisfied with its functioning, saying that it needs more transparency in decision-making; in certain instances, the respondents reported not having been consulted to make any decisions. However, some of the customary laws of the SEGs are important for sustainable community development. This is the case for the SCDF.

Impacts of Sustainable Community Development Framework: Some impacts of the customary laws based on SCDF of the Santal communities are described below—

- *Impacts on Land Management for Agriculture and Livelihood:* The land is central to Santal life; land inheritance and land management are guided according to Hindu Rules (Sarker et al., 2016) instead of customary law. This framework will help to activate new laws according to their customs in the second stage. Absentee landlordism, tenancy, and landlessness were unknown in the traditional Santal community that was supposed to be guided by the SCDF. This kind of impact in the community undoubtedly benefits everyone relatively well off. The impact of the SCDF is to make the community sustainable.
- *Impacts on Agricultural Activities*: The SEGs have high regard and respect for the soil, which feeds them and their children. Some festivals and dances are held before or after sowing to thank God for a bountiful harvest. Rice is the main crop of Santal, and traditionally, they are agricultural migrants. However, they cultivate the land using modern technology. Moreover, those who did not have land worked as agri-laborers in the field. The rich become more affluent, and the poor become landless tenants or agricultural wage laborers. Diversification of cultivation to commercial crops is also found in the field. The SCDF will work on these discrimination issues by activating laws.
- *Impact on Cultural Distinctiveness*: This SCDF is a part of the government that collaborates to establish the community as a unique unit in society. It is important for people to adhere to customary laws to ensure human rights and security. According to the scenarios presented, the SCDF will improve after a certain period of time if it begins to be implemented.
- *Good Academic Knowledge Practice in the Ethnic Studies*: The Santals community came from India to sustain the agricultural economy, but they are now under threat of being sustained despite their identity. After fifty years, they did not have any collective name or number, including the total population, which is also dubious to all. In this context, this framework will help them logically and legally develop under this framework's guidance. Studies show that in India, there are a good number of universities for studying ethnic or minority communities, but in Bangladesh, we did not have any single department for their academic research despite more than one hundred universities working there. Two international treaties guide this framework to lead the Santal people, who will be inspired to set up a sound academic knowledge practice. The long-term coexistence changed the Santal community and transformed various sections, which is one of the premises of this study. Bangladesh is an ancient part of the Indian subcontinent.

Furthermore, to understand our ancient Bengal history, all the books on which we rely (British administrator cum ethnographers like Hunter, 1876, 1878; Bodding, 1942; Malley, 1910; Risely, 1892; Dalton, 1872) contain ethnographic details of the socioeconomic profile of the Santal community. Their representation of customary law could have been more intended than strengthening customary power, and the purpose of their writing was to control the community. On the other hand, there was the potential to incorporate customary law into legislation. When the researcher of this project observes customary law in South Africa being incorporated within the framework of legislation, a dilemma arises (Saussine & Murphy, eds,2007; Pulea,1993). Why did the British ruler not adopt customary law in our region during that period? Rather, the East India British Company instigated the blaze between the state and community people, and the event's result continued. Ethnic groups have always struggled for 'self-control' or 'self-determination.' It is a calamity that colonialist and neo-colonialist writings on history have not taken into account, many of which tribal movements took place in the country (Doshi,1990). As a result, political consciousness grew among the SEGs.

CONCLUSION

Human rights have no boundaries; hence, they are universal and political (Aghahosseini,2007), and the state is the implementing tool that wants to ensure that in the interest of public welfare. When two Santal farmers did not receive water in the paddy field from the government-controlled irrigation project, they were threatened instead of receiving water. Finally, both peasants have paid by themselves, committing suicide. Academicians cannot keep this side-line as an isolated incident, but rather, this reflects, of course, brutally, the violence of human rights of the Santals community (The Daily Star, 2022). Like activists say, fingers at the weakness of human rights. GoB compensated the two families, but there was no way to give their lives back; in such an incident, the government needed to implement fundamental structural reforms as required to ensure human rights.

The chapter recommended a few words by proposing a framework for improving the Santals community, including—

- First, the Santals people need constitutional recognition;
- Second, it is time be fitting matter to ratify the agreements of UNDRIP-2007 and ILO 169; and
- Third, they have to give political rights to enjoy the human rights articulated in the proposed framework.

Here, we critically discuss the history since the birth of Bangladesh, when the highest level of authority of the state advised them to "become a Bengali"; then, the rest is, to all, an inherent phenomenon. The question of the protection of human rights arose for all. It is necessary to know minority groups' sensitivity to this issue of 'self-determination.' Otherwise, human rights will worsen and become critical to ensure sustainable community development for the smooth reach of the SDGs of 2030.

REFERENCES

Aghahosseini, M. (2007). *Claims of dual nationals and the development of customary international law: issues before the Iran-United States Claims Tribunal*. BRILL. doi:10.1163/ej.9789004156982.i-310

Amanda, T. L. (2018). Customary Law and the Domain of Federal Common Law today. *Customary Law Today*, 233-254.

Barkat, A. (2016). *Political economy of unpeopling of indigenous peoples: The case of Bangladesh*. MuktoBuddhiProkasana.

Benjaminsen, T. A., & Svarstad, H. (2021). *Political ecology: A critical engagement with global environmental issues*. Springer Nature. doi:10.1007/978-3-030-56036-2

Besra, L. (2014). *A Critical Review of Democracy and Governance Challenges in Bangladesh with special refences to a human rights-based approach for the Development of marginalized indigenous people*. [PhD Thesis, Flinders of Institute of Public Policy Management, Australia].

Biermann, F., Hickmann, T., & Sénit, C. A. (Eds.). (2022). *The Political Impact of the Sustainable Development Goals: Transforming Governance Through Global Goals?* Cambridge University Press. doi:10.1017/9781009082945

Chakma, N., & Maitrot, M. (2016). *How ethnic minorities became poor and stay poor in Bangladesh: A qualitative enquiry.* EEP/Shiree.

Constitution of Bangladesh. (2019). Ministry of Law, Justice, and Parliamentary Affairs, GoB.

Du Pisani, J. A. (2006). Sustainable development–historical roots of the concept. *Environmental Sciences (Lisse)*, *3*(2), 83–96. doi:10.1080/15693430600688831

Grober, U. (2007). *Deep roots-a conceptual history of' sustainable development.*

Hasan, M. M. (2020). *Mining conflict, indigenous peoples and environmental justice: The case of Phulbari coal project in Bangladesh,* [PhD thesis, York University].

Hossain, M. S., Sharifuzzaman, S. M., Nobi, M. N., Chowdhury, M. S. N., Sarker, S., Alamgir, M., Uddin, S. A., Chowdhury, S. R., Rahman, M. M., Rahman, M. S., Sobhan, F., & Chowdhury, S. (2021). Seaweeds farming for sustainable development goals and blue economy in Bangladesh. *Marine Policy*, *128*, 104469. doi:10.1016/j.marpol.2021.104469

Jeje, Y. (2006). *Southern Alberta Landscapes: Meeting the Challenges Ahead: Export Coefficients for Total Phosphorus, Total Nitrogen and Total Suspended Solids in the Southern Alberta Region: A Review of Literature.* Alberta Environment.

Mahapatra, S. (1986). *Modernization and ritual: Identity and Change in Santal society.* Oxford University Press.

Mamun, M. (Ed.). (2021). *Subaltern, Revolt and Armed Resistance in Bangladesh (1763-1950).* Kothaprokash.

Meadows, D. H., Meadows, D. L., Randers, J., & Behrens, W. W. (2018). The limits to growth. In *Green Planet Blues*. Routledge. doi:10.4324/9780429493744-3

Mebratu, D. (2017). Systems concept of sustainability and sustainable development. In *Sustainable development policy and administration* (pp. 85–112). Routledge. doi:10.4324/9781315087535-4

Mohsin, A. (2002). *The Politics of Nationalism: The Case of the Chittagong Hill Tracts Bangladesh* (2nd ed.). The University Press Limited.

Mohsin, A. (2022). The Chittagong Hill Tracts, Bangladesh. In The Emergence of Bangladesh (pp. 251-258). Palgrave Macmillan

Parris, T. M., & Kates, R. W. (2003). Characterizing and measuring sustainable development. *Annual Review of Environment and Resources*, *28*(1), 559–586. doi:10.1146/annurev.energy.28.050302.105551

Paul, B. D. (2008). A history of the concept of sustainable development: Literature review.The Annals of the University of Oradea. *Economic Sciences Series*, *17*(2), 576–580.

Pulea, M. (1993). *An Overview of Constitutional and Legal Provisions Relevant to Customary Marine Tenure and Management Systems in the South Pacific*. USP.

Rist, G. (2014). *The history of development: from Western origins to global faith*. Bloomsbury Publishing.

Roy, P., Chowdhury, J. S., Abd Wahab, H., & Saad, R. B. M. (2022). Ethnic Tension of the Bangladeshi Santal: A CDA of the Constitutional Provision. In Handbook of Research on Ethnic, Racial, and Religious Conflicts and Their Impact on State and Social Security (pp. 208-226). IGI Global. doi:10.4018/978-1-7998-8911-3.ch013

Roy, P. K. (2024). *Customary Law and Sustainable Community Development: A Study of the Santals of Bangladesh,* [PhD Thesis, Universiti Malaya].

Roy, P. K., Abd Wahab, H., & Hamidi, M. (2023). A Philosophical Discussion of Sustainable Development: A Case From the Bangladeshi Santal Community. Handbook of Research on Implications of Sustainable Development in Higher Education, (pp. 97-114). IGI Global. doi:10.4018/978-1-6684-6172-3.ch005

Roy, R. D., & Chakma, P. (2010). The Chittagong Hill Tracts Accord & Provisions on Lands, Territories, Resources and Customary Law. *Hope and Despair: Indigenous Jumma Peoples Speak on the Chittagong Hill Tracts Peace Accord*. Tetebba. http://tebtebba. org/index. php/all-resources/category/8-books

Sarker, M. A. R., Khan, N. A., & Musarrat, K. M. (2016). Livelihood and vulnerability of the Santals community in Bangladesh. *The Malaysian Journal of Social Administration*, *12*(1), 38–55. doi:10.22452/mjsa.vol12no1.2

Saussine, A. P., & Murphy, J. B. (Eds.). (2007). *The nature of Customary Law*. Cambridge University Press. doi:10.1017/CBO9780511493744

Sen, A. (2009). *The Idea of Justice*. Allan lane Penguin Books.

Sen, A. (2017). Elements of a theory of human rights. In *Justice and the capabilities approach* (pp. 221–262). Routledge. doi:10.4324/9781315251240-6

Sneddon, C., Howarth, R. B., & Norgaard, R. B. (2006). Sustainable development in a post-Brundtland world. *Ecological Economics*, *57*(2), 253–268. doi:10.1016/j.ecolecon.2005.04.013

Tobin, B. (2014). *Indigenous peoples, customary law and human rights-why living law matters*. Routledge. doi:10.4324/9781315778792

ADDITIONAL READING

Chowdhury, J. S., & Roy, P. K. (2023). A Philosophical Reflection of SDG 4 and Our Education Policy: Justified Self-Interest vs. Common Interest. *Positive and Constructive Contributions for Sustainable Development Goals*, 200-219.

Debnath, M. K. (2010). *Living on the Edge: The predicament of a rural indigenous Santal community in Bangladesh*. University of Toronto.

Debnath, M. K. (2020). A community under siege: Exclusionary education policies and indigenous Santals* in the Bangladeshi context. *Third World Quarterly*, *41*(3), 453–469. doi:10.1080/01436597.2019.1660634

Holmberg, J., & Sandbrook, R. (2019). Sustainable development: what is to be done? In *Policies for a small planet* (pp. 19–38). Routledge. doi:10.4324/9780429200465-1

Mitlin, D. (1992). Sustainable development: A guide to the literature. *Environment and Urbanization*, *4*(1), 111–124. doi:10.1177/095624789200400112

Roy, P., Chowdhury, J. S., Abd Wahab, H., Saad, M. R. B., & Parahakaran, S. (2021). Christianity, COVID-19, and marginal people of Bangladesh: An experience from the Santal Community. In Handbook of Research on the Impact of COVID-19 on Marginalized Populations and Support for the Future (pp. 65-82). IGI Global.

Roy, P. K., Abd Wahab, H., & Hamidi, M. (2023). Achieving the Sustainable Development Goals: A Case Study of the Ministry of Chittagong Hill Tracts Affairs, Bangladesh. In Positive and Constructive Contributions for Sustainable Development Goals (pp. 161-180). IGI Global.

KEY TERMS AND DEFINITIONS

Development: In the Santal community, development occurs when the community feels a positive change that smooths their lives without destroying their traditions.

Ethnic Groups: According to the Government of Bangladesh, there are fifty ethnic groups. Nineteen of those live in the northern area of Bangladesh. The ethnic communities are Santals, Orao, Rajbangshi, and Mushohor are a few of these names.

Sustainable: Whatever the meaning of Sustainable in the text, we understand that it is the nurturing of nature based on community-based guidelines. So, the Santal community says they have a Customary law to protect nature with love and humanity called Sustainability.

Chapter 5
Taxing Tomorrow:
Eco-Fiscal Dynamics for Sustainable Development

Ali Gökhan Gölçek
https://orcid.org/0000-0002-7948-7688
Niğde Ömer Halisdemir University, Turkey

ABSTRACT

This chapter explores the role of ecological taxation in sustainable development, focusing on Uruguay and Chile's strategies. It discusses "taxing tomorrow," a concept that emphasizes using fiscal policies to preemptively address sustainability challenges by internalizing environmental costs. The analysis covers eco-fiscal policies like carbon taxes and congestion charges, demonstrating their impact on reducing environmental degradation and promoting sustainable behaviors. By comparing Uruguay and Chile, the chapter highlights how different approaches can reflect specific national contexts and contribute to achieving the United Nations' sustainable development goals (SDGs). This comparative insight underlines the importance of adaptable ecological taxes in global sustainability efforts, offering lessons on integrating these policies into broader economic and environmental strategies.

INTRODUCTION

As the world navigates the complexities of sustainable development, the United Nations' Sustainable Development Goals (SDGs) have emerged as a guiding agenda for global efforts. Adopted in 2015, the SDGs outline a comprehensive agenda aimed at addressing critical challenges such as environmental degradation, climate change, poverty, and inequality. In line with these goals, the exploration of innovative policy tools has gained momentum, with taxation emerging as a key instrument in this endeavor. In this context, the necessity of examining how fiscal policies, and taxation in particular, can play a significant role in shaping a sustainable future and how they can be utilized to support the SDGs has become imperative. This exploration underscores the importance of taxation beyond its immediate revenue-generating function for countries, highlighting its significance in creating a long-term sustain-

DOI: 10.4018/979-8-3693-2758-6.ch005

able future. Accordingly, this section is constructed around the concept of "*taxing tomorrow*," a term coined to summarize the idea of actively and effectively using fiscal policies to preempt and mitigate the challenges of sustainable development.

The urgent need to fundamentally restructure economic and social systems towards sustainability has become one of the main focal points of the 21st century. Traditional fiscal policies, largely designed without considering environmental externalities, have often proven inadequate in addressing the increasing pressures on planetary boundaries and have sometimes had counterproductive effects (Rockström et al., 2009). In this regard, taxation, traditionally the primary tool for generating revenue, possesses promising potential as a fundamental instrument of state intervention to reorient economic incentives and direct behaviors towards more sustainable objectives. This potential impact is supported by the recognition that fiscal policies can significantly influence behaviors, investment decisions, and ultimately the trajectory of economic development (Mintrom, 2019). Within this context, eco-fiscal policies, encompassing various environmental and ecological taxes, have emerged as a dynamic approach to aligning fiscal systems with sustainability principles.

The concept of eco-fiscal policies is based on the principle of internalizing externalities. Both negative and positive externalities are known as the impacts of economic activities on third parties, which are not reflected in market prices. Environmental externalities, such as pollution and resource depletion, are particularly significant in the discourse of sustainable development. Eco-fiscal policies aim to incorporate the social and environmental costs of economic activities into the price mechanism, thereby correcting the resulting market failures and guiding consumers and producers towards more sustainable choices.

Carbon taxes, one of the foremost forms of environmental taxation, exemplify this approach. By levying a tax on the carbon content of fossil fuels, carbon taxes create an economic incentive to reduce greenhouse gas emissions, thereby contributing to climate action (SDG-13). The effectiveness of carbon taxes in reducing emissions has been demonstrated in numerous countries through studies indicating that they can lead to significant reductions in carbon dioxide emissions (Ali & Kirikkaleli, 2023; Haites, 2018; Timilsina, 2009). Beyond carbon taxes, the spectrum of environmental taxes includes various other measures designed to address specific environmental challenges. For instance, the plastic bag tax aims to deter the use of single-use plastic bags, targeting the issue of plastic pollution and thereby contributing to the goal of responsible consumption and production (SDG-12) (Hussain et al., 2020; Nielsen et al., 2019; Ritch et al., 2009). Similarly, congestion charges aim to reduce urban traffic congestion and related emissions, aligning with the goal of sustainable cities and communities (SDG-11) (González-Aliste et al., 2023; Gu et al., 2018; Ye, 2012).

The impact assessment of environmental taxes is indeed a multifaceted inquiry that extends beyond their environmental effects. Therefore, a comprehensive evaluation can reveal the revenue-generating potential of these taxes (Sandmo, 2004) and how these revenues can be allocated to advance the Sustainable Development Goals. Moreover, since the assessment includes the effects of environmental taxes on equity, ensuring that these taxes do not disproportionately burden vulnerable populations is crucial for maintaining social cohesion and advancing the goal of reducing inequalities (SDG-10).

The global perspective on eco-fiscal policies is characterized by a wide variety of implementation experiences. The study emphasizes the advantages of taxing tomorrow for a sustainable future, drawing on examples of countries that actively utilize environmental taxes. The successes achieved by various countries are significant in demonstrating the potential of environmental taxes to create meaningful change. On the other hand, it is impossible to overlook the challenges that may arise in the design and implementation of these policies. Indeed, learning from these experiences is crucial for improving eco-fiscal policies and enhancing their effectiveness in supporting sustainable development.

The first two sections of the study establish the background and conceptual framework. In this section, the spectrum of environmental taxes is explained, including the historical background of carbon tax, plastic bag tax, and congestion charge. The conceptual and operational nuances of the carbon tax are elucidated, examining its roles in reducing emissions and promoting renewable energy investments. Moreover, significant tools serving unique roles in environmental management, such as the plastic bag tax, congestion charge, and green subsidies, are introduced, highlighting the importance of environmental taxation. In conclusion, the adoption of well-designed environmental taxes is seen to support the decoupling of economic growth from harmful environmental impacts, thereby encouraging a transition towards a more circular and regenerative model.

In the third section, an impact assessment of the mentioned taxes has been conducted. Within this context, the efficacy, allocation, and fairness of environmental taxes have been debated. This section evaluates the tangible impacts of environmental taxes on environmental protection, carbon footprint reduction, and resource optimization through empirical data and case studies. The roles of environmental taxes in financing SDG initiatives, green infrastructure, and community resilience projects have been emphasized, and the strategic allocation of revenues generated from these taxes has been discussed. Ultimately, it has been concluded that environmental taxes are a significant tool in achieving sustainable development goals and combating climate change. These taxes are seen as playing a critical role in balancing economic growth with environmental protection and creating a more livable world for future generations.

The fourth section of the study focuses on the transition to renewable energy and environmental sustainability, examining the experiences of different countries with eco-fiscal policy implementation. This section analyzes both promising practices and the persistent challenges encountered by various countries, discussing findings on the future design and implementation of eco-fiscal reforms. Case studies are conducted on two countries in Latin America: Uruguay, which has recently emphasized significant eco-fiscal policies and operates within the "*taxing tomorrow*" framework, and Chile, which has taken important steps in environmental taxation but faces challenges in fully realizing the potential of its eco-fiscal initiatives. This comparative analysis aims to shed light on the key factors contributing to the success or shortcomings of eco-fiscal policies and provide significant contributions to achieving sustainable development goals.

In the conclusion section of the study, the transformative potential of environmental taxes in guiding global efforts towards achieving the Sustainable Development Goals (SDGs) is reiterated. It is concluded that eco-fiscal policies, with their adaptable and long-term structure based on changing environmental imperatives, are an effective tool for a sustainable future. As we progress towards a sustainable future, "*taxing tomorrow*" emerges not just as a financial strategy but as a call to action, urging the utilization of the power of eco-fiscal policies today to create a developing, equitable world for future generations.

BACKGROUND

Ecological taxation, also known as environmental or green taxation, encompasses a set of fiscal instruments designed to address environmental externalities (Fullerton et al., 2008). Simply put, traditional economic activities often generate environmental costs – such as pollution, resource depletion, and habitat

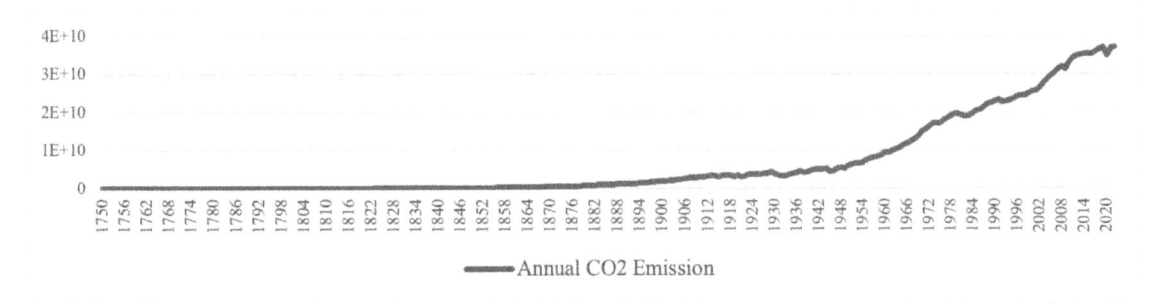

Figure 1. Annual CO2 emission (fossil fuels and industry)
(Ritchie et al., 2023)

━━ Annual CO2 Emission

destruction – that are not accounted for in market transactions (Pigou, 1932). Ecological taxes aim to correct this imbalance by imposing a financial cost on these previously unpriced environmental harms (Baranzini et al., 2000). In other words, eco-taxes internalize these costs, prompting fundamental shifts towards less environmentally damaging choices in production and consumption patterns (Goulder & Parry, 2008). Thus, green taxation serves as a crucial mechanism in the pursuit of sustainable development, aligning economic incentives with the imperative to protect and preserve the environment.

The need for innovative fiscal tools like green taxation arises from the escalating ecological crisis humanity faces, primarily driven by climate change resulting from greenhouse gas emissions, posing existential risks to ecosystems, agricultural systems, and human security (IPCC, 2022). Figure 1 clearly illustrates the sharp trajectory of the dramatic increase in annual CO2 emissions from fossil fuels and industry since the onset of the Industrial Revolution, especially noting the rapid rise in recent decades (Ritchie et al., 2023). This trend signifies not only a deepening dependence on fossil fuels but also reflects the increasing intensity of industrial activities worldwide. Furthermore, the graph reveals a concerning correlation: as emissions rise, so does the potential for severe climate change-related risks, underscoring the urgency of integrating environmental taxation into economic systems.

The rising curve of CO2 emissions represents a multidimensional threat, indicating an intensification of the greenhouse effect, an acceleration of global warming, and consequent severe weather conditions, rising sea levels, and deteriorating ecosystems. This increase in emissions can exacerbate food and water insecurity (Hasegawa et al., 2018), trigger health crises due to heatwaves and pollution (Grigorieva & Lukyanets, 2021), and lead to population displacements through climate-induced migration (Reuveny, 2007). Additionally, biodiversity loss caused by habitat destruction and overexploitation threatens vital ecosystem services essential for human well-being (Dasgupta, 2021). This escalating trend in emissions underscores the need for a fundamental shift in addressing the climate crisis, a shift that the integration of environmental taxation into economic systems can help catalyze.

Considering the clear and present dangers posed by rising CO2 emissions, the adoption of environmental taxation becomes a strategic response. This shift represents a move from reactive to proactive measures, not only fostering corrective actions but also promoting innovation and long-term sustainability. Societies can strategically realign economic signals through eco-taxes, encouraging investment in greener alternatives while deterring activities contributing to environmental degradation. This fiscal approach bridges the gap between current practices and the desired paradigm where economic growth is harmonized with environmental protection, laying the groundwork for diverse and specific eco-tax designs.

The specific design of eco-taxes varies significantly. While some directly target emissions (e.g., carbon tax), others focus on pollutants, resource usage, or environmentally harmful products (Fullerton & Stavins, 1998). More importantly, ecological taxation encompasses not only the introduction of new taxes but also the critical reform of subsidies that disproportionately support environmentally harmful activities (UNEP, 2022). This comprehensive approach ensures that eco-taxes not only deter environmentally damaging practices but also pave the way for more sustainable and equitable economic activities.

Although traditional regulatory approaches, such as mandated pollution limits, have played a significant role in environmental protection, their limitations are becoming increasingly apparent. Command-and-control regulations often fall short in addressing widespread pollution sources or the need for rapid transitions across the economy. In this context, market-based instruments like environmental taxation offer a complementary approach, utilizing price signals to facilitate widespread change among various economic actors (Stavins, 2003).

The rationale behind environmental taxes extends beyond narrowly defined environmental outcomes. Well-designed eco-taxes have the potential to address income inequality, which is exacerbated by environmental degradation and poses a barrier to effective climate action (Piketty, 2014). Additionally, environmental taxes can generate significant revenue that could offset the costs of other taxes (like income or labor taxes), finance substantial environmental investments, or support communities disproportionately affected by pollution or the transition to a greener economy (Labeaga & Labandeira, 2020). Therefore, eco-taxes are increasingly recognized not merely as tools for environmental management but as integral components of broader fiscal and social policy frameworks aimed at achieving sustainable and inclusive growth.

In conclusion, the potential benefits of ecological taxation are multifaceted, extending from direct environmental improvements to broader economic and social transformations. Eco-taxes, leveraging economic incentives, catalyze behavioral and investment shifts that are crucial for addressing complex challenges like environmental degradation, climate change, and social inequality. However, fully capitalizing on this potential requires a thorough understanding of the diverse instruments encompassed within the environmental taxation framework.

CAN TAXES SAVE THE PLANET? THE SPECTRUM OF ENVIRONMENTAL TAXES AND THEIR IMPACTS

With the growing recognition of the potential of environmental taxation, it is crucial to examine not only the various types of environmental taxes implemented worldwide but also their tangible effects on promoting environmental sustainability and economic resilience. Each tax instrument targets specific environmental issues, from carbon emissions to plastic waste, and possesses unique mechanisms and impacts. This section explores the range of environmental taxes, their historical contexts, design mechanisms, and most importantly, their effectiveness in reducing environmental harm and encouraging sustainable behaviors.

A cornerstone of climate policy, the carbon tax, exemplifies how financial instruments can drive significant change. By putting a price on greenhouse gas emissions, it sends a strong economic signal, encouraging a shift from polluting fossil fuels to cleaner alternatives. However, environmental issues extend beyond carbon emissions. Therefore, a holistic understanding of the spectrum of environmental taxes is essential.

Plastic bag taxes demonstrate how targeted financial measures can effectively address specific waste streams, reduce plastic pollution, and promote reusable alternatives. Congestion charges offer another example of targeted intervention, using price signals to alleviate traffic congestion, improve air quality, and create more livable urban areas. Additionally, the reform or elimination of environmentally harmful subsidies, which often support unsustainable industries and practices, plays a crucial role in complementing the implementation of new eco-taxes.

Understanding the multifaceted nature of ecological taxation, including its various tools and impacts, equips policymakers with a comprehensive toolkit to tackle environmental challenges. By strategically combining taxes, fees, and subsidy reforms, governments can design effective fiscal strategies that balance environmental, economic, and social considerations. This section will provide a comprehensive overview of this critical policy area by examining the history and mechanisms of various environmental taxes and evaluating their real-world impacts.

Carbon Tax: Transforming Energy Systems

The carbon tax, central to effective climate policy, serves as a fundamental mechanism designed to correct a primary market failure: the lack of pricing for greenhouse gas (GHG) emissions, the main drivers of climate change (Nordhaus, 1993). By imposing a cost on each ton of carbon dioxide equivalent (CO2e) emitted, carbon taxes create a robust economic incentive to shift away from fossil fuels towards lower-carbon energy sources, technologies, and practices. As a crucial component of contemporary climate policy, carbon taxes are implemented globally to reduce greenhouse gas emissions, increasingly accepted as an effective economic instrument.

A carbon tax is an eco-fiscal tool applied to the carbon content of fossil fuels, primarily taxing the CO_2 emissions resulting from fuel combustion. Based on the Pigouvian tax principle (Pigou, 1932), it aims to internalize the social cost of carbon emissions by incorporating environmental negative externalities into market prices.

The concept of carbon tax began to take shape towards the end of the 20th century, a period marked by the rising momentum of the environmental movement and the consolidation of climate change science. The establishment of the Intergovernmental Panel on Climate Change (IPCC) in 1988 provided a platform that helped elevate the issue of climate change and the need for carbon taxation in international policy discussions (IPCC, 2022). The practical application of carbon taxation began to be debated post-1990s, with Nordhaus (1993) presenting a detailed quantitative model of its economic impacts, paving the way for policy experimentation. Finland took a pioneering step in implementing carbon taxation in 1990, followed closely by other Scandinavian countries (Sumner et al., 2011), demonstrating that carbon taxes could be politically acceptable and economically feasible without significantly harming economic growth. The Kyoto Protocol of 1997, despite focusing on cap-and-trade mechanisms, included carbon taxation in the international dialogue on climate change (UNFCCC, 1998).

The specific designs of carbon taxes vary, with some policies directly targeting emissions through measures like carbon taxes, while others aim at controlling pollutants, regulating resource use, or managing environmentally harmful products (Burgers & Weishaar, 2018; Weisbach & Metcalf, 2009). This flexibility allows countries to tailor their carbon tax policies to their unique economic structures and environmental challenges. The nuanced application of carbon taxes highlights their role not only in promoting immediate environmental benefits but also in catalyzing long-term sustainable innovation in various national contexts.

The transformative potential of carbon taxes on global energy systems is both profound and crucial for the future of sustainable development. As countries implement carbon taxes, a shift from traditional to innovative, low-carbon alternatives is likely to be facilitated. The inherent pricing mechanism of carbon taxes directly influences energy consumption, consumption patterns, and investment decisions, encouraging a shift towards renewable and cleaner options. By making the use of fossil fuels financially discouraging, carbon taxes motivate both energy producers and consumers to reduce their carbon footprints and seek energy-efficient solutions.

The effectiveness of carbon taxes in achieving emission reductions is supported by a growing body of empirical evidence. Studies have demonstrated their impact on various fronts:

Carbon taxes have demonstrated varying degrees of effectiveness in reducing greenhouse gas emissions across different regions. In Australia, the implementation of a carbon tax at A\$23 per tonne in 2012 significantly cut emissions by 70 Mt, accounting for a 12% reduction from the base year, aligning with Australia's commitment under the Copenhagen Accord to reduce emissions by 80% below 2000 levels by 2050, while a compensation plan helped mitigate economic impacts (Meng et al., 2013). Similarly, in Ireland, a tax of 10-15 euros per tonne of CO_2 enabled the achievement of a 25.8% reduction from 1998 levels, affecting minimal economic welfare while shifting production and consumption patterns towards less carbon-intensive alternatives (Wissema & Dellink, 2007). British Columbia saw a 5 to 15% reduction in fuel consumption and GHG emissions from 2007 to 2012 due to its carbon tax (Haites, 2018). In China, a carbon tax rate of 200 CNY/ton significantly decreased emissions across various sectors (Zhao et al., 2023).

Furthermore, carbon taxes are designed not only to curb emissions but also to motivate significant behavioral changes across various sectors and communities. By financially incentivizing more sustainable practices, these policies aim to reshape consumption patterns and operational behaviors. In British Columbia, the implementation of North America's first revenue-neutral carbon tax led to substantial reductions in fuel use and emissions by incentivizing energy efficiency through gradual tax increases and economic rebates, benefiting especially lower-income households (Litman, 2009). Similarly, in Catalonia, a carbon tax on food effectively reduced greenhouse gas emissions and shifted consumer preferences towards healthier, lower-carbon diets (Dogbe & Gil, 2018). In the UK, carbon pricing mechanisms have spurred companies and individuals to adopt greener practices, significantly lowering carbon footprints across multiple sectors (Herweg & Schmidt, 2022). Furthermore, research on the aviation industry has shown that carbon tax incentive programs can successfully reduce emissions, as evidenced by a study utilizing airline data and algorithms (Qiu et al., 2020). These examples illustrate the versatile impact of carbon taxes in promoting sustainable behaviors and technological advancements globally.

In conclusion, carbon taxes have emerged as pivotal instruments in the global response to climate change, effectively addressing the urgent need for reduced greenhouse gas emissions and fostering significant behavioral shifts towards sustainability. By implementing these taxes, governments are not merely applying a fiscal measure; they are fundamentally reorienting economic systems to reflect the true environmental costs of carbon emissions. This policy tool has proven its versatility and effectiveness across diverse economic sectors and geographical regions, from reducing reliance on fossil fuels in British Columbia to promoting sustainable food consumption in Catalonia. The empirical evidence supports the efficacy of carbon taxes in driving both immediate and long-term environmental benefits, catalyzing innovations in technology and sustainable practices that align with the broader goals of the Paris Agreement. As the world continues to grapple with the pressing challenges of climate change, carbon taxes offer a robust strategy for encouraging a shift towards renewable energy sources, enhancing energy efficiency, and achieving a greener, more resilient future. Their ongoing refinement and adaptation will be crucial in ensuring that these policies remain effective in the face of evolving economic landscapes and environmental imperatives. Ultimately, carbon taxes not only symbolize a commitment to sustainable development but also demonstrate actionable progress towards a more sustainable and equitable global society.

Plastic Bag Tax: Curbing a Global Waste Stream

Single-use plastic bags, epitomized by their omnipresence, have become a widespread environmental scourge. These bags contribute to overflowing landfills, pollution of waterways, and disruption of wildlife and ecosystems (UNEP, 2018). The proliferation of single-use plastic bags has emerged as a critical environmental issue. In response to this growing crisis, governments and municipalities worldwide have adopted various fiscal measures to combat the issue of plastic bag pollution. Plastic bag taxes, implemented through fees or bans, aim to reduce their usage and encourage the shift to reusable alternatives.

Similar to carbon taxes, plastic bag taxes are designed to correct a market failure by internalizing the environmental costs of plastic bag production and disposal, which are not reflected in the market price. They target this environmental issue at its source by altering consumer behavior. Typically applied at the point of sale as small charges, these taxes make reusable bags a more attractive option. For instance, Ireland introduced a plastic bag tax in 2002, leading to a significant reduction in plastic bag usage (Convery et al., 2007). Similarly, San Francisco became the first U.S. city to ban single-use plastic bags in major supermarkets and pharmacies in 2007, setting a precedent for other cities and states (McKinley, 2007). Countries like Denmark and Bangladesh have also implemented their versions of plastic bag taxes and bans, showcasing these initiatives' global reach in combating plastic pollution (Nielsen et al., 2019; Shawon et al., 2023).

The effectiveness of plastic bag taxes can be quantified through various metrics such as reductions in bag usage, decreases in environmental pollution, and changes in consumer behavior. Research consistently shows that plastic bag taxes lead to significant reductions in plastic bag consumption and waste. Studies in Portugal found that a voluntary fee led to a 64% reduction in plastic bag consumption (Luís & Spínola, 2010), while a mandatory tax resulted in a 74% reduction (Martinho et al., 2017). Similar findings were reported in Serbia, where environmental taxes were found to positively impact consumer behavior (Đurović-Todorović et al., 2024). However, the effectiveness of these policies can vary, as seen in Padang, where a non-free plastic bag policy was not perceived as adequate by nearly half of the respondents (Wirna-Putri et al., 2021).

Plastic bag taxes not only change individual behavior but also influence the practices of retailers and manufacturers. Research consistently shows that plastic bag taxes have a significant impact on consumer behavior, leading to a reduction in plastic bag use (Convery et al., 2007; He, 2012; Seo & Kudo, 2022). These taxes also influence the practices of retailers and manufacturers, with supermarkets and hypermarkets playing a key role in providing alternatives such as reusable bags (Martinho et al., 2017). The success of these taxes is contingent on factors such as enforcement, consumer attitudes, and socioeconomic characteristics (He, 2012). Furthermore, the taxes can raise awareness of environmental issues and foster further pro-environmental behavior (Seo & Kudo, 2022; Thomas et al., 2019).

Furthermore, by curbing plastic bag consumption, these taxes contribute to various environmental benefits. Fewer plastic bags end up in landfills, reducing the burden on waste management systems. They also help to mitigate plastic pollution in oceans and waterways, protecting marine life and ecosystems (Abate & Elofsson, 2024; Mentis et al., 2022; Oosterhuis et al., 2014).

This comprehensive overview underscores the multifaceted benefits of plastic bag taxes not only in reducing immediate consumption but also in catalyzing broader shifts towards sustainability. By effectively altering both consumer habits and industrial practices, these taxes demonstrate a powerful tool for ecological conservation, encouraging societies worldwide to embrace more environmentally responsible behaviors.

Plastic bag taxes serve as a pivotal instrument in the global battle against plastic pollution, demonstrating their efficacy in instigating substantial behavioral and industrial changes. These measures not only curtail the immediate prevalence of plastic waste but also instill a culture of environmental responsibility among consumers and businesses alike. By internalizing the environmental costs of plastic bag usage, these taxes foster a shift towards more sustainable consumption practices and encourage the adoption of reusable alternatives. As nations continue to confront the escalating challenges of plastic pollution, the experiences gained from existing plastic bag tax implementations offer critical insights for refining and expanding these policies. Ultimately, these taxes are not just mechanisms for reducing waste but catalysts for a broader environmental ethos, paving the way towards a more sustainable future where ecological considerations are integral to everyday decision-making and policy frameworks. The continued evolution and adaptation of these taxes will be essential in ensuring their effectiveness and acceptance, as we strive to protect our ecosystems and enhance the quality of life on our planet.

Congestion Tax: Improving Urban Livability

The relentless roar of traffic in congested cities has become synonymous with modern life. Cities around the world face numerous challenges due to rapid urbanization and population growth. One of the most significant challenges is traffic congestion, which has become a major issue affecting the livability and efficiency of cities. As urban centers continue to grow, traffic congestion has emerged as a critical problem, significantly impacting air quality, public health, and urban productivity. Exhaust fumes pollute the air, contributing to respiratory illnesses and other health hazards (WHO, 2022). Furthermore, traffic congestion intensifies transport-related greenhouse gas emissions, exacerbating climate change. In response to these intertwined problems, a growing number of cities are turning to an innovative policy tool: congestion taxes.

Urban congestion is typically characterized by excessively crowded road networks during peak times, leading to prolonged travel times and increased emissions. The effects of congestion extend beyond mere inconvenience, impacting broader issues such as economic efficiency, air quality, and public health. The complexity of the traffic congestion problem necessitates innovative approaches in urban planning and policymaking.

The idea of traffic congestion pricing is not new; its roots trace back to the early 20th century when economist Arthur Pigou proposed a tax to address externalities not accounted for by the free market. However, the practical application of this theory did not materialize until the late 20th century.

Congestion taxes are designed to address a fundamental problem within transportation systems. When motorists are not charged the true cost of their journey—including delays imposed on others, air pollution, and climate impacts—they overuse a limited resource (road space) particularly during peak hours. This leads to an inefficient outcome for society. Congestion taxes aim to correct this market failure by placing a price on the negative externalities of excessive traffic. By doing so, they encourage drivers to

Taxing Tomorrow

reconsider their travel choices, potentially shifting to public transport, carpooling, cycling, walking, or adjusting their travel times.

n 1975, Singapore pioneered the modern concept of congestion pricing with the Area Licensing Scheme and in 1998 transitioned to the Electronic Road Pricing (ERP) system, which uses electronic fee collection to manage vehicle flow into the central business district (Phang & Toh, 2004). Following Singapore's success, other cities began to recognize the potential benefits of congestion taxes. London implemented its congestion charge in 2003, significantly reducing vehicle traffic and improving air quality within the charging zone (Green et al., 2020). Stockholm followed in 2007 with its congestion tax, which was initially met with public skepticism but soon demonstrated tangible benefits in traffic reduction and environmental improvements, leading to increased public support (Eliasson, 2008). These pioneering cities illustrate the potential of congestion taxes to make a positive difference in the lives of urban dwellers.

Congestion taxes not only alleviate traffic congestion but also yield numerous benefits across various dimensions. The effectiveness of congestion taxes can be evaluated through their impact on reducing vehicle congestion, improving air quality, and promoting shifts towards sustainable urban mobility.

Studies consistently show that congestion pricing effectively reduces traffic volume in charged zones. Martin & Thornton (2017) found that charges targeted at peak times or central areas are particularly successful in alleviating congestion. Triantafyllos et al. (2019) both demonstrated the effectiveness of congestion pricing in reallocating traffic volumes and reducing total traffic, with the latter also highlighting the potential for reducing emissions.

Moreover, research consistently shows that congestion taxes lead to a reduction in traffic volumes, which in turn improves air quality (Johansson et al., 2009). For example, the London congestion charging scheme significantly reduced NOX and PM10 emissions (Beevers & Carslaw, 2005), while a study in New York City found that cordon pricing reduced particulate matter inventory by up to 17.5% (Baghestani et al., 2020).

Congestion taxes, such as those implemented in Stockholm and New York City, have been shown to improve air quality and subsequently lead to positive public health outcomes (Ghassabian et al., 2024; Johansson et al., 2009). These taxes have been linked to reductions in ambient air pollution and a decrease in the rate of acute asthma attacks among children (Simeonova et al., 2021).

Research suggests that congestion taxes can indeed incentivize a shift towards more sustainable modes of transportation. Munnich (2010) further supports this, highlighting the success of congestion pricing in reducing congestion and increasing transit ridership in cities like Singapore, London, and Stockholm. Begg (2004) emphasizes the need for a combination of measures, including both incentives and disincentives, to achieve a truly sustainable transport system.

These findings collectively reinforce the multi-faceted advantages of congestion taxes, from enhancing urban air quality to fostering healthier communities and promoting greener transit options. By strategically managing urban mobility, congestion taxes not only address immediate environmental and health concerns but also lay the groundwork for more sustainable, resilient urban development.

Congestion taxes have proven to be powerful instruments for reshaping urban environments, offering a pragmatic solution to the enduring challenges of urban congestion. By effectively pricing the social costs of traffic, these taxes not only alleviate immediate traffic congestion but also catalyze broader environmental and public health improvements. They encourage a cultural shift towards sustainable transport options, reducing dependency on private vehicle use and fostering a more balanced urban mobility landscape. Furthermore, the success of congestion taxes in pioneering cities underscores their potential as a scalable and adaptable approach that can be tailored to the specific needs and conditions of urban centers worldwide. Looking forward, the integration of congestion taxes with other urban planning initiatives promises to enhance their effectiveness and contribute to the creation of more sustainable, equitable, and resilient cities. As urban populations continue to grow, the role of congestion taxes in promoting sustainable urban development becomes increasingly vital, offering a clear path forward in our collective journey towards achieving greener, more livable urban spaces.

Green Subsidies: Accelerating Sustainable Transitions

As global awareness of environmental sustainability increases, governments and policymakers tend to use green subsidies as a critical tool to accelerate the transition to sustainable practices. Green subsidies can be defined as financial incentives provided by governments to support activities and technologies that are environmentally friendly and contribute to reducing carbon emissions. These subsidies play a significant role in shifting markets and consumer behaviors from fossil fuels to renewable energy sources and sustainable agriculture, thereby promoting sustainable development.

Green subsidies encompass a range of financial incentives provided by the government, including direct cash grants, tax reductions, and price supports, aimed at promoting environmentally sustainable practices. These measures reduce the economic burden of adopting green technologies and behaviors, making sustainable options more attractive and financially viable for both businesses and consumers (OECD, 2007). The conceptual roots of green subsidies date back several decades and have expanded significantly following major international environmental agreements. Initial efforts focused on supporting renewable energy technologies and conservation efforts. The establishment of the United Nations Framework Convention on Climate Change (UNFCCC) and subsequent agreements such as the Kyoto Protocol and the Paris Agreement have intensified the implementation of green subsidies as part of broader strategies to achieve emission reduction targets.

Globally, the scope and impact of green subsidies vary. For example, Germany's Energiewende, which includes strong feed-in tariffs and investment grants, has effectively accelerated the country's transition to renewable energy, significantly increasing the share of energy produced from renewable sources (Bruns et al., 2011). In the United States, federal tax credits for solar and wind projects have played a crucial role in doubling renewable energy capacity over the past decade (EIA, 2022).

The introduction of green subsidies has led to a significant reduction in the cost of renewable technologies and has encouraged their widespread adoption beyond initial projections. For example, the cost of solar photovoltaic (PV) panels has decreased substantially due to market expansion driven by subsidies (Barbose et al., 2015; Jung & Feng, 2020). Beyond energy, subsidies have catalyzed the adoption of electric vehicles, water conservation technologies, and sustainable agricultural practices, each contributing to the reduction of carbon footprints and environmental degradation.

Green subsidies are indispensable in the global shift towards sustainability. By reducing the cost barrier to green technology adoption, they play a pivotal role in accelerating the transition to a sustainable economy. As environmental imperatives become increasingly urgent, the strategic application of green subsidies will continue to shape sustainable practices across the globe.

GLOBAL PERSPECTIVES: SUCCESS STORIES AND CAUTIONARY TALES – A COMPARATIVE LOOK AT URUGUAY AND CHILE

The mounting urgency of the climate crisis and the interconnected challenges of environmental degradation have spurred a growing global interest in ecological taxation as a vital fiscal tool. Ecological taxes, by internalizing environmental costs into market prices, aim to shift economic incentives towards sustainability. Their ability to discourage environmentally harmful activities, promote innovation, and generate revenue for climate-related investments makes them an increasingly prominent feature of policy debates worldwide.

Within this global context, Latin America offers valuable insights into the implementation of ecological taxes. The region grapples with unique social and environmental challenges, providing rich case studies on the diverse forms these fiscal instruments can take. This section examines the contrasting experiences of Uruguay and Chile. Both nations have embarked on an ecological taxation journey but with distinct approaches shaped by their respective political landscapes, economic structures, and environmental priorities.

A compelling case study emerges when we juxtapose the experiences of Uruguay and Chile in their implementation of ecological taxation. While close geographically, these Latin American nations offer contrasting socioeconomic and environmental landscapes that uniquely shape their approaches to eco-fiscal policy. This comparative analysis holds the potential to reveal valuable insights into the complexities and transformative power of such policies when tailored to diverse national contexts.

A key point of divergence lies in the countries' economic structures. Uruguay boasts a sizable agricultural sector that plays a significant role in its economy. In contrast, Chile traditionally derives economic strength from mining and other resource-extraction industries (Atienza et al., 2021; Korinek, 2013). This fundamental difference necessitates distinct considerations when crafting ecological taxes. To have a meaningful impact, taxes must target the most prominent sources of environmental harm within each country's specific economy.

Furthermore, Uruguay and Chile prioritize different environmental challenges. While both nations contend with issues like pollution and the escalating climate crisis, specific areas of focus differ. Uruguay places great emphasis on sustainable agriculture practices and the conservation of its rich biodiversity. Chile, on the other hand, faces the consequences of its industrialized economy, struggling with severe air and water pollution (Pino et al., 2015). Logically, their ecological tax agendas are molded by these differing environmental pressures.

Another layer of complexity arises when examining the socio-political contexts within which ecological taxation operates. Uruguay benefits from a comparatively stable political system where environmental protection generally enjoys broad public support. Historically, Chile's political landscape has experienced more volatility, potentially generating a less predictable climate for fiscal reform (González, 2020; OECD, 2015). Understanding how ecological taxation operates within these varied social and political environments will provide essential insights for other nations considering similar policies.

Uruguay: Emerging Model With Targeted Focus

Uruguay has embarked on a notable journey of economic transformation by adopting ecological taxation as a cornerstone of its sustainability strategy. The country's targeted approach, focusing on specific sectors with well-defined environmental goals, serves as a valuable example for policymakers aiming to effectively implement financial instruments that promote environmental responsibility.

A significant example of Uruguay's targeted approach is the carbon tax on fossil fuels. Implemented with the broader goal of decarbonizing the economy, this tax acts as a deterrent to the use of polluting energy sources and encourages the transition to renewable energies. This strategic measure is complemented by incentives targeting specific sectors with significant environmental footprints, such as agriculture. These targeted financial measures promote practices like crop rotation, soil conservation, and efficient water management, contributing to sustainability and the preservation of biodiversity (ECLAC, 2015; Hall, 2023).

Uruguay's comprehensive climate strategy is evidenced by its second Nationally Determined Contribution (NDC) presented in December 2022, which includes absolute unconditional reduction targets for major greenhouse gases (GHGs) like CO_2, CH_4, and N_2O. The commitment not to exceed emissions of 9,267 $GgCO_2$, 818 $GgCH_4$, and 32 GgN_2O by 2030 demonstrates a solid pathway toward emission stabilization and carbon neutrality. Additionally, Uruguay's new commitments include a 10% reduction in HFC emissions by 2030, in line with the Kigali Amendment to the Montreal Protocol (UNDP, 2024).

Agriculture plays a crucial role in Uruguay's economy, contributing to 70% of the country's exports. It is also a significant source of GHG emissions, accounting for about 75% of total emissions, with 46% stemming from the enteric fermentation of 12 million cattle. Methane, primarily produced by livestock, constitutes 91% of these emissions. Consequently, the beef and dairy sectors have become focal points of Uruguay's climate change mitigation and adaptation efforts (Meza & Rodriguez, 2022). Uruguay's comprehensive approach includes measures to reduce methane emissions. The country is one of the 150 signatories of the Global Methane Pledge, aiming to reduce methane emissions by 30% by 2030 (Hall, 2023). These efforts reflect Uruguay's proactive stance on addressing climate change and its leadership in promoting sustainable environmental practices on the global stage.

To achieve these ambitious climate goals, Uruguay has strategically used revenue from ecological taxes to support its sustainability agenda. Emphasizing revenue generation from ecological taxes serves multiple purposes. These tax revenues have created positive effects on the economy, employment, and the environment (Morales-Olmos & Siry, 2009) First, they function as a deterrent to environmentally harmful activities (Bluffstone, 2003; Ivanov et al., 2024; Steenwegen, 2000). Second, the revenue stream, often earmarked for specific purposes, becomes a powerful tool for accelerating the transition to sustainability. Revenue from eco-taxes is allocated to investments in renewable energy infrastructure, expansion and improvement of public transport networks, and initiatives to mitigate the potential impacts of the transition on affected workers and communities (Labeaga & Labandeira, 2020; Parente, 2023; Wright & Mallia, 2003). Transparency in the use of these revenues strengthens public support for ecological taxation, highlighting its potential for both environmental and social benefits.

These targeted investments have enabled Uruguay to make significant strides in the renewable energy sector. The country has made substantial investments in biomass, solar, and wind energy, achieving a transition to 98% renewable electricity (Market, 2024). This transition has not only reduced the country's carbon footprint but also saved over half a billion dollars annually that would have been spent on fossil fuel imports (Shannon, 2022). Uruguay's roadmap for green hydrogen production, aimed at positioning the country as a leading gas exporter, is expected to generate $2.1 billion in revenue and create up to 34,000 jobs by 2040 (MIEM, 2022).

In addition, Uruguay's emphasis on sustainable practices in the agricultural sector has yielded positive results. Farmers are adopting promoted sustainable practices, improving soil health, and contributing to ecosystem restoration (FAO, 2022). This sector-specific approach acknowledges the disproportionate environmental impact of certain sectors and adopts a nuanced strategy to address these critical areas for tangible environmental improvements.

Uruguay's success in ecological taxation and the adoption of renewable energy underscores the importance of strong political will and public support. The country consistently ranks environmental protection as a high priority, reflecting its societal commitment to sustainability (Knox, 2018). The participatory process in developing the NDC, which included an open digital platform for public contributions and comments, further demonstrates Uruguay's commitment to inclusive and transparent policymaking.

Despite promising early successes, Uruguay's journey highlights ongoing challenges. Targeted financial instruments are effective in certain sectors, but broader impacts necessitate extending them to other activities contributing to environmental degradation. Continuous monitoring and evaluation are crucial to track the long-term effectiveness of policies, identify unintended consequences, and allow policymakers to make adjustments, ensuring that the ecological taxation strategy remains responsive to dynamic and evolving challenges (Waylen et al., 2019).

In conclusion, Uruguay's model of targeted ecological taxation and broader sustainability initiatives provides a compelling case study for other countries. The integration of financial measures with environmental goals, complemented by public investments in renewable energy and a participatory approach to policy development, underscores the potential of ecological taxes to deliver significant environmental and economic benefits. As Uruguay continues to develop and expand its strategies, it offers valuable lessons in balancing economic growth with environmental stewardship.

Chile: Promise Amidst Complexities

Chile, with its historically resource-driven economy and complex energy mix, faces a unique set of hurdles and opportunities in its pursuit of ecological taxation. Recognizing the urgency of addressing climate change and environmental degradation, the country has embarked on a path towards fiscal reform, demonstrating a commitment to balancing economic growth with environmental stewardship. However, implementing effective and equitable ecological taxes in a context heavily reliant on resource extraction, particularly mining, presents a considerable challenge.

Chile's carbon tax, introduced in 2017, represents a significant step towards mitigating greenhouse gas emissions. It applies to carbon dioxide emissions from stationary sources, primarily targeting power plants and industrial facilities (NDC Partnership, 2019). This policy aligns with Chile's ambitious climate goals outlined in its Nationally Determined Contribution (NDC), which includes a commitment to reducing CO_2 emissions per GDP unit by 30% below 2007 levels by 2030 and potentially an even more ambitious 45% reduction conditional on international support (Government of Chile, 2020).

Chile's carbon tax implementation involved a series of critical steps, including identifying establishments subject to taxation, quantifying emissions, declaration and consolidation of emissions data, tax calculation and payment, and finally, payment prorating by the National Electricity Coordinator (NDC Partnership, 2019). The implementation process was supported by a robust Measurement, Reporting, and Verification (MRV) system, ensuring transparency and accountability in emissions tracking.

While Chile's broader approach to ecological taxation aims to drive change across a wider range of economic sectors, the complexities associated with its reliance on mining are undeniable. This sector is a major contributor to the national economy but also a significant source of environmental degradation, particularly in terms of water pollution, air pollution, and waste generation (Martínez, 2020). Therefore, crafting a tax policy that incentivizes environmental responsibility while maintaining the competitiveness of the mining sector poses a delicate balancing act for policymakers.

Research suggests that the initial carbon tax rate of $5 per tonne of CO_2 might be insufficient to achieve significant emission reductions (Martínez, 2020). To achieve the desired environmental outcomes, some experts propose a rate of 26 USD per ton of CO_2-equivalent, highlighting the need for potential revisions to the existing policy (García-Benavente, 2016). Additionally, concerns have been raised about the potential economic impacts of taxing both producers and households, as opposed to solely targeting producers, which could potentially lead to a 2% decrease in GDP (García-Benavente, 2016). However, despite these initial challenges, Chile's proactive approach to climate change and environmental protection is commendable. The government's commitment to phasing out coal-fired plants by 2040 and promoting renewable energy sources through various initiatives, such as the promotion of solar and wind energy, signifies a determination to transition towards a greener future (Ministerio de Energia, 2021). Moreover, the revenue generated from the carbon tax, amounting to over USD 298.3 million in 2018, can be leveraged to fund these ambitious climate goals and support the development of sustainable infrastructure (NDC Partnership, 2019).

Ensuring equity and social justice in the implementation of ecological taxes remains a critical consideration for Chile. It is essential to prevent disproportionate burdens on specific sectors and vulnerable communities while fostering public acceptance and participation in the transition process. Transparent communication about the rationale behind ecological taxation and the strategic use of the generated revenue are key steps towards building trust and achieving a just and sustainable transition.

Chile's ongoing journey with ecological taxation underscores the importance of adapting policy measures to the unique challenges and opportunities presented by its specific context. The country's focus on fostering public engagement, strengthening institutional capacity, and continuously evaluating policy effectiveness provides a valuable model for other nations seeking to balance environmental protection with economic growth.

Chile's recent legal and policy developments, such as the Framework Law on Climate Change, which sets a binding target to reach net zero emissions by 2050 and requires comprehensive adaptation plans for vulnerable sectors (Government of Chile, 2022), demonstrate a strong commitment to comprehensive climate action. Additionally, the integration of nature-based solutions and circular economy principles into its updated NDC further solidifies Chile's commitment to sustainable development (Government of Chile, 2020).

While the road ahead is marked by challenges, Chile's proactive stance on climate change and environmental protection, combined with its ongoing efforts to refine and expand its ecological tax policies, presents a promising pathway towards a sustainable and resilient future. The country's experiences offer valuable lessons for other nations grappling with similar dilemmas, highlighting the importance of comprehensive and context-specific approaches to environmental taxation.

Comparative Analysis: Lessons Learned

The contrasting experiences of Uruguay and Chile illuminate a crucial lesson when implementing ecological taxes: the effectiveness of policy design hinges on its alignment with the specific economic and environmental conditions of the nation in question. Uruguay's choice of targeted taxes allows the country to zero in with precision on the key sectors contributing to its environmental challenges. Chile, on the other hand, has opted for an initially broader approach with its carbon tax, aiming to affect a wider range of economic activities with a single policy instrument. The outcomes of these contrasting strategies are likely to be distinct and provide valuable insights for other nations embarking on ecological tax reform.

The rationale behind Uruguay's sectoral focus lies in the recognition that certain economic activities have disproportionate environmental impacts. In their case, agriculture presents a major area of concern. Taxes designed to shift practices within this specific sector, incentivizing sustainable farming and biodiversity protection, offer the potential for outsized impact compared to a more diluted, one-size-fits-all tax. By pinpointing the most significant sources of environmental harm, countries can prioritize their policy interventions for maximum efficacy.

Chile's broader-scope carbon tax aims to influence a wider range of economic sectors. The potential advantage of this approach lies in its ability to stimulate change across many industries simultaneously. Its focus on large emitters reflects a goal of achieving significant reductions from the most polluting sources. Importantly, such a carbon tax also generates substantial revenue, a critical asset for financing Chile's green transition initiatives. However, this broader approach necessitates careful attention to its distributional impacts to avoid undermining specific industries central to the national economy or disproportionately burdening certain businesses or consumers.

As Uruguay and Chile continue on their journeys with ecological taxes, a comparative analysis promises to reveal the unique strengths and potential shortcomings of both targeted and broader approaches. It is crucial to remember there's no single "*perfect*" answer. The optimal design depends on various factors:

- *Environmental Priorities*: A nation facing acute pollution may need a different tax approach than one focused on biodiversity loss.
- *Economic Structure*: The mix of industries within an economy dictates where a tax will have the biggest environmental impact versus the biggest economic disruption.
- *Level of Development*: Emerging economies must balance environmental goals with the need for growth, and this can shape their tax choices.

The experiences of Uruguay and Chile underscore the importance of continuous learning and adaption in eco-fiscal policy. Ongoing monitoring to assess both the environmental and economic effects of different strategies is key for policymakers. This will allow for evidence-based adjustments to ensure ecological taxes successfully contribute to a sustainable and prosperous future.

Beyond economic and environmental profiles, a pivotal factor shapes the trajectory of ecological taxation in both Uruguay and Chile: the interplay between political will and public support. The prevailing political climate, the strength of environmental movements, and the broader public sentiment towards sustainability initiatives all play a crucial role in determining the viability, design, and ultimately, the success of eco-tax policies.

Uruguay provides an example of ecological tax implementation facilitated by a relatively stable political landscape and a populace with a well-established concern for environmental issues. Public opinion polls consistently indicate that Uruguayans value environmental protection and support policy initiatives aligned with this priority. This broad public consensus creates a conducive environment for policymakers to propose and implement green fiscal reforms with a stronger likelihood of long-term support. Strong political leadership that recognizes and responds to this public mandate further paves the way for successful eco-tax implementation.

The political landscape in Chile, on the other hand, presents a more complex picture. Historically characterized by a greater degree of volatility, the political establishment must navigate a sometimes

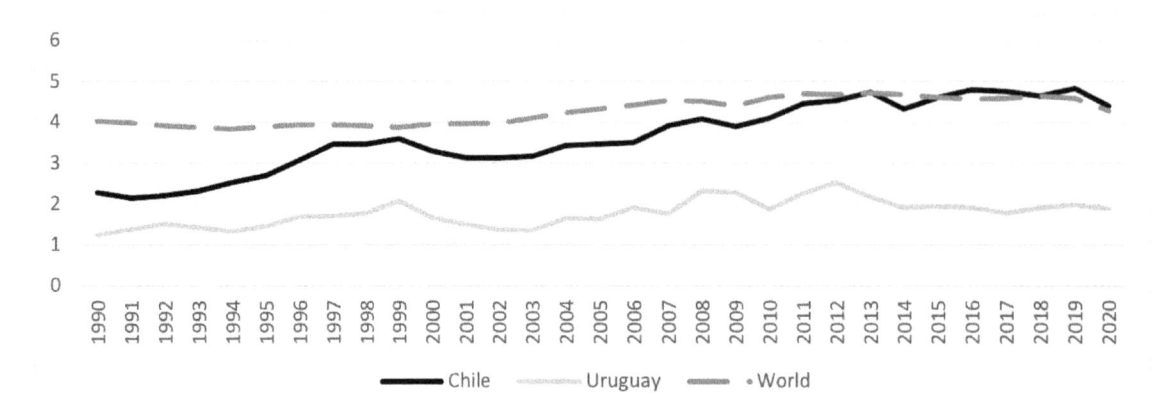

Figure 2. CO2 emission (metric tons per capita)
(World Bank, 2024)

shifting terrain when it comes to public opinion on environmental issues. While a growing awareness of climate change and the imperative of green transformation is evident, political polarization can at times pose challenges to enacting ambitious policies in this domain.

To achieve success in ecological taxation, Chilean policymakers must invest heavily in building broader public consensus. Proactive educational campaigns and transparent communication about the aims and intended benefits of eco-taxes will be crucial. Furthermore, strategically aligning green fiscal initiatives with measures that address social concerns, such as potential price increases or impacts on certain industries, will be vital for winning broader public support and demonstrating that the transition towards sustainability is also an equitable one.

The question of how revenue generated from ecological taxes is utilized is of paramount importance for both the effectiveness and public acceptance of these fiscal instruments. Uruguay and Chile offer interesting case studies on contrasting approaches to revenue allocation and the resulting implications.

Uruguay stands out with its commitment to transparency and targeted spending of its eco-tax revenue. The government explicitly designates proceeds for funding renewable energy development, enhancing public transport networks, and supporting communities and workers potentially affected by the transition to a greener economy. This alignment between the source of the revenue (environmental taxes) and its designated use sends a powerful signal and builds confidence in the government's commitment to the ecological transformation.

Furthermore, Uruguay's emphasis on investing in green infrastructure and supporting those impacted by eco-taxes underscores its focus on fostering a just and equitable transition. By proactively addressing potential hardships, Uruguay aims to mitigate the regressive effects often associated with ecological taxes and build broader acceptance.

Chile's approach to eco-tax revenue appears less concrete at this stage. While the country signals an intention to invest in green initiatives, specific allocation plans and mechanisms remain to be fully articulated. One potential challenge for Chile arises from its reliance on certain dominant industries, like mining. Securing revenue for sustainability initiatives through ecological taxation while preserving the economic competitiveness of these industries requires careful balancing. Transparent communication of revenue plans will be critical to maintain trust and public support amidst these competing interests.

Furthermore, understanding the quantitative impact of these policies on greenhouse gas emissions provides a clearer picture of the effectiveness of Uruguay's and Chile's strategies. Analyzing trends in CO2 emissions per capita over the past three decades highlights the tangible outcomes of their respective approaches. The following graph illustrates the CO2 emissions trends for Uruguay, Chile, and the world average, offering a comparative perspective on their environmental performance and the global context.

While the CO2 emissions graph offers a limited snapshot, it hints at potential early successes for Uruguay's eco-fiscal policies. The relative stability of Uruguay's emissions trajectory stands in contrast to the global trend of rising per capita CO2 emissions. This suggests that Uruguay's targeted approach, focusing on its key emission source – agriculture – might be yielding positive environmental results.

The CO2 emissions per capita for Chile have shown a relatively stable trend over the past three decades, with slight fluctuations. The initial implementation of the carbon tax in 2017, aimed at reducing emissions from power plants and industrial facilities, has yet to produce a significant downward trend. This stability indicates that the current tax rate and policy measures may not be sufficient to drive substantial reductions in emissions. The need for higher tax rates and broader application across various sectors is evident to achieve meaningful environmental outcomes.

In contrast, Uruguay's CO2 emissions per capita demonstrate a more noticeable decline, particularly in the last decade. The targeted approach to ecological taxation, coupled with significant investments in renewable energy, has contributed to this downward trend. Uruguay's focus on sectors with substantial environmental impacts, such as agriculture and energy, has proven effective in reducing emissions. The comprehensive climate strategy, including ambitious NDC targets and participation in international commitments like the Global Methane Pledge, underscores Uruguay's proactive stance in combating climate change.

The world average CO2 emissions per capita have shown a gradual increase, reflecting the global challenges in addressing climate change. The rising trend highlights the need for more aggressive and coordinated efforts worldwide to reduce emissions and transition to sustainable energy sources.

The graph clearly illustrates the contrasting trajectories of Chile and Uruguay in terms of CO2 emissions. While Uruguay's targeted and strategic policies have yielded positive results, Chile's broader approach requires further refinement and more robust measures. The comparison with the world average emphasizes the urgency for countries to adopt effective environmental policies to achieve global climate goals.

However, several caveats are important. The graph doesn't isolate the specific impact of Uruguay's eco-taxes. Other factors, such as technological advancements or changes in agricultural practices unrelated to the taxes, could also be contributing to the observed stability. Further research delving into the specific impacts of Uruguay's eco-tax policies on agricultural practices and land-use patterns would be necessary to definitively attribute success to its eco-fiscal strategy.

In Chile's case, it's too early to assess the effectiveness of its carbon tax definitively. The policy is still in its early stages of implementation. The graph doesn't reveal a clear downward trend in emissions yet, but this doesn't necessarily signal ineffectiveness. The broader scope of Chile's carbon tax, encompassing various sectors, makes it more challenging to isolate its specific environmental impact within a short timeframe. Additionally, the success of any eco-tax policy hinges not just on its design but also on how the generated revenue is used.

Here, transparency and strategic allocation of revenue become crucial. If Chile utilizes its carbon tax revenue to fund green initiatives like renewable energy development or public transport improvements, the environmental benefits may not be immediately reflected in emissions data but could manifest over time through a systemic shift towards a lower-carbon economy.

In conclusion, the graph reinforces the lessons learned from Uruguay and Chile's experiences. Uruguay serves as a model of successful ecological taxation and renewable energy adoption, demonstrating the benefits of targeted and well-implemented policies. Conversely, Chile's experience highlights the challenges of broader tax policies and the need for higher tax rates and sector-specific strategies to achieve significant emission reductions. These insights can guide other nations in developing effective and sustainable environmental policies.

CONCLUSION: CHARTING THE WAY FORWARD WITH ECO-FISCAL POLICY

In the realm of sustainable development, the notion of "*taxing tomorrow*" represents a transformative approach, aligning fiscal instruments with the environmental imperatives of our time. Eco-fiscal policies, embodying the essence of this concept, offer a strategic blueprint for harnessing the power of taxation to catalyze a shift towards a sustainable, resilient, and equitable future. As the global community stands at the crossroads of ecological uncertainty and economic opportunity, the imperative to embed sustainability into the core of fiscal policy has never been more pressing.

The journey of eco-fiscal reform is one of innovation, pragmatism, and foresight. By internalizing the environmental costs of economic activities, these policies incentivize the market to operate within the planet's ecological boundaries, fostering a transition to low-carbon, resource-efficient economies. Carbon taxes, plastic bag levies, and congestion charges are not mere revenue tools; they are mechanisms for steering societal behavior and investments towards sustainable pathways, echoing the principle of paying forward for the planet's well-being.

The experiences of nations like Uruguay and Chile underscore the diversity and adaptability of eco-fiscal policies. Uruguay's targeted eco-tax initiatives demonstrate the potential for sector-specific fiscal tools to drive substantial environmental improvements, while Chile's broader carbon tax approach reflects a commitment to systemic change across multiple sectors. These varying strategies highlight the importance of contextually crafted policies, attuned to the unique ecological, economic, and social landscapes of each country.

As the way forward is charted, it is crucial to recognize that eco-fiscal policies are not standalone solutions but integral components of a comprehensive strategy for sustainable development. They should be designed to complement regulatory frameworks, innovation incentives, and investment in green infrastructure, ensuring a holistic approach to environmental and economic challenges. The integration of these policies within the broader agenda of the Sustainable Development Goals (SDGs) offers a roadmap for harmonizing economic growth with environmental stewardship.

The future of eco-fiscal policy necessitates a commitment to continuous learning, adaptation, and global cooperation. As the impacts of these policies unfold, it is vital to monitor their environmental, economic, and social outcomes, adapting strategies to enhance their effectiveness and equity. International collaboration can amplify the benefits of eco-fiscal reforms, sharing insights, experiences, and best practices to foster a global transition towards sustainability.

"*Taxing tomorrow*" is more than a fiscal strategy; it is a call to action for harnessing the transformative power of eco-fiscal policies to secure a sustainable future. It embodies the resolve to invest in the planet's health, ensuring that economic practices contribute to the well-being of current and future generations. Advancing eco-fiscal policies is not just about reshaping tax systems; it is about redefining the very essence of progress, steering the global community towards a future where economic prosperity and environmental sustainability are inextricably linked, ensuring that the legacy left behind is one of resilience, equity, and enduring prosperity.

REFERENCES

Abate, T. G., & Elofsson, K. (2024). Environmental taxation of plastic bags and substitutes: Balancing marine pollution and climate change. *Journal of Environmental Management*, *359*, 120868. doi:10.1016/j.jenvman.2024.120868 PMID:38692024

Ali, M., & Kirikkaleli, D. (2023). Carbon taxes, resources efficiency, and environmental sustainability in a developed country. *International Journal of Sustainable Development and World Ecology*, 1–10. doi:10.1080/13504509.2023.2296492

Atienza, M., Fleming-Muñoz, D., & Aroca, P. (2021). Territorial development and mining. Insights and challenges from the Chilean case. *Resources Policy*, *70*, 101812. doi:10.1016/j.resourpol.2020.101812 PMID:34173424

Baghestani, A., Tayarani, M., Allahviranloo, M., & Gao, H. O. (2020). Evaluating the Traffic and Emissions Impacts of Congestion Pricing in New York City. *Sustainability (Basel)*, *12*(9), 3655. doi:10.3390/su12093655

Baranzini, A., Goldemberg, J., & Speck, S. (2000). A future for carbon taxes. *Ecological Economics*, *32*(3), 395–412. doi:10.1016/S0921-8009(99)00122-6

Barbose, G., Darghouth, N. R., Weaver, S., Feldman, D., Margolis, R., & Wiser, R. (2015). Tracking US photovoltaic system prices 1998-2012: A rapidly changing market. *Progress in Photovoltaics: Research and Applications*, *23*(6), 692–704. doi:10.1002/pip.2482

Beevers, S. D., & Carslaw, D. C. (2005). The impact of congestion charging on vehicle emissions in London. *Atmospheric Environment*, *39*(1), 1–5. doi:10.1016/j.atmosenv.2004.10.001

Begg, D. (2004). Pricing Solutions for Sustainable Transport. *Environmental Science, Economics, Engineering*. https://www.semanticscholar.org/paper/Pricing-solutions-for-sustainable-transport-Begg/8390497aab52231cc82949ea694b0025e31960a9

Bluffstone, R. A. (2003). Environmental Taxes in Developing and Transition Economies. SSRN *Electronic Journal*. doi:10.2139/ssrn.461539

Bruns, E., Ohlhorst, D., Wenzel, B., & Köppel, J. (2011). *Renewable Energies in Germany's Electricity Market: A Biography of the Innovation Process*. Springer Dordrecht. doi:10.1007/978-90-481-9905-1

Burgers, I. J., & Weishaar, S. E. (2018). *Designing carbon taxes is not an easy task: Legal perspectives*. EconStor. https://www.econstor.eu/handle/10419/179313

Convery, F., McDonnell, S., & Ferreira, S. (2007). The most popular tax in Europe? Lessons from the Irish plastic bags levy. *Environmental and Resource Economics*, *38*(1), 1–11. doi:10.1007/s10640-006-9059-2

Dasgupta, P. (2021). *Final Report- The Economics of Biodiversity*. UK Government. https://www.gov.uk/government/publications/final-report-the-economics-of-biodiversity-the-dasgupta-review

Dogbe, W., & Gil, J. M. (2018). Effectiveness of a carbon tax to promote a climate-friendly food consumption. *Food Policy*, *79*, 235–246. doi:10.1016/j.foodpol.2018.08.003

Đurović-Todorović, J., Đorđević, M., & Stojanović, M. (2024). The Impact of Environmental Taxes on the Reduction of Plastic Bag Consumption in the Republic of Serbia. *TEME*, *767*, 767. doi:10.22190/TEME220529048D

ECLAC. (2015). *Uruguay Can Move Ahead on Implementing Green Taxes*. ECLAC. https://www.cepal.org/en/news/uruguay-can-move-ahead-implementing-green-taxes

EIA. (2022). *Annual Energy Outlook 2021*. EIA. https://www.eia.gov/outlooks/aeo/tables_side.php

Eliasson, J. (2008). Lessons from the Stockholm congestion charging trial. *Transport Policy*, *15*(6), 395–404. doi:10.1016/j.tranpol.2008.12.004

FAO. (2022). *Agroecology a win-win for Uruguay's farmers, environment, and economy*. FAO. https://www.fao.org/support-to-investment/news/detail/ru/c/1601307/

FullertonD.LeicesterA.SmithS. (2008). *Environmental Taxes*. https://ssrn.com/abstract=1179867 doi:10.3386/w14197

Fullerton, D., & Stavins, R. (1998). How economists see the environment. *Nature*, *395*(6701), 433–434. doi:10.1038/26606

García-Benavente, J. M. (2016). Impact of a carbon tax on the Chilean economy: A computable general equilibrium analysis. *Energy Economics*, *57*, 106–127. doi:10.1016/j.eneco.2016.04.014

Ghassabian, A., Titus, A. R., Conderino, S., Azan, A., Weinberger, R., & Thorpe, L. E. (2024). Beyond traffic jam alleviation: Evaluating the health and health equity impacts of New York City's congestion pricing plan. *Journal of Epidemiology and Community Health*, *78*(5), 273–276. doi:10.1136/jech-2023-221639 PMID:38195634

González, J. (2020). Political economy of inequality in Chile: historical institutions, taxation, and elite power. In P. Anand, S. Fennell, & F. Comim (Eds.), *Handbook of BRICS and Emerging Economies* (pp. 746–785). Oxford University Press., doi:10.1093/oso/9780198827535.003.0028

González-Aliste, P., Derpich, I., & López, M. (2023). Reducing Urban Traffic Congestion via Charging Price. *Sustainability (Basel)*, *15*(3), 2086. doi:10.3390/su15032086

GoulderL. H.ParryI. W. H. (2008). *Instrument Choice in Environmental Policy*. https://ssrn.com/abstract=1117566

Government of Chile. (2020). *Chile's Nationally Determined Contribution*. UNFCCC. https://unfccc.int/sites/default/files/NDC/2022-06/Chile%27s_NDC_2020_english.pdf

Government of Chile. (2022). *A milestone in Chile's environmental history: From today, we have our first Framework Law on Climate Change*. Government of Chile. https://www.gob.cl/en/news/a-milestone-in-chiles-environmental-history-from-today-we-have-our-first-framework-law-on-climate-change/

Green, C. P., Heywood, J. S., & Navarro Paniagua, M. (2020). Did the London congestion charge reduce pollution? *Regional Science and Urban Economics*, *84*, 103573. doi:10.1016/j.regsciurbeco.2020.103573

Grigorieva, E., & Lukyanets, A. (2021). Combined Effect of Hot Weather and Outdoor Air Pollution on Respiratory Health: Literature Review. *Atmosphere (Basel)*, *12*(6), 790. doi:10.3390/atmos12060790

Gu, Z., Liu, Z., Cheng, Q., & Saberi, M. (2018). Congestion pricing practices and public acceptance: A review of evidence. *Case Studies on Transport Policy*, *6*(1), 94–101. doi:10.1016/j.cstp.2018.01.004

Haites, E. (2018). Carbon taxes and greenhouse gas emissions trading systems: What have we learned? *Climate Policy*, *18*(8), 955–966. doi:10.1080/14693062.2018.1492897

Hall, S. (2023). *Uruguay is a sustainability success story-here's why*. WeForum. https://www.weforum.org/agenda/2023/01/uruguay-sustainable-energy-renewables/

Hasegawa, T., Fujimori, S., Havlík, P., Valin, H., Bodirsky, B. L., Doelman, J. C., Fellmann, T., Kyle, P., Koopman, J. F. L., Lotze-Campen, H., Mason-D'Croz, D., Ochi, Y., Pérez Domínguez, I., Stehfest, E., Sulser, T. B., Tabeau, A., Takahashi, K., Takakura, J., van Meijl, H., & Witzke, P. (2018). Risk of increased food insecurity under stringent global climate change mitigation policy. *Nature Climate Change*, *8*(8), 699–703. doi:10.1038/s41558-018-0230-x

He, H. (2012). Effects of environmental policy on consumption: Lessons from the Chinese plastic bag regulation. *Environment and Development Economics*, *17*(4), 407–431. doi:10.1017/S1355770X1200006X

Herweg, F., & Schmidt, K. M. (2022). How to Regulate Carbon Emissions with Climate-Conscious Consumers. *Economic Journal (London)*, *132*(648), 2992–3019. doi:10.1093/ej/ueac045

Hussain, A., Javed, Z., Kishwa, F., Bangash, M. K., Raza, H. M. Z., & Farooq, M. (2020). Impact of single use polyethylene shopping bags on environmental pollution, a comprehensive review. *Pure and Applied Biology*, *9*(3). Advance online publication. doi:10.19045/bspab.2020.90209

IPCC. (2022). *Climate Change 2022: Impacts, Adaptation and Vulnerability*. IPCC. https://www.ipcc.ch/report/ar6/wg2/

Ivanov, M. O., Pinskaya, M. R., & Bogachov, S. V. (2024). Ecological tax as a tool for leveling the negative impact on the environment. *BIO Web of Conferences*, *83*, 04003. 10.1051/bioconf/20248304003

Johansson, C., Burman, L., & Forsberg, B. (2009). The effects of congestions tax on air quality and health. *Atmospheric Environment*, *43*(31), 4843–4854. doi:10.1016/j.atmosenv.2008.09.015

Jung, S. H., & Feng, T. (2020). Government subsidies for green technology development under uncertainty. *European Journal of Operational Research*, *286*(2), 726–739. doi:10.1016/j.ejor.2020.03.047

Knox, J. H. (2018). *Report of the Special Rapporteur on the Issue of Human Rights Obligations Relating to the Enjoyment of a Safe, Clean, Healthy and Sustainable Environment on his mission to Uruguay*. Digital Library. https://digitallibrary.un.org/record/1475218?ln=en&v=pdf

Korinek, J. (2013). *Mineral Resource Trade in Chile: Contribution to Development and Policy Implications*. https://doi.org/10.1787/5k4bw6twpf24-en

Labeaga, J. M., & Labandeira, X. (2020). Economics of Environmental Taxes and Green Tax Reforms. *Sustainability (Basel), 12*(1), 350. doi:10.3390/su12010350

Litman, T. (2009). Evaluating Carbon Taxes as an Energy Conservation and Emission Reduction Strategy. *Transportation Research Record: Journal of the Transportation Research Board, 2139*(1), 125–132. doi:10.3141/2139-15

Luís, I. P., & Spínola, H. (2010). The influence of a voluntary fee in the consumption of plastic bags on supermarkets from Madeira Island (Portugal). *Journal of Environmental Planning and Management, 53*(7), 883–889. doi:10.1080/09640568.2010.490054

Market, S. (2024). *The Uruguay Way: Achieving Energy Sovereignty in the Developing World*. Earth.org. https://earth.org/the-uruguay-way-achieving-energy-sovereignty-in-the-developing-world/

Martin, L. A., & Thornton, S. (2017). Can Road Charges Alleviate Congestion? SSRN *Electronic Journal*. doi:10.2139/ssrn.3055522

Martínez, S. (2020). Environmental Taxation in Chile: A Critical Analysis. *Latin American Legal Studies, 6*, 119–158. doi:10.15691/0719-9112Vol6a7

Martinho, G., Balaia, N., & Pires, A. (2017). The Portuguese plastic carrier bag tax: The effects on consumers' behavior. *Waste Management (New York, N.Y.), 61*, 3–12. doi:10.1016/j.wasman.2017.01.023 PMID:28131637

McKinley, J. (2007). San Francisco Board Votes to Ban Some Plastic Bags. *The New York Times*. https://www.nytimes.com/2007/03/28/us/28plastic.html

Meng, S., Siriwardana, M., & McNeill, J. (2013). The Environmental and Economic Impact of the Carbon Tax in Australia. *Environmental and Resource Economics, 54*(3), 313–332. doi:10.1007/s10640-012-9600-4

Mentis, C., Maroulis, G., Latinopoulos, D., & Bithas, K. (2022). The effects of environmental information provision on plastic bag use and marine environment status in the context of the environmental levy in Greece. *Environment, Development and Sustainability*. doi:10.1007/s10668-022-02465-6 PMID:35729922

Meza, L. E., & Rodriguez, A. G. (2022). *Nature-Based Solution and the Bioeconomy*. ECLAC-Natural Resources and Development Series No. 210.

MIEM. (2022). *Green Hydrogen Roadmap in Uruguay*. GUB. https://www.gub.uy/ministerio-industria-energia-mineria/sites/ministerio-industria-energia-mineria/files/documentos/noticias/Green Hydrogen Roadmap in Uruguay.pdf

Ministerio de Energia. (2021). *Planning Together the Future of Energy in Chile*. https://energia.gob.cl/sites/default/files/documentos/pelp2023-2027_informe_preliminar_ingles.pdf

Mintrom, M. (2019). *Public Policy: Investing for a Better World*. Oxford University Press.

Morales-Olmos, V., & Siry, J. P. (2009). Economic Impact Evaluation of Uruguay Forest Sector Development Policy. *Journal of Forestry, 107*(2), 63–68. doi:10.1093/jof/107.2.63

Munnich, W. L. (2010). Enhancing Livability and Sustainability by Linking Congestion Pricing with Transit. *Environmental Science, Engineering, Economics.* https://www.semanticscholar.org/paper/Enhancing-Livability-and-Sustainability-by-Linking-Munnich-Lee/5a93cf156f932fda9d93e9f1ea8899742c783838

Nielsen, T. D., Holmberg, K., & Stripple, J. (2019). Need a bag? A review of public policies on plastic carrier bags – Where, how and to what effect? *Waste Management (New York, N.Y.), 87,* 428–440. doi:10.1016/j.wasman.2019.02.025 PMID:31109543

Nordhaus, W. D. (1993). Rolling the 'DICE': An optimal transition path for controlling greenhouse gases. *Resource and Energy Economics, 15*(1), 27–50. doi:10.1016/0928-7655(93)90017-O

OECD. (2007). *Subsidy Reform and Sustainable Development: Political Economy Aspects.* OECD. https://www.oecd-ilibrary.org/environment/subsidy-reform-and-sustainable-development_9789264019379-en

OECD. (2015). *Chile: Policy Priorities for Stronger and More Equitable Growth.* OECD. https://www.oecd.org/chile/chile-policy-priorities-for-stronger-and-more-equitable-growth.pdf

Oosterhuis, F., Papyrakis, E., & Boteler, B. (2014). Economic instruments and marine litter control. *Ocean and Coastal Management, 102,* 47–54. doi:10.1016/j.ocecoaman.2014.08.005

Parente, S. A. (2023). The New Horizons of Tax Law between Energy Policies and Ecological Transition: The Case of Energy Communities. *Teka Komisji Prawniczej PAN Oddział w Lublinie, 16*(2), 267–278. doi:10.32084/tkp.8029

Partnership, N. D. C. (2019). *Chile's Carbon Tax: An Ambitious Step towards Environmentally Friendly Policies and Significant Greenhouse Gas Emission Reductions.* NDC. https://ndcpartnership.org/knowledge-portal/good-practice-database/chiles-carbon-tax-ambitious-step-towards-environmentally-friendly-policies-and

Phang, S.-Y., & Toh, R. S. (2004). Road Congestion Pricing in Singapore: 1975 to 2003. *Transportation, 43*(2), 16–25. https://www.jstor.org/stable/20713563

Pigou, A. C. (1932). *The Economics of Welfare.* Macmillan.

Piketty, T. (2014). *Capital in the Twenty-First Century.* Harvard University Press. doi:10.4159/9780674369542

Pino, P., Iglesias, V., Garreaud, R., Cortés, S., Canals, M., Folch, W., Burgos, S., Levy, K. P., Naeher, L., & Steenland, K. (2015). Chile Confronts its Environmental Health Future After 25 Years of Accelerated Growth. *Annals of Global Health, 81*(3), 354. doi:10.1016/j.aogh.2015.06.008 PMID:26615070

Qiu, R., Xu, J., Xie, H., Zeng, Z., & Lv, C. (2020). Carbon tax incentive policy towards air passenger transport carbon emissions reduction. *Transportation Research Part D, Transport and Environment, 85,* 102441. doi:10.1016/j.trd.2020.102441

Reuveny, R. (2007). Climate change-induced migration and violent conflict. *Political Geography, 26*(6), 656–673. doi:10.1016/j.polgeo.2007.05.001

Ritch, E., Brennan, C., & MacLeod, C. (2009). Plastic bag politics: Modifying consumer behaviour for sustainable development. *International Journal of Consumer Studies*, *33*(2), 168–174. doi:10.1111/j.1470-6431.2009.00749.x

Ritchie, H., Rosado, P., & Roser, M. (2023). *CO2 and Greenhouse Gas Emissions*. https://ourworldindata.org/co2-and-greenhouse-gas-emissions

Rockström, J., Steffen, W., Noone, K., Persson, Å., Chapin, F. S. III, Lambin, E. F., Lenton, T. M., Scheffer, M., Folke, C., Schellnhuber, H. J., Nykvist, B., de Wit, C. A., Hughes, T., van der Leeuw, S., Rodhe, H., Sörlin, S., Snyder, P. K., Costanza, R., Svedin, U., & Foley, J. A. (2009). A safe operating space for humanity. *Nature*, *461*(7263), 472–475. doi:10.1038/461472a PMID:19779433

Sandmo, A. (2004). Environmental Taxation and Revenue for Development. In A. B. Atkinson (Ed.), *New Sources of Development Finance* (pp. 33–57). Oxford University Press Oxford. doi:10.1093/0199278555.003.0003

Seo, Y., & Kudo, F. (2022). Charging plastic bags: Perceptions from Japan. *PLOS Sustainability and Transformation*, *1*(5), e0000011. doi:10.1371/journal.pstr.0000011

Shannon, N. G. (2022). What Does Sustainable Living Look Like? Maybe Like Uruguay. *New York Times*. https://www.nytimes.com/2022/11/20/podcasts/the-daily/uruguay-sustainable-living.html

Shawon, I. H., Haider, M. Z., & Oni, F. A. (2023). Effectiveness of banning plastic bag in Bangladesh for environmental protection. *Khulna University Studies*, 112–118. doi:10.53808/KUS.SI.2023.ICES.A40-ss

Simeonova, E., Currie, J., Nilsson, P., & Walker, R. (2021). Congestion Pricing, Air Pollution, and Children's Health. *The Journal of Human Resources*, *56*(4), 971–996. doi:10.3368/jhr.56.4.0218-9363R2

Stavins, R. N. (2003). Experience with Market-Based Environmental Policy Instruments. In K.-G. Mäler & J. R. Vincent (Eds.), *Handbook of Environmental Economics* (Vol. 1, pp. 355–435). North-Holland. doi:10.1016/S1574-0099(03)01014-3

Steenwegen, C. (2000). Can Ecological Taxes Play a Role in Diminishing the Health Impacts of Waste Management? In P. Nicolopoulou-Stamati, L. Hens, & C. V. Howard (Eds.), *Health Impacts of Waste Management Policies* (pp. 199–213). Springer. doi:10.1007/978-94-015-9550-6_13

Sumner, J., Bird, L., & Dobos, H. (2011). Carbon taxes: A review of experience and policy design considerations. *Climate Policy*, *11*(2), 922–943. doi:10.3763/cpol.2010.0093

Thomas, G. O., Sautkina, E., Poortinga, W., Wolstenholme, E., & Whitmarsh, L. (2019). The English Plastic Bag Charge Changed Behavior and Increased Support for Other Charges to Reduce Plastic Waste. *Frontiers in Psychology*, *10*, 266. doi:10.3389/fpsyg.2019.00266 PMID:30863332

Timilsina, G. R. (2009). Carbon tax under the Clean Development Mechanism: A unique approach for reducing greenhouse gas emissions in developing countries. *Climate Policy*, *9*(2), 139–154. doi:10.3763/cpol.2008.0546

Triantafyllos, D., Illera, C., Djukic, T., & Casas, J. (2019). Dynamic congestion toll pricing strategies to evaluate the potential of route-demand diversion on toll facilities. *Transportation Research Procedia*, *41*, 731–740. doi:10.1016/j.trpro.2019.09.121

UNDP. (2024). *Climate Promise: Uruguay*. UNDP. https://climatepromise.undp.org/what-we-do/where-we-work/uruguay

UNEP. (2018). *Single-use plastics: A roadmap for sustainability*. UNEP. https://www.unep.org/resources/report/single-use-plastics-roadmap-sustainability

UNEP. (2022). *State of Finance for Nature. Time to act: Doubling investment by 2025 and eliminating nature-negative finance flows*. UNEP. https://www.unep.org/resources/state-finance-nature-2022

UNFCCC. (1998). *Kyoto Protocol to the United Nations Framework Convention on Climate Change*. UNFCCC. https://unfccc.int/resource/docs/convkp/kpeng.pdf

Waylen, K. A., Blackstock, K. L., van Hulst, F. J., Damian, C., Horváth, F., Johnson, R. K., Kanka, R., Külvik, M., Macleod, C. J. A., Meissner, K., Oprina-Pavelescu, M. M., Pino, J., Primmer, E., Rîşnoveanu, G., Šatalová, B., Silander, J., Špulerová, J., Suškevičs, M., & Van Uytvanck, J. (2019). Policy-driven monitoring and evaluation: Does it support adaptive management of socio-ecological systems? *The Science of the Total Environment*, *662*, 373–384. doi:10.1016/j.scitotenv.2018.12.462 PMID:30690371

WeisbachD.MetcalfG. E. (2009). *The Design of a Carbon Tax*. https://ssrn.com/abstract=1327260 doi:10.2139/ssrn.1327260

WHO. (2022). *Ambient (outdoor) air pollution*. WHO. https://www.who.int/news-room/fact-sheets/detail/ambient-(outdoor)-air-quality-and-health

Wirna-Putri, N., Pristi-Rahmah, S., Djafri, D., Sandra-Olivia, I., & Winanda-Putri, U. (2021). The effectiveness of the non-free plastic bag policy to reduce plastic waste in the community of Padang. *E3S Web of Conferences*, *331*, 02022. doi:10.1051/e3sconf/202133102022

Wissema, W., & Dellink, R. (2007). AGE analysis of the impact of a carbon energy tax on the Irish economy. *Ecological Economics*, *61*(4), 671–683. doi:10.1016/j.ecolecon.2006.07.034

Wright, S., & Mallia, C. (2003). The Potential of Eco-Taxes as Instruments for Sustainability: An Analysis of the Critical Design Elements. *The Journal of Transdisciplinary Environmental Studies*, *2*(2), 1–14. https://journal-tes.ruc.dk/wp-content/uploads/2021/05/Stuart-og-Christina_lav-1.pdf

Ye, S. (2012). Research on Urban Road Traffic Congestion Charging Based on Sustainable Development. *Physics Procedia*, *24*, 1567–1572. doi:10.1016/j.phpro.2012.02.231

Zhao, A., Song, X., Li, J., Yuan, Q., Pei, Y., Li, R., & Hitch, M. (2023). Effects of Carbon Tax on Urban Carbon Emission Reduction: Evidence in China Environmental Governance. *International Journal of Environmental Research and Public Health*, *20*(3), 2289. doi:10.3390/ijerph20032289 PMID:36767655

ADDITIONAL READING

Alper, F. O., Golcek, A. G., & Alper, A. E. (2024). The relationship between environmental taxes and renewable energy in Europe: A pathway to sustainable development? In *Reference Module in Social Sciences*. Elsevier. doi:10.1016/B978-0-44-313776-1.00211-7

Espinosa, C., & Fornero, J. (2014). Welfare analysis of an optimal carbon tax in Chile. *Revista de Análisis Económico, 29*(2), 75–111. doi:10.4067/S0718-88702014000200004

OECD. (2021). *Taxing Energy Use for Sustainable Development*. OECD. https://www.oecd.org/tax/tax-policy/taxing-energy-use-for-sustainable-development.htm

Torrecillas, C., Fernandez, S., & Garcia-Garcia, C. (2023). Drivers to increase eco-efficiencies in Uruguay, Peru, and Panama. *Energy Policy, 183*, 113832. doi:10.1016/j.enpol.2023.113832

KEY TERMS AND DEFINITIONS

Carbon Footprint: Carbon footprint refers to the total amount of greenhouse gases (GHGs) that a person, organisation, activity or product emits both directly and indirectly into the atmosphere over its life cycle. These emissions are mainly measured in carbon dioxide equivalent (CO2e), a metric that takes into account the varying warming potential of different GHGs.

Carbon Tax: A carbon tax is a financial charge imposed on the carbon content of fossil fuels. Its primary goal is to reduce greenhouse gas emissions by making the use of carbon-intensive fuels more expensive, thus encouraging a shift towards cleaner energy sources. This tax is based on the Pigouvian principle, which aims to internalize the social cost of carbon emissions, reflecting the environmental damage in the market prices.

Eco-Fiscal Policy: Eco-fiscal policies refer to the use of fiscal tools such as taxes, subsidies, and other financial incentives to promote environmental sustainability. These policies aim to correct market failures by internalizing environmental externalities, guiding consumers and producers towards more sustainable choices. Examples include carbon taxes, plastic bag taxes, and congestion charges.

Nationally Determined Contributions (NDC): Nationally determined contributions (NDCs) are at the heart of the Paris Agreement and the achievement of its long-term goals. NDCs embody efforts by each country to reduce national emissions and adapt to the impacts of climate change. The Paris Agreement (Article 4, paragraph 2) requires each Party to prepare, communicate and maintain successive nationally determined contributions (NDCs) that it intends to achieve. Parties shall pursue domestic mitigation measures, with the aim of achieving the objectives of such contributions.

Chapter 6
Advancing Sustainable Development Goals (SDGs) Through Public–Private Partnerships (PPPs)

Siriyama Kanthi Herath
https://orcid.org/0000-0002-6443-9739
Clark Atlanta University, USA

Laksitha Maheshi Herath
New York University, USA

Marlissa Jones Phillips
https://orcid.org/0000-0002-1940-7535
Clark Atlanta University, USA

ABSTRACT

This chapter discusses public-private partnerships (PPPs) and the role they play in sustainability development. It emphasizes the PPP's role in speeding up sustainable development using good governance, active participation across all stakeholder groups, and fulfilling legal and sector-specific standards and requirements. It offers a viewpoint on PPPs as crucial collaborative tools that promote sustainable development while encouraging the preservation of good governance, active stakeholder engagement, and adherence to ethical standards to guarantee their success. The contributions of PPPs to SDGs fulfillment are analyzed by secondary literature review and real case examples.

INTRODUCTION

For years, Public-Private Partnerships (PPPs) have been shown to be the main tool used for overcoming the development obstacles in providing vital infrastructure and services due to the strengths that public

DOI: 10.4018/979-8-3693-2758-6.ch006

and private sectors offer (UN, 2016). This chapter insists on devising anti-poverty strategies primarily through partnerships for sustainable development, meaning PPPs that are often effective and cover any theme or area they may apply to. The 2030 Agenda for Sustainable Development adopted by all UN member states gave access to PPPs. Because of the holistic nature of the Sustainable Development Goals (SDGs), it required many partners to engage in the fight against poverty and other socioeconomic challenges. The role of PPPs has proven to be very high in achieving SDGs.

In 2015, the UN laid the foundation for robust relationships between governments or public and private sectors and reached for voluntarism and cooperation in the achievement of collaborative and joint efforts that will be oriented toward sustainable development. Those international trends and innovations in PPPs are continually changing and adopting them employing SDGs support according to a UN Office for Partnerships 2021 report (UN Office for Partnerships, 2021).

In addition, studying the best-practice models of PPPs offers invaluable insights into current trends and effective strategies that they employ to move up the SDGs faster, offering relevant guidance for maximizing the role of PPPs to promote the SDGs agenda. For example, the Asian Development Bank illustrates that knowledge transfers from successful projects have influential role in terms of learning from case studies and benchmarking, pushing for the implementation of similar approaches in the future (ADB, 2020). These insights are clear demonstrations of the robustness of institutional structures, the clarity in the regulatory framework and the dedication of politicians in the execution of PPP projects (UN DESA, 2023).

The Sustainable Development Goals pose a significant turning point in the world's collective actions towards the realization of a fairer, productive, and, of course, sustainable world (Steiner, 2018; Vargas et al., 2021). What needs to be highlighted is that when it comes to resolving global issues like poverty, inequalities, and climate change, PPPs would be a strategic tool of gathering resources, expertise, and technology, to successfully attain development goals.

In this chapter, the contributions of PPPs to SDGs fulfillment are analyzed by secondary literature study and real case examples. The PPPs mean complexity and hazards, which moreover intensify the need ever more of transparency, accountability, and equity for the whole processes of the PPPs to become cooperative despite being very promising (IMF, 2020).

This study is conducted using a holistic approach to advance PPPs in which sustainability input is increased. The main objective of the study is to evaluate the effect of PPPs on different sectors and the context, learn the important factors for the successes and failures of these partnerships, and offer a workable solution to the stakeholders, practitioners and policymakers. In doing so, we shall build a platform of dialog, knowledge-sharing and a collective learning process which will tremendously accelerate the pace at which the world will achieve significant equality, sustainability, and prosperity. Some objectives of this research include the following.

a. *Comprehensive exploration of the impact of PPPs on advancing SDGs:* This study chapter covers the details pertaining to PPPs from numerous sectors. This exploratory study focuses on the practical cases from where the real outcomes and lessons are learned, both from the cases of success and unsuccess.
b. *Identification of key success factors and challenges faced by PPPs*: Research endeavors in depth conducting case studies and literature review, to access and bring to light the elements and factors that lead to the success and failures of such programs.

c. *Recommendations that can enhance PPP efficiency in supporting Sustainable Development Goals (SDGs):* The derived recommendations stated in detail this chapter after a thorough investigation. PPPs are enhanced as a result. The chapter outlines the measures that should be taken to create sustainable development objectives. Decision actors, in this example of policy makers, developers, and others associated should refer to these recommendations as a given in this manner of perception when it comes to overcoming the challenges of PPP implementation and the squeezing out of the best possible outcomes from PPPs in the SDGs framework.

METHODOLOGY

This literature analysis primarily relies on an extensive review and amalgamation of relevant findings from secondary literature to explore the dynamics of public-private partnerships (PPPs) and their contribution to sustainable development. The qualitative analysis methodology involves identifying recurrent themes and significant elements contributing to successful PPPs. By delving into recorded experiences, the study aims to uncover the nuanced dynamics associated with both success factors and obstacles hindering PPPs in supporting sustainable development. Table 1 outlines the methodology of this literature review that explores the relationship between Public-Private Partnerships (PPPs) and achieving Sustainable Development Goals (SDGs).

Although original data was not collected for this chapter, its methodology includes a circumstantial amount of information available in scholarly works and official documents. This literature-driven approach covers various aspects of PPP dynamics, recovery factors, and challenges as documented by previous researchers. This literature-driven approach covers various aspects of PPP dynamics, recovery factors, and challenges as documented by previous researchers. Also, it applies the principles of Sustainable Development Goals (SDGs) to inform policy and practice in PPP initiatives.

Because this chapter relies on secondary literature, case study analysis is the core of this research. Through a comprehensive review of academic articles, reports, and documented materials, the study will select PPP initiatives prevalent in different geographic areas and sectors. The literature-based approach used here also helps a brief discussion on the historical development and challenges faced by PPPs in relation to selected SDGs.

LITERATURE REVIEW

Public-Private Partnerships (PPPs) serve as crucial policy instruments globally, easing cooperation between government agencies and private firms (World Bank, 2023). The 2023 World Bank report accentuates PPPs' role in delivering sustainable infrastructure by focusing on the idea of risk sharing and efficient project administration, allowing governments to access private sector capital and expertise for public infrastructure development (World Bank, 2023).

While public-private partnerships (PPP) are increasingly recognized as a method for addressing infrastructure projects with limited funding, lack of prior experience, and the necessity of sharing the burden of implementation between the state and the private sector (Zhai and al., 2021). Simultaneously, the popularity of collaboration between the private and public sectors has been growing worldwide in the time related to the last decade, with more countries introducing this pattern (Wang & Ma, 2021;

Table 1. Literature review methodology for PPPs & SDGs

Step	Description	Purpose
1. Literature Review	Conduct an extensive review of secondary sources on Public-Private Partnerships (PPPs) & Sustainable Development Goals (SDGs) Sources include academic articles, reports, & documented materials related to PPPs	Gain a comprehensive understanding of PPPs, SDGs, & the relationship between them
2. Qualitative Analysis	Analyze the literature to identify: • Recurrent themes: Common threads or patterns related to successful PPPs • Contributing elements: Factors that contribute to successful PPPs in achieving SDGs • Success factors: Practices & approaches associated with successful PPPs for SDGs • Obstacles: Challenges hindering PPPs from supporting sustainable development • Historical development: Historical context & past issues faced by PPPs related to SDGs	Identify key themes, factors, & challenges related to PPPs & SDGs
3. Case Study Selection	Based on the literature review, select a set of PPP initiatives: • Criteria: Widespread adoption across different geographic areas & sectors • Purpose: Analyze case studies to understand how PPPs address specific SDGs	Choose diverse case studies that showcase real-world applications of PPPs for SDGs
4. Policy & Practice Implications	Analyze the findings from the literature review & case studies to: • Inform policy development related to PPPs & SDGs • Identify best practices for practitioners involved in PPP projects	Translate research findings into real-world applications for policy & practice

Zhai et al., 2021; Strasser et al., 2021). Concerning The World Bank report, 135 countries and territories – public-private partnerships (PPPs) – have put together contracts according to b2b type for public infrastructure construction on a fee basis, i.e. involving hospitals, and roads (2018).

The central concern of this literature review is on the intersection of PPPs and SDGs, demonstrating the parts played by PPPs as we aim to achieve SDGs' goals. The 'Lit Review' in this chapter looks at the concept of PPPs and how it is interwoven to the SDGs hoping that its complexity would be explained in terms of the effect it has on achieving one SDGs to another.

Partnering with the private investor to offer a public infrastructure service is crucial as this contributes to achieving the unity sustainable development goals (SDGs). It is important to share the risk and optimally utilize the available human resources to improve the service to the target community. The partnership now has 5 components of the UN Global Goals namely - Powers, Planet, Peace, and Prosperity (Farazmand, 2018). This is in a way that PPPs are one of the stakeholders which provide the resources and carried out projects to give positive results to decrease pollution and help gain these goals (Farazmand, 2018; Akomea-Frimpong et al., 2023).

Blockchain technology introduces a new engineering scheme that helps find difficulties in the way of the Public-Private Partnerships (PPP) and, after finding them, proposes changes holding to sustainable development. The application of blockchain introduces to the ledger system that is not controlled by any central authority and where records cannot be changed, offering an alternative to escrow – a trusted third party in online transactions, that reduced transaction risks and fostered stakeholders' trust (Tafuro et al., 2023).

Moreover, not only does the blockchain technology make it possible to record transaction that are more conveniently readable and transparent, but the traditional budget documentation cannot be underestimated as it considers both financial accountability and oversight. Through the usage of a clear sequential framework, we shall be able to delve into the basic roles of comprehensive budgeting practices when it comes to the complete success of interactions between the private and public sectors.

The actual auditing documentation should be included in PPP contracts, irrespective of whether, from an accounting point of view, it can be done immediately, but until a budget period set in the document has been exhausted. The roles of private sector partnerships (PPP) may be regarded as insufficiently treated in governance, and a lack of financial and technical capability can produce unwanted side effects in the administration of PPP projects (Joseph et al., 2022).

Additionally, as PPPs started to play a primary role in MNE-state relations in the late 1990s, MNEs can utilize PPPs as a conduit for solidifying a new role for business in the community. In Ghana, PPP projects date as early as 1965 with the building of the Akosombo Dam (Joseph et al., 2022).

The available data testifies therefore that PPPs as a model can be utilized to fashion solutions to the most complex SDGs as well as 1, 2, and 4 (Eden and Wagstaff, 2020). The purpose of the three SDGs which are focused on the destruction of poverty, zero hunger, and quality education is to be both formidable and global in nature and that implies that the responsibility of eradicating the three will have to be carried by the governments, private sectors and civil society. The PPs provide one of the only forums wherein the structure of resources, knowledge, and innovative solutions made to resolve the major challenges by the local government are organized on a global level.

Moreover, PPPs can be also a tool for containing the social and environmental components of sustainable development, creating an environment in which social objectives like poverty, hunger, and inequality education would be tackled with (Malik and Kaur, 2020). Nonetheless, the outturn of a PPP project may differ for various nations, which will involve both victories and failures. Such fluctuation accentuates the requirement of steady management, monitoring, and review to ensure that PPP Projects progressively facilitate sustainable company objectives with minimal adverse effects.

Dickson and Thaler (2020) argued that the adoption of R&R models where both the government and the private sector would be entrusted with implementing PPPs was necessary to promote sustainability. By including external regulatory rules and elements at the internal organizational levels, PPPs can become an integrated part of the system of sustainability goals. This, in turn, may bring a responsible business mindset and environmental stewardship to corporate activities.

In the context of this literature review, the intention is to provide in-depth literature on the role of PPPs in the sustainable development process which will discuss their challenges, opportunities, and ways to achieve further achievements. The study also aims to identify PPPs as a tool for achieving the 17 sustainable development goals and provide lessons learned and areas requiring further study and research during sustainable development.

This exposition covers the PPP importance in tackling the infrastructure problems, as well as identifying technological innovations and fully supporting sustainable development goals. It highlights the idea that PPP is not about governments alone but encompasses the efficiency, collaboration and alignment so as to harness the potentials PPPs create in helping to achieve global sustainability objectives Thanks to the continuous communication, new ideas, and partnerships, PPPs have great potential to be major tools with the ability to drive positive change and, ultimately, the future for everyone will become more environmentally friendly.

EVOLUTION PUBLIC-PRIVATE PARTNERSHIP: TRACING HISTORICAL ROOTS AND MODERN ADAPTATIONS

For years, Public-Private Partnerships (PPPs) have shown to be the main tool used for overcoming the development obstacles in providing vital infrastructure and services due to the strengths that each faction (public and private) offer (UN, 2016). Above all, this section of the article insists on devising anti-poverty strategies primarily through partnerships for sustainable development, meaning PPPs that are often effective and cover any theme or area they may apply to.

Historically, PPPs have been around the corner ever since the times of the ancient civilizations wherein private contractors undertook massive infrastructure projects like roads, bridges, and canals. Though the modern notion of PPPs is evidenced in the 1970s when policymakers started contemplating private-sector involvement as this was considered a solution to budgetary immobility and to deliver speedy delivery of desired services. Between the 1980s and the 1990s, a resurgence of privatization and de-regulation policies occurred which placed the private sector as the main player in the delivery of previously publicly run services and infrastructures.

In the long run, forms of the PPP were modified in response to the factors like changes in the policy of governments, financial shocks and new requirements which arise among people. Firstly, transport and utilities sectors become the main target area of PPPs, but now PPPs have also spread to the education, health, environment sphere Scientific and technical developments and financial possibilities have formed the basis of the union of complex and high-powered contracts, while also such forms of cooperation as performance-based contracting and a joint venture have been widely spread.

In summary, PPPs' evolution echoes a growing adaptability of human systems to social-economic changes. Its roots can be traced back to early cultures, with modern adaptations fueled by continuously changing technology and governance models. By unceasingly making amendments and innovations, PPPs have immensely become the necessary mechanisms for accomplishing public services delivery challenges and driving development projects that show sustainability nationwide in different areas.

Intersecting Paths: PPPs and the Sustainable Development Goals

The plan of action, established by the United Nations in 2015 as one of the components of the 2030 Agenda for Sustainable Development, was the Sustainable Development Goals (SDGs), comprising 17 interlinked goals to address worldwide issues such as poverty, inequalities, climate change, and environmental issues. The goals of these strategies offer a structured structure based on the SMART criteria to solve current emerging issues and share the responsibility of inclusive development and sustainability until 2030.

Inalienable from the SDGs is an inclusive approach that demonstrates how social, economic, and environmental components of sustainable development are correlated. The aims establish a goal, which is to give everyone the chance of food, education and healthcare to live in a peaceful place, where many people can prosper and be happy. Targets play the role of directing force in governments, businesses, civil society organizations, individuals, and the general society to points where the next stage consists of a future based on equality, fairness, and well-being.

The meeting place for Public-Private Partnerships (PPPs) and the SDGs will be decisive because PPPs use different skills, expertise and resources unleashed to reach the SDG goals. Involving the PPP in all steps of the SDGs can address those needed goals to provide essential services, infrastructure development, and serve sustainability challenges (Wachira et al., 2022). PPPs make it possible for the government, industries, and the public to work together in developing sustainable economies in which they all can enjoy social inclusion and care for the environment which is promoted through the expertise of the private sector resources and financing.

An assessment of the factors on how PPPs link with the SDGs would involve the scrutiny of the congruence of PPP projects with distinct SDG targets besides mainstreaming the overarching SDG goals. Through the collaboration of partners that consist of local organizations and international agencies using both innovations and novel techniques, the scope of the problem is improved and the movement towards SDGs (Sustainable Development Goals) is achieved.

In this way, the synergy of PPPs with the SDGs can be seen as an interactional strategy for solving the world's problems and ensuring priorities for sustainable economic development. PPPs give a strategic approach to accessing affordable and quality education, sanitation, health care, and renewable energy. With innovative solutions implemented in their partnerships, PPPs are playing a central role in the attainment of the SDGs, as no one is left behind in the journey to a fair, robust, and green future.

INTEGRATION OF RELEVANT THEORETICAL FRAMEWORKS

The use of suitable theoretical frameworks or models is essential to explore the details of PPP and the multifaceted roles played by these models in supporting the principles of sustainable development in the broader scheme of affairs. They also provide the reader with some fundamental knowledge of the different PPP aspects, their mechanisms, structure and the issues they are facing in the institutional setting, decision-making, and systems. Table 2 summarizes theoretical frameworks such as Institutional Theory, Governance Theory, and Systems Thinking that can be used to analyze Public-Private Partnerships (PPPs) and their role in achieving Sustainable Development Goals (SDGs).

One theoretical framework named Institutional Theory explains the importance of formal and informal institutions in defining the strategic management and performance of firms. In this context, PPP Institutional Theory becomes another useful tool to distinguish the institutions that would consist, including laws, norms, and culture. The chapter would be better if it were dedicated to the analysis of the formation and consequences of these organizations, and in addition to studying how PPPs affect institution formation, governance, and performance, the chapter should its impact on community development and policy outcomes.

Another theory is the Governance Theory, which focuses on how different institutions can make decisions and are accountable while also considering their distribution and power. The theory offers the participants a multi-level perspective regarding this segmentation, the responsibility and control of which is shared by the public and private sectors as well as with the transparency expectations that each stakeholder is accountable. The implementation tutoring of the PPP tool is important, and as chapter decides the best way to do it, addresses the governance challenges, and explains the SDGs recommendations that will lead to the success of SDGs.

Additionally, a system thinking approach recommends a timely illustration of the complex and interconnected nature of sustainable development. This paradigm stresses the concept of the mutual causal connection, complexity and unpredictability as critical features of socio-ecological relationships and offers insights into the fundamental contributors of sustainability obstacles. The chapter can provide systems thinking approach for events in understanding PPP projects both from the macro level and the

Table 2. Theoretical frameworks for analyzing PPPs & sustainable development

Theoretical Framework	Description	Benefits for Research
Institutional Theory	Examines how formal, informal, & cultural factors (norms, regulations) influence the formation, performance, & governance of PPPs.	• Understands the institutional context of PPPs • Analyzes the evolution & impact of rules, norms, & practices on public-private partnerships • Explores how PPPs shape institutions & vice versa
Governance Theory	Focuses on decision-making, accountability, & power distribution within PPPs, including the roles & responsibilities of public & private sectors, & stakeholder engagement.	• Evaluates the effectiveness of governance tools used in PPPs for achieving SDGs • Identifies governance challenges & best practices • Provides recommendations for improving governance systems in PPPs
Systems Thinking	Recognizes the interconnectedness & interdependence of challenges & solutions in sustainable development. It highlights feedback loops & unforeseen consequences.	• Identifies systemic drivers of sustainability issues in PPPs • Analyzes the potential cumulative effects of economic, social, & environmental objectives • Develops solutions that address systemic problems. • Analyzes both macro & micro-level impacts of PPP projects • Identifies leverage points for interventions to reduce risks

micro level of concerns. Along with that, it can point out the leverage points and offer interventions at the system level to reduce risks and improve development outcomes.

Merging these theoretical schemas into the assessment structure of PPPs logically enhances the apprehension of their meaning in the concept of sustainable growth. These frameworks will be the ones guiding empirical materials interpretation and extraction of hidden matters and mechanisms causing projects to perform better. In other words, they will uncover what drives PPP. Among the others, theory building in the PPP area becomes possible when new outcomes and perspectives emerge, thereby providing better quality in this field than ever before.

EMPIRICAL STUDIES AND CASE EXAMPLES

To bolster the persuasiveness of the arguments presented and to lay a more solid foundation for policymaking, a highly effective approach is to incorporate additional case studies and instances of successful Public-Private Partnership (PPP) initiatives aligned with Sustainable Development Goals (SDGs). For this purpose, the analysis of the case studies offers an opportunity to understand the stages as well as the outcomes of the PPP projects, hence helping the achievement of the prescribed targets relating to sustainable development. Using the following case studies is a way to explore this issue in detail. Table 3 summarizes case studies highlighting Public-Private Partnerships (PPPs) successfully contributing to specific Sustainable Development Goals (SDGs) around the globe.

Case Study: Green Energy Infrastructure Development (SDG7 Investment)—Germany

Germany's ambitious Energiewende (energy transition) plan, in which renewable sources of energy from coal and nonrenewable sources like wind and solar power are used (UN, 2021). In the center of the plan stands what is officially known as the Public-Private Partnership (PPP), which includes governmental bodies, private energy companies, and local communities in building up new infrastructure, including wind farms and solar parks. These joint ventures have generated groundbreaking discoveries in environment-friendly energy innovation, reduction of carbon emissions, and development of energy independence within the scope of SDG 7 (Affordable and Clean Energy).

Case Study: Healthcare Service Delivery (a sub-target of SDG 3) —India

India is engaged with partnerships by the Private Sector to accomplish the dream of efficient healthcare in the districts previously kept away from this sector (UN India, 2023). A case study is how health Intercontinental Narayana Health System and government health agencies have co-created hospitals and clinics with the provision of affordable care to the common folk in the rural sector. These partnerships combine the prowess that the private sector has in filling medical gaps like surgical procedures, diagnostic services and primary care against the underserved population. Such endeavors have this effect greatly for the Sustainable Development Goal (SDG) 3 (Good Health and Well-being).

Case Study: Spatial Public Transport Infrastructure (SDG11) —Colombia

The implementation of a Bus Rapid Transit (BRT) system in Bogotá, Colombia serves as a notable example of a successful Public-Private Partnership (PPP) in public transport infrastructure (UN-Habitat, 2021). A policy, in which inter-agency collaboration of government, private transport operators, and development banks is involved. Utilizing the TransMilenio network, a host of mobile transport gains have been encountered, congestion notches, and a whole lot of local and national service contributions, serving millions of people around. The further development of local public transport enables us to ensure the goals of SDG 11 (Sustainable Cities and Communities).

Case Study: Water and Sewage Services SDGs (6) —Senegal

The Water and Sanitation Department of Dakar, Senegal demonstrates the PPP initiative (Public-Private Partnership), driven by the goal of widening access to clean drinking water coupled with sanitation services, particularly in urban sites (UN Water, 2022). This participative initiative is AMONG the Coastlines government, international development non-governmental organizations, and private sector water firms. The project much pos positive results by using infrastructure improvements, capacity-building efforts community involvement to achieve its goal - SDG 6 (Water and Sanitation).

Case Study: Education Facility Building (SDG 4) —Kenya

In Kenya, PPPs (Public-Private Partnerships) become crucial instruments that are deployed to solve the issues of over-populated classrooms and inadequate learning facilities to accommodate the rising

Table 3. Empirical studies and case examples: PPPs supporting SDGs

SDG	Case Study	Description	Contribution to SDG
SDG 7: Affordable & Clean Energy	Green Energy Infrastructure Development **(Germany)**	Germany's Energiewende plan uses PPPs to involve private companies & communities in developing renewable energy infrastructure (wind farms, solar parks)	Increased clean energy projects, reduced carbon emissions, & supported energy independence
Sub-target of SDG 3: Good Health & Well-being	Healthcare Service Delivery **(India)**	India partners with private healthcare providers to improve access in underserved areas	Increased access to affordable healthcare services (surgeries, diagnostics, primary care) for the poor in rural areas
SDG 11: Sustainable Cities & Communities	Spatial Public Transport Infrastructure **(Colombia)**	Bogotá's Bus Rapid Transit (BRT) system, a PPP involving government, private operators, & development banks, improves mobility, reduces congestion, & expands access for millions	TransMillenial system improves mobility, reduces congestion, & expands access to public transport
SDG 6: Clean Water & Sanitation	Water & Sewage Services (Senegal)	Dakar Water & Sanitation Project uses a PPP with the government, NGOs, & private water companies to improve access to clean water & sanitation	Increased access to clean drinking water & sanitation services in cities
SDG 4: Quality Education	Education Facility Building **(Kenya)**	Bridge International Academies partners with local governments to build low-cost, high-quality schools for disadvantaged communities	Increased access to quality education through technology, innovative teaching methods, & community involvement

number of students (Kenya UN, 2024). For instance, in the dialogue between Bridge International Academies and local authorities, there were cases of innovative solutions to the construction of low-cost, high-quality schools for underprivileged communities. It could provide an example for other partners involved (Ministry of Education, 2017). These collaborations help technology and innovative teaching styles, the community, and society to be utilized to the maximum bringing better results to the achievement of Goal 4 (Quality Education).

Besides, this study represents a congregation of handy information for policymakers, operators and researchers eager to learn about the practical work of PPPs and their outcomes connected to the attainment of the Sustainable Development Goals. Through contrastive and instructive case studies, stakeholders make a cognitive transition toward that goal and learn the necessary steps for the PPP scheme establishment. Besides this, these insights are not only levering the arguments for PPPs but also, give practical lessons to promote appropriate partnerships to address obstacles to development.

ADDRESSING INFRASTRUCTURE GAPS: THE ROLE OF PPPs

Public-Private Partnerships (PPPs) have emerged as very effective tools for meeting the demands of long-term financing in the construction of infrastructure and development for both countries and at the same time, with increasing public demands and limited government resources. PPPs are a noteworthy pathway for infrastructure investment, with the annual infrastructure investment being contributed by developed countries' governments ten percent and three percent of the global infrastructure investment (Fay et al., 2018; Narbaev, 2022; Uddin & Zaman, 2022; Herath & Herath, 2023). PPPs are considered the key element in this process of economic development of transitioning countries by providing funds, know-how, and managing risks.

A PPP is not only a catalyst for officials' expenditure but also for economic expansion by producing jobs and innovation. These platforms act as meeting grounds to assist the partnership between the public and private sectors. In doing so, development challenges can be handled through various ways. The PPPs have traditionally been viewed as a tool for countries with developed economies, while in the last years they have proven also convenient for the developing and underdeveloped countries – where these merge resources, professional and innovation skills to meet common objectives of development.

Undoubtedly, the unpredictability related to infrastructure investment, the economic factors, political considerations, and social issues, in addition to the intricacies of the global financial markets have resulted in a slowdown in the investment of funds (Gardner, Henry 2023, and Ramey,2021). Investors are involved in a search for additional sources of guaranteed returns and risk management measures considering existing ones and other hindrances related to the investment in the transport infrastructure, particularly in developing countries / Developing countries face various barriers to investment in infrastructure, transport being the most important and pivotal one of those. Investors, traditionally acting in a profit-maximizing role, are always present in the search for cost-effective.

In summary, PPPs give the infrastructure and development sector a solution to mobilize the resources, experience and the ability to innovate from the public and private sectors. Not yet PPPs could be referred to as a useful instrument to bring about economic growth, and even sustainable development, though they do also encounter some difficulties like investment uncertainties and fiscal restraints.

THE USE OF PPPs IN IMPLEMENTATION OF THE SUSTAINABLE DEVELOPMENT GOALS

PPPs are a key instrument for giving an impulse to SDG implementation by motivating innovation, using private investors, and making knowledge transfer more efficient. Haque et al. (2020) have stressed the role of PPPs in sustainable development through the establishment of various facets such as prudent infrastructure development, health systems, the education sector, and environmentally conscientious sustainability. Success stories drawn from different sectors present the way PPPs contribute to the set SDG targets by highlighting their potential to create conditions for inclusive and sustainable growth.

In many situations, there already exists a wealth of data and reports from which SDG projects using PPP systems have successfully delivered results. Such systems, for example, the George Dukmejian courthouse building in Long Beach, California, and the infrastructural developments like the I-595 reversible managed lanes in Broward County, Florida, have an unambiguous proof of the fact that PPPs help in the sustainability of the development (Anderson & Ratiu, 2017). Nevertheless, successfully finished PPP projects is a function of factors like the partners' selection process, performance indicators, and the implementation mechanisms for procurement (Anderson & Ratiu, 2018; Dolla & Laishram, 2018).

Eden and Wagstaff (2020) have made it known why public-private partnerships (PPPs) play a vital role in realizing women's empowerment and gender equality, especially as regards Sustainable Development Goal 5. In addition to that, Joseph et al. (2022) also lists the pros of PPP projects in SDG6 (clean water and sanitation), showing a case of a PPP project from Ghana. Paradoxically, the PPPs' pluses also have an opposite angle with the cases faced, as they include budgetary constraints, regulatory changes, and capital costs (Ahmad et al., 2018).

Eden and Wagstaff (2020) highlight the use of PPPs in improving gender equality and women empowerment and consequently in the attainment of SDG 5. Apart from Joseph et.al.'s (2022) discussions on how PPP projects could attain SDG6 (clean water and sanitation) with an example from Ghana. However, public-private partnerships have barriers including budgetary strictures, policy changes, and capital charges (Ahmad et al., 2018).

Institutional structures and decision-making processes which are key to the success or failure of PPP are greatly affected by the project's planners (Elena et al., 2020). Dolla and Laishram (2018) propose a PPP lifecycle framework, which includes phases of procurement, construction, commissioning, and operation, to guide the implementation of PPP projects efficiently. One of the core propositions of the United Nations Smart Cities agenda is the deployment of novel technologies and smart innovation into PPP projects (Haque et al., 2020). Also, there are different PPP models closely held by the distinct features and connections between them. This opulently reveals the diversity of private sector involvement in sustainable development (Farazmand, 2018; Haque et al., 2020).

In general, PPPs are a tool providing a basis for achieving SDGs through realizing the potential of resources and bringing innovation and teamwork between the public and private sectors. Thus, the key issue is overcoming obstructing factors such as regulatory barriers, economic viability, and the establishment of regulatory mechanisms that can force the promotion of sustainable development goals.

CRITICAL ANALYSIS OF CHALLENGES AND LIMITATIONS

Public-Private Partnership Programs (PPPs) have recently been positively highlighted as key instruments in innovation and resolution of infrastructure development, social services delivery, and economic growth problems across the globe. Though PPPs are a source of unique positive initiatives, gamut of uncertainties and conditions are associated with them too. The PPPs hold tremendous promise and to achieve full potential in harnessing their advantages a thorough investigation of the challenges they face in different contexts is necessary.

One of the complexities in developing PPPs stems from the fact that both tasks in question are not as simple as they sound. PPP projects are most likely to be multi-faceted with a wide range of interests that complicate matters while aligning the interests of all stakeholders and making setting priorities impossible. It is worth noting that this complexity can stem from the engagement of numerous governmental entities, private companies, local communities, and many other actors with their aims and priorities (UN Office for Partnerships, 2021). Yet putting the regulation framework in place and working the legal laws contribute to the project only facing postponements or extra expenditures.

Moreover, the distribution of risks and obligations between the government and private partners is formed for a diverse variety of challenges. PPP contracts generally argue upon risk transfer mechanisms where the competence tanks are assigned by each party regarding project achievements, provision of financial resources and management of operations. Nonetheless, such assessments of risk as well as their management may be complex, particularly in situations where the projects' performance is hard to anticipate, and external circumstances change frequently (OECD, 2022). For example, in space missions, risks such as noise, lasers, and space radiation must be carefully evaluated, highlighting the intricate nature of risk management in PPPs.

Sustainability in terms of finance and viability are the other major challenges for PPPs, more so in low-income economies with great challenges reserving the capital markets. Government and private sectors may find themselves in a situation where they have insufficient resources to implement the projects for multiple reasons. As a result, there is a need for collaboration through PPPs. Nevertheless, it poses the challenge of financing procurement for long-term projects, which implies among others the ability to forecast well the revenue sources and the cost-recovery measures (World Bank, 2023). Funding for the PPPs is one of the major r elements that needs to be a framework to ensure equity and the financial sustainability of the services provided.

Lastly, it is the social and political issues that can severely affect the execution of such PPP schemes in the developing countries. Housing shortages, unsuitable infrastructure, and limited access to basic services have been the problematic solutions in most areas (Kavishe & Chileshe, 2019). Illustratively, Tanzania experiences rapid population growth and urbanization which worsens the housing shortage problem. Consequently, the government has opted for Public-Private Sector Partnerships (PPP)as an approach to associate affordable housing solutions. Likewise, in Nigeria and Albania development of infrastructure through project are also faced with numerous problems including unsustainable planning design, political interference, or regulation constraints mechanisms. (Babatunde et al., 2018; Berisha et al., 2022).

Unlike public financing where there is a possibility of a longer and more dynamic perspective, the PPPs offer innovative solutions to pressing society's hindrances but also involve numerous complexities and uncertainties. Addressing these barriers, whether financing or outsourcing, must be considered so that PPP projects may have a definite and lasting impact. Policy makers, practitioners, and stakeholders can gain more insight into the in-depth granularity of the structure of projects, identification, and management of risks, and stakeholders' engagement which will help them to develop successful frameworks for realizing the untapped possibilities through the PPP approach in different contexts. The PPP initiative is fraught with many challenges from project structuring to governance models and balance of risks among the government and private sector partners. The unique hurdles are a great deal, and it goes from the difficulty of coordination to the implementation of regulations as well as the duration of financial viability.

The design of the public-private partnership model that considers structural organization and governance as the key criteria is the most considerable challenge with this model. Involving parties in PPP schemes is commonly more complicated than working with single partners due to multiple stakeholders with different orientations and goals. The uncertainty in views among the various relevant people like the governments, private companies, and local people with divergent goals and motives, are the key causes of coordination troubles (UN Office for Partnerships, 2021). Working with all the stakeholders concerned may lead to problematic scenarios for decision-making, and this could in turn cause slow project progress.

Moreover, it is challenging for PPP to be implemented itself over segments, which involve regulatory obstacles and legal limits. One of the trickiest components of PPP is the creation of the necessary regulatory framework and the management of legal complexities that brings about the major challenge. These problems are not static; they can materialize in complex and multi-faceted forms, one of the given examples include, getting permits and approvals, complying with regulatory requirements and handling legal disputes (OECD, 2022). The depth of regulatory compliance adds layers of complexity to project implementation that normally leads to the prolongation of the process and boosts a project's cost.

Aside from that, the division of liability and obligation between the government and private sectors seems to be a formidable barrier to perfecting PPP implementation. Representatives from the PPP usually accept risk-sharing agreements, committing to some risks related to project performance, finance, and operations for each party. Yet, the right way to calculate and distribute risk may not be a simple task, though this may be more complicated in projects with uncertain outcomes or changing external factors (World Bank, 2023). An illustration, crew members on a voyage are required to consider many situations such as noise, lasers, and space radiation. These activities, therefore, reinforce the prominent role of risk provision in PPP projects.

The main issue in the public-private partnership model, based on structural organization and governance, being the determining aspect, should be what that issue is. Part of the deal with PPP schemes is that they need to be handled more complexly than transactions with single players because the latter have unique orientations and interests in addition to those of the best of the parties. Moreover, the widespread differing opinions shared by the relevant actors including governments, private corporations, and locals of varying goals and >motives are the chief factors for coordination problems (UN Office for Partnerships, 2021). The involvement and collaboration with the interested players may create scenarios that could fail in the decision-making issues resulting in slower project operation.

Meantime, it is very complex for PPP to function in the private sector itself throughout the areas that are expressly involved with certain regulatory problems and legal limits. One key challenge that the PPP framework faces is the building of the required regulation system and dispute settlement mechanism, which in turn is a major obstacle of legal complexity standing on the PPP way. These issues do not just stand out, they materialize in complex and diversified forms, such as permitting processing, dealing with regulatory requirements, and management of litigations (OECD, 2022). With the depth of regulatory compliance being involved, the complexity of implementation is boosted and results in the prolongation of the process, which also removes a project's budget on the longer side.

It is also worth noting that the task of dividing responsibilities as well as obligations between two parties: the public and private sector is the most challenging obstacle towards the full development of PPP implementation. The tender of the PPP workshops PPP typically implies the acceptance of risks associated with how the project will be performed, financed, and administered for each of the parties involved. Rather, risk imbalance may not be a straight-cut endeavor, though this could be more complex with projects that have uncertain outcomes or those that frequently change in each environment (World Bank, 2023). Since the voyage involves crew members, they must study scenarios like the exhibition of noises, lasers and space radiation. These activities consequently enable the preeminent part of risk sharing in PPP projects.

The ability to bring finances is the main guiding principle when PPP is going about the establishment. The most critical issue faced by the PPP projects in a moderate economy might relate to their funding; this is especially true in the case of narrowing access to the financial markets. The states and the businesses cannot face the projects whose resources would be expensive to be assumed, then PPP collaboration comes on board to make the presumption possible. Unlike others, PPP investment sustainability and having the balance between "equitable access" and meeting service requirements is a highly impeding hindrance (Kavishe & Chileshe, 2019). The potential sources of income, sources, and sustainability of financial resources which are the basis for the success of PPP projects s to be done prior to a plan being put in place for the long term.

This research analysis on PPP in Tanzania shows that a committed professional team to oversee the projects, routine monitoring at the site and inspections, government support and guarantees, extensive monitoring mechanisms, sustainable selection of PPP proposals, and building trust and integrity among stakeholders are the success factors of PPP in Tanzania (Kavishe and Chileshe, 2019). It is evident that these success factors support the notion that good management, stakeholders' involvement, and openness are among the necessary factors to achieve the objectives of PPP aimed at curbing housing shortages.

Moreover, ICT infrastructure projects in Nigeria and Albania offer a good example of how complicated PPP implementation can be. A study that was conducted in Nigeria showed that there were seventy factors associated with PPP infrastructural projects, during the development phase, construction phase, and operation phase (Babatunde et al., 2018). Risks were grouped according to these two parameters; those that occurred more often and were more severe were put in the most urgent category, requiring immediate countermeasures. Likewise, an Albanian study showed several fields for PPP implementation and spoke about its cognitive success factors like the macro-micro conditions, suitable consortium structure, partnership based on cooperation and community involvement, trusted concessionaire consortia, and an appropriate investment environment (Berisha et al., 2022). The fact that these case studies point out the significance of risk management, stakeholder integration, and institutional backing in PPP projects, highlights their role and credibility in these projects.

The other point is that there is also a case study from Australia that highlights the problematic of PPP infrastructure projects. Australia has several obstacles such as insufficient business cases, weak independence of transport long agencies, political influence, and less objectivity in public finance offices (Godfrey, et al., 2019). These hurdles prove the critical importance of clear policymaking, stringent oversight systems, and accountability structures in PPP deals.

By the end of the day, four countries' case study from Tanzania, Nigeria, Albania, Australia give us a clear picture of the hindrances and options when the PPP model is implemented in the private sector and all over the globe. Through the dissecting of these case studies, the policy makers, practice, and other stakeholders will gain a deeper understanding of the dynamics behind the PPP projects and realize what the means for the success of the PPP projects are. The success and sustainability of any PPP enterprise hinges on effective governance, stakeholder engagement, risk management, and institutional support; these are the critical aspects that need attention if PPP is to become an effective tool for addressing poor infrastructure, climate change and global pandemics.

Developing a mixed set of measures to overcome the difficulties in utilizing the mode of Public-Private Partnership as the way forward requires implementation of solutions such as transparency, risk management, policies, sharing of information, innovations, and technology integration.

Transparency has an upper hand when it comes to public-private partnerships (PPPs), because it is a source of trust between stakeholders, and it is a process that keeps one accountable. Through the enhancement of disclosure, the government can allow the access of information, including schedules, budgets, and performance, to the stakeholders. This transparency helps all concerned people with circumstances to evaluate the efficiency of PPP scheme and keep partners of the project responsible for their activities (Heydari et al., 2021).

Solid risk management should be considered another effective approach to overcoming this option's hindrances. Effective risk management methodology comprehends risk assignment, evaluation as well as hazard substance control throughout the project's whole lifecycle. Through robust risk management solutions and business continuity plans, the stakeholders can forecast ahead of the time and respond to issues that they are not expecting, thus reducing the impact of disasters on projects (Heydari et al., 2021).

The issue becomes vital, especially for the successful realization of PPP projects with a long-term perspective in mind. It is one of the essential functions of barriers between the subfields of science that distinct roles, responsibilities, and procedures are to be set, which resultantly, create clarity and make the implementation of the projects smoother. Additionally, in doing so, regulatory oversight contributes to compliance with legal and regulatory requirements, and that creates protection around the interests of all parties.

And yes, lessons and innovations are the foundation of the project. Because errors are bound to occur, participants can learn from their past and have a chance to re-examine what they have done wrong. Demonstrating the most efficient strength, facilitating better performance of the operations and signaling the progress of the performance would permit stakeholders in the project to improve the PPP outcome by keeping the projects on track. Not only can digitalization, blockchain and big data improvements lead to project performance, but they could also help in its accountability, transparency and responsibility. Thus, along with collaborating and sharing knowledge and capabilities among stakeholders, it will be possible to improve capacity building and risk-sharing within PPP projects.

The formation of common grounds for stakeholders to exchange expertise, resources and lessons learned would reinforce the hybrids of private and public sectors and, by this, effort lessen the potential risk implications. Moreover, setting the culture of incorporating innovations and experiments is favorable as stakeholders will be eager to try more tactics and implement these solutions, thus resulting in continuous improvement in PPP projects (World Bank, 2019).

Overcoming the challenges associated with PPP mechanisms implies an integrated strategy that involves transparency, effective risk management, supportive regulatory environment, dissemination of knowledge, innovation and technology adaptation. Particularly through by applying these measures, the policymakers, practitioners and all the other stakeholders can ensure the best effectiveness, efficiency and durability of the PPP projects to finally get a success of the Sustainable development initiatives.

The PPPs of tomorrow with related trends and innovations appear likely to bring forth exciting solutions that will lead to overcoming the global challenges through sustainable development goals achievement. Another trend is seen in the growing popularity of the social investing and entrepreneurship which sees the social, economic, and environmental factors as interlinked factors that can catalyze the long-term sustainable developments (Global Impact Investing Network, 2023). This trend is a clear indicator that PPP has become more multifaceted such that it goes beyond achieving development goals that solely have economic impact but incorporates social and environmental as well.

One of the contemporary technological advances that have a significant bearing on the rise of public–private partnerships is the fast emergence of this type of cooperation. Digital technologies such as blockchain, data analytics, and digital platforms provide opportunities to do projects the right way, check on the users of the resources, and rectify in case of any errors or noncompliance (World Bank, 2023). Utilizing these technical tools, the PPPs may simplify the procedures, reduce the transaction costs, and create teamwork among the stakeholders; the latter is the goal (Herath & Herath, 2024a).

Moreover, orientation of PPPs to the United Nations Sustainable Development Goals (SDG) is crucial because it proofs the effectiveness thereof and their contribution to the improvement of the state of global development. The United Nations Office for Partnerships stresses that development of the relevant partnerships in areas of climate change, poverty, poverty and inequality resonates as the most critical issue in the world (UN Office for Partnerships, 2021). Integrating SDGs in PPP projects helps the stakeholders to put SDGs into determined actions which leads to reaching the sustainable development targets and more equitable societies are achieved.

However, aside from the social aspect, the sinking of social investments, entrepreneurship, and technological breakthrough adopting innovative funding mechanisms can lead PPP projects to be more resolute and scalable. For instance, the impact investing approach of deploying capital to achieve impact would be suited for socially and environmentally beneficial results besides the financial return to investors (Global Impact Investing Network, 2023). The attraction of impact-oriented investment from PPP's investors is one of the main sources of funding, and this allows the latter to increase the number of communities in which they intervene, especially in the fields which are poorly funded.

In addition, developing ESG (Environmental, Social, and Governance) criteria framework into PPP projects can emphasize its effect and sustainability. ESG criteria give the stakeholders an instrument for the evaluation of environmental and social risk factors and investments' opportunities. That is why these factors are considered on decision-making and business activities procedures of stakeholders (Heydari et al., 2021).

PPPs, like any other concept or framework, will innately be subject to evolution and adapting to address the intricate challenges of the 21st century. Through leveraging new emerging trends and innovations, integration of SDGs and having EGG criteria will be the essential keys for allowing PPPs to work as the new engine for sustainable development and social and environmental change. As the world is facing increasingly complex challenges and an increasing number of them go beyond borders, the governments, businesses, and civil society entities stand together shaping a more prepared, inclusive, and sustainable future for everyone.

Future trends and the novel techniques of PPPs provide a hopeful vision of how global challenges can be tackled, and sustainable goals can be attained. With the use of social enterprise, entrepreneurship, technology advancements, pioneering financing mechanisms, and ESG indicators, PPPs can leverage their advantages and create an overall better world, which is fairer, wealthy, and stable.

The public-private partnership structures have been acknowledged as indispensable tools that are exclusively suited at tackling international problems such as providing services like infrastructure design, economic liberation, or running social services (Thuraiswamy et al., 2018; Tiwari et al., 2020). Nevertheless, these trilateral partnerships are not an exception because they come with influencing factors that bring with them their operational uncertainties. It will probably be more detailed to investigate and overcome the hindrances they pursue through different levels of processes to holistically evaluate their possibilities and, finally, to get them properly used. Major hurdles like project design, structural reform, risk parsing, and monetary exploitation have been predominant disruptions to long-term PPP survival. The case studies from numerous countries and industry types offer a rich source of information on this topic, with lessons on the related challenges and recommended solutions.

Moreover, this section underlines the significance of making informed risk management decisions and fostering effective stakeholder engagement. Overcoming these challenges needs a varied approach, knowing that improving transparency, warming risk management, empowering regulatory regimes, knowledge sharing, innovative approaches, and SD in line with the organizations should be worked on. As we look ahead, policymakers, practitioners, and other stakeholders must align with that to improve the success and sustainability of PPP projects and eventually help us achieve our number one goal, which is economic development.

SIGNIFICANCE OF THE STUDY

This study carries substantial implications for various stakeholders, including academia, policymakers, and practitioners alike.

Academic Contribution

This research intends to add to the existing knowledge on the results of PPPs (public-private partnerships) regarding sustainability by broadly looking at the entire additive process of this partnership for the purpose of achieving the goals of sustainable development by looking into the factors that determine whether the partnership will be successful or not. The research aims at diving deeper into these components and thereby builds a sustainable way for PPPs to be applied in the advancement of the sustainable development goals.

The study will furnish stakeholders working from across multiple sectors, inclusive of policymakers, practitioners, and others, who play a role in attaining the SDGs by 2030, with essential insights for discharging this objective. The role of the PPPs in small and medium private sector development in attaining the SDGs has not been fully unpacked, however, the document provides prolific insights and strategies for improving their influence. Thanks to this study, the policymakers will be armored with solid evidence underpinning their policies, they will be able to coordinate their efforts effectively and will support the implementation of the agenda through long-term endeavors.

The work presented in the chapter acts as a medium for thought and theories and as a source of information on what is needed to boost PPPs and their capacity to drive a sustainable pace of development.

Informed Policymaking

The study's outcome casts a crucial objective for those governing implementing PPPs as the most effective means of achieving SDGs. The interest of studying the latest discoveries and innovations in PPPs may be true, but this is not the end of the story, since it may also open windows on the ways they are relevant to the UN SDGs. The report of the UN Office for Partnerships, published in 2021, is the perfect example where this phenomenon is highlighted. This fact confirms the idea that achieving global goals such as eliminating poverty, ensuring environmental conservation, and reducing inequality all involve the creation of strategic partnerships.

As the final part of this research, a lot of collected data from this study will undoubtably give policymakers a clear vision that PPPs are the most critical tool for the full scale and global implementation of SDGs. Highlighting the noticing of The World Economic Forum in 2023 about the necessity for setting knowledge-driven infrastructure as a key to PPPs, further push requires comprehensive frameworks and capacity-building arrangements.

Additionally, setting up informed policies will be the major outcome of this project. The experiences will have the policymakers assess and track the results as they formulate protocols substantial enough to support effective public-private sector cooperation with negotiations that need to consider sector-specific hindrances and geographical considerations. The approach to creating the base for the effective PPP system implies certain formulations can result in the achievement of sustainable development goals.

The study's outcomes are in an important position to guide a policy which has the base of evidence as well as takes into consideration sustainable results. Through knowledge about the cornerstone of PPP effectiveness, quality sinews and credible factors that drive SDG implementation, policymakers have the evidence they need to make the right decisions by allocation resources strategically, involving stakeholders and implementing the activities that have the SDGs contribution at the focus.

In essence, the study's outcomes allow the policymakers to accept PPPs as innovators in the transformation of the developing world using the sustainable development framework conditioned by evidence-based, best practices, inclusivity, equity and the principle of environmental sustainability.

Guidance for Practitioners

It is necessary to emphasize that this study aims to create an operational mainstreaming plan that tells everybody who is directly or indirectly involved in the activities how to make use of the tools as well as giving them a detailed guide on the steps of implementation of the measures implemented in the past. It will be able to take advantage of the situation due to its thorough scanning of then prevailing programs. Alongside the fast-growing attention towards PPPs in SDGs implementation, higher cautiousness is required when dealing with such arrangements, which are still in the beginning of their development. Instantly following this specific, the 2021 UN Office for Partnerships report declares the urgency of the drawbacks being PPPs as possible for the SDGs program to be realized mainly for the issue of global climate response, poverty eradication and inequality.

In the forthcoming investigation, the knowledgeable outcome is likely to be the key object on which the policymakers can rely for understanding regarding the significance of PPP in promoting the SDGs. This is the 2023 study set forth by the World Economic Forum, which notes the role of capacity dedicated knowledge-based partnerships within discerning frameworks and highlighting capacity development. Furthermore, intensive analysis concerning the outcomes of well-performing PPP operations from OECD's 2022 documents can help solve these challenges by sharing successful experiences and practices.

Following the guidance given will be a major step in taking part in the exploration of past and present PPP projects, from which previous lessons and deep insights are derived. It is important to realize that lessons are drawn from both successful and failed projects, aiming to determine the freedom or bias parameters that lead to their being either a success or a failure. By attempting to fully grasp the complex factors that inform successful PPP ventures and based on their deep understanding of these determinants' stakeholders can create/devise sophisticated methods for improving their performance in future scenarios and thus the PPPs can impact positively the realization of the development goals and the promotion of economic growth.

Developing through the lining of protruding patterns and coming antinomic factors surrounding the Public-Private Partnerships (PPPs) is paramount in releasing their potential to make sustainable development as well as supporting the achievement of Sustainable Development Goals (SDGs) from the United Nations. Reinforcing this notion, the UNOPS chapter entitled "Main Report" from 2021 underscores the imperative of developing PPPs with a clear focus on the resolution of persistent planetary crises such as climate change prevention, eradication of poverty, and the reduction of social injustices.

The findings gathered from the comprehensive research in this chapter include a broad spectrum of PPP implementation facets, from meticulous project preparation to the active engagement of stakeholders, meticulous risk management, and diligent performance tracking. In addition, the overarching aim of this research endeavor is to serve as a source of inspiration for practitioners, showcasing exemplary strategies and fostering a culture of innovation within their respective organizations.

Moreover, the research's essential constituent is the extensive analysis of the inestimable acquisition of knowledge and of the cliffhangers that many PPP projects have encountered and were not met with the desired goals. PPP processes can be fortified, and negative impacts avoided. To achieve this, participants will be empowered to recognize brakes on their way and prefer strong solutions to break these down barriers enabling the PPP initiatives to thrive.

Lastly, the primary contribution of this study lies mainly in its capacity to bring together theoretically informed policymaking and pragmatic actions, thereby propelling the advancement of public-private partnerships towards the realization of a sustainable environment. The implementation of public-private partnerships as a way of going about both local commitments and international commitments towards a sustainable environment would be an outcome. Still, it is projected that the realization of results from the research will be a guide for the decision-makers makers; to understand the diverse strategic planning options they have and help them develop strong partnerships that would be aimed at nurturing global development that is both sustainable and equitable.

CONCLUSION, RECOMMENDATIONS, AND LESSONS LEARNED

The role of Public-Private Partnerships (PPPs) in advancing sustainable development targets is multifaceted and pivotal. Through an extensive case review, the study has identified key lessons and best practices essential for boosting progress towards the Sustainable Development Goals (SDGs). Central to PPP success are appropriate governance structures, transparent decision-making processes, and the effective allocation of risks and responsibilities. These elements lay the groundwork for fostering cooperation, building trust, and incentivizing accountability, thus ensuring the long-term achievement of sustainable development objectives.

The creation of democratic, as well as versatile, PPPs turn into a powerful instrument for handling environmentally sustainable development challenges of the future by exploiting the benefits of the public and private sectors. The developments that fall under the public and private sector umbrella focus on the reallocation of their resources by joint research, developmental technologies, and the support of new growth by this multiplier effect on SDGs. But the key to customizing PPPs is intensive planning, robust governance systems with integrity and fairness. All that contributes to making PPPs to be more beneficial and available to all.

The study of the adaptiveness of PPPS showed that they can bring new points of view to approaches and business conditions that organize sustainable development strategies. Thus, it was demonstrated that PPPS are always open to modifications, and they are looking for more effective methods of how to take sustainable development hurdles. PPPs' strengths to combine the sectors' resources, smartness, and introductions of innovations are the balancers in the way to deal with development issues and progress toward achieving SDGs (Yin et al, 2023). Supporting elements to the functioning of PPP have also been highlighted, among which bulging leadership, stakeholders' active engagement, and stringent accountability mechanisms have been itemized as a priority for a successful implementation. on. The realization of this collection of guidelines is of great value, as it can guide practitioners, policymakers and stakeholders in using PPPs as a tool option for development purposes.

Despite the fact PPPs have advantages, they require you to overcome obstacles and risks. Governance, concerns about sustainability, and social and environmental effects to any actions must be identified otherwise there is no way to act on any of those concerned. The idea of ethics in PPPs being clear, not biased in favor of anything, and taking responsibility for delivering equal results is what makes them work properly. Developing a conducive environment for PPPs is imperative for the future and necessitates relentless knowledge sharing, capacity-building, and inter-sectoral collaboration by stakeholders.

Herath & Herath (2024) suggest that integrating artificial intelligence within the public and private sectors would be a great solution for managing ethical issues related to PPP projects. For them to function optimally as change agents and make substantial contributions to the SDGs stipulated in the 2030 Agenda for Sustainable Development, innovation and learning must be promoted in PPPs.

To conclude, PPPs are an indispensable means of initiating closer collaboration between a broad variety of stakeholders and progressing significantly towards sustainable development goals. In this way,

Table 4. Key variables

Academic Contribution	Examines how Public-Private Partnerships (PPPs) originated & affect progress towards Sustainable Development Goals (SDGs), informing solutions
Case Studies	Deep dives into specific PPP projects to understand their real-world context
Challenges & Risks	Acknowledges persistent problems in PPPs like governance, sustainability, & social/environmental impacts on achieving equitable development
Ethical Considerations	Emphasizes ethical research practices like confidentiality & informed consent to protect participants' rights & ensure trust
Governance & Accountability	Focuses on setting up proper governance structures, stakeholder engagement, & accountability frameworks to prevent corruption & ensure positive development outcomes
Governance Theory	Provides a framework for fair, accountable, & transparent PPP implementation, examining tools, challenges, & best practices
Impact Investing	Invests in projects tackling environmental & social issues while aiming for financial returns
Inclusivity	Ensures participation of marginalized groups in decision-making & project benefits
Informed Consent	Obtains permission from participants potentially affected by research, acknowledging their contribution & protecting their privacy
Infrastructure Development	The process of creating, financing, building, & maintaining physical structures that support the economy, society, & environment (e.g., transportation, energy, water)
Innovation	The creation of new technologies, approaches, or solutions to improve PPP projects & sustainable development
Innovation & Learning Culture	Promotes an environment for PPP players to learn, adapt, & become agents of change for achieving SDGs
Institutional Theory	Analyzes the role of formal & informal institutions (rules, norms, cultures) in shaping PPP implementation
Interdisciplinary Approach	Combines different perspectives & knowledge from various fields to understand PPPs' role in achieving SDGs
Policy Fortification	Strengthens policy by incorporating evidence & analysis for more effective goal achievement
Policy Implications	Provides real-world insights to policymakers for evidence-based decisions & strategic policy formulation for sustainable development
Practical Guidance for Practitioners	Offers actionable recommendations for improving project outcomes by analyzing successful strategies & best practices
Public-Private Partnership (PPP)	Collaboration between governments & private entities for joint investment, risk-sharing, & responsibility in building infrastructure, providing services, or developing projects
Risk Management	Identifies, assesses, & mitigates potential risks (financial, operational, legal, environmental) to ensure project success
Sustainable Development Goals (SDGs)	17 interconnected global goals adopted by the UN in 2015 to address poverty, inequality, environmental issues, & promote peace by 2030
Systems Thinking	Analyzes the interconnectedness of different elements within a system (e.g., a PPP project) to understand their combined effects

they function as stimuli to change in numerous sectors and nations and pave the way to the equitable, inclusive, strong, and sustainable future through interdisciplinary methods and as evident in the given case studies.

REFERENCES

Ahmad, E., Vinella, A., & Xiao, K. (2018). Contracting arrangements and public private partnerships for sustainable development. *Public Sector Economics*, *42*(2), 145–169. doi:10.3326/pse.42.2.8

Akomea-Frimpong, I., Jin, X., Osei-Kyei, R., & Tumpa, R. J. (2023). A critical review of public–private partnerships in the COVID-19 pandemic: Key themes and future research agenda. *Smart and Sustainable Built Environment*, *12*(4), 701–720. doi:10.1108/SASBE-01-2022-0009

Anderson, B. B., & Ratiu, C. (2019). Stakeholder considerations in public-private partnerships. *World Journal of Entrepreneurship, Management and Sustainable Development*, *15*(3), 212–221. doi:10.1108/WJEMSD-04-2018-0046

Asian Development Bank (ADB). (2020). *Knowledge Transfer for Successful Public-Private Partnerships: A Compendium of Case Studies*. ADB.

Babatunde, S. O., Perera, S., & Adeniyi, O. (2019, February 22). (2028). Identification of critical risk factors in public-private partnership project phases in developing countries: A case of Nigeria. *Benchmarking*, *26*(2), 334–355. doi:10.1108/BIJ-01-2017-0008

Berisha, A., Kruja, A., & Hysa, E. (2022). Perspective of Critical Factors toward Successful Public–Private Partnerships for Emerging Economies. *Administrative Sciences*, *12*(4), 160. doi:10.3390/admsci12040160

Cheng, Z., Huanming, W., Xiong, W., Dajian, Z., & Cheng, L. (2021). Public–private partnership as a driver of sustainable development: Toward a conceptual framework of sustainability-oriented PPP. *Environment, Development and Sustainability*, *23*(1), 1043–1063. doi:10.1007/s10668-019-00576-1

Dolla, T., & Boeing, S. L. (2018). Procurement of low carbon municipal solid waste infrastructure in India through public-private partnerships. *Built Environment Project and Asset Management*, *8*(5), 449–460. doi:10.1108/BEPAM-10-2017-0087

Eden, L., & Wagstaff, M. F. (2021). Evidence-based policymaking and the wicked problem of SDG 5 Gender Equality. *Journal of International Business Policy*, *4*(1), 28–57. doi:10.1057/s42214-020-00054-w

Elena, P., Liesl, R., & Cummings, M. E. (2020). Diaspora investment promotion via public–private partnerships: Case-study insights and IB research implications from the Succeed in Ireland initiative. *Journal of International Business Policy*, *3*(1), 23–37. doi:10.1057/s42214-019-00044-7

Farazmand, A. (2018). *The Role of Partnerships in the Implementation of the Sustainable Development Goals*. Sustainable Development Goals.

Fay, M., Martimort, D., & Straub, S. (2018). Funding and financing infrastructure: The joint-use of public and private finance. *Journal of Development Economics*, *150*, 102629. Advance online publication. doi:10.1016/j.jdeveco.2021.102629

Gardner, C., & Henry, P. B. (2023). The Global Infrastructure Gap: Potential, Perils, and a Framework for Distinction. *Journal of Economic Literature*, *61*(4), 1318–1358. doi:10.1257/jel.20221530

Global Impact Investing Network. (2023). *The Global Impact Investing Network Landscape Report 2023*. GIIN.

Godfrey, C. M., Gurmu, A. T., & Tivendale, L. (2019). Investigation of the challenges facing public-private partnership projects in Australia. *Construction Economics and Building*, *19*(1).

Grossi, G., & Argento, D. (2022). The fate of accounting for public governance development. *Accounting, Auditing & Accountability Journal*, *35*(9), 272–303. doi:10.1108/AAAJ-11-2020-5001

Haque, M. N., Saroar, M., Fattah, M. A., & Morshed, S. R. (2020). Public-Private Partnership for achieving sustainable development goals: A case study of Khulna, Bangladesh. *Public Administration and Policy*, *23*(3), 283–298. doi:10.1108/PAP-04-2020-0023

Helmy, R., Khourshed, N., Wahba, M., & Alaa Abd, E. B. (2020). Exploring Critical Success Factors for Public Private Partnership Case Study: The Educational Sector in Egypt. *Journal of Open Innovation*, *6*(4), 142. doi:10.3390/joitmc6040142

Herath, S. K., & Herath, L. M. (2023). Key Success Factors for Implementing Public-Private Partnership Infrastructure Projects. In C. Popescu, P. Yu, & Y. Wei (Eds.), *Achieving the Sustainable Development Goals Through Infrastructure Development* (pp. 1–38). IGI Global. doi:10.4018/979-8-3693-0794-6.ch001

Herath, S. K., & Herath, L. M. (2024). Investigation Into the Barriers to AI Adoption in ESG Integration and Identification of Strategies to Overcome These Challenges. In A. Derbali (Ed.), *Social and Ethical Implications of AI in Finance for Sustainability* (pp. 286–311). IGI Global. doi:10.4018/979-8-3693-2881-1.ch013

Herath, S. K., & Herath, L. M. (2024a). Corporate Social Responsibility (CSR) and Sustainable Development (SD) in the Digital Age. In A. Erturk, S. Colbran, E. Coşkun, F. Theofanidis, & O. Abidi (Eds.), Convergence of Digitalization, Innovation, and Sustainable Development in Business (pp. 162-184). IGI Global. doi:10.4018/979-8-3693-0798-4.ch008

Heydari, M., Lai, K. K., & Xiaohu, Z. (2021). *Risk management in public-private partnerships*. Routledge. doi:10.4324/9781003112051

International Monetary Fund. (2024, April 12). *World Economic Outlook: April 2024*. IMF. https://www.imf.org/en/Publications/WEO

Jahromi, F. S., & Jahromi, F. S. (2023). Policy and legal frameworks for underground natural gas storage in Iran. *Utilities Policy*, *80*(C), 101471. doi:10.1016/j.jup.2022.101471

Joseph Gerald, T. N., Kwame, A. D., Buabeng, T., & Maloreh-Nyamekye, T. (2022). Governance and effectiveness of public–private partnership in Ghana's rural-water sector. *International Journal of Public Sector Management*, *35*(7), 709–732. doi:10.1108/IJPSM-05-2021-0129

Joudyian, N., Doshmangir, L., Mahdavi, M., Jafar, S. T., & Gordeev, V. S. (2021). Public-private partnerships in primary health care: A scoping review. *BMC Health Services Research*, *21*(1), 1–18. doi:10.1186/s12913-020-05979-9 PMID:33397388

Katharina, S., & Thaler, J. (2020). Partnering for good? An analysis of how to achieve sustainability-related outcomes in public–private partnerships. *Business Research*, *13*(2), 485–5. doi:10.1007/s40685-019-0097-3

Kavishe, N., & Chileshe, N. (2019). Critical success factors in public-private partnerships (PPPs) on affordable housing schemes delivery in Tanzania: A qualitative study. *Journal of Facilities Management*, *17*(2), 188–207. doi:10.1108/JFM-05-2018-0033

Kenya U. N. (2024). *Sustainable Development Goal 4 Quality Education*. UN. https://kenya.un.org/en/sdgs/4/key-activities

M., H. & Margot, H. (2022). Reflecting on twenty years of international agreements concerning water governance: insights and key learning. *International Environmental Agreements: Politics, Law and Economics, 22*(2), 317-332.

Ma, M., Wang, N., Mu, W., & Zhang, L. (2022). The Instrumentality of Public-Private Partnerships for Achieving Sustainable Development Goals. *Sustainability (Basel)*, *14*(21), 13756. doi:10.3390/su142113756

Malik, S., & Kaur, S. (2021). Multi-dimensional public–private partnership readiness index: a sub-national analysis of India. Transforming Government: People. *Process and Policy*, *15*(4), 483–511.

Ministry of Education Republic of Kenya. (2017). *Education for Sustainable Development Policy for the Education Sector*. Ministry of Education Republic of Kenya. https://www.education.go.ke/sites/default/files/2022-05/Education-for-Sustainable-Development-Policy-for-the-Education-Sector.pdf

Mishenina, H., & Dvorak, J. (2022). Public–Private Partnership as a Form of Ensuring Sustainable Development of the Forest Management Sphere. *Administrative Sciences*, *12*(4), 156. doi:10.3390/admsci12040156

Narbaev, T. (2022). A meta-analysis of the public-private partnership literature reviews: Exploring the identity of the field. *International Journal of Strategic Property Management*, *26*(4), 318–331. doi:10.3846/ijspm.2022.17860

Ncube, T., Murray, U., & Dennehy, D. (2023). Digitalising Social Protection Systems for Achieving the Sustainable Development Goals: Insights from Zimbabwe. *Communications of the Association for Information Systems*, *53*, 53. doi:10.17705/1CAIS.05306

OECD (Organisation for Economic Co-operation and Development). (2022). *Public-Private Partnerships: A Toolkit for Decision-makers*. OECD.

Ramey V. A. (2021, April). The Macroeconomic Consequences of Infrastructure Investment. CEPR Discussion Paper No. DP15998. SSRN. https://ssrn.com/abstract=3846053

Solomon, O. B., Perera, S., & Adeniyi, O. (2019). Identification of critical risk factors in public-private partnership project phases in developing countries: A case of Nigeria. *Benchmarking*, *26*(2), 334–355. doi:10.1108/BIJ-01-2017-0008

Steiner, A. (2018). The Extraordinary Opportunity of the 2030 Agenda for Sustainable Development. *European Journal of Development Research*, *30*(2), 163–165. doi:10.1057/s41287-018-0131-x

Strasser, S., Stauber, C., Shrivastava, R., Riley, P., & O'Quin, K. (2021). Collective insights of public-private partnership impacts and sustainability: A qualitative analysis. *PLoS One*, *7*(16), e0254495. doi:10.1371/journal.pone.0254495 PMID:34283847

Tafuro, A., Dammacco, G., & Costa, A. (2023). A Conceptual Study on the Role of Blockchain in Sustainable Development of Public–Private Partnership. *Administrative Sciences*, *13*(8), 175. doi:10.3390/admsci13080175

The World Bank. (2018). *Procuring Infrastructure Public-Private Partnerships: A Guide for Public Authorities*. The World Bank. https://ppp.worldbank.org/public-private-partnership/sites/ppp.worldbank.org/files/documents/Procuring_Infrastructure_PPPs_2018_EN.pdf

Thuraiswamy, R., & Rogan, J. M. (2018). Public-private partnerships for delivering social infrastructure in developing countries. *International Journal of Public Sector Management*, *31*(7), 867–889.

Tiwari, A., & Pandey, C. M. (2020). Public–private partnerships: A way forward for sustainable infrastructure development in India. *International Journal of Sustainable Development and Planning*, *15*(7), 835–846.

Uddin, S. A., & Zaman, S. (2022). Assessing value for money in public–private partnership projects: A conceptual framework. *International Journal of Construction Project Management*, *17*(2), 242–257.

UN Department of Economic and Social Affairs (UN DESA). (2023). *The Sustainable Development Goals Report 2023*. UNDDESA. https://unstats.un.org/sdgs/report/2023/.

UN Office for Partnerships. (2021). *Public-Private Partnerships and the 2030 Agenda for Sustainable Development: Fit for Purpose?* UN. https://www.un.org/en/desa/public-private-partnerships-and-2030-agenda-sustainable-development-fit-purpose

United Nations. (2015). *Transforming our world: The 2030 Agenda for Sustainable Development*. UN. https://sdgs.un.org/2030agenda

United Nations. (2016). *Public-Private Partnerships and the 2030 Agenda for Sustainable Development: Fit for purpose?* UN. https://sdgs.un.org/publications/public-private-partnerships-and-2030-agenda-sustainable-development-fit-purpose-18018

United Nations. (2018). *Sustainable Development Goal 11: Make cities and human settlements inclusive, safe, resilient and sustainable*. UN. https://sustainabledevelopment.un.org/sdg11

United Nations. (2021). *SDG7 Energy Compact of Germany; A next Decade Action Agenda to advance SDG7 on sustainable energy for all, in line with the goals of the Paris Agreement on Climate Change*. UN. https://un.org/sites/un2.un.org/files/germany.pdf

UNWater. (2022). *Country Acceleration Case Study - Senegal*. UNWater. https://www.unwater.org/publications/country-acceleration-case-study-senegal

Vargas, G., & De La Vega- Navarro, A. (2021). Public-Private Partnerships for a Sustainable Urban Development: A Literature Review. *Sustainability*, *13*(24), 14222.

Wachira, J. M., Karimi, N., & Mberia, D. K. (2022). Critical success factors influencing the effectiveness of public-private partnerships (PPPs) in infrastructure development projects: A case study of Kenya. *Journal of Public Procurement*, *22*(3), 399–422.

Yin, J., Li, H., & Wang, Y. (2023). Public-private partnership and responsible innovation: A framework based on a systematic literature review. *Technological Forecasting and Social Change*, *192*, 120452.

KEY TERMS AND DEFINITIONS

Academic Contribution: Examines how Public-Private Partnerships (PPPs) originated & affect progress towards Sustainable Development Goals (SDGs), informing solutions.

Case Studies: Deep dives into specific PPP projects to understand their real-world context.

Challenges & Risks: Acknowledges persistent problems in PPPs like governance, sustainability, & social/environmental impacts on achieving equitable development.

Ethical Considerations: Emphasizes ethical research practices like confidentiality & informed consent to protect participants' rights & ensure trust.

Governance and Accountability: Focuses on setting up proper governance structures, stakeholder engagement, & accountability frameworks to prevent corruption & ensure positive development outcomes.

Governance Theory: Provides a framework for fair, accountable, & transparent PPP implementation, examining tools, challenges, & best practices.

Impact Investing: Invests in projects tackling environmental & social issues while aiming for financial returns.

Inclusivity: Ensures participation of marginalized groups in decision-making & project benefits.

Informed Consent: Obtains permission from participants potentially affected by research, acknowledging their contribution & protecting their privacy.

Infrastructure Development: The process of creating, financing, building, & maintaining physical structures that support the economy, society, & environment (e.g., transportation, energy, water).

Innovation and Learning Culture: Promotes an environment for PPP players to learn, adapt, & become agents of change for achieving SDGs.

Innovation: The creation of new technologies, approaches, or solutions to improve PPP projects & sustainable development.

Institutional Theory: Analyzes the role of formal & informal institutions (rules, norms, cultures) in shaping PPP implementation.

Interdisciplinary Approach: Combines different perspectives & knowledge from various fields to understand PPPs' role in achieving SDGs.

Policy Fortification: Strengthens policy by incorporating evidence & analysis for more effective goal achievement.

Policy Implications: Provides real-world insights to policymakers for evidence-based decisions & strategic policy formulation for sustainable development.

Practical Guidance for Practitioners: Offers actionable recommendations for improving project outcomes by analyzing successful strategies & best practices.

Public-Private Partnership (PPP): Collaboration between governments & private entities for joint investment, risk-sharing, & responsibility in building infrastructure, providing services, or developing projects.

Risk Management: Identifies, assesses, & mitigates potential risks (financial, operational, legal, environmental) to ensure project success.

Sustainable Development Goals (SDGs): 17 interconnected global goals adopted by the UN in 2015 to address poverty, inequality, environmental issues, & promote peace by 2030.

Systems Thinking: Analyzes the interconnectedness of different elements within a system (e.g., a PPP project) to understand their combined effects.

Chapter 7
Role of Public-Private Partnership Under China's BRI Framework of Sustainable Development in Central and Eastern Europe

Mukesh Shankar Bharti
https://orcid.org/0000-0002-3693-7247
Amity University, India

Yogendra Singh
Amity University, India

ABSTRACT

This chapter aims to discuss the role of public-private partnership (PPP) under China's Belt and Road Initiative (BRI) in Central and Eastern European countries (CEECs) in the achievement of sustainable development goals. The purpose of this chapter is to explain more broadly major BRI-related sustainable development programs in CEE countries under the PPP model. Moreover, the neo-realist approach of study involved describing China's deeper trade and economic connectivity in this region under the BRI framework of the '17+1' cooperation. This chapter relies on a theoretical discussion of the soft power politics of China's successful connectivity in the CEE countries under the BRI projects. The role of the '17+1' framework of economic cooperation and PPP model in the infrastructural development under China's flagship economic project BRI relies on the qualitative approach to scientific study.

INTRODUCTION

China's BRI-related infrastructure projects are establishing deeper partnerships with countries in Central and Eastern Europe. As part of the BRI projects, the "17+1" economic cooperation framework enables

DOI: 10.4018/979-8-3693-2758-6.ch007

in-depth partnership between China and the CEE countries. Since the launch of several BRI-related projects in the CEE region, the importance of the public-private partnership (PPP) model has been increased in the context of BRI projects. In infrastructure development projects, private companies win tenders for government projects and contractual models have multiplied since the liberalization, privatization and globalization (LPG) taking shape across the world. The public-private partnerships (PPPs) have become a popular approach for financing and developing projects under the Belt and Road Initiative (BRI). PPPs involve collaboration between government agencies and private sector entities to deliver public infrastructure or services. By leveraging private sector expertise and capital, PPPs can help fill the financial gap for large-scale projects (Dinwiddie, 2020). The choice of PPP model depends on various factors, including the nature of the project, financing requirements, risk appetite, and regulatory framework. Governments must carefully assess these factors to determine the most suitable approach for each BRI project. Effective risk allocation mechanisms and clear contractual arrangements are essential to ensure the success and sustainability of PPPs under the BRI.

The sustainable development has gained prominence on international policy agendas, with concepts like "green development," "inclusive and sustainable economy," and "sustainable investment" featuring prominently in both formal and informal statements and policies. Sustainable development considerations are increasingly integrated into trade agreements and negotiations. This includes provisions aimed at promoting environmental conservation, labor rights, and social welfare. Beijing has incorporated BRI framework of cooperation in the CEECs and their policymakers aim to foster a more inclusive, resilient, and sustainable global economy through the expansion of the new silk road projects in the former communist block of Europe (Yin, 2019). The harnessing the potential of PPPs, the BRI can play a significant role in advancing progress towards the SDGs by addressing infrastructure gaps, promoting regional integration, and fostering sustainable economic growth in participating countries (China Council for International Cooperation on Environment and Development (CCICED) Secretariat, 2022). However, it's essential for stakeholders to ensure that BRI projects are designed and implemented in a manner that maximizes their positive impacts while minimizing potential risks and negative externalities.

PPPs have emerged as a valuable tool for governments and private sector entities to collaborate in addressing infrastructure gaps, improving public service delivery, and fostering sustainable development. As countries continue to face evolving challenges and resource constraints, PPPs are expected to remain a prominent mechanism for leveraging private sector participation and investment in addressing public needs. Many countries and regions around the world have embraced PPPs as a key strategy for infrastructure development and public service delivery (Wang et al., 2018). Governments in both developed and developing countries have established legal and regulatory frameworks to facilitate PPP implementation, and international organizations have promoted PPP best practices and knowledge sharing (Hodge & Greve, 2007). The adoption of the PPP model in China's BRI projects in the CEECs reflects a collaborative and cooperative approach to infrastructure development and economic cooperation between public and private sector actors. By leveraging the PPP model, China and the CEECs aim to address infrastructure deficits, promote sustainable development, and enhance regional connectivity as part of the broader BRI initiative.

METHODS

It utilizes content analysis to investigate China's Belt and Road Initiative (BRI) framework of partnership with CEE countries, particularly in terms of political and economic cooperation since 2015, and how this framework relates to investments in PPP projects. The BRI is a global infrastructure development strategy initiated by China, aiming to promote economic cooperation and connectivity among countries across Asia, Africa, and Europe through infrastructure projects, trade, and investment. PPP projects are a common approach in infrastructure development, involving collaboration between public and private sectors to finance, build, and operate infrastructure projects. The study seeks to provide empirical insights into how China's BRI framework influences the decision-making processes and investments in PPP projects in CEE countries, shedding light on the dynamics of infrastructure development and international cooperation in the context of China's global economic strategy. To describe China's Belt and Road Initiative (BRI) projects in Central and Eastern European Countries (CEECs) under the Public-Private Partnership (PPP) framework, this study can utilize primary and secondary resources to provide a comprehensive understanding of these initiatives.

REVIEW OF LITERATURE

Guo et al., (2023) explain the public-private partnerships (PPPs) indeed have the potential to significantly contribute to infrastructure development in the Central and Eastern European (CEE) countries of the European Union. These partnerships can help mobilize private sector resources, expertise, and innovation to address infrastructure gaps and promote economic growth. However, despite their potential benefits, the successful implementation of PPPs in the CEE region has faced several challenges. Political changes and institutional weaknesses in some CEE countries can affect the continuity and effectiveness of PPP projects. Political instability can lead to policy reversals, delays in decision-making, and changes in project priorities, which can deter private sector investment. (Guo et al., 2023) discuss the utilization of China's PPP cases in the Central and Eastern European (CEE) countries provides valuable insights into the determinants of successful PPP projects under the Belt and Road Initiative (BRI) framework. The study suggests that several factors influence the attraction of commercial investment in PPP projects in the CEE region, with local government characteristics playing a significant role. A conducive business environment characterized by transparent regulations, investment incentives, political stability, and effective governance can enhance the attractiveness of PPP projects to commercial investors in the CEE countries.

Wang et al., (2024) elucidate the term "public-private partnership" (PPP) encompasses a wide range of contractual arrangements and collaborative models between public and private entities. These partnerships are often utilized as alternatives to traditional government procurement methods for delivering public infrastructure, services, and projects. China's entrepreneurs winning bids to partner in infrastructure development projects in the Central and Eastern European (CEE) countries under the Belt and Road Initiative (BRI) is a notable trend. This phenomenon reflects China's increasing presence and investment in the region as part of its broader BRI strategy. Chinese firms, particularly state-owned enterprises (SOEs) and construction companies, possess extensive experience and expertise in infrastructure development gained from domestic and international projects. Their track record of successfully implementing infrastructure projects, including roads, railways, ports, and energy facilities, enhances their credibility and competitiveness in bidding processes. (Rosell & Saz-Carranza, 2020) characterise the success and capacity for Public-Private Partnerships (PPPs) are significantly influenced by the institutional quality of a country's governance. Institutional quality encompasses factors such as transparency, rule of law, regulatory efficiency, and government effectiveness. In the context of PPPs, strong institutional quality fosters an enabling environment for collaboration between the public and private sectors, mitigates risks, and ensures the efficient implementation and management of PPP projects. The Central and Eastern European (CEE) countries, being deeply associated with China's Belt and Road Initiative (BRI) investment in the region, can benefit from PPP models to address infrastructure needs and promote economic development. Moreover, building trust and partnerships between public and private stakeholders, improving project preparation and procurement capacity, and promoting best practices in PPP governance and management are critical for maximizing the benefits of BRI investments through PPPs in the CEE region.

Delamotte (2020) elucidates China's investments in European infrastructure and energy sectors, as well as its participation in the Belt and Road Initiative in the region, have garnered significant attention in recent years. China's acquisition of the Greek port of Piraeus, as well as investments in the ports of Trieste and Genoa in Italy, demonstrate its interest in expanding maritime connectivity and trade routes in Europe. China's investment in Portugal's national electricity company and its interest in the port of Sines reflect its focus on securing energy resources and infrastructure in Europe. These investments enable China to diversify its energy sources and enhance its energy security while also contributing to Europe's energy transition and infrastructure development. China has committed to massive investments in Central European countries, including infrastructure projects, industrial partnerships, and trade agreements. These investments aim to strengthen economic ties between China and Central European countries, promote regional development, and facilitate China's access to European markets. More than 20 European countries, including EU members, non-EU members, and EU applicant countries, are part of China's Belt and Road Initiative. These countries have signed cooperation agreements with China to promote infrastructure development, trade facilitation, and people-to-people exchanges under the BRI framework (Bharti, 2023a, 2024; Brattberg, 2020).

China's attempts to exploit divisions in CEE countries or undermine EU unity may provoke backlash and resentment from other EU member states, regional allies, or civil society groups. This could lead to diplomatic tensions, trade disputes, or increased scrutiny of China's activities in the region. China may seek to establish itself as a dominant economic and political actor in the countries of CEE. Encouraging China to adopt a "One Europe" policy reflects the EU's commitment to promoting unity and solidarity among its member states. China to pursue a "One Europe" policy, as advocated by German Foreign Minister Sigmar Gabriel in August 2017, highlights the importance of European unity and cohesion in dealing with external partners such as China. Moreover, the Central and Eastern Europeans' "European sentiment" is important, it may not be sufficient to address their concerns or counter China's influence in the region. Poland and other CEE countries in coordinated EU efforts on China, France, Germany, and Italy can counter China's attempts to divide and influence Europe. This can contribute to a more unified and assertive EU stance on China, enhancing the EU's ability to defend its interests and values in its relations with China (Gaspers, 2018; Herrero & Xu, 2017; Jensen & Malesky, 2018; J. Zeng, 2017; Y. Zeng, 2024).

THEORETICAL BACKGROUND AND CONCEPTUAL EXPLANATION

Casady et al., (2019) use institutional theory to conceptualize PPP institutional maturity as the evolution of legitimacy, trust, and capacity within the PPP process over time. They argue that transparency plays a crucial role in enhancing these three aspects of institutional maturity. Legitimacy refers to the perceived appropriateness and acceptance of PPPs by stakeholders, trust relates to confidence and reliance on the PPP process and its outcomes, while capacity encompasses the ability of institutions to effectively design, implement, and manage PPP projects. The negative fiscal conditions in Southern Europe have indeed incentivized the region to promote Public-Private Partnerships (PPPs) as a means of addressing infrastructure needs and leveraging private sector resources and expertise. Southern European countries, such as Greece, Italy, Portugal, and Spain, have faced significant fiscal challenges in recent years, including high levels of public debt, budget deficits, and limited fiscal space for public investment. Southern European governments have turned to PPPs as an alternative financing mechanism to fund infrastructure projects without adding to their debt burden. PPPs allow governments to shift some of the financial risks and responsibilities to private sector partners, thereby reducing the immediate budgetary impact of infrastructure investments (van den Hurk et al., 2016).

Analyzing Public-Private Partnerships (PPPs) within an economics background provides valuable insights into the underlying economic principles, incentives, and outcomes associated with PPP arrangements. when developing theoretical models to discuss Public-Private Partnerships (PPPs), this can draw upon three primary knowledge backgrounds. Firstly, Economics provides insights into the efficiency, incentives, and outcomes associated with PPP arrangements. Secondly, applying network and governance theories, it can gain insights into the complexities of PPP governance, decision-making processes, and policy outcomes. These theoretical perspectives help elucidate the dynamics of cooperation, coordination, and conflict resolution between public and private sectors in PPP projects, informing efforts to enhance the effectiveness, accountability, and sustainability of collaborative arrangements in public infrastructure and service delivery. Network theory emphasizes the interconnectedness and relationships among various actors involved in PPPs, including government agencies, private companies, civil society organizations, and other stakeholders. Governance theory focuses on the mechanisms and processes of collective decision-making, coordination, and control in multi-actor environments, such as PPPs. Thirdly, Stakeholder theory emphasizes the importance of identifying, understanding, and managing the interests and expectations of various stakeholders involved in PPP projects (Wang et al., 2018). In the context of PPPs, stakeholders may include government agencies, private companies, investors, local communities, civil society organizations, and regulatory bodies. Stakeholder theory helps to assess the impacts of PPP projects on different stakeholders, anticipate potential conflicts or challenges, and develop strategies to enhance stakeholder collaboration and alignment of interests.

Institutional theory views PPPs as institutional arrangements embedded within broader social, cultural, and political contexts. Institutional theorists argue that achieving legitimacy is as crucial as achieving efficiency in PPP implementation, as legitimacy enhances the project's credibility, acceptance, and long-term sustainability (Hodge & Greve, 2007; Wang et al., 2018). Institutional theory helps researchers understand how PPP projects are shaped by institutional norms, rules, and expectations, and how actors navigate institutional pressures and constraints to achieve project objectives. These theoretical perspectives inform strategies for stakeholder engagement, organizational management, and institutional governance in PPP implementation, contributing to improved project outcomes and societal impacts. The arguments relating to what leads to a successful Public-Private Partnership (PPP) often stem from two main theoretical perspectives, as believed by some Dutch scholars: Resource Dependency Theory posits that organizations depend on external resources to survive and thrive. In the context of PPPs, this theory suggests that successful partnerships are characterized by a careful allocation and management of resources, including financial, human, and technological resources. Contract Theory focuses on the design and implementation of contractual agreements between public and private partners in PPPs (Kort et al., 2015; Steijn et al., 2011). This perspective emphasizes the importance of clear, comprehensive contracts that specify rights, responsibilities, incentives, and performance metrics to align interests and mitigate risks. These two theoretical perspectives offer complementary insights into the factors influencing PPP success and effectiveness.

The preliminary and classic theory of network effectiveness, which focuses on balancing multiple stakeholder values including principals, agents, and clients, is indeed a valuable framework for understanding and evaluating the effectiveness of Public-Private Partnership (PPP) networks. However, as you rightly pointed out, this framework may overlook the potential value conflicts that can arise between different levels of government involved in PPP projects. In the context of PPPs, conflicts between central and local governments can arise due to divergent priorities, objectives, and interests. Central governments may prioritize broader policy goals such as sustainability development, national economic growth, and social welfare, while local governments may be more concerned about relieving financial burdens, stimulating local economic development, and meeting immediate infrastructure needs. This approach promotes more inclusive, responsive, and sustainable PPP governance arrangements, contributing to better outcomes for all stakeholders involved (Provan & Milward, 1995).

CHINA-EUROPE FREIGHT CORRIDOR

China-Europe freight trains have emerged as an important mode of transportation in cross-continent trade, offering speed, reliability, and connectivity for businesses and countries participating in the Belt and Road Initiative (Mingyang & Yeping, 2024). The BRI, launched by China in 2013, aims to enhance connectivity and cooperation between China and countries in Asia, Europe, Africa, and beyond through infrastructure development, trade facilitation, and economic integration. The China-Europe freight trains are a key component of the BRI's transportation and logistics network, providing a faster and more cost-effective alternative to traditional maritime shipping and air freight. These trains connect major cities and industrial hubs in China with destinations in Europe, traversing vast distances across Eurasia and passing through multiple countries along the route. The Chinese government initiated the China-Europe intercontinental freight train service in 2011, which has since become known as the China Railway Express within the context of the Belt and Road Initiative (BRI) (Kundu & Sheu, 2019). The China Railway Express (CR) Express is a key component of China's efforts to strengthen trade and connectivity between China and Europe, as well as other regions along the BRI corridor. The CR exemplifies the strategic significance of rail transportation within the broader framework of the Belt and Road Initiative, serving as a vital artery for trade, investment, and connectivity between China and Europe, as well as other countries along the BRI corridor. The China Merchants Group (CMG) and Huajian Group represent two significant players within the Belt and Road Initiative (BRI), shedding light on the intricate relationship between state-owned enterprises (SOEs) and private companies in China's global economic endeavors.

In Europe, BRI-related construction works primarily target economies with a strong need for infrastructure development, particularly in Central, Eastern, and Southeastern Europe (CESEE). These regions are considered crucial gateways to Western European markets due to their strategic geographical location and connectivity potential. Several factors contribute to the focus on CESEE economies for BRI-related construction projects. The focus on CESEE economies for BRI-related construction works underscores the region's importance as a key node in the BRI network, linking East and West and facilitating economic cooperation and integration across continents. By investing in infrastructure development in CESEE, the BRI aims to unlock the region's growth potential, promote connectivity, and contribute to shared prosperity and development (Gruebler, 2021).

The diplomatic initiative "16+1," later renamed "17+1," aimed to enhance cooperation between Central and Eastern European countries (CEEC) and China. Initially, it involved 11 European Union (EU) Member States from Central and Eastern Europe, all of which joined the EU in 2004 or later, excluding Malta and Cyprus. Additionally, five Western Balkan countries participated in the initiative. The "17+1" initiative provided a platform for dialogue and collaboration between China and the CEEC and Western Balkan countries, enabling them to address common challenges, explore opportunities for mutual benefit, and foster closer ties. However, the initiative also raised concerns among some EU member states and institutions about its potential implications for EU unity, transparency, and adherence to EU standards and regulations (Bharti, 2022a, 2022b, 2023b). In recent years, the "17+1" initiative has undergone changes and faced criticism, leading to discussions about its effectiveness and future direction. Some participating countries have expressed reservations or scaled back their involvement, while others continue to seek opportunities for cooperation with China within the framework of the initiative. Overall, the "17+1" initiative remains a significant aspect of China's engagement with Central and Eastern Europe and the Western Balkans, albeit with evolving dynamics and considerations.

BELT AND ROAD INITIATIVE AND THE SDGs

The Belt and Road Initiative (BRI) is often characterized as a joint development project rather than an aid project. It's an ambitious global infrastructure and economic development strategy. Many of the projects under the BRI are undertaken by Chinese companies as commercial ventures, aiming to generate returns on investment rather than providing aid. These investments often involve partnerships with local businesses and governments. The Sustainable Development Goals (SDGs) were adopted by the United Nations in September 2015 as a universal call to action to end poverty, protect the planet, and ensure prosperity for all by 2030. They succeeded in the Millennium Development Goals (MDGs), which were in place from 2000 to 2015. While the MDGs primarily focused on reducing poverty and improving social indicators, the SDGs are more comprehensive and address a wider range of issues, including environmental sustainability, economic development, and social inclusion (Jin, 2018). The Chinese permanent representative, Ambassador Jieyi Liu, argued that the Belt and Road Initiative (BRI) could promote the fulfillment of the Sustainable Development Goals (SDGs) during a high-level UN meeting. China has often emphasized the potential synergies between the BRI and the SDGs, highlighting how the BRI's focus on infrastructure development, connectivity, and economic cooperation aligns with the objectives of the SDGs (Hong, 2016).

António Guterres, the Secretary-General of the United Nations, has indeed expressed support for the Belt and Road Initiative (BRI) on various international occasions. His remarks underscore the alignment between the BRI and the UN's 2030 Agenda for Sustainable Development, which encompasses the Sustainable Development Goals (SDGs). Guterres acknowledges that the BRI is in line with the 2030

Agenda for Sustainable Development. This indicates recognition of the potential synergies between the BRI's objectives and the SDGs, particularly in areas such as infrastructure development, poverty alleviation, and economic cooperation. Guterres's support for the BRI reflects the UN's recognition of the initiative's potential to advance sustainable development and address global challenges through cooperation and partnership among countries (Dong et al., 2018). However, it's important to note that while the BRI holds promise, its implementation must adhere to principles of transparency, sustainability, and inclusivity to ensure that its benefits are shared equitably and contribute to the well-being of all stakeholders. The Secretary-General suggests that the BRI can contribute to making economic globalization more balanced and inclusive.

Central and Eastern European (CEE) countries, as participants in the BRI, can benefit from China's support for their sustainable development goals under the UN's agenda. Through collaboration with China on BRI projects, these countries can access resources, technology, and expertise to advance their environmental and developmental objectives in alignment with the SDGs.

The Central and Eastern European countries may be performing relatively well in implementing SDG 15 compared to other regions, there may still be challenges and areas for improvement. Environmental issues such as deforestation, land degradation, and loss of biodiversity continue to pose threats in these countries, albeit to varying degrees. The majority of Central and Eastern European (CEE) countries are making progress or maintaining achievement in implementing SDG 15, with ten out of sixteen countries on track or maintaining achievement. Additionally, four countries are showing a moderately improving trend, indicating that they are making strides toward fulfilling the targets outlined in SDG 15 (CCICED, 2020). However, two countries are experiencing stagnation in their efforts to implement SDG 15, suggesting that they may be facing challenges or obstacles in addressing issues related to terrestrial ecosystems, forest management, desertification, land degradation, and biodiversity conservation.

China has become a member of the European Bank for Reconstruction and Development (EBRD), while many European Union (EU) member states have joined the Asian Infrastructure Investment Bank (AIIB). These memberships reflect efforts to promote cooperation and investment in infrastructure projects, particularly in regions such as the Balkans where there is a need for development and connectivity (Ping & Zuokui, 2017). Loan programs have been established for the private sector in the Balkans to facilitate their participation in projects backed by China in the region. These programs aim to provide financial support and incentives for businesses to engage in infrastructure development and other initiatives supported by China's investments. This study highlights ensuring transparency and accountability in BRI projects and activities is essential for building trust and facilitating coordination with other initiatives in CEECs. Concerns about the lack of transparency and accountability in BRI projects may hinder efforts to find suitable operational modalities for coordination. The BRI is framed as a commercial initiative, with a focus on leveraging market-based investments and economic growth initiatives. By engaging the private sector and adhering to market rules and international laws, the BRI aims to create opportunities for businesses and stimulate economic development along its routes.

DISCUSSION AND KEY FINDINGS

The findings indicate a mixed picture of progress in implementing SDG 15 across CEE countries, with some making notable advancements, others showing improvement, and a few facing challenges or stagnation. Continued efforts to strengthen environmental governance, promote sustainable land management practices, and enhance biodiversity conservation are essential to ensure the long-term sustainability of terrestrial ecosystems in the region. Collaboration among governments, civil society organizations, businesses, and international partners is crucial to address the complex environmental challenges outlined in SDG 15 and achieve the sustainable development goals set forth by the United Nations. On the other hand, the CEE countries of refusing Chinese funding that is linked to sovereign guarantees. Instead, alternative forms of funding agreements are suggested, such as public-private partnership schemes or concession agreements, particularly for major infrastructure projects like railroads and highways (Bharti, 2023a). The BRI is seen as an accelerator for achieving the Sustainable Development Goals (SDGs). By generating development dividends tied to market-based investments and economic growth initiatives, the BRI has the potential to advance progress towards the SDGs, particularly in areas such as poverty alleviation, infrastructure development, and sustainable resource management.

The alignment between the Belt and Road Initiative (BRI) and the global sustainable development framework, particularly the Sustainable Development Goals (SDGs) outlined in Agenda 2030. The five priorities of the BRI align closely with the objectives of the SDGs. These priorities, which include policy coordination, infrastructure connectivity, trade facilitation, financial integration, and people-to-people bonds, reflect the core elements of sustainable development such as economic growth, social inclusion, and environmental sustainability. Agenda 2030 complements the BRI by emphasizing sustainability as a critical aspect. By aligning with the SDGs, the BRI enhances its credibility and is seen as an important instrument for furthering sustainable human development across participating countries. This alignment reinforces the BRI's long-term vision of promoting economic integration and societal development along the ancient Silk Road routes. In today's globalized world, economic and social linkages transcend individual countries. The BRI recognizes this reality by promoting connectivity and cooperation among countries, fostering regional and global integration. Environmental sustainability, being a regional and global issue, is inherently embedded in the SDGs and is essential for the success of the BRI. The SDGs encompass economic, social, and environmental aspects, reflecting a holistic approach to sustainable development (Horvath, 2016). By embracing the SDGs, the BRI aims to enhance the integration of economies and societies along the ancient Silk Road routes in a sustainable manner, ensuring that development benefits are shared equitably and that environmental resources are preserved for future generations.

The BRI to serve as a crucial coordinating device for infrastructure development plans, aligning with the objectives outlined in Agenda 2030, particularly the Sustainable Development Goals (SDGs).

Coordination for Infrastructure Development: The BRI can provide a framework for coordinating infrastructure development plans among a large set of countries. Given the significant costs associated with misallocating resources in infrastructure investment, effective coordination is crucial for maximizing the impact and efficiency of investments in infrastructure projects.

Alignment with SDGs: The BRI's alignment with the SDGs enables it to contribute to overarching objectives related to sustainable development, including trade, investment, social progress, and environmental sustainability. By coordinating efforts to achieve the SDGs, the BRI can promote the greater good and long-term human development across participating countries.

Win-Win Strategy: Linking the BRI and SDGs is seen as a win-win strategy. It enables the integration of SDGs into local development contexts, enhances coordination among interrelated goals, and ensures that BRI projects positively impact critical social issues such as inequality and inclusiveness.

Enhanced Image for China: Implementing the BRI in alignment with the SDGs can enhance China's image as a leading country in South-South Cooperation. By prioritizing partner country development and supporting adaptation to shifting patterns of development financing, China can demonstrate its commitment to mutual benefit and inclusive development cooperation.

Strong Institutions and Mechanisms: Strong institutions and mechanisms are essential for informing sound political decision-making in all BRI countries. Robust governance structures, transparent processes, and effective oversight mechanisms can help ensure accountability, mitigate risks, and enhance the credibility of BRI initiatives.

Alignment with Development Objectives: Building strong ties among BRI countries ensures buy-in and commitment to common sustainable development objectives. By promoting dialogue and cooperation, countries can identify shared priorities, leverage synergies, and address common challenges, ultimately contributing to inclusive and sustainable development outcomes.

Facilitation by SDG Framework: The Sustainable Development Goals (SDGs) provide a global, multilaterally adopted agenda that can facilitate dialogue and communication on the BRI. By serving as a common reference point, the SDG framework helps align different national development strategies with global and regional development goals, enhancing coherence and coordination among BRI countries.

Engagement of Stakeholders: Effective engagement of stakeholders, including governments, private actors, and local communities, is critical for the success of BRI projects. Formal and informal dialogue mechanisms facilitate communication, foster collaboration, and ensure that diverse perspectives are considered in decision-making processes.

Chinese investments had been increasing until 2017 but experienced a drop in 2018. This indicates a period of growth followed by a decline in investment activity. The share of investments in Europe as a portion of overall Chinese investments varied over time. It ranged from 6.5% in 2010 to 38.9% in 2017, indicating significant fluctuations in investment patterns. The European Union's 16 countries (EU16) emerged as the primary targets for Chinese investments in Europe. In contrast, the "17+1" countries, referring to Central and Eastern European countries, played a minor role in attracting Chinese investments. In 2017, there was a notable investment in the EFTA region, particularly the acquisition of Swiss seed and agrochemicals producer Syngenta by China National Chemical Corporation (ChemChina). This acquisition amounted to USD 43 billion and represented a significant investment in the region. The PRC's ambassador to Switzerland in 2019, describing the Syngenta acquisition as a mistake, may indicate a response to criticism from Swiss politicians. There were calls for government intervention in sales of Swiss companies to foreign investors, suggesting concerns about the impact of foreign acquisitions on national interests (Gruebler, 2020).

ROLE OF NATIONAL DEVELOPMENT FINANCIAL INSTITUTIONS

National development financial institutions, such as the China Development Bank (CDB) and the Export-Import Bank of China (Chexim), played a crucial role in providing initial financing for BRI projects. These institutions took the lead in providing funding, which helped attract private sector investment. CDB and Chexim were instrumental in "blood making" for the BRI, referring to the provision of crucial financial support to kickstart infrastructure projects. Their involvement helped bridge the gap in financing and encouraged further investment from both public and private sectors. Due to their large reserve assets, CDB and Chexim emerged as major lenders for infrastructure projects along the Belt and Road. CDB, for instance, provided substantial loans totaling USD 170 billion to BRI countries by June 2017, with significant amounts disbursed annually to support infrastructure development (Liu et al., 2020).

Chexim's concessional loans, export credits, and development loans with guaranteed repayment and low interest rates were crucial sources of funding for BRI infrastructure projects. These financing mechanisms helped address the challenges associated with long-term investment repayment and incentivized participation in BRI initiatives.

Scope and Significance of PPP Projects

In 2017, China established a PPP framework specifically for BRI projects. This initiative aims to facilitate long-term cooperation between the government and the private sector in infrastructure development and the provision of public services. China signed a Memorandum of Understanding with the United Nations Economic Commission for Europe (UNECE) to jointly promote the application of the PPP model to BRI projects. This collaboration enhances the adoption of best practices and standards in PPP implementation. PPP projects under the BRI cover various industries, including transportation, renewable energy, electric power, and oil and gas. These projects span multiple countries along the Belt and Road and contribute to infrastructure development and economic growth in the region. PPPs play an important role in the BRI by leveraging private sector expertise, resources, and innovation in infrastructure development. They also contribute to addressing the diverse needs and challenges of countries along the Belt and Road, reflecting differences in natural resources, population structure, legal systems, investment environments, and policy frameworks.

The World Bank and the United Nations Economic Commission for Europe (UNECE) provide broad descriptions of Public-Private Partnerships (PPPs), emphasizing their role in financing, designing, implementing, and operating public sector facilities and services. The private sector brings capital and expertise to deliver projects on time and within budget. The public sector retains responsibility for providing services to the public in a manner that benefits the public and promotes economic development and an improvement in the quality of life. The collaborative nature of PPPs, where the strengths of both the public and private sectors are leveraged to achieve shared objectives. PPPs are seen as a means to address infrastructure needs, improve service delivery, and stimulate economic development while ensuring accountability and value for money. PPPs are described as mechanisms for financing, designing, implementing, and operating public sector facilities and services. The private sector brings capital and expertise to deliver projects on time and within budget. The public sector retains responsibility for providing services to the public in a manner that benefits the public and promotes economic development and an improvement in the quality of life (Baxter, 2022).

The public sector in emerging economies turns to PPPs as a means of leveraging private sector expertise, capital, and innovation to bridge the funding gap and deliver essential infrastructure and services. PPPs allow governments to access additional funding and resources while transferring risks to the private sector, thereby enabling the timely and cost-effective delivery of projects aligned with national development priorities.

There is a lack of research specifically focused on understanding the interrelationship between the BRI and the SDGs. While there is existing literature on the BRI and the SDGs separately, there is a need for further investigation into how BRI projects contribute to achieving the SDGs. Despite the growing number of BRI projects, there is limited evidence on their specific aims, development, implementation, effectiveness, and impact in terms of the SDGs. This gap hinders policymakers' ability to assess the contribution of BRI projects to sustainable development outcomes. There is a clear need for policy-oriented research to evaluate BRI projects' performance, outcomes, and impact concerning the

SDGs (Renwick et al., 2018). Establishing a comprehensive research program focused on collecting and analyzing project-focused evidence would help address this knowledge gap. A BRI-wide research program would significantly contribute to closing the knowledge gap, providing critical data on meeting SDG targets and goals. It would also strengthen evidence-based policymaking and future strategic development cooperation efforts.

Transit and Logistical Potential

Despite the presence of transit and logistical infrastructure in CEE countries, their potential remains largely untapped. This suggests that these countries are not fully integrated into the transportation routes of the Northern route of the BRI. Ports in Poland and the Baltic countries, which could serve as key nodes along the Northern route, are not extensively involved in BRI-related transportation activities. This indicates a missed opportunity for these countries to capitalize on their strategic geographical location and maritime infrastructure. The main transport and logistics centers for Chinese goods, such as Duisburg and Hamburg in Germany, are already operating at full capacity. This presents challenges for expanding their capacities to accommodate the growing volume of goods transported along the BRI routes (Smotrytska, 2020). The uneven distribution of cargo flows, combined with the insufficient technological level of transport and logistics infrastructure in CEE countries, poses challenges to the development of China-Europe ties. This uneven distribution may result in suboptimal routes and increased transportation costs.

The increasing number of Chinese investments and relations in Europe, as evidenced by initiatives like the 17+1, indicates that China has become a significant player in European affairs. This development suggests a deeper and more complex engagement with Europe than initially anticipated by both Beijing and European capitals. The reality of China's growing influence in Europe necessitates that China acknowledges its position as a "European power." Similarly, European countries need to engage in mature and meaningful discussions about China's influence, moving beyond simplistic categorizations of friend or foe, rival or ally. The evolving cooperation between China and Central and Eastern European (CEE) countries demonstrates the complexity of international relations, where actors can simultaneously play multiple contradictory roles. This complexity challenges traditional notions of alliances and partnerships. Economic Implications: Ignoring China's emergence as a major player in Europe can have significant economic consequences for the European Union. The BRI initiative has highlighted the importance of engaging with China and leveraging its influence for mutual benefit.

CONCLUSION

This research indicates that China's economic diplomacy towards Central and Eastern Europe does not appear to be driven by a strategy aimed at dividing Europe or benefiting China at Europe's expense. Instead, China's engagement with CEE countries is primarily motivated by economic interests, geopolitical considerations, and a desire to foster closer ties with European partners (Bharti, 2022b; Garlick, 2019). The region offers opportunities for Chinese companies to expand their presence in Europe, access new markets, and participate in infrastructure projects, while CEE countries benefit from Chinese investment, technology transfer, and market access. The paper highlights uncertainties and risks associated with Chinese Belt and Road Initiative (BRI) activities in Europe from an economist's perspective. These risks include potential debt traps, financial dependency, the establishment of foreign production networks, circumvention of public procurement rules, and the deterioration of standards. In light of these risks, the paper provides policy recommendations, particularly in the context of recent EU investment initiatives such as the Invest EU program. These recommendations aim to address the challenges posed by Chinese BRI activities and promote better coordination and complementarity between European and Chinese efforts.

China's BRI presents an opportunity to advance sustainable development goals, including environmental objectives, both domestically and internationally. By closely linking the BRI with the 2030 SDGs and prioritizing environmental governance, China can contribute to broader global efforts to address environmental challenges and promote sustainable development along the BRI route and beyond. China recognizes the importance of involving various stakeholders, including private and international actors, in the BRI's institution-building process. This approach reflects a departure from traditional state-driven governance models and emphasizes collaboration among different actors to achieve geopolitical and geostrategic goals in CEECs (Coenen et al., 2021). China expects companies to take a leading role in implementing the vision of a "green BRI." By involving the private sector, China aims to leverage their expertise, resources, and innovation to promote environmentally sustainable practices in BRI projects.

The BRI represents an opportunity to harness market forces and economic incentives to drive sustainable development, enhance regional cooperation, and accelerate progress towards the SDGs. By integrating economic, social, and environmental considerations into its projects and initiatives, the BRI can contribute to inclusive and sustainable development outcomes that benefit participating countries and communities. By embracing the SDGs, the BRI enhances its credibility, promotes inclusive development, and contributes to the achievement of global sustainable development objectives. Moreover, linking the BRI and SDGs is viewed as a strategic approach to maximizing the positive impact of infrastructure investments and promoting sustainable development outcomes. By prioritizing coordination, inclusiveness, and long-term human development goals, the BRI can enhance its credibility, effectiveness, and perceived value among partner countries and international stakeholders. The study also indicates that adoption of PPPs within the BRI framework reflects China's commitment to fostering cooperation between the public and private sectors to promote sustainable development and infrastructure investment along the Belt and Road. By leveraging PPPs, countries can address infrastructure gaps, enhance connectivity, and drive economic growth in the region.

China's development finance model on the approach of traditional donors to international development, particularly in the context of the emergence of the Total Official Support for Sustainable Development (TOSSD) framework proposed by the Organization of Economic Cooperation and Development (OECD). The OECD has introduced the TOSSD framework as a new international statistical framework for monitoring official resources and private finance mobilized by official interventions in support of sustainable development. This framework aims to capture the diverse sources and instruments of development finance, including those associated with emerging providers like China. By and large, China has provided support to countries in Central and Eastern Europe (CEE) in various areas, including environmental protection and sustainable development. China actively implements the 2030 Agenda for Sustainable Development and the Sendai Framework for Disaster Risk Reduction 2015-2030 (Center for International Knowledge on Development, 2023). These frameworks provide guidance for countries to address disaster risks and enhance resilience.

REFERENCES

Baxter, D. (2022, May 12). *Public-Private Partnerships and Sustainable Development Goals*. IDEES. https://revistaidees.cat/en/public-private-partnerships-and-sustainable-development-goals/

Bharti, M. S. (2022a). China's BRI in Central and Eastern European Countries: The Role Of '17+1' Framework for Regional Economic Cooperation. *Athenaeum Polish Political Science Studies*, 76(4), 241–262. doi:10.15804/athena.2022.76.13

Bharti, M. S. (2022b). The Economic Integration of the Central and Eastern European Countries into the European Union: Special Reference to Regional Development. *Copernicus Political and Legal Studies*, 1(2), 11–23. https://doi.org/doi.org/10.15804/CPLS.20222.01

Bharti, M. S. (2023a). EU's energy policy and assessing Europe's spiraling energy security crises. In M. S. Ö. Özcan (Ed.), *Analyzing Energy Crises and the Impact of Country Policies on the World* (pp. 101–118). IGI Global. doi:10.4018/979-8-3693-0440-2.ch006

Bharti, M. S. (2023b). Global Development and International Order Transition: The Role of China. In M. O. Dinçsoy & H. Can (Eds.), *Optimizing Energy Efficiency During a Global Energy Crisis* (pp. 200–212). IGI Global. doi:10.4018/979-8-3693-0400-6.ch013

Bharti, M. S. (2023c). The Sustainable Development and Economic Impact of China's Belt and Road Initiative in Ethiopia. *East Asia (Piscataway, N.J.)*, 40(2), 175–194. doi:10.1007/s12140-023-09402-y PMID:37065271

Bharti, M. S. (2024). Impact of Industry 4.0 Technologies for Advancement of Supply Chain Management (SCM) Sustainability. In M. R. Khan, N. R. Khan, & N. Z. Jhanjhi (Eds.), *Convergence of Industry 4.0 and Supply Chain Sustainability* (1st ed., pp. 157–175). IGI Global. doi:10.4018/979-8-3693-1363-3.ch007

Brattberg, E. (2020, February 19). *The EU and China in 2020: More Competition Ahead*. Carnegie. https://carnegieendowment.org/2020/02/19/eu-and-china-in-2020-more-competition-ahead-pub-81096

Casady, C. B., Eriksson, K., Levitt, R. E., & Scott, W. R. (2020). (Re)defining public-private partnerships (PPPs) in the new public governance (NPG) paradigm: An institutional maturity perspective. *Public Management Review*, 22(2), 161–183. doi:10.1080/14719037.2019.1577909

CCICED. (2020, September). *Green BRI and 2030 Agenda for Sustainable Development*. BU. https://www.bu.edu/gdp/files/2020/09/SPS-4-1-Green-BRI-and-2020-Agenda-for-Sustainable-Development.pdf

Center for International Knowledge on Development. (2023, September). *China's Progress Report on Implementation of the 2030 Agenda for Sustainable Development*. MFA. https://www.mfa.gov.cn/eng/topics_665678/2030kcxfzyc/202310/P020231018367257234614.pdf

China Council for International Cooperation on Environment and Development (CCICED) Secretariat. (2022). Green BRI and 2030 Agenda for Sustainable Development. In Green Consensus and High-Quality Development (pp. 375–445). Springer Singapore. doi:10.1007/978-981-16-4799-4_8

Coenen, J., Bager, S., Meyfroidt, P., Newig, J., & Challies, E. (2021). Environmental Governance of China's Belt and Road Initiative. *Environmental Policy and Governance*, 31(1), 3–17. doi:10.1002/eet.1901

Delamotte, G. (2020). Dealing with China: A European Perspective. *Asia-Pacific Review*, *27*(2), 109–123. doi:10.1080/13439006.2020.1826681

Dinwiddie, A. N. (2020). China's Belt and Road Initiative: An Examination of Project Financing Issues and Alternatives. *Brooklyn Journal of International Law*, *45*(2), 745–776.

Dong, L., Yang, X., & Li, H. (2018). The Belt and Road Initiative and the 2030 Agenda for Sustainable Development: Seeking linkages for global environmental governance. *Zhongguo Renkou Ziyuan Yu Huanjing*, *16*(3), 203–210. doi:10.1080/10042857.2018.1487745

Garlick, J. (2019). China's Economic Diplomacy in Central and Eastern Europe: A Case of Offensive Mercantilism? *Europe-Asia Studies*, *71*(8), 1390–1414. doi:10.1080/09668136.2019.1648764

Gaspers, J. (2018, March 2). Divide and Rule. *Berlin Policy Journal*. https://berlinpolicyjournal.com/divide-and-rule/

Gruebler, J. (2020, August). *The People's Republic of China Connecting Europe?* Asian Development Bank Institute. https://www.adb.org/sites/default/files/publication/634751/adbi-wp1178.pdf

Gruebler, J. (2021). China connecting Europe? *Asia Europe Journal*, *19*(1), 77–101. doi:10.1007/s10308-021-00616-4 PMID:34248452

Guo, J., Del Barrio Álvarez, D., Yuan, J., & Kato, H. (n.d.). Determinants of the formation process in public-private partnership projects in developing countries: Evidence from China. *Local Government Studies*, 1–24. doi:10.1080/03003930.2023.2198221

Herrero, A. G., & Xu, J. (2017). China's Belt and Road Initiative: Can Europe Expect Trade Gains? *China & World Economy*, *25*(6), 84–99. doi:10.1111/cwe.12222

Hodge, G. A., & Greve, C. (2007). Public–Private Partnerships: An International Performance Review. *Public Administration Review*, *67*(3), 545–558. doi:10.1111/j.1540-6210.2007.00736.x

Hong, P. (2016). Jointly Building the 'Belt and Road' towards the Sustainable Development Goals. Department of Economic and Social Affairs, United Nations. https:// ssrn.com/abstract =2812893

Horvath, B. (2016). *Identifying Development Dividends along the Belt and Road Initiative*. UNDP. https://www.undp.org/sites/g/files/zskgke326/files/migration/cn/139e87df8c74c6731e5da60079ce6c88d59e7fe6e5282c3a8f4c472955315493.pdf

Jensen, N. M., & Malesky, E. J. (2018). Incentives to Pander: How politicians Use Corporate Welfare for Political Gain. In N. M. Jensen & E. J. Malesky (Eds.), *Incentives to Pander: How Politicians Use Corporate Welfare for Political Gain* (pp. v–v). Cambridge University Press. https://www.cambridge.org/core/product/8AF81E7336F02EA245DFC3684F20E98F doi:10.1017/9781108292337

Jin, L. (2018). Synergies between the Belt and Road Initiative and the 2030 SDGs: From the perspective of development. *Economic and Political Studies*, *6*(3), 278–292. doi:10.1080/20954816.2018.1498990

Kort, I., Verweij, S., & Klijn, E.-H. (2015). In search for effective public-private partnerships: An assessment of the impact of organizational form and managerial strategies in urban regeneration partnerships using fsQCA. *Environment and Planning. C, Government & Policy*, *34*(5), 777–794. doi:10.1177/0263774X15614674

Kundu, T., & Sheu, J.-B. (2019). Analyzing the effect of government subsidy on shippers' mode switching behavior in the Belt and Road strategic context. *Transportation Research Part E, Logistics and Transportation Review, 129*, 175–202. doi:10.1016/j.tre.2019.08.007

Liu, H., Xu, Y., & Fan, X. (2020, June 29). *Development finance with Chinese characteristics: financing the Belt and Road Initiative*. RBPI. https://www.redalyc.org/journal/358/35863121008/html/#B6

Mingyang, T., & Yeping, Y. (2024, January 31). China-Europe freight trains under BRI stabilize transport amid Red Sea tensions. *Global Times*. https://www.globaltimes.cn/page/202401/1306453.shtml#:~:text=China%2DEurope%20freight%20trains%20under%20the%20Belt%20and%20Road%20Initiative,cargo%20space%20on%20the%20trains

Ping, H., & Zuokui, L. (2017). *How the 16+1 Cooperation promotes the Belt and Road Initiative*. SHA. https://sha.static.vipsite.cn/media/thinktank/attachments/0127811c10d2e4b9c9090b6240f73362.pdf

Provan, K. G., & Milward, H. B. (1995). A Preliminary Theory of Interorganizational Network Effectiveness: A Comparative Study of Four Community Mental Health Systems. *Administrative Science Quarterly, 40*(1), 1–33. doi:10.2307/2393698

Renwick, N., Gu, J., & Gong, S. (2018, September). *The impact of BRI investment in infrastructure on achieving the Sustainable Development Goals*. Assets Publishing. https://assets.publishing.service.gov.uk/media/5be9560ced915d6a166edb35/K4D_Helpdesk_BRI_REPORT_2018_final.pdf

Rosell, J., & Saz-Carranza, A. (2020). Determinants of public–private partnership policies. *Public Management Review, 22*(8), 1171–1190. doi:10.1080/14719037.2019.1619816

Smotrytska, M. (2020, October 1). *Belt and Road in Central and East Europe: Roads of opportunities*. Modern Diplomacy. https://moderndiplomacy.eu/2020/10/01/belt-and-road-in-central-and-east-europe-roads-of-opportunities/

Steijn, B., Klijn, E.-H., & Edelenbos, J. (2011). Public Private Partnerships: Added Value by Organizational from OR Management? *Public Administration, 89*(4), 1235–1252. doi:10.1111/j.1467-9299.2010.01877.x

van den Hurk, M., Brogaard, L., Lember, V., Helby Petersen, O., & Witz, P. (2016). National Varieties of Public–Private Partnerships (PPPs): A Comparative Analysis of PPP-Supporting Units in 19 European Countries. *Journal of Comparative Policy Analysis, 18*(1), 1–20. doi:10.1080/13876988.2015.1006814

Wang, H., Sun, X., & Shi, Y. (2024). Commercial investment in public–private partnerships: The impact of government characteristics. *Local Government Studies, 50*(1), 230–260. doi:10.1080/03003930.2023.2198217

Wang, H., Xiong, W., Wu, G., & Zhu, D. (2018). Public–private partnership in Public Administration discipline: A literature review. *Public Management Review, 20*(2), 293–316. doi:10.1080/14719037.2017.1313445

Yin, W. (2019). Integrating Sustainable Development Goals into the Belt and Road Initiative: Would It Be a New Model for Green and Sustainable Investment? *Sustainability (Basel), 11*(24), 69–91. doi:10.3390/su11246991

Zeng, J. (2017). Does Europe Matter? The Role of Europe in Chinese Narratives of 'One Belt One Road' and 'New Type of Great Power Relations.'. *Journal of Common Market Studies, 55*(5), 1162–1176. doi:10.1111/jcms.12535

Zeng, Y. (2024). Riding the Trojan Horse? EU Accession and Chinese Investment in CEE Countries. *Journal of Contemporary China, 33*(147), 486–501. doi:10.1080/10670564.2023.2196507

ADDITIONAL READING

Adarov, A., Gruebler, J., & Holzner, M. (2018). What does China's Belt and Road Initiative mean for CESEE and how should the EU respond? In *WIIW Forecast Report*. Vienna: WIIW. https://wiiw.ac.at/p-4644.html

Brînză, A. (2018, March 20). Redefining the Belt and Road Initiative: The BRI is not about physical routes in Eurasia. It is a global strategy. *The Diplomat*. https://thediplomat.com/2018/03/redefining-the-belt-and-road-initiative/

Chance, A. (2017, October 31). The Belt and Road Initiative and the future of globalization: Xi Jinping's signature policy is about more than just infrastructure. *The Diplomat*. https://thediplomat.com/2017/10/the-belt-and-road-initiative-andthe-future-of-globalization/

Clarke, M. (2017, July). The Belt and Road Initiative: China's new grand strategy? Asia Policy. *National Bureau of Asian Research, 24*(1), 71–79. doi:10.1353/asp.2017.0023

García-Herrero, A., & Xu, J. (2017). China's Belt and Road Initiative: Can Europe expect trade gains? *China & World Economy, 25*(6), 84–99. doi:10.1111/cwe.12222

Hurley, J., Morris, S., & Portelance, G. (2019). Examining the debt implications of the Belt and Road Initiative from a policy perspective. Journal of Infrastructure. *Policy and Development, 3*(1), 139–175.

Joo, F. (2019). Chinese consortium signs contract for Budapest – Belgrade upgrade. *International Railway Journal.* https://www.railjournal.com/regions/ europe/budapest-belgrade-upgrade-contract-signed/

Pavlićević, D. (2019). Structural power and the China–EU–Western Balkans triangular relations. *Asia Europe Journal, 17*(4), 453–468. doi:10.1007/s10308-019-00566-y

Ralev, R. (2018). China offers 18-yr loan to Hungary for overhaul of rail link to Serbia. *SeeNews*. https://seenews.com/news/china-offers-18-yr-loan-tohungary-for-overhaul-of-rail-link-to-serbia-597483

Wolff, P. (2016). *China's "Belt and Road" Initiative – challenges and opportunities (Report Prepared For the Annual Meeting of The Asian Development Bank)*. Bonn: German Development Institute / Deutsches Institut für Entwicklungspolitik (DIE).

Xinhua. (2018a, June 14). UN official stresses links between China's Belt and Road Initiative and UN's 2030 Agenda. *People's Daily Online*. http://en.people.cn/n3/2018/0614/c90000-9471123.html

KEY TERMS AND DEFINITIONS

Central and Eastern Europe (CEE): Central and Eastern Europe (CEE) refers to a region in Europe that encompasses countries located between Western Europe and Eastern Europe. While there is no universally agreed-upon definition of CEE, it generally includes countries that were formerly part of the Eastern Bloc during the Cold War, as well as those that underwent political and economic transitions following the collapse of communism in the late 20th century. The region is characterized by its diverse cultural, historical, and geopolitical dynamics. Central and Eastern Europe experienced significant geopolitical shifts during the 20th century, including the partitioning of territories, World War I and II, the rise of communism, and the Cold War division between the Eastern Bloc (led by the Soviet Union) and the Western Bloc (led by the United States).

Public-Private Partnership (PPP): Public-Private Partnership refers to a collaborative arrangement between government entities and private sector organizations to jointly undertake projects or provide public services. PPPs leverage the strengths of both sectors to address infrastructure development, service delivery, and other societal needs while sharing risks, responsibilities, and resources. PPPs represent a collaborative approach to addressing infrastructure needs and delivering public services by leveraging the strengths of both public and private sectors. By sharing risks, resources, and responsibilities, PPPs can enhance efficiency, innovation, and quality in infrastructure development and service delivery while promoting sustainable development and economic growth.

Sustainable Development: Sustainable development is a concept that emphasizes meeting the needs of the present without compromising the ability of future generations to meet their own needs. It encompasses economic, social, and environmental dimensions and seeks to balance economic growth, social equity, and environmental protection to ensure the well-being of current and future generations. Sustainable development aims to achieve a harmonious and equitable balance between economic development, social progress, and environmental protection, while also addressing global challenges such as poverty, inequality, climate change, and biodiversity loss. Sustainable development is a holistic and forward-looking approach to development that seeks to balance economic, social, and environmental priorities to ensure the well-being of current and future generations. It requires transformative changes in policies, practices, and behaviors at all levels to address global challenges and build a more resilient, inclusive, and sustainable future for all.

The Belt and Road Initiative (BRI): The Belt and Road Initiative (BRI), also known as the One Belt One Road (OBOR) initiative, is a global development strategy launched by the Chinese government in the late 2013. The initiative aims to enhance connectivity and cooperation between countries in Asia, Europe, and Africa through infrastructure development, trade facilitation, investment, and people-to-people exchanges. The BRI comprises two main components: the Silk Road Economic Belt and the 21st Century Maritime Silk Road.

Chapter 8
Assessment of Critical Raw Materials by Addressing Sustainable Development Goals Using Fuzzy MCDM Approach

Elifcan Göçmen-Polat
Munzur University, Turkey

ABSTRACT

Critical raw materials (CRMs), constituting the first step of the industry, are vital to meet sustainable development. With increasing digital technology and green transition efforts under the scope of twin transformation, demand for CRMs has increased, and supply interruption is expected in the future. All countries should plan the supply chain of CRMs in the context of the green and digital transition. The sustainable development goals (SDGs) have presented a reference based on sustainability metrics. In the chapter, hesitant-fuzzy analytical hierarchy process-based order preference technique based on similarity to ideal solutions (HF-AHP based TOPSIS) has been developed to evaluate the critical raw materials in the context of sustainability. Most relevant goals with the CRMs are obtained as SDG 1, SDG 3, SDG 5, SDG 6, SDG 7, SDG 8, SDG 9, SDG 11, SDG 17. The findings show how raw materials have important strengths and weaknesses in sustainable development. Policies recommended for the most important CRMs are effective road maps in the context of twin transformation.

INTRODUCTION

The role of critical raw materials (CRMs) is critical in the deployment of zero-carbon and environmentally friendly technologies, contributing to climate balance and human well-being. Raw materials are associated with high expectations for various policy objectives, including greenhouse gas reduction, energy security, and regional development. Raw materials play an essential role in driving economic growth and prosperity in modern societies, and they are crucial for advancing the Sustainable Development Goals (SDGs) across multiple domains. The SDGs comprise 17 goals aimed at achieving various

Assessment of Critical Raw Materials by Addressing Sustainable Development Goals

Table 1. Strategic goals involving CRMs and SDGs

Strategic Goals		Raw Material Lists	
What percentage of the country's consumption shares will be extracted from its territory?	What percentage of material transactions will take place in the country?	Critical raw material list	Strategic raw material list
What percentage of consumption will be covered by recycling?	What should be the maximum percentage of critical raw materials to be sourced from a single country?		
Circular Economy and Sustainability		**Risk Monitoring and Mitigation**	
Reporting of critical raw materials within the scope of SDGS	Strengthening circularity by including recycling	Strategic partnerships	(friend-shoring) (near-shoring) / Strategic stock

sustainability objectives, including no poverty, zero hunger, good health and well-being, quality education, gender equality, clean water and sanitation, affordable and clean energy decent work and economic growth, industry, innovation and infrastructure, reduced inequality, sustainable cities and communities, responsible consumption and production, climate action, life below water, life on land, peace justice and strong institutions, partnerships for the goals and encompassing a total of 169 sub-goals. The positive and negative implications of raw materials (RMs) are reflected across multiple dimensions of the SDGs. The production of RMs can yield substantial environmental and social detriments, especially within developed nations. However, their utilization in high-tech applications, transportation and energy infrastructure, industrial processes, and medical components underlines their indispensable role in driving economic development and promoting human well-being. While their production may contribute to greenhouse gas emissions, their utilization in renewable energy applications can mitigate climate change. Moreover, the extraction and manufacturing of raw materials may lead to water resource pollution, yet RMs are crucial for the development of green technologies and water purification techniques. While the RM sector positively contributes to the economy through its involvement in foreign trade and employment generation, it also raises concerns due to inadequate working conditions and adverse social impacts. In this context, strategic goals including the relation between the SDGs and CRMs are presented in Table 1.

In the current global landscape, marked by heightened international competition in recent years, all countries have inclined towards formulating strategic plans to maintain their geopolitical influence. Coordinating these strategic plans with the SDGs is necessity for advancing not only economic prosperity but also environmental and social well-being. These raw materials play a pivotal role in enhancing global competitiveness and ensuring the sustainability of the European industry (Theodosopoulos, 2020). The EU produces various solutions against the dependence on imports of these raw materials and the supply risk. In this context, methods such as partial or complete substitution of critical materials and increasing recycling amounts are recommended as solutions (Rizzo et al., 2020). In ensuring sustainable development, trade-offs conducted in the scope of economic growth and issues such as social life and environmental awareness are often overlooked. The fact that sustainable development encompasses various dimensions such as environmental, social, and economic aspects, and that these dimensions require integration with specific sectors, highlights the complexity of achieving sustainability. Therefore, exploring the intersection of interconnected goals, the simultaneous advancement of these goals, and adopting a win-win approach in sustainable development would be the right strategy. Instead of addressing the economic growth target and the clean technology target separately, integrating them under the title defined as the green economy or circular economy can help sustainability efforts. Additionally, critical raw material supply chains need to be considered in the context of environmental, social, and management aspects, in addition to diversification in the supply chain. The issue of raw materials should be addressed to prevent environmental pollution, destruction of nature, carbon emissions, and violations of human rights and labor. While incorporating the contributions of raw materials within the framework of SDGs, cooperation between the public and private sectors should be ensured to overcome obstacles such as insufficient financial and human resources and a lack of awareness of global scenarios. To achieve progress in sustainable development and raw material unity, there is a need to coordinate the efforts of government institutions and sector experts. A strategic partnership approach is required between low- and high-income countries to manage raw material supply processes sustainably. Finally, the extent to which raw materials will affect the SDGs depends on investments in education, scientific, and technological developments, enabled by a result-oriented and accountable system. With globalization and technological developments, supply chains have become much more complex. The sustainable supply chain problem of CRMs under the headings of environmental impacts, resource criticality, and responsible sourcing using life cycle assessment should be evaluated. When assessing the environmental impacts of raw materials, factors such as the deterioration of ecological balance and global warming should be considered. When evaluating resource criticality, global competition, and supply disruptions should be considered, along with natural risks when evaluating responsible sourcing. The chapter responds to the theoretical problem of balancing the use of CRMs with SDGs between globalization and technological progress. It emphasizes the need for integrating economic, social, and environmental considerations for strategic alignment with SDGs to achieve sustainability.

LITERATURE REVIEW

Apart from the industry and government, most researchers in the literature also address the relationship between SDGs and CRMs. Since there has been a new policy change in recent years (Xie et al., 2023) as a transition from a linear economy to a circular economy, the effects of air and water pollution, climate change (Salvi et al., 2023), agriculture and biodiversity, secondary production are evaluated in the context of CRMs. In addition to the mentioned green criteria, price with considerable variability (Torrubia et al., 2023), socio-economic indicators are included in the evaluation of the geostrategic, security, social aspects of CRMs (Leal Filho et al., 2023). Cherepovitsyn et al. (2023) discuss rare earth elements, emphasizing their strategic importance and their potential environmental impacts during extraction. Thus, they recommend key strategies to balance their production processes to achieve the SDGs. Pouresmaieli et al. (2023) conduct a scientometric review of sustainable development, focusing on the negative ecological impacts, as well as the positive economic and social benefits of mining. They concluded that small-scale mining holds significant importance for economies and emphasized the necessity of clear regulations aligned with the principles of sustainable development. Zhou (2023) investigates the necessity of sustainability integration to mining. The author discusses the impacts of mineral resources, methods named criticality assessment, material flow analysis, life cycle analysis, processes of mining, manufacturing, recycling, reusing in the context of sustainability. Pozo-Gonzalo (2023) examines the relationship between metals and SDGs 7 and 13. The findings indicate that SDG 7, which emphasizes clean and affordable energy, and SDG 13, focusing on climate action, are dependent on metals such as lithium, cobalt, and rare earth elements. Fulfilling the demand for these metals necessitates their recovery from secondary resources. Shaikh (2020) evaluates the CRMs chain under the headings of environment effects of CRMs, resource criticality, and responsible sourcing using life cycle assessment. To address the environmental impacts of CRMs, factors such as deterioration of ecological balance and global warming, resource criticality, global competition, supply disruptions, responsible sourcing, terrorism, and natural risks are considered within the context of sustainability. Tamzok (2019) discusses that the mining industry can play an important function in line with sustainable development goals. Therefore, it is considered important to develop a policy framework for this purpose and to ensure that all legal regulations and practices in the industry comply with this framework. This framework is for the Turkish mining industry is defined, based on basic human, moral and scientific principles.

This study is the first to examine the roles of the SDGs in evaluating CRMs using fuzzy decision-making methods. Findings regarding critical raw materials and their connections with the SDGs will be examined through the presented methodology named Hesitant Fuzzy Analytical Hierarchy Process (HF-AHP)-based TOPSIS. Performance criteria of the CRMs related to SDGs are weighted by researchers and experts. Then, TOPSIS is used as a decision-making method to assign alternative raw materials with the shortest distances to the ideal best points and alternatives with the farthest distances to the negative ideal worst points. The most influential CRMs are identified using the rankings of the TOPSIS. Additionally, mapping the roles of the CRMs in the SDG framework is a first in Turkey. CRMs are popular mainly in the context of energy and climate goals. Thus, other roles of CRMs are presented, and negative effects of the CRMs are investigated to be evaluated as opportunities.

CRMs CONTRIBUTE TO SDGs

The strategies and policies developed by the EU regarding CRMs prioritize reducing dependence on CRMs in technologies required for the net zero emission target (such as renewable energy sources, electric motors, and batteries). The increasing demand for green technologies and products is expected to drive demand for CRMs as well (Rietveld et al., 2022). Countries that prioritize investment in production and technology have facilitated the spread of renewable energy and interactive technologies. With the rapid development of green technologies, the protection of the environment and human well-being, construction of a circular economy, and the increasing dependence on strategic raw materials in low-carbon applications, intensive efforts should be made to evaluate raw materials using a comprehensive framework. These efforts should include reducing raw material consumption, promoting recycling and reuse, developing green technologies, and adopting sustainable resource management practices. Wind turbines, solar panels, and electric vehicles are of strategic importance for low-carbon transitions, and green growth is achieved thanks to the strategic raw materials in these low-carbon products. Therefore, the scarcity of these materials affects the green transition, which is important in combating climate change (Pommeret et al., 2022). Based on strategic raw materials, resource availability and sustainability are essential to increase reliance on green resources (Domaracka et al., 2022). Recycling is an essential parameter for raw materials policy as it overcomes supply risks associated with strategic raw materials. Due to the global economy facing rising supply risks of critical raw materials, attention has turned to alternative secondary critical raw materials. For example, alternative reuse applications have been provided in the production of cement and pig iron with the bauxite residues generated in aluminum production. However, since bauxite residues contain significant amounts of valuable elements, benefits such as environmental/animal health, emission reduction, solid waste storage reduction, occupational

Table 2. Relation of SDGs and CRMs

Sustainable Development Goal	Indicator
No poverty	Ratio of raw material foreign trade volume to national income
Zero hunger	Raw material rich soil quality statistics
Good health and well-being	Number of diseases and deaths caused by harmful chemicals from raw materials
Quality education	Raw material training inventory
Gender equality	Number of women/men working in the sector
Clean water and sanitation	Water efficiency, wastewater treatment, rate of CRMs utilized in recycling and reuse technology
Affordable and clean energy	Usage share of CRMs in the energy sector, Renewable energy statistics
Decent work and economic growth	Import dependency ratio, Usage share and added value of raw materials in manufacturing sectors, Market concentration value
Reduced inequality	Projects to improve the regulation and supervision of global raw material markets and institutions
Sustainable cities and communities	Number of electric vehicles that improve air quality for sustainable urbanization
Climate action	Substitution index
Life below water	Marine and coastal ecosystems
Life on land	Number of land works destroyed and corrected in raw material extraction activities
Peace, justice, and strong institutions	Number of non-discriminatory laws and policies for global raw material trade
Partnerships for the goals	Number of multi-stakeholder partnerships

Source: (Polat, 2023).

health, and safety, etc., are obtained rather than economic value gain in the recovery of critical raw materials (Ujaczski et al., 2018). The relationship between SDGs and CRMs is presented in Table 2.

CRMs in SDG-7 and SDG-13

Clean energy issues face challenges such as cost inflation, supply chain bottlenecks and high installation costs in the global markets. However, the clean energy sector is the fastest growing area of global energy investments. How fast clean energy will grow in the coming years and how it will respond to policy and market incentives are expected to differ in three main scenarios. In the first scenario, incentives for clean energy will continue to increase rapidly, reducing costs while expanding financing and investment opportunities for clean energy projects. In this scenario, demand of coal, oil, natural gas will decrease, while clean energy sector will grow rapidly. In the second scenario, policy and market incentives will continue steadily, so that financing and investment opportunities for clean energy projects will increase and the decline in costs will begin to slow. The clean energy sector continues to grow rapidly, but the decline for coal, oil and natural gas demand may be slightly slower. In the third scenario, policy, and market incentives slow or stop, in which financing and investment opportunities for clean energy projects may be limited, and costs may rise. The clean energy sector continues to grow, but this growth may be slower than in other scenarios. It is also thought that the decline in coal, oil and natural gas demand may be slower than other scenarios. These scenarios show how clean energy projects will respond to future growth potential and changes in the energy market. Policy makers, investors and industry leaders should take these scenarios into account and determine their strategies for clean energy projects and shape the future of the sector (IEA, 2023). With the new global energy economy emerging towards clean energy transitions, countries are competing for sustainable growth with both political and economic decisions (Cozzi et al., 2020). The fact that the world public opinion has reached a consensus that the model of economic growth based on fossil fuels is unsustainable, indeed reflects an increase in awareness about the negative effects of climate change and global warming. This awareness draws attention to the importance of green technology by emphasizing the necessity of a new and sustainable economic model, considering the environmental damage caused by energy sources based on fossil fuels and their contribution to climate change. Adopting a low-carbon economy model will not only bring environment benefits but can also bring financial and social benefits. By contributing to the renewable energy, it could open job options and support economic growth. Additionally, energy efficiency and the transition to clean energy sources can increase energy security and reduce energy costs (Yalçın, 2010). Green technology represents an approach that aims to minimize environmental impacts and preserve natural resources. This technology aims to minimize environmental impacts by addressing issues such as environmental sustainability, energy efficiency, waste reduction and renewable energy sources. Some important points regarding the environmental dimension of clean technology are:

- *Energy efficiency*: Green technologies are designed to increase energy efficiency. In this way, energy consumption is reduced, and environmental impacts are minimized.
- *Renewable energy sources*: Renewable energy inputs such as sun, wind, water, and biomass have less environment effects than fossil fuel. Green technologies support environmental sustainability by using these renewable energy sources.
- *Waste reduction and recycling*: Green technologies help reduce waste materials and promote recycling. In this way, depletion of natural resources is prevented, and environmental pollution is reduced.
- *Clean production technologies*: Clean production technologies used in industrial processes minimize environmental impacts by reducing waste and emissions. • Environmentally friendly materials: Green technologies encourage the use of environmentally friendly materials. The production and use of these materials reduces environmental impacts (Qamar et al., 2021).

According to United Nations Population Fund (UNFPA) data, world population would reach 9.7 billion and the world economy will quadruple in 2050. This increase will bring with it negative effects such as high industrial product consumption, loss of biodiversity, and increase in global warming. Countries feel the need to take some precautions against this situation; They signed the Paris Agreement in 2015 and the UN SDGs in the same year. These initiatives aim to minimize the impact of climate change, reduce emissions and limit carbon footprint. To achieve these goals, policies such as increasing renewable energy investments and conversion to green technology have become more important (Hiçyılmaz et al., 2022). The main goals of the transformation to green technology can be listed as reducing increasing carbon emissions, electronic conversion with low energy consumption, and recycling waste electronics into the system. In this way, it will be possible to reduce energy consumption and electronic waste, increase the performance of technological products, provide savings and competitive advantage, and therefore prevent air pollution and reduce the carbon footprint. In addition, there are nuclear energy, hydroelectric energy, and renewable energy sources. For this reason, Turkey and other countries need to take the necessary measures to reduce carbon dioxide emissions. Countries need to turn to renewable energy sources instead of fossil fuels. These measures include investing in these sources, efficient energy implementing policies to minimize carbon emissions, reducing dependence on fossil fuels. In addition, it is important to invest in clean energy sources such as nuclear energy and use these resources effectively (Aydın and Aydoğdu, 2022). There are steps that Turkey also needs to take in this regard. More investments in renewable energy sources across the country, increasing energy efficiency and implementing guidelines to minimize carbon emissions will help Turkey adopt a sustainable approach in the energy sector. As a result, considering the rising energy demand and environmental damage of fossil fuel, all countries, including Turkey, need to turn to renewable energy sources and take measures to reduce carbon emissions. In this way, it will be possible to get rid of fossil fuels that harm the environment, and a sustainable energy policy will be adopted (Kumcu and Özyörük, 2023). It assessed the importance and potential availability of critical raw material deposits for three critical industries in the EU (renewable energy, defense, and aerospace) and proposed measures to alleviate import dependence. Wind turbine generators have been evaluated as the cost-effective technology for EU green energy production, and it has been emphasized that the critical raw materials needed for these technologies are boron, dysprosium, niobium, neodymium, and praseodymium. In addition, by 2025, permanent magnets containing Neodymium-Iron-Boron (NdFeB) are expected to be used in applications such as electric bicycles and electric motors by 90-100%. However, the most suitable raw materials for wind energy are listed as borate, gallium, germanium, indium, and silicon metal (Lewicka, 2021). In their study, Ferro and Bonollo (2019) tried to identify the most suitable raw materials for recycling to reduce the supply risk of critical raw materials. It has been concluded that titanium alloy used in aviation, automotive, medical and chemical industries is the most suitable raw material for recycling, while magnesium is not suitable for recycling (Ferro and Bonollo, 2019) China, which has many critical raw material reserves, was not very active for wind energy until the Renewable Energy Law came into force in 2006. However, it has achieved significant growth in this field by increasing its installed capacity by 166% after 2006 (Yang et al., 2020). In addition, countries such as China, the EU and India have implemented important policies for electric cars on a national scale. These policies are expected to have a strong effect on importance of the lithium mine and its value in the global sector (Hache et al., 2019)

CRMs in SDG-11

David and Koch (2019) focus on data security, surveillance, or the impact of companies on urban development in recent criticisms of smart cities, while also focusing on material foundations of smart city technologies and interconnected resource problems. they brought to the agenda. To reduce this deficiency in the urban planning literature, this study linked the urban planning literature on smart cities with the literature on critical raw material mining and recovery from scrap metals. To explain such problems in the study, the smart city and CRM connection was examined from the perspective of the relevant literature, while referring to the smart city field. Results of the study showed that CRMs are an essential basis for smart city applications.

CRMs in SDG-13

The stages of obtaining ores have negative effects on air, water, and soil emissions. In the study, the technological, economic, and social effects, as well as the environmental effects on human health of the process called metal purification are presented (Ujaczki et al., 2018). In their study on the social effects of mining, Mancinia and Sala (2018) discussed the undesirable impacts of mining processes in high-risk prone. The negative effects of mining activities in high-risk areas have been defined as poor working conditions, child labor, work accidents resulting in death and injuries, poor housing conditions and lack of union activities.

CRMs in SDG-1, SDG-2, SDG-8

To take part in the global market, countries need continuous development in many branches such as economy, technology, industry, communication, and renewable energy. However, with the modernization in the industry, critical raw materials have become vital for many sectors (Erkara, 2023). The need for raw materials is increasing rapidly due to the increasing demand for new technologies in the EU and the rapid economic development of the newly joined countries. However, dependence on China and China's supply restrictions also bring demand imbalance and price instability (Cerny et al., 2021). Problems in the supply of CRMs can have important effects on the economies of countries. This may be due to a variety of factors, including geopolitical risks, export restrictions and trade barriers. Possible supply problems can lead to delays and disruptions in production, which can damage companies' reputation and cause customer loss. At the same time, extending production times may cause delays in product delivery and heavy economic losses (Islam et al., 2019). However, supply risk may cause a decrease in production, especially in sectors dependent on raw materials, and thus demand-driven inflationary pressures (Manberger, 2023).

Karaman (2021) discussed about graphite mineral deposits in Turkey in the context of the country's economy. Bertrand et al. (2006) aimed to minimize the import dependency of CRMs for EU industries. In their academic study in 2021, Konuk et al., discussed the world natural graphite related to economic growth. It is thought that the phosphate enterprise, which was put into operation in the region in the academic studies of Karademir and Bilinir in 2020, can make a great contribution to the development of the region as well as to the unemployment problem in Mazıdağı. In Veral's academic study in 2018, the Circular Economy Package, with an action plan and legal regulation proposal on waste, green and competitive low-carbon economy was investigated. In this study, the strategies of some member countries will be examined by touching on the developments and new measures after the adoption of the Circular Economy Package in the European Union. Jin et al. (2016), emphasized that the World Trade Organization is important in the use of materials for some rare earth elements in defense industries for many industries and country economies. This study includes a good understanding of the current and future potential status of critical raw materials and the measures that can be taken by stakeholders against the critical raw material supply risk. Mancini et al., (2018) conducted a social assessment for the supply chain of CRMs in European Commission report they prepared. They stated that CRMs have a strategic importance to improve the competitiveness of the EU industry. Therefore, the supply of sustainable and safe raw materials from local sources and the international market has been determined as the main goal. For the EU, it has been reported that social risk outcomes as governance indicators used in criticality assessment may be suitable for main assessment of material flow for estimating the social impacts of import dependence or to assess the results in trading.

CRMs in SDG-9, SDG-17

The development in display technologies and the rapid spread of portable electronic devices have caused to a rapid increase of indium demand, which is used extensively in these technologies. However, the demand for cobalt, a component of lithium-ion batteries, has increased due to the development of technologies such as mobile phones and laptops (Tercero, 2019). As is known, critical raw materials are indispensable components, especially in the production of high-tech products. The rapid increase in the world population and the increase in living standards along with technological developments cause an increase in demand for high-tech products, and therefore the demand for critical raw materials is increasing rapidly (Michal and Zuzana, 2021). In the Industrial and Technology Strategy Report published by the Ministry of Industry and Trade, the strategy components are grouped under 5 headings: high-technology, digital transition, entrepreneurship, human capital, and infrastructure. It is planned to determine technological competencies and sectoral road maps with high technology and innovation, and to develop strategic materials for priority sectors. These main sectors are listed as follows:

- Chemical
- Pharmaceutical and medical device
- Motor land vehicles
- Rail systems
- Machine
- Defense
- Designated as aviation and space.

Electric vehicles, robotic applications, sensors, armor, wearable technology, renewable energy, and unmanned aerial vehicles have been determined as priority sectors, and it is planned to produce the raw materials needed by these sectors from existing resources or to develop them as new high-performance materials as a result of R&D studies. In addition, it is planned to assign universities to develop alternatives for strategic minerals and materials and to encourage industrial collaborations. R&D, ecosystem understanding, and centers of excellence, research and development studies are aimed to be result-oriented, with the principle of pre-competitive cooperation with stakeholders, when necessary, focused on high technology and independent of location. Active Participation in the Development of Technology Standards, Test Centre and Certification: It is aimed to ensure proactive participation in international studies by preparing the necessary regulations in areas where international legislation will direct the emerging markets, such as 5G, robots and autonomous vehicles (2023 Industry strategy document, 2019).

By addressing the SDG17, EU countries make strategic collaborations to meet these raw material needs with a secure supply chain and try to reduce the supply risk for critical raw material needs through economic agreements (Demirtaş et al., 2017).

MATERIAL AND METHOD

In this section, we introduce the HF-AHP methodology, which stands for Hesitant Fuzzy Analytical Hierarchy Process, to evaluate the subheadings of the SDGs. HF-AHP employs Hesitant Fuzzy Sets (HFS) and Linguistic Sets to determine the criterion weights, leveraging decision maker preferences to

Assessment of Critical Raw Materials by Addressing Sustainable Development Goals

assign these weights effectively. The rationale behind selecting HF-AHP lies in its ability to accommodate hesitant decisions often encountered among experts in the field. Subsequently, TOPSIS is employed to rank CRMs based on the obtained criteria weights. The selection of five experts is based on their extensive expertise in CRMs and their involvement in coordinating CRM projects within the university. These experts bring a wealth of knowledge and experience, ensuring a comprehensive and insightful assessment of the SDG subheadings pertaining to CRMs.

The raw material foreign trade volume (SDG 1), number of diseases and deaths caused by harmful chemicals from raw materials (SDG 3), number of women/men working in the sector (SDG 5), ratio of raw materials used in water efficiency (SDG 6), usage share of raw materials in the energy sector (SDG 7), import dependency ratio (SDG 8), added value of raw materials in manufacturing sectors (SDG 9), number of electric vehicles for sustainable urbanization (SDG 11), number of multi-stakeholder partnerships (SDG 17) were evaluated under the SDG headings.

HF-AHP

To decide the weights, HF-AHP is utilized. This method is used to determine the criteria weight including Hesitant Fuzzy Sets (HFS) and Hesitant Fuzzy Linguistic Expression Sets (HF-LS) and F-AHP. In this process, linguistic terms are defined, D= [D0, D1,..., Dn) (Step 1) and then used for binary comparisons of dimensions (Step 2). Data envelopes are generated for these comparisons, env[dij] (Step 3), which are then tabulated with corresponding triangular fuzzy numbers (TFNs) (Step 4), data envelopes env[dij] are converted to data envelopes (Step 5), these TFNs are calculated to find the mean of each criterion i (Step 6), geometric mean for each criterion i, $r_i = \left(\sum_{j=1}^{n} d_{ij}\right)^{1/n}$ i= 1,2,...,n (Step 7), followed by the calculation of fuzzy weights for each criterion, $w_i = r_i \otimes (r_1 \otimes r_2 \otimes .. \otimes r_n)^{-1} = (lw_i, mw_i, uw_i)$, (Step 8). The FNs are clarified using the area center method, $M_i = \frac{lw_i + mw_i + uw_i}{3}$, (Step 9) and then normalized to calculate each criterion's weight, $N_i = \frac{M_i}{\sum_{i=1}^{n} M_i}$, (Step 10). These steps systematically convert linguistic definitions into fuzzy weights, facilitating decision-making in uncertain environments (Göçmen, 2021).

TOPSIS

TOPSIS (Technique for Order of Preference by Similarity to Ideal Solution), which is a decision-making approach introduced by Chen and Hwang in 1992, is used for ranking the CRMs to prioritize their importance in the context of the sustainability. This method suggests assigning options based on their proximity to the ideal solution, considering the shortest distances as ideal and the farthest distances as negative ideal. However, it does not account for the relative importance of distances, as noted by Oprivicić and Tzeng in 2004. TOPSIS offers several advantages, including its straightforward mathematical logic,

Figure 1. TOPSIS method algorithm
(Sánchez-Lozano et al, 2013)

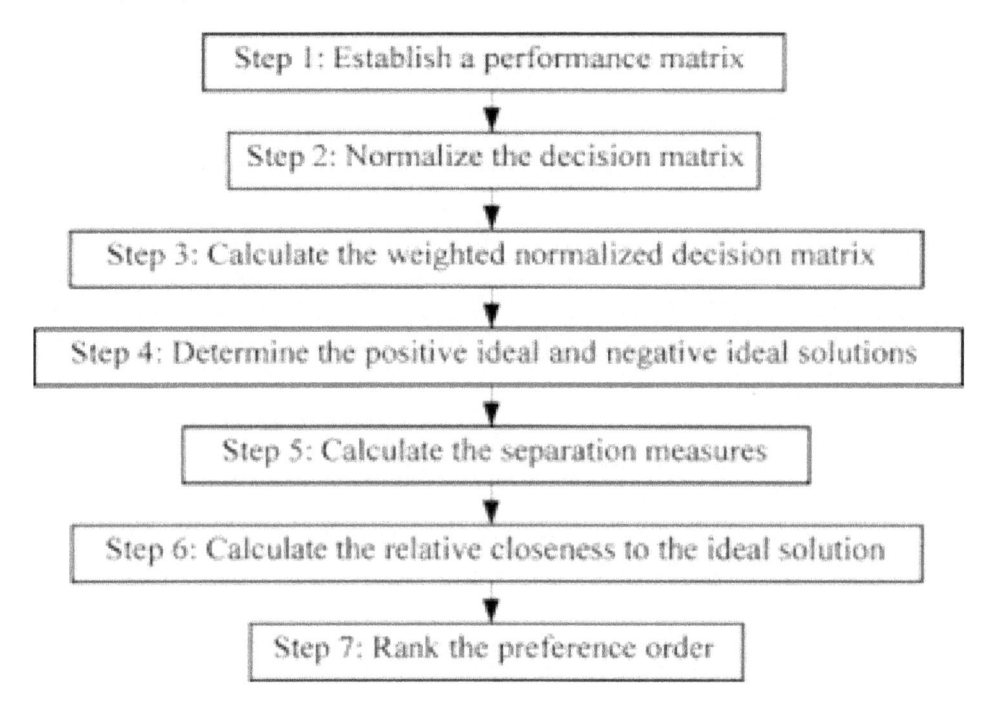

```
Step 1: Establish a performance matrix
        ↓
Step 2: Normalize the decision matrix
        ↓
Step 3: Calculate the weighted normalized decision matrix
        ↓
Step 4: Determine the positive ideal and negative ideal solutions
        ↓
Step 5: Calculate the separation measures
        ↓
Step 6: Calculate the relative closeness to the ideal solution
        ↓
Step 7: Rank the preference order
```

fast determination of optimal alternatives, and incorporation of relative criteria weights, as highlighted by Wang et al. in 2018. The steps of this methodology are illustrated in Figure 1.

RESULT

In this section, the integrated methodology is presented to evaluate the CRMs associated with the SDGs. The findings can be used to form the CRM lists. Despite the literature reviews use the only two criteria to assess the CRM lists, this study provides the importance of the various criteria. Here, results of HF-AHP method are obtained via similar scoring of the decision makers. The results are obtained using the steps of the presented methodology:

Step 1: Linguistic expressions are presented as:

S = {Equally Important [EQ], Weakly Important [WI], Strongly Important [SI], Very Strongly Important [VSI], Absolutely Important [AI]}. These sets are formed due to the expert's hesitant decisions.

Step 2: In this step, five decision makers compare the dimensions shown in Table 1. Experts have some hesitancy to provide their decisions through dimensions. For instance, first decision maker decides the SDG9 is more strongly important than SDG3 while the other decides as very strongly important (Table 3).

Step 3: Generating data envelopes of dimension expressions is demonstrated in Table 3. For example, Expert 1 defines the SDG9 is weakly important [WI] than SDG8 while the other expert defines as strongly important [SI].

Step 4: Linguistic definitions, corresponding and inverse TFNs are demonstrated in Table 4.

And finally, de-fuzzified and normalized weights of the criteria are provided in Table 5.

Assessment of Critical Raw Materials by Addressing Sustainable Development Goals

Table 3. An instance for pairwise comparison

AI	VSI	SI	WI	Dimension	EQ	Dimension	WI	SI	VSI	AI
	✓	✓		SDG9		SDG3				
				SDG6		SDG7	✓	✓		
		✓	✓	SDG8		SDG16				

Table 4. The envelope of linguistic terms

Dimension	SDG9	SDG8	SDG7	SDG11	SDG17	SDG3	SDG1	SDG5	SDG6
SDG9	[EQ]	[WI, SI]	[VSI]	[VSI]	[VSI]	[VSI]	[VSI]	[VSI]	[VSI]
SDG8	-	[EQ]	[SI]	[SI]	[WI]	[VSI]	[SI]	[VSI]	[VSI]
SDG7	-	-	[EQ]	[WI,SI]	-	[WI, SI]	[WI, SI]	[WI]	[WI,SI]
SDG11	-	-	-	[EQ]	-	[WI]	[WI]	[WI]	[WI]
SDG17	-	-	[SI]	[VSI]	[EQ]	[VSI]	[WI]	[VSI,SI]	[VSI]
SDG3	-	-	-	-	-	[EQ]	-	-	-
SDG1	-	-	-	-	-	[SI,VSI]	[EQ]	[WI,SI]	[WI]
SDG5	-	-	-	-	-	[WI]	-	[EQ]	[WI]
SDG6	-	-	-	-	-	[WI]	-	-	[EQ]

The table provides a comparison of the dimensions based on their de-fuzzified and normalized weights. The dimension, namely SDG9 with the highest normalized weight indicates its relative importance. SDG 9, focusing on industry, innovation, is linked to CRMs due to their vital role in the industrial applications such as production of high-tech goods, and with the global population growth, rising living standards, and technological progress. The demand for such materials is escalating rapidly.

In Figure 2, rare earth elements are ranked first due to their utilization in clean technologies and their significance in driving economic growth and fostering technological innovation. Additionally, lithium and nickel, essential elements in green technologies, are identified as important CRMs. The chart also demonstrates the criticality of these raw materials, with high-ranked materials being associated with SDGs 7-8-9-17 objectives. Rare earth elements are critical to achieving SDGs 7, 8, 9, and 17 by supporting the development of clean energy technologies, fostering economic growth and industrialization,

Table 5. Expressions with corresponding TFNs

Linguistic terms	TFN	Inverse TFN
Equally Important [EQ]	(1, 1, 1)	(1, 1, 1)
Weakly Important [WI]	(2, 3, 4)	(1/4, 1/3, 1/2)
Strongly Important [SI]	(4, 5, 6)	(1/6, 1/5, 1/4)
Very Strongly Important [VSI]	(6, 7, 8)	(1/8, 1/7, 1/6)
Absolutely Important [AI]}	(9, 9, 9)	(1/9, 1/9, 1/9)

Table 6. De-fuzzified (Mi) and normalized (Ni) relative weights of criteria

Dimension	M_i	N_i
SDG9	0.456	0.448
SDG8	0.376	0.370
SDG7	0.087	0.084
SDG11	0.047	0.045
SDG17	0.185	0.179
SDG3	0.028	0.027
SDG1	0.052	0.050
SDG5	0.033	0.031
SDG6	0.022	0.021

and facilitating global partnerships for sustainable development. The digital and green transitions in the coming years necessitate the availability of these raw materials.

DISCUSSIONS

Discussions of the SDGs obtained with high weights in relation to CRMs is summarized below:

SDG1-In many countries, growth and development of the raw material sector is the determinant of getting rid of poverty. Its utilization as input across various sectors fundamental to the country's economy, along with its contribution to foreign trade, reveals the significance of raw materials as a pivotal parameter affecting poverty within the nation. The raw materials sector has the potential to stimulate local economies, generate employment opportunities, and increase incomes and trade volumes. Value added and employment within raw material sector can be regarded as key indicators.

SDG3- CRMs utilized in the medical sector play a vital role in enhancing human well-being. For instance, tantalum is employed in prosthetic tools, while niobium and titanium are utilized in the magnetic coils of resonance imaging devices. Conversely, negative indicators include increased incidences of cancer resulting from cobalt sulfate inhalation and radiation exposure attributed to uranium.

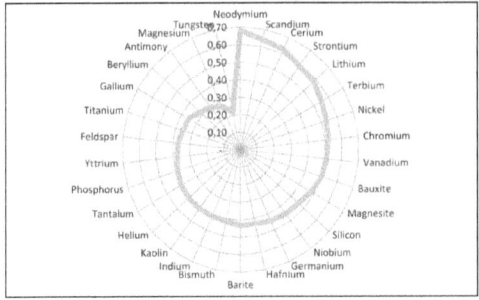

Figure 2. TOPSIS scores for CRMs

SDG5- The issue of gender equality cannot be found in raw material-related studies. However, social, economic, and political inequalities created by gender discrimination can disrupt the achievement of economy, decent work, education, health, and decision-making goals. Female participation in large-scale mining remains notably low. The prevalence of initiatives aimed at enhancing women's involvement can serve as a pivotal indicator in this regard.

SDG6- Mining activities, mineral extraction, ore processing, and similar processes contribute to the release of pollutants into water, soil, and air. These pollutants and hazardous substances have adverse effects on water quality, potentially leading to toxicity and contaminating groundwater supplies through leaks.

SDG7-Due to Turkey's increasing focus on renewable energy and green technologies, the demand and supply gap for these materials is expected to increase exponentially. To address the challenges posed by this transition, policies need to be formulated to fulfill future demands for these materials. Strategic raw material supplies are at risk in connection with green technologies involving large amounts of raw materials.

SDG-8- The rising of innovative technologies, population increasing, and changing resource control models will increase the demand for CRMs in the coming years. Rising concerns increase the importance of critical raw materials effective in economic growth (Polat et al., 2023). A green strategy centered on raw materials facilitates the transition from a linear economy to a green circular economy. Consequently, strategic material provisions are imperative for Turkey's green transition, ensuring fulfillment of the demand for these materials. It is imperative to explore investments in raw material substitution to mitigate potential shortages.

SDG11- It is crucial to mitigate adverse environmental impacts by placing particular emphasis on air quality and waste management. Particles emitted into the air during raw material recycling and the volume of electronic device waste, containing strategic raw materials, serve as significant indicators. The number of electric vehicles can be given as an indicator that can be evaluated positively. Electric vehicles, which incorporate materials sourced from lithium and cobalt mines, contribute to the establishment of sustainable cities by enhancing air quality through reduced emissions.

SDG17- The raw material dilemma can be addressed through a game theory approach, wherein producer and consumer nations engage in cooperation or confrontation. Producer countries employ power strategies concerning their raw materials, while consumer nations implement impact strategies via waste recycling and efficient resource utilization. Consequently, policies for raw material cooperation should be devised between nations. Key indicators within the domain of raw materials may include the number of cooperation agreements and programs established with countries boasting intensive raw material production. Additionally, fostering and supporting partnerships among public, public-private, and non-governmental entities in formulating raw material policies is essential.

CONCLUSION

The rapid population growth, increased demand for technological knowledge and products, and rising consumption patterns have propelled countries into a competitive race, both domestically and in the global market. This technological knowledge-based competition has led countries to prioritize the effective utilization of existing raw materials and the identification and procurement of industrially critical raw materials. In this race, countries encounter challenges such as the risk of access to raw materials, supply crises with nations possessing these resources, environmental impacts, import dependency, supply risks, and trade restrictions (Şahin, 2011). Critical raw materials (CRMs) are indispensable for countries' development and growth objectives, yet their supply is often jeopardized by geopolitical factors and environmental concerns (Filho et al., 2023). By addressing the SDGs, rare earth elements are obtained as the most related materials used in the clean technologies and the economic growth. SDGs 7,8,9, and SDG 17 are particularly intertwined with CRMs, with parameters such as the energy sector, import dependency, value addition in manufacturing sectors, and multi-stakeholder partnerships being closely associated with CRMs.

Future studies should assess CRMs in conjunction with other SDG objectives. Notably, reducing inequalities and promoting gender equality are critical aspects within the mining sector. Furthermore, quality education forms the foundation of the mining sector's value chain. State-of-the-art applications-based supply chain planning, incorporating security and safety considerations (Göçmen, 2021), along with leveraging big data through popular machine learning methods, could enhance the evaluation of CRMs and their alignment with SDGs.

REFERENCES

Aydın, S. G., & Aydoğdu, G. (2022). Makine öğrenmesi algoritmaları kullanılarak Türkiye ve AB ülkelerinin CO2 emisyonlarının tahmini. *Avrupa Bilim ve Teknoloji Dergisi*, (37), 42–46.

Bertrand, G., Cassard, D., Arvanitidis, N., & Stanley, G. (2016). Map of critical raw material deposits in Europe. *Energy Procedia*, 97, 44–50. doi:10.1016/j.egypro.2016.10.016

Černý, I., Vaněk, M., Maruszewska, E. W., & Beneš, F. (2021). How economic indicators impact the EU internal demand for critical raw materials. *Resources Policy*, 74, 102417. doi:10.1016/j.resourpol.2021.102417

Chen, S. J., & Hwang, C. L. (1992). Fuzzy multiple attribute decision making methods. In *Fuzzy multiple attribute decision making* (pp. 289–486). Springer. doi:10.1007/978-3-642-46768-4_5

Cherepovitsyn, A., Solovyova, V., & Dmitrieva, D. (2023). New challenges for the sustainable development of the rare-earth metals sector in Russia: Transforming industrial policies. *Resources Policy*, 81, 103347. doi:10.1016/j.resourpol.2023.103347

Cozzi, L., Gould, T., Bouckart, S., Crow, D., Kim, T. Y., McGlade, C., & Wetzel, D. (2020). *World energy outlook 2020*. International Energy Agency.

David, M., & Koch, F. (2019). "Akıllı, yeterince akıllı değil!" Akıllı şehir konseptlerinde kritik hammadde kullanımının öngörülmesi: Akıllı şebeke örneği. *Sürdürülebilirlik*, 11(16), 4422.

Demirtaş, M., Turan, A., Car, E., & Yücel, O. (2017). Kritik Hammaddeler. *Metalurji ve Malzeme Mühendisleri Odası Dergisi*, 183, 28–33.

Domaracka, L., Matuskova, S., Tausova, M., Senova, A., & Kowal, B. (2022). Efficient Use of Critical Raw Materials for Optimal Resource Management in EU Countries. *Sustainability (Basel)*, 14(11), 6554. doi:10.3390/su14116554

Erkara, E. (2023). Kritik Malzemeler ve Arz Riski Yaratan Faktörler. İklim değişikliği ekonomisi çalıştayı. Eskişehir.

Ferro, P., & Bonollo, F. (2019). Design for recycling in a critical raw materials perspective. *Recycling*, *4*(4), 44. doi:10.3390/recycling4040044

Filho, W. L., Kotter, R., Özuyar, P. G., Abubakar, I. R., Eustachio, J. H. P. P., & Matandirotya, N. R. (2023). Understanding Rare Earth Elements as Critical Raw Materials. *Sustainability (Basel)*, *15*(3), 1919. doi:10.3390/su15031919

Göçmen, E. (2021). A maturity model for assessing sustainable project management knowledge areas: A case study within a logistics firm. *Journal of Advanced Research in Natural and Applied Sciences*, *7*(4), 536–555. doi:10.28979/jarnas.958605

Göçmen, E. (2021). Smart airport: Evaluation of performance standards and technologies for a smart logistics zone. *Transportation Research Record: Journal of the Transportation Research Board*, *2675*(7), 480–490. doi:10.1177/03611981211019740

Hache, E., Seck, G. S., Simoen, M., Bonnet, C., & Carcanague, S. (2019). Critical raw materials and transportation sector electrification: A detailed bottom-up analysis in world transport. *Applied Energy*, *240*, 6–25. doi:10.1016/j.apenergy.2019.02.057

Hiçyılmaz, B. (2022). Avrupa Birliği Kritik Hammaddeler Yasası. İklim değişikliği ekonomisi çalıştayı. Eskişehir.

IEA. (2023), *World Energy Outlook 2023*. IEA, Paris https://www.iea.org/reports/world-energy-outlook-2023, License: CC BY 4.0 (report); CC BY NC SA 4.0 (Annex A)

Islam, M. A., Rashed, C. A. A., & Hasan, J. (2019). Raw Materials Shortage and Their Impact on the Manufacturing Business-an Empirical Study in the Pharmaceutical Sector of Bangladesh. *Review of General Management*, *29*(2).

Karademir, Ö. Ü. N., & Bilinir, A. G. Ş. (2020). *Mazidaği (Mardin)'daki Fosfat Madeninin Sosyo-Ekonomik Etkileri.*

Karaman, M. (2021). Grafit Cevherleşmelerinin Sentinel-2 Uydu Görüntülerinden Belirlenmesinde En Uygun Bant Kombinasyonları. *Avrupa Bilim ve Teknoloji Dergisi*, (25), 749–757. doi:10.31590/ejosat.945779

Konuk, A., Gürsoy, Y. H., & Hakan, A. K. (2021). Doğal Grafit İhracatı Yoğunlaşmasının Ekonomik Büyüme Üzerindeki Etkisi. *Eskişehir Osmangazi Üniversitesi Mühendislik ve Mimarlık Fakültesi Dergisi*, *29*(3), 316–327. doi:10.31796/ogummf.964124

Kumcu, S., & Özyörük, B. (2023). Sürdürülebilir yeşil bir kalkınma için salınan karbonun yakalanması, depolanması ve kullanımına yönelik bir araştırma. *Niğde Ömer Halisdemir Üniversitesi Mühendislik Bilimleri Dergisi*, *12*(2), 386–394.

Leal Filho, W., Kotter, R., Özuyar, P. G., Abubakar, I. R., Eustachio, J. H. P. P., & Matandirotya, N. R. (2023). Understanding Rare Earth Elements as Critical Raw Materials. *Sustainability (Basel)*, *15*(3), 1919. doi:10.3390/su15031919

Lewicka, E., Guzik, K., & Galos, K. (2021). On the possibilities of critical raw materials production from the EU's primary sources. *Resources*, *10*(5), 50. doi:10.3390/resources10050050

Manberger, A. (2023). Critical Raw Material Supply Matters and the Potential of the Circular Economy to Contribute to Security. *Inter Economics*, *58*(2), 74–78. doi:10.2478/ie-2023-0016

Mancini, L., Eynard, U., Eisfeldt, F., Ciroth, A., Blengini, G., & Pennington, D. (2018). Social assessment of raw materials supply chains. *A life-cycle-based analysis*. Luxemburg.

Mancini, L., & Sala, S. (2018). Social impact assessment in the mining sector: Review and comparison of indicators frameworks. *Resources Policy*, *57*, 98–111. doi:10.1016/j.resourpol.2018.02.002

Michal, C., & Zuzana, Š. (2021). Critical raw materials as a part of sustainable development. *Multidiszciplináris Tudományok*, *11*(5), 12–23. doi:10.35925/j.multi.2021.5.2

Opricovic, S., & Tzeng, G. H. (2004). Compromise solution by MCDM methods: A comparative analysis of VIKOR and TOPSIS. *European Journal of Operational Research*, *156*(2), 445–455. doi:10.1016/S0377-2217(03)00020-1

Polat, E. G., Yücesan, M., & Gül, M. (2023). A comparative framework for criticality assessment of strategic raw materials in Turkey. *Resources Policy*, *82*, 103511. doi:10.1016/j.resourpol.2023.103511

Pommeret, A., Ricci, F., & Schubert, K. (2022). Critical raw materials for the energy transition. *European Economic Review*, *141*, 103991. doi:10.1016/j.euroecorev.2021.103991

Pouresmaieli, M., Ataei, M., & Qarahasanlou, A. N. (2023). A scientometrics view on sustainable development in surface mining: Everything from the beginning. *Resources Policy*, *82*, 103410. doi:10.1016/j.resourpol.2023.103410

Pozo-Gonzalo, C. (2023). UN Sustainable Development Goals 7 and 13. How sustainable are the metals in our journey to clean energy storage? *RSC Sustainability*, *1*(4), 662–664. doi:10.1039/D3SU90020G

Qamar, M. Z., Ali, W., Qamar, M. O., & Noor, M. (2021). Green technology and its implications worldwide. *The Inquisitive Meridian*, *3*, 1–11.

Rietveld, E., Bastein, T., van Leeuwen, T., Wieclawska, S., Bonenkamp, N., Peck, D., & Poitiers, N. (2022). *Strengthening the security of supply of products containing Critical Raw Materials for the green transition and decarbonisation*. European Parliament.

Rizzo, A., Goel, S., Luisa Grilli, M., Iglesias, R., Jaworska, L., Lapkovskis, V., Novak, P., Postolnyi, B. O., & Valerini, D. (2020). The critical raw materials in cutting tools for machining applications: A review. *Materials (Basel)*, *13*(6), 1377. doi:10.3390/ma13061377 PMID:32197537

Salvi, A., Arosio, V., Compagnoni, L. M., Cubiña, I., Scaccabarozzi, G., & Dotelli, G. (2023). Considering the environmental impact of circular strategies: A dynamic combination of material efficiency and LCA. *Journal of Cleaner Production*, *387*, 135850. doi:10.1016/j.jclepro.2023.135850

Sánchez-Lozano, J. M., Teruel-Solano, J., Soto-Elvira, P. L., & García-Cascales, M. S. (2013). Geographical Information Systems (GIS) and Multi-Criteria Decision Making (MCDM) methods for the evaluation of solar farms locations: Case study in south-eastern Spain. *Renewable & Sustainable Energy Reviews*, *24*, 544–556. doi:10.1016/j.rser.2013.03.019

Shaikh, N. U. R. (2020). *Tool to assess raw material social supply risks* [Master's thesis, University of Waterloo].

Tercero, L. A., (2019). *Report on the future use of critical raw materials*. SCRREEN project, Deliverable D, 2.

Theodosopoulos, V. (2020). *The Geopolitics of Supply: towards a new EU approach to the security of supply of critical raw materials?* Institute for European Studies Policy Brief.

Torrubia, J., Valero, A., Valero, A., & Lejuez, A. (2023). Challenges and Opportunities for the Recovery of Critical Raw Materials from Electronic Waste: The Spanish Perspective. *Sustainability (Basel)*, *15*(2), 1393. doi:10.3390/su15021393

Ujaczki, É., Feigl, V., Molnár, M., Cusack, P., Curtin, T., Courtney, R., O'Donoghue, L., Davris, P., Hugi, C., Evangelou, M. W. H., Balomenos, E., & Lenz, M. (2018). Re-using bauxite residues: Benefits beyond (critical raw) material recovery. *Journal of Chemical Technology and Biotechnology*, *93*(9), 2498–2510. doi:10.1002/jctb.5687 PMID:30158737

Wang, C. N., Nguyen, V. T., Duong, D. H., & Thai, H. T. N. (2018). A hybrid fuzzy analysis network process (FANP) and the technique for order of preference by similarity to ideal solution (TOPSIS) approaches for solid waste to energy plant location selection in Vietnam. *Applied Sciences (Basel, Switzerland)*, *8*(7), 1100. doi:10.3390/app8071100

Xie, J., Xia, Z., Tian, X., & Liu, Y. (2023). Nexus and synergy between the low-carbon economy and circular economy: A systematic and critical review. *Environmental Impact Assessment Review*, *100*, 107077. doi:10.1016/j.eiar.2023.107077

Yalçın, A. Z. (2010). Sürdürülebilir kalkınma için düşük karbon ekonomisinin önemi ve Türkiye için bir değerlendirme. *Balıkesir Üniversitesi Sosyal Bilimler Enstitüsü Dergisi*, *13*(24), 186–203.

Zhou, L. (2023). Towards sustainability in mineral resources. *Ore Geology Reviews*, *160*, 105600. doi:10.1016/j.oregeorev.2023.105600

Chapter 9
Analysing the Role and Contribution of Tourism in Achieving Sustainable Development Goals

Pramendra Singh
https://orcid.org/0000-0002-9142-265X
Lovely Professional University, India

Manisha Seal
https://orcid.org/0000-0003-0380-0647
Jyoti Nivas College (Autonomous), India

Disha Sharma
Amity University, Raipur, India

ABSTRACT

This chapter examines tourism's role in achieving sustainable development goals (SDGs), analyzing its contributions across all seventeen goals. Through extensive literature review and report analysis, it explores how tourism catalyzes economic growth, job creation, poverty alleviation, and uplifts marginalized communities. The chapter highlights responsible tourism's potential for environmental sustainability, cultural understanding, peace, and tourism's impact on critical issues like gender equality, education, and health. It also investigates the role different stakeholders play to achieving these SDGs. By recognizing and maximizing tourism's contributions, stakeholders can collectively build a more equitable, resilient, and sustainable future. The descriptive chapter, based on secondary data and literature review, aims to deepen understanding of the tourism-SDG relationship, offering insights for researchers, academics, and industry professionals to maximize their interrelationship's benefits.

DOI: 10.4018/979-8-3693-2758-6.ch009

INTRODUCTION: EVOLUTION OF SUSTAINABLE DEVELOPMENT GOALS

Originally, the inception of sustainable development (SD) emerged to address environmental concerns as observed by the first appearance of the term in the World Charter for Nature (Jackson, 1983 & UN, 1992). These concerns are indicated and elaborated in Agenda 21 of the Earth Summit in 1992 (UN, 1992). This summit was a great endeavour to reconcile two significant distinctive aspects such as economic progression and environmental protection by conserving and preserving the natural resources to ensure sustainable development at global level (Meadows et al., 1972).

Subsequently, the World Summit on social development held at Copenhagen in 1995 (UN, 1995) elucidates sustainable development's vital role in acquiring universal social development effectively adding to the contemporary meaning of sustainable development which is also recognised by World Summit on sustainable development organised at Johannesburg in 2002 (UN, 2002). In a following year at the United Nation's Summit the concept of green economy was deliberated representing its significant role in eradication of poverty and its liaison with eco-friendly sustainable development (UN, 2012).

Finally, in the year 2015 September, the United Nations formally embraced and declared the 17 Sustainable Development Goals (SDGs) as an essential part of 2030 Agenda for global sustainable development (UN, 2015). The millennium development goals which are very much related to sustainable development goals (SDGs) address prevalent global issues like poverty, starvation, disease, unmet schooling, gender discrimination, and environmental degradation (Sachs, 2012). The goals encompass all these burning challenges which must be handled tactfully, strategically and must be eradicated from the globe.

The involvement of stakeholders is significant in attaining these goals which must be practised responsibly keeping in view the circumstances associated with tourism occurrences in tourist destinations globally. The perception of tourism stakeholder, their knowledge and their level of understanding concerning sustainable development goals (SDGs) are the predominate factor in determining the successful achievement of SDGs worldwide through tourism. The declaration of sustainable development goals striving to create sense of consciousness among the stakeholders worldwide aimed to set of global guidelines to be embraced by government & non-governmental organizations, civil society, and business entity globally as responsible stakeholders (Jones et al., 2015). The application of sustainable development approach as set of principles or guidelines in attaining SDGs with every business operational activity is yet to be achieved by stakeholders (Sachs, et al., 2019).

LINKING TOURISM WITH SUSTAINABLE DEVELOPMENT GOALS

With the declaration of SDGs by United Nations, it advocates on imperative role of all member nations of UN in accomplishing strategic political and financial commitments towards attaining sustainable development. Tourism can be treated as a device to attain sustainable development goals. This global travel & tourism industry is a prime driving force towards achieving international understanding and world peace by creating a common platform for the member nations to establish economic relations (Jones et al., 2017). It opens up pathways for the global society to interact with each other. It creates opportunities for people living in the world to visit and explore various countries in different continents learn about their culture, historical background, religious faith and way of living which expands the horizon of knowledge and tolerance level of global citizens to ensure universal harmony.

Tourism patronizes global culture including the most deprived section of the society located in any region of the world. The tribal societies residing in the most distinctive and remote geographical areas of the world like Amazon rainforest, Nicobar Island, and dispersed areas of African regions etc. are also the integral part of the global society connecting with main land and its economical as well as technological progression through the concept of tribal tourism. Tourism carries tremendous capacity to create economic opportunities for the labour forces residing in the world. As it creates employment opportunities for skilled, semi-skilled and unskilled labour force residing in different regions of the world.

It also opens up multiple avenues of entrepreneurial prospects to support and to contribute to the international trade and commerce. The tourism business is a great source of foreign exchange earnings for a nation and a relevant contributor to the country's revenue to enhance its gross domestic product (GDP) and maintain favourable balance of payment (Archer & Fletcher 1990). Tourism is also instrumental in bringing out regional development and achieving economic diversification for a nation by boosting local trade and commercial activities.

Jones et al., (2015) thrown light on interest and awareness created by tourism business stakeholders concerning social, economic, and environmental impact of tourism on the global society by indicating achievements of SDGs. The leading stakeholder United Nations World Tourism Organization stated that tourism is capable in accomplishing all the goals of sustainable development directly or indirectly (UNWTO, 2015). Similarly, the prominent global tourism organization the Pacific Asia Travel Association (2015) claimed that attaining the SDGs is primary concern of global tourism business and affirms that tourism industry is possibly the most apt industry to achieve SDGs as compared to any other industry. Scheyvens, (2018) interprets a great example of attaining sustainable development goals through the concept of agro tourism and rural tourism by accomplishing SDG no.1 eliminating poverty and SDG no. 2 end hunger since agri base tourism and rural tourism exhibits agricultural, rustic cultural, handicraft, rural lifestyle, rural fairs, and festivals as tourist attractions to the tourists. In return it creates economic benefits in the form of numerous employment opportunities and entrepreneurial prospects for the indigenous community.

The concept of rural tourism advocates conservation and preservation of nature and its ecosystem to exhibit its natural aesthetic beauty as tourism resources to the tourists which helps in achieving SDG no.13 related to combatting climate change issues. Tourism industry is a labor intensive in nature creates huge amount of career prospects for human resource especially for female gender. It creates a safe place for women pursuing career prospects in tourism and hospitality industry by seeking SDG no.5 gender equality and women empowerment (UNWTO, n.d.).

CONTRIBUTION OF TOURISM IN ACHIEVING ALL THE 17 SDGS

Tourism holds significant potential to make substantial contributions, wielding the ability to contribute to the objectives of all 17 goals within the set (Trupp & Dolezal, 2020). Tourism serves as a catalyst for sustainable development by attracting foreign investment, bolstering local businesses, creating employment opportunities, generating tax revenue, increasing personal income, fostering cultural exchange, and preserving art, traditions, and natural landscapes such as national parks and reserves (Verhun & Bondarchuk, 2022). The development of tourism is positively correlated with sustainable economic growth, emphasizing the importance of fostering a more impactful dialogue and partnership among stakeholders, including governments, the travel industry, and community networks, to garner local support

Analysing the Role and Contribution of Tourism in Achieving Sustainable Development Goals

Table 1. Role of tourism & SDGs

SDG No.	SDG	How tourism contributes in achieving the SDG	Outcomes	Suggested By
1	No poverty	Builds human capital assets among poor through skill development, revenue is invested for pro-poor services, promotes community inclusive tourism products & activities, ensures participative approach	Leads to better job prospects, reduces economic disparity, gives opportunity to work and earn, gives equal say in policy & other matters	(Croes, 2014; Medina-Muñoz et al., 2016)
2	Zero hunger	Slum and pro-poor tourism cares for needy and take tourism to them	Brings socio-economic benefits for poor	(Obrien, 2011)
3	Good health and well-being	Health, wellness, spa, medical, yoga and adventure tourism encourage tourists and hosts to actively engage in physical and mental activities	Keeps tourists and host organizers healthy and mentally strong	(Koncul, 2012)
4	Quality education	Tourism trains and educates human resources through elementary, university, skill based, vocational based education	Increases literacy, improves skills, empowers human resources, brings social change & improves quality of life	(Buhalis et al., 2023)
5	Gender Equality	Provides equal and favourable job & entrepreneurial opportunities at all levels of involvement	Eliminates gender bias discrimination against women	(Zhang & Zhang, 2021)
6	Clean water and sanitation	Tourism destinations are kept sanitized and clean water facility is ensured for all	Reduces waste, proper & clean water supply, waste water management	(Frone & Frone, 2013)
7	Affordable and clean energy	Adopting alternative & renewable sources of energy for accommodation, transportation etc.	Reduces carbon emissions, saves energy	(Işik et al., 2017; Kelly & Williams, 2007)
8	Decent work and economic growth	Provides job, encourage investment, boost local economy, stimulates the growth of other sectors	People get job, start enterprises, government gets taxes, industries get revenue hence ensures overall economic growth	(Garidzirai & Pasara, 2020; Gökovali & Bahar, 2006)
9	Industry, innovation and infrastructure	Develops infrastructure for roads, parks, airports, accommodation units, other projects as well as drives innovation for product development & service delivery	Encourages new ideas, innovation in diverse areas along with infrastructure development	(Khadaroo & Seetanah, 2007; Mandic et al., 2018)
10	Reduced inequalities	Inclusive tourism seeks social cohesion, provides equal opportunities to all irrespective of gender, race, religion, age etc.	Equal & fair opportunities for job, work, education and participate in tourism	(Chin et al., 2023; Peña-Sánchez et al., 2020; Sabina & Nicolae, 2013)
11	Sustainable cities and communities	City resources are promoted for urban tourism and provides local communities various economic and other opportunities	Makes cities & destinations liveable, safe, prosperous and improves social condition	(Hernandez-Garcia, 2013; Setyaningsih et al., 2016)
12	Responsible consumption and production	Motivates environment friendly behaviour and consumption, delivers eco-friendly products, frames regulations for responsible tourism	Ensures durability of tourism resources, protection of environment & culture, enhances destination image	(Mehmetoglu, 2009; Sharpley, 2021)
13	Climate action	Adapting to diversification of tourism products and applying reforms & innovation in resource management, waste management, physical planning, land management, coastal management etc.	Helps to negate or counter the effects of climate change on destination	(Gómez-Martín et al., 2014.; Mycoo, 2014; Njoroge, 2015)
14	Life below water	Creates awareness and education among stakeholders to protect & conserve marine resources & habitat, frames regulations for adherence & monitoring	Sustains marine eco-system, protects species & local coastal environment	(Marlina et al., 2020; Trave et al., 2017)
-15	Life on land	Provides support and resources for natural-cultural conservation and community welfare	Conserves resources and improves social living conditions	(Kaffashi et al., 2015; Tisdell, 2003)
16	Peace, justice and strong institutions	Encourages cross-cultural engagement, gives fair economic opportunities, involves multi-organizational inputs & participation for tourism development	Dispels negative stereotypes, fosters goodwill among communities, gives equal treatment, contributes to building peace & harmony	(Castañeda & Burtner, 2010; Levy & Hawkins, 2009; Pratt & Liu, 2016)
17	Partnerships for the goals	Fosters partnership & collaboration among government bodies, private organizations, local communities, tourists, destination managers, researchers & educational institutions	Achieves sustainable development & industry growth and wellbeing of all	(Feyers et al., 2020; Selin, 1999)

for the expansion of the travel industry (Lisha et al., 2021). A great foundation and robust monitoring ensure the positive impacts of tourism in achieving sustainable development goals (Kimbu & Tichaawa, 2018). Tourism plays a vital role in achieving Sustainable Development Goals (SDGs) by encouraging sustainable consumptive patterns, fostering innovation, embracing responsible tourism practices, and can achieve it further by addressing climate change challenges (Dube, 2020).

Tourism significantly impacts poverty reduction by creating jobs, utilizing taxes for local initiatives, and supporting infrastructure. It promotes sustainable agriculture, emphasizing food production, agritourism, and regional stability. The sector's dependence on contact-intensive services during COVID-19 underscores the importance of clean facilities and reinvesting tourism-generated taxes in local healthcare. With a large workforce potential, tourism fosters inclusive development, advocates for skilled workers, and raises awareness about SDG contributions. It plays a vital role in water access, security, and hygiene, champions renewable energy, and contributes to economic growth, particularly in developing countries.

Responsible tourism management unlocks job creation, rural development, economic diversification, cultural awareness, and inclusiveness. Sustained infrastructure investment is crucial for tourism development, influencing policies for sustainability. Tourism reduces inequalities, promotes urban well-being, adopts sustainable practices, and addresses climate change challenges. Coastal tourism emphasizes integrated development for marine ecosystem conservation and a blue economy. It strategically fosters biodiversity appreciation, linking conservation to community well-being. Multicultural tolerance is promoted, along with human rights, justice, and cross-sectoral partnerships for SDGs, contributing to the 2030 Agenda.

CRITICISM TO TOURISM'S CONTRIBUTION TO SDGs

The negative impacts of tourism present a significant challenge in achieving sustainable development goals. Tourism, while contributing to economic growth, often brings about adverse consequences for destination communities and the environment. Issues such as environmental degradation, cultural erosion, and socio-economic inequalities are common challenges associated with mass tourism. These negative impacts span economic, socio-cultural, and environmental dimensions, creating complex challenges for destination communities (Buhalis et al., 2023). The strain on local resources, pollution, and disruption of traditional lifestyles hinders the pursuit of sustainability objectives. Striking a balance between tourism-driven economic benefits and the preservation of local ecosystems and communities is imperative for overcoming these challenges and advancing towards sustainable development goals in the tourism sector.

In the realm of tourism development, the engagement of local communities doesn't guarantee automatic positive outcomes; instead, poor areas often bear the brunt of various negative impacts associated with tourism (Croes, 2014). In many areas, especially the developing and underdeveloped countries, most of the economic benefits are derived by the affluent and resourceful people. The economic disparity keeps on growing in absence of proper mechanism to check the participation of local community and resource output sharing among all stakeholders. Economic leakage is also one of the possible negative impacts which may create an imbalance in a society. The rising prices of commodities and services for non-tourism associated local people may further affect their economic condition.

The tourism industry may also witness the disparity in terms of ensuring equal participation by all genders. Women in rural and semi-urban areas may not get equal opportunity to participate and excel in tourism. Within the tourism industry, gender inequalities prevalent in broader society find echoes, underscoring the need for more inclusive practices to rectify existing disparities (Zhang & Zhang, 2021). Recognizing and addressing these gender disparities within the tourism sector can contribute to creating a more equitable and socially responsible industry.

The tourism industry is also considered to be one of the major polluters of the environment through various modes of transportation, accommodation units, activities and sightseeing etc. The amount of energy required to operate tourism transportation and business cannot be fulfilled by sustainable source of energy. The energy demands of the tourism sector present a looming threat, particularly if met through non-renewable sources without adequate pollution control (Kelly & Williams, 2007). To navigate this challenge, it is essential to explore and implement sustainable energy solutions in the tourism industry.

As per the United Nations Environment Program (UNEP), tourism is also one of the major contributors to plastic waste. As per it, eight out of ten tourists visit coastal areas and they generate eight million tons of plastic that enter the ocean as waste every year. Tourist activities, including pollution and congestion, contribute to environmental degradation, resulting in escalated living costs for locals and the potential economic unviability of the destination for both residents and tourists (Garidzirai & Pasara, 2020 & Khadaroo & Seetanah, 2007). Unplanned tourism development exacerbates these challenges, risking the overall quality of the tourist experience (Mandic et al., 2018). In the race for international competitiveness, the crucial concept of sustainability is often overshadowed, leading to adverse effects on the local environment and the overall tourism experience (Peña-Sánchez et al., 2020). Furthermore, the combined impact of tourists and unchecked tourism development significantly contributes to global warming, amplifying environmental concerns on a global scale (Sharpley, 2021). Many of the destinations have faced the brunt of uncontrolled development and tourism activities.

Addressing these multifaceted challenges necessitates a comprehensive and sustainable approach to tourism development that fosters positive outcomes for both local communities and the environment while ensuring the long-term viability of tourism destinations. It demands a paradigm shift towards responsible tourism practices, thoughtful planning, and robust regulations to strike a balance between the economic benefits of tourism and the well-being of destination communities and their natural surroundings.

TOURISM STAKEHOLDERS AND THEIR INVOLMENT IN ACHIEVING SDGs

Tourist being the primary stakeholder in tourism industry has a greater contribution in revival and rejuvenation of indigenous culture and its communities placed in an ancient cities and town. A tourist with curiosity towards culture nurtures and preserves the community and its identity along with its ancient cities (Artal-Tur et al., 2020). As the visitor being explorers, adventurers, students, researchers and backpackers or a cultural tourist would be curious to visit numerous cities and towns to experience their culture, customs and ethnic practices leading to sustainability of global cities and its communities by accomplishing SDG no.11.

The suppliers from the primary sector as an ancillary service provider to tourism occurrences. Agriculturist, handicraft makers, textile, wood craft manufacturer and transportation sector are the representatives of suppliers who supports directly or indirectly the tourism industry contributes to fulfilling the sustainable development goal no. 9 i.e. industry, innovation and infrastructure and SDG no. 12. i.e., responsible consumption and production. Torres, (2003) elucidates agriculture being a source of food for the host community in a tourist destination to cater local cuisines to the tourist. Decelle, (2004) identifies innovation as a part and parcel of tourism sector leading to emergence of new business ideas. Tourism

Table 2. Role of stakeholders in achieving SDG

S. No.	Tourism Stakeholders	Participation in achieving SGDs
1.	Tourist e.g. Backpackers, families, luxury, business, adventure, students	Tourist visiting in tourist destinations such as cities, rural areas and its local communities helps in accomplishing the goal SDG11
2.	Suppliers e.g. farmers, Service providers, manufacturers	Farmers and several manufacturers being ancillary service provider of tourism promote SDG 9, SDG 12
3.	Employees e.g. waiters, taxi drivers, tour managers, holiday planner, Customer relationship managers	Achieves SDG 1, SDG 2, SDG 8
4.	Education e.g. Students, employees undertaking training and development, education providers, educational institutes	Generates great learning experience for tourist and the tourism service provider also seeking SDG 4
5	Utilities and Infrastructure e.g. power plants, utility companies, road maintenance	Creation of infrastructure for better accessibility and to support tourism occurrences helps in achieving SDG 9
6	NGOs e.g. The tourism society, The Travel Foundation	The NGOs operates in tourism sector with a view to support tourists' destinations and its community SDG 11, SDG 13, SDG 15
7	Micro Small and Medium Enterprises (MSME) e.g. small enterprises supporting restaurants, hotels, homestays	MSME supports SDG 5, SDG 10 & SDG 8
8	Transport e.g. airlines, transport providers, cruises, trains	Enables to achieve SDG 9
9	Tourism Organisations & Operators e.g. travel agent, DMO, tour operators	Helps in achieving SDG 8, SDG 9, SDG 11
10.	Government e.g. local, regional, national	Acquires SDG 6, SDG 7, SDG 8 SDG 9
11.	Communities e.g. host community, guest community, global community.	Achieves SDG 11, SDG 16
12.	Collaborative efforts all of the above stakeholders	Initiates SDG 16, SDG 17

advocates responsible usage of resources and production of services, pleasant experiences denoting the attainment of SDG no.12.

Employees being another important stakeholder representing all the segments of tourism sector such as waiters, taxi drivers, tour managers, holiday representatives, customer relation officer are the significant stakeholders responsible for driving the tourism industry help us in achieving SDG no1, SDG no. 2 and SDG no. 8. The sustainable development goal no. 1 no poverty and goal no. 2 zero hunger are achieved through the creation of abundant employment prospects for skilled and semi-skilled manpower available in society ensuring decent, respectable work and economic growth of all involved in catering tourism services as sustainable development goal no.8. (Robinson, et al., 2019).

The universities, tourism and hospitality educational institutions and training centers at international level being significant stakeholder responsible for skilling manpower and creating tourism and hospitality professional ensuring the fulfilment of SDG no. 4 i.e. quality education imparted to the human resource employed in tourism and hospitality industry. The term tourism is itself is lifetime learning experience for the tourists with an exposure related culture, nature geography and the historical background of the tourist destination visited by the tourist (Falk, et al., 2012). Katircioğlu, (2010) reveals the long-lasting relationship between international tourism and higher education creating a greater impact on economic growth of the nation.

Another important stakeholder like road connectivity, highways, power supply, water supply, telecommunications and numerous modes of transportation networks representing utilities and infrastructure of a nation are an important part of tourism infrastructure as well helps in achieving sustainable development goals no. 9 i.e. Industry, innovation and infrastructure. Seetanah, et al., (2011) identifies infrastructure as one most necessary factor in international destination development for the tourists which exhibits positive linkage with tourism occurrences.

The non-governmental organizations (NGO) such as the tourism society, the travel foundations support tourist destinations, and its local communities to seek economic development though tourism practices aiming to sustainable development of the whole region and achieving SDG no.1 (No poverty) SDG no.11 (sustainable cities and communities), SDG no. 13 (climate change) and SDG no. 15. (Life on land). Hoque (2022) elucidates that the NGOs primarily serve the local community of a tourist destination by attaining no poverty. The local NGOs are the initiators to encourage ecotourism norms and sustainable practices among the tourist and guest communities to conserve and preserve the natural ecosystem of the tourist destination leading to better life on land and an initiative towards reduction of climate change or global warming (Horochowski, & Moisey, 1999).

Being a strong stakeholder of tourism sector the micro small and medium tourism enterprises (MSME) such as e.g., travel agent, restaurant, hotel, homestay serves to achieve SDG no.5, SDG no.10 & SDG no.8 gender equality, reduced inequalities and decent work and economic growth for the professionals working in tourism related MSME dedicated to women empowerment. Zhang & Zhang, (2020) advocate on gender equality and significant role of women in tourism industry being service industry contributing to achieving sustainable development goal no. 5 and 6. Bianchi & de Man, (2021) investigates a strong linkage between better life and economic growth of tourism professional including skilled and semi-skilled labors being served in tourism industry.

Transportation being an important part of tourism industry which denotes the term travel as the most prominent stakeholder in tourism ensuring a successful achievement of SDG no.9 i.e., Industry, innovation and infrastructure. Tourism and transport are two sides of a coin which cannot be separated from each other which enables to achieve sustainable development goal no. 9. Transport is an integral part of the tourism industry for mobilizing tourists from one place to another (Page & Connell, 2014).

Tourism Organizations and Operators including travel agents, Destination Management Organizations, travel bloggers as important stakeholders strive to achieve SDG no.8. SDG no. 9. SDG no.11. Aleksandrov (2014) reveals the role destination management organizations in creating economic benefits, employment opportunities through tourism business for the local community and strategies to conserve the natural and cultural resources of tourist destination as cities and towns. The government of nation at local level, regional level and central level play an important role in attaining SDG no.6, SDG no.7, SDG no.8, SDG no. 9 through tourism promotion. As it is a primary responsibility of a government to ensure clean water and sanitation condition, affordable and clean energy availability to host and guest both the communities. Government ensures creation of decent job prospects and bringing economic development through tourism industry, innovative ideas and tourism infrastructure.

The government policy on tourism brings out effective guidelines for tourism planning and development and creates economic opportunities (Vujko & Gajić, 2014) contributing to sustainable development goals. Finally, the communities including host and guest communities are relevant body in achieving SDG no. 11 and SDG no. 16 i.e. sustainable cities and communities and seeking international peace, justice and strong institutions though the platform created by tourism for the world. Var & Ap, (2013) seeks to identify tourism as a forum to promote world peace among the nations of the world. The conclusive observation reveals that the collaborative efforts of above-mentioned multiple stakeholders will lead to better achievement of sustainable development goal no. 17 partnerships for the goals to make the world a better place to live by contributing maximum in accomplishment of sustainable development goals.

CONCLUSION

The study provides a comprehensive overview of the evolution of the concept of sustainable development (SD) and its incorporation into the global agenda through various United Nations (UN) summits and declarations. The focus then shifts to the pivotal role of tourism in achieving the 17 Sustainable Development Goals (SDGs) established in 2015. The involvement of stakeholders is emphasized as a critical factor in the successful realization of these goals, with a particular emphasis on tourism stakeholders. The study highlights tourism as a powerful tool for fostering international understanding, cultural exchange, and economic development. It explores how tourism contributes directly and indirectly to each of the 17 SDGs, ranging from poverty reduction and zero hunger to climate action and partnerships for the goals. Notable examples, such as agro tourism and rural tourism, illustrate how specific tourism practices align with and support individual SDGs.

The contribution of tourism to each SDG is further detailed in Table 1, showcasing the multifaceted impact of the industry on global development. The examples provided in the table demonstrate how tourism can be a force for positive change, promoting economic growth, environmental sustainability, and social well-being. However, the study also acknowledges the criticisms and challenges associated with tourism's contribution to SDGs. The negative impacts, such as environmental degradation, cultural erosion, and socio-economic inequalities, pose significant obstacles to achieving sustainable development through tourism. The need for a balanced approach that considers the well-being of destination communities and ecosystems is underscored.

The final section of the study introduces a preview of tourism stakeholders and their roles in achieving SDGs. A detailed table categorizes various stakeholders, from tourists and suppliers to governments and communities, outlining their specific contributions to different SDGs. This section emphasizes the interconnectedness of these stakeholders and the necessity for collaborative efforts to realize SDGs. In essence, the study emphasizes the potential of tourism as a catalyst for sustainable development but calls for a mindful and responsible approach to address its associated challenges. The engagement of diverse stakeholders and the adoption of sustainable practices are deemed essential for tourism to fulfil its role in advancing the global agenda for sustainable development.

Implications and Recommendations

To effectively balance tourism growth with sustainability goals, destinations can adopt several key frameworks and models. Firstly, establishing robust Destination Management Organizations (DMOs) is essential. These entities serve as the coordinating body for stakeholders, facilitating the development of sustainable tourism policies and implementing comprehensive destination management plans. Embracing the Triple Bottom Line (TBL) approach is also crucial, ensuring that economic, social, and environmental considerations are integrated into all tourism development strategies. Certification programs such as Green Globe etc. can incentivize businesses to adhere to sustainable practices, offering assurance to tourists concerned about environmental impact. Community-Based Tourism (CBT) initiatives empower residents, fostering their involvement in decision-making processes and ensuring that tourism benefits are distributed equitably. Investing in sustainable infrastructure projects, including transportation networks and renewable energy systems, is vital to support tourism growth while minimizing environmental degradation.

REFERENCES

Aleksandrov, K. (2014). The role of DMO for sustainable development of a tourist destination–Bulgaria case study. *Journal of Tourism Research*, *9*(2), 198–209.

Archer, B., & Fletcher, J. (1990). Tourism: its economic importance. In *Horwath Book of Tourism* (pp. 10–25). Palgrave Macmillan UK. doi:10.1007/978-1-349-11687-4_2

Artal-Tur, A., Villena-Navarro, M., & Alamá-Sabater, L. (2020). The relationship between cultural tourist behaviour and destination sustainability. In *Culture and Cultures in Tourism* (pp. 71–85). Routledge. doi:10.4324/9780429054891-8

Bianchi, R. V., & de Man, F. (2021). Tourism, inclusive growth and decent work: A political economy critique. *Journal of Sustainable Tourism*, *29*(2-3), 353–371. doi:10.1080/09669582.2020.1730862

Buhalis, D., Leung, X. Y., Fan, D., Darcy, S., Chen, G., Xu, F., & Tan, W.-H. G., Nunkoo, R., & Farmaki, A. (2023). Editorial. Tourism Review (Vol. 78, Issue 2, pp. 293–313). Emerald Publishing. doi:10.1108/TR-04-2023-620

Castañeda, Q., & Burtner, J. (2010). Tourism as "A Force for World Peace" The Politics of Tourism, Tourism as Governmentality and the Tourism Boycott of Guatemala. *The Journal of Tourism and Peace Research*, *1*(2), 1–21.

Chin, W. L., Tham, A., & Noorashid, N. (2023). Distribution of (In)Equality and Empowerment of Community-Based Tourism: The Case Study of Brunei Darussalam. *International Journal of Hospitality & Tourism Administration*, 1–32. doi:10.1080/15256480.2023.2175287

Croes, R. (2014). *Issue 3* (Vol. 6). Tourism and poverty reduction in Latin America: Where does the region stand? Worldwide Hospitality and Tourism Themes. Emerald Group Publishing Ltd., doi:10.1108/WHATT-03-2014-0010

Decelle, X. (2004). A conceptual and dynamic approach to innovation in tourism (pp. 1-16). Paris: OEcD.

Dube, K. (2020). Touris and sustainable development goals in African context. *International journal of economics and finance studies*, *12*(1), 88-102. doi:10.34109/ijefs.202012106

Falk, J. H., Ballantyne, R., Packer, J., & Benckendorff, P. (2012). Travel and learning: A neglected tourism research area. *Annals of Tourism Research*, *39*(2), 908–927. doi:10.1016/j.annals.2011.11.016

Feyers, S., Stein, T., & Klizentyte, K. (2020). Bridging worlds: Utilizing a multi-stakeholder framework to create extension-tourism partnerships. *Sustainability (Basel)*, *12*(1), 1–23. doi:10.3390/su12010080

Frone, S. M., & Florin Frone, D. (2013). Sustainable Tourism and Water Supply and Sanitation Development in Romania. *Journal of Tourism and Hospitality Management, 1*(3).

Garidzirai, R., & Pasara, M. T. (2020). An analysis of the contribution of tourism on economic growth in South African provinces: A panel analysis. *Geo Journal of Tourism and Geosites, 29*(2), 554–564. doi:10.30892/gtg.29214-489

Gökovali, U., & Bahar, O. (2006). Contribution of tourism to economic growth: A panel data approach. *Anatolia, 17*(2), 155–167. doi:10.1080/13032917.2006.9687184

Gómez-Martín, M. B., Armesto-López, X. A., Cors-Iglesias, M., & Muñoz-Negrete, J. (2014). Adaptation strategies to climate change in the tourist sector: The case of coastal tourism in Spain. *Tourism (Zagreb), 62*(3), 293–308.

Hernandez-Garcia, J. (2013). Slum tourism, city branding and social urbanism: The case of Medellin, Colombia. *Journal of Place Management and Development, 6*(1), 43–51. doi:10.1108/17538331311306122

Hoque, M. A., Lovelock, B., & Carr, A. (2022). Alleviating Indigenous poverty through tourism: The role of NGOs. *Journal of Sustainable Tourism, 30*(10), 2333–2351. doi:10.1080/09669582.2020.1860070

Horochowski, K., & Moisey, R. N. (1999). The role of environmental NGOs in sustainable tourism development: A case study in northern Honduras. *Tourism Recreation Research, 24*(2), 19–30. doi:10.1080/02508281.1999.11014872

Işik, C., Dogan, E., & Ongan, S. (2017). Analyzing the tourism–energy–growth nexus for the top 10 most-visited countries. *Economies, 5*(4), 40. doi:10.3390/economies5040040

Jackson, P. (1983). A World Charter for Nature. *Ambio, 12*(2), 133–134.

Jones, P., Hillier, D., & Comfort, D. (2015). 'Sustainability in the Hospitality Industry: Some Personal Reflections on Corporate Challenges and Research Agendas'. *International Journal of Contemporary Hospitality Management, 28*(1), 36–67. doi:10.1108/IJCHM-11-2014-0572

Jones, P., Hillier, D., & Comfort, D. (2017). The sustainable development goals and the tourism and hospitality industry. *Athens Journal of Tourism, 4*(1), 7–18. doi:10.30958/ajt.4.1.1

Kaffashi, S., Radam, A., Shamsudin, M. N., Yacob, M. R., & Nordin, N. H. (2015). Ecological conservation, ecotourism, and sustainable management: The case of Penang National Park. *Forests, 6*(7), 2345–2370. doi:10.3390/f6072345

Katircioğlu, S. T. (2010). International tourism, higher education and economic growth: The case of North Cyprus. *World Economy, 33*(12), 1955–1972. doi:10.1111/j.1467-9701.2010.01304.x

Kelly, J., & Williams, P. W. (2007). Modelling tourism destination energy consumption and greenhouse gas emissions: Whistler, British Columbia, Canada. *Journal of Sustainable Tourism, 15*(1), 67–90. doi:10.2167/jost609.0

Khadaroo, J., & Seetanah, B. (2007). Transport infrastructure and tourism development. *Annals of Tourism Research, 34*(4), 1021–1032. doi:10.1016/j.annals.2007.05.010

Kimbu, A. N., & Tichaawa, T. M. (2018). Sustainable development goals and socio-economic development through tourism in central Africa: Myth or reality? *Geo Journal of Tourism and Geosites, 23*(3), 780–796. doi:10.30892/gtg.23314-328

Koncul, N. (2012). Wellness: A new mode of tourism. Ekonomska Istrazivanja (Vol. 25, Issue 2, pp. 525–534). doi:10.1080/1331677X.2012.11517521

Levy, S. E., & Hawkins, D. E. (2009). Peace through tourism: Commerce based principles and practices. *Journal of Business Ethics, 89*(S4, SUPPL. 4), 569–585. doi:10.1007/s10551-010-0408-2

Lisha, L. (2021). The relationship between tourism development and sustainable development goals in Vietnam. *Caudemos de Economia, 44*, 42–49. doi:10.32826/cude.v1i124.504

Mandic, A., Mrnjavac, Ž., & Kordic, L. (2018). Tourism infrastructure, recreational facilities and tourism development. *Tourism and Hospitality Management, 24*(1), 41–62. doi:10.20867/thm.24.1.12

Marina., S. & Astina, I., K. (2020). Sustainable marine ecotourism management: A case of marine resource conservation based on local wisdom of Bojo Mola community in Wakatobi national park. *GeoJournal of Tourism and Geosites, 32*(4), 1317–1323. https://doi.org/ doi:10.30892/gtg.3

Meadows, D. H., Meadows, D. L., Randers, J., & Behrens, W. (1972). *Club of Rome. The limits to growth.*

Medina-Muñoz, D. R., Medina-Muñoz, R. D., & Gutiérrez-Pérez, F. J. (2016). The impacts of tourism on poverty alleviation: An integrated research framework. *Journal of Sustainable Tourism, 24*(2), 270–298. doi:10.1080/09669582.2015.1049611

Mehmetoglu, M. (2009). Predictors of sustainable consumption in a tourism context: A CHAID approach. *Advances in Hospitality and Leisure, 5*, 3–23. doi:10.1108/S1745-3542(2009)0000005005

Mycoo, M. (2014). Sustainable tourism, climate change and sea level rise adaptation policies in Barbados. *Natural Resources Forum, 38*(1), 47–57. doi:10.1111/1477-8947.12033

Njoroge, J. M. (2015). Climate change and tourism adaptation: Literature Review. *Tourism and hospitality management, 21*(1), 95-108.

Obrien, P. W. (2011). Business, Management and Poverty Reduction: A Role for Slum Tourism? *Journal of Business Diversity, 11*(1), 33–46.

Page, S., & Connell, J. (2014). Transport and tourism. *The Wiley Blackwell Companion to Tourism*, 155-167. Wiley.

Peña-Sánchez, A. R., Ruiz-Chico, J., Jiménez-García, M., & López-Sánchez, J. A. (2020). Tourism and the SDGs: An analysis of economic growth, decent employment, and gender equality in the European Union (2009-2018). *Sustainability (Basel), 12*(13), 5480. doi:10.3390/su12135480

Pratt, S., & Liu, A. (2016). Does Tourism Really Lead to Peace? A Global View. *International Journal of Tourism Research, 18*(1), 82–90. doi:10.1002/jtr.2035

Robinson, R. N., Martins, A., Solnet, D., & Baum, T. (2019). Sustaining precarity: Critically examining tourism and employment. *Journal of Sustainable Tourism, 27*(7), 1008–1025. doi:10.1080/09669582.2018.1538230

Sabina, J. M., & Nicolae, J. C. (2013). Gender Trends in Tourism Destination. *Procedia: Social and Behavioral Sciences*, *92*, 437–444. doi:10.1016/j.sbspro.2013.08.698

Sachs, J. D. (2012). From millennium development goals to sustainable development goals. *Lancet*, *379*(9832), 2206–2211. doi:10.1016/S0140-6736(12)60685-0 PMID:22682467

Sachs, J. D., Schmidt-Traub, G., Mazzucato, M., Messner, D., Nakicenovic, N., & Rockström, J. (2019). Six transformations to achieve the sustainable development goals. *Nature Sustainability*, *2*(9), 805–814. doi:10.1038/s41893-019-0352-9

Scheyvens, R. (2018). Linking tourism to the sustainable development goals: A geographical perspective. *Tourism Geographies*, *20*(2), 341–342. doi:10.1080/14616688.2018.1434818

Seetanah, B., Juwaheer, T. D., Lamport, M. J., Rojid, S., Sannassee, R. V., & Subadar, A. U. (2011). Does infrastructure matter in tourism development? *University of Mauritius research journal, 17*, 89-108.

Selin, S. (1999). Developing a Typology of Sustainable Tourism Partnerships. *Journal of Sustainable Tourism*, *7*(3&4), 260–273. doi:10.1080/09669589908667339

Setyaningsih, W., Nuryanti, W., Prayitno, B., & Sarwadi, A. (2016). Urban Heritage Towards Creative-based Tourism in the Urban Settlement of Kauman - Surakarta. *Procedia: Social and Behavioral Sciences*, *227*, 642–649. doi:10.1016/j.sbspro.2016.06.127

Sharpley, R. (2021). On the need for sustainable tourism consumption. *Tourist Studies*, *21*(1), 96–107. doi:10.1177/1468797620986087

Tisdell, C. (2003). Economic Aspects of Ecotourism: Wildlife-based Tourism and its Contribution to Nature. *Sri Lankan journal of agricultural economics, 5*(1), 83-95. http://ageconsearch.umn.edu

Torres, R. (2003). Linkages between tourism and agriculture in Mexico. *Annals of Tourism Research*, *30*(3), 546–566. doi:10.1016/S0160-7383(02)00103-2

Trave, C., Brunnschweiler, J., Sheaves, M., Diedrich, A., & Barnett, A. (2017). *Are we killing them with kindness? Evaluation of sustainable marine wildlife tourism. Biological Conservation* (Vol. 209). Elsevier Ltd., doi:10.1016/j.biocon.2017.02.020

Trupp, A., & Dolezal, C. (2020). Tourism and the Sustainable Development Goals in Southeast Asia. ASEAS - Austrian. *Journal of Southeast Asian Studies*, *13*(1), 1–16. doi:10.14764/10.ASEAS-0026

UN. (1992). Earth Summit: Agenda 21. Rio de Janerio, Brazil: United Nations (UN).

UN. (1995). *Copenhagen Declaration on Social Development.* World Summit for Social Development, Copenhagen.

UN. (2002). *Report of the world summit on sustainable development.* Johannesburg, South Africa, UN.

UN System Task Team. (2012). *Realizing the Future We Want for All. Report to the Secretary-General.* UN.

United Nations World Tourism Organisation. (2015). *Tourism and the Sustainable Development Goals.* UN. http://cf.cdn.unwto.org/sites/all/files/pdf/sustainable_deve lopment_goals_brochure.pdf

United Nations World Tourism Organisation/ Pacific Asia Travel Association. (2015). Global Trends Shaping Tourism in Asia Pacific. UN. http://www.hotelsandtravel ler.com/review/unwtopata-report-

UNWTO. (n.d.). *Tourism and the sustainable development goals*. UNWTO. publication/tourism-and-sustainable-development-goal

Var, T., & Ap, J. (2013). Tourism and world peace. In *Global tourism* (pp. 63–76). Routledge.

Verhun, A. M. & Bondarchuk, J. A. (2022). Role of tourism industry growth in attaining sustainable development goals in a modern globalized world. *Journal of strategic economics of research, 1*(6), 8-16. doi:10.30857/2786-5398.2022.1.1

Vujko, A., & Gajić, T. (2014). The government policy impact on economic development of tourism. *Ekonomika Poljoprivrede, 61*(3), 789–804. doi:10.5937/ekoPolj1403789V

Zhang, J., & Zhang, Y. (2020). Tourism and gender equality: An Asian perspective. *Annals of Tourism Research, 85*, 103067. doi:10.1016/j.annals.2020.103067

Zhang, J., & Zhang, Y. (2021). A qualitative comparative analysis of tourism and gender equality in emerging economies. *Journal of Hospitality and Tourism Management, 46*, 284–292. doi:10.1016/j.jhtm.2021.01.009

Chapter 10
Moving Sustainable Development Goals (SDG-5) Forward:
Challenges, Enablers, and Policy Implications for Mumpreneurs in Developing Countries

Nurul Hidayana Mohd Noor
https://orcid.org/0000-0003-2262-2524
Faculty of Administrative Science and Policy Studies, Universiti Teknologi MARA, Malaysia

Noralina Omar
Department of Social Justice and Administration, Universiti Malaya, Malaysia

ABSTRACT

Sustainable entrepreneurship positively impacts the 2030 United Nations (UN) Agenda and Goal 5. The chapter aims to discover mumpreneurs' entrepreneurial challenges and enablers. Mumpreneurs are the key to economic growth, and without attention to the gender dimension in economic development, Malaysia is unlikely to achieve its growth targets. This chapter employed a qualitative research approach under the interpretive research paradigm. Using purposive sampling, 20 mumpreneurs were selected as key informants. The chapter found various entrepreneurial challenges, including lack of financial assistance, poor business location, poor customer management, weak marketing strategy, product delivery issues, poor management, and shift competition. The enablers identified are capital and aid, motivation, business skills, innovation, network, technology absorption, and business support. This chapter contributes to the literature on entrepreneurship in general and specifically to the literature on female entrepreneurs from the perspective of developing country economies.

DOI: 10.4018/979-8-3693-2758-6.ch010

INTRODUCTION

Malaysia is a federal country located in Southeast Asia. Malaysia has two main areas separated by the South China Sea: Peninsular Malaysia and East Malaysia. Women are a large part of the Malaysian population. Women's significant contribution to the country's development has long been recognized as wives, mothers, and children. According to sources from the Department of Statistics Malaysia, in 2023, the estimated population of Malaysia was 33.4 million compared to 32.7 million in 2022. The population includes 17.5 million men and 15.9 million women (Pfordten, September 2023). The report also shows that the female labor force in Malaysia is 6.60 million persons compared to the male labor force, which is 10.40 million persons. The increase in the participation of women in the labor force shows that the involvement of women in national development activities is becoming more prominent and positive.

Women are the main driving force of the family and national development (Wells, 2021). Starting from home, the role of women is very significant. Sustainable Development Goals (SDGs) are global agreements encouraging changes towards sustainable development (Iqbal et al., 2024). This development agreement is based on human rights and equality to encourage social, economic, and environmental development. Goal five of the 17 SDGs is gender equality, namely achieving gender equality and empowering all women and girls (Eden & Wagstaff, 2021). Gender equality is a human right and a necessary foundation for a peaceful, prosperous, and sustainable world (Castro Núñez et al., 2020). Women represent half the world's population, yet gender inequality hinders social progress (Fisher & Ryan, 2021). According to the 2023 Sustainable Development Goals Report by the United Nations (UN), approximately 2.4 billion adult women still need equal economic opportunities. Furthermore, 178 countries maintain legal barriers that prevent women's full economic participation (Carlsen & Bruggemann, 2022). The findings of this study were obtained from 50 international and regional agencies based on data from more than 200 countries and regions.

Women's empowerment is the basis for smoothing the gender gap line. Malaysian Statistics Department Report 2022 shows that the Malaysian Gender Gap Index (MGGI) 2021 is 0.707. Malaysia ranked 103rd, far behind other regional countries such as Thailand, Indonesia, and Singapore (Department of Statistics Malaysia, November 2022). Therefore, women's empowerment needs to be improved. The issue of gender equality and women's empowerment has become a global topic. Many countries face this problem mainly regarding women's involvement in developing the economic sector. Although many statistics and reports report on the issue of equality for this gender, there is still no precise mechanism that can be applied or implemented to overcome this problem (Dang & Nguyen, 2021). In the meantime, the responsibility and burden of working mothers have caused the statistics of unmarried women and single women to increase yearly (Jephcott et al., 2023). The government should intensify its efforts to empower women to be competitive and move forward. The synergy of women's competitiveness needs to be improved to optimize human capital and the nation's productivity (Neumann, 2021).

Women's involvement in business is increasing and growing. Efforts and persistence in running a business prove a high ability of women because the business field requires various strategies to succeed (Salmony & Kanbach, 2022). Therefore, this article aims to identify the challenges and driving factors of women and mothers in the field of entrepreneurship in Malaysia. This article uses a qualitative approach to collect data from mumpreneurs. "Mumpreneurs" describes mothers involved in entrepreneurial activities. Mumpreneurs is a new emerging trend that describes women who start or manage their ventures besides taking the role of being a mother. The term "Mumpreneur" was conceptualized by Patricia Cobe and Ellen H. Parlapiano. Along with men, women also take advantage of the opportunity to enliven the field of entrepreneurship in Malaysia. However, the field of entrepreneurship is not easy and is linked with isolation and stress, and emotional hardships (Wang et al., 2020).

Women's role is not only in managing the household but as a contributor to the family economy. They must get up early in the morning to manage children and families, go out to work an average of eight to ten hours a day, return home late afternoon or early night, and continue the tasks as a wife and mother. This scenario has caused them to become tired and emotionally full of tension (Rodrigues et al., 2023). Adhikari (2022) shows that people who experience higher stress are women. When the working woman is married, her responsibilities and duties are focused on her career alone and her husband and children. In addition, the pressure will be higher when childcare duty is fully responsible for women. According to Chávez Rivera et al. (2021), stress causes less free time and excessive homework, childcare issues, lack of communication with spouse, and fatigue. Time is the key for every woman in today's era. Every available moment is necessary and best used; every free minute should be filled efficiently, and clock-in and clock-out must be accurate and precise. At home, they do not stop thinking about increasing the family's income due to the high standard of living. No matter how high a woman's rank is, giving full attention to their children is more important after becoming a mother (Dhaliwal, 2022).

Among the challenges in managing business faced by mumprenuers is lack of capital and high fixed costs, slow economic activity, slow cash flow rates, tax problems, loss of critical customers, inefficient management, problems with partners, and poor financial management (Babina et al., 2024; Bilan et al., 2020; De Clercq & Brieger, 2022; Lestari et al., 2020). Problems after operating a business include marketing and labor problems, administrative problems, and personal problems (Röglinger et al., 2022). On the other hand, Afshan et al. (2021) and Hillson (2023) have obtained a different conclusion. Where in their study, they found that most mumpreneurs face the problem of lack of business training, lack of management experience, lack of experience in terms of financial skills, lack of advice and guidance, lack of experience in hiring external services, lack of respect, and lack of peer participation. Adikaram and Razik (2023) also think that other problems include difficulty obtaining loans and prejudice against women or a credibility gap due to the assumption that women are incapable of managing their businesses.

Mumpreneurs face problems because of gender stereotypes, especially in finance and banking, which men dominate (De Clercq & Brieger, 2022). They need a guarantor or business advisor to obtain a loan from a bank or financial institution. Many mumpreneurs used personal savings to start businesses (Noor & Isa, 2020). Therefore, researchers emphasize the need for more exploration of the challenges and enablers that occur in the context of developing countries. Such an understanding will help relevant parties, such as policymakers, to remove the challenges and barriers women entrepreneurs face and foster an environment that inspires women to become entrepreneurs. Although there are many studies on women entrepreneurs in general, there needs to be more understanding of the specific context of mumpreneurs in Malaysia.

To increase entrepreneurial competition in the market, Belitski et al. (2020) advise that business success requires careful training. To avoid sluggish conditions occurring in business, individuals should maintain competitive activity. According to Wach et al. (2020), the general measurement of an entrepreneur's success in business is the level of business profit obtained, i.e., whether it is lower than the industry average, equal to the industry average, or higher than the industry average.

At the same time, the factors that determine the success of entrepreneurs include capitalization, planning, record keeping and financial control, professional advisors, management experience, industry experience, education level, workforce, economic conditions, production of products and services, marketing skills, business status, and business maturity (Al-Fadhat, 2022; Kaciak & Welsh, 2020; Mohd

Noor et al., 2024). According to Kaciak and Welsh (2020), the success factors of entrepreneurs include the availability of raw resources, motivation of entrepreneurs, industry knowledge, technology, communication skills, interpersonal skills, and risk-taking. With the above background and recognizing the need for research, this study aims to provide qualitative insights into the challenging factors that could hinder the success of women entrepreneurs and identify the growth drivers of mumpreneurs. Research on women's entrepreneurship is essential in creating new knowledge and promoting women's entrepreneurship and gender equality. Towards this, this study aims to address three pertinent research questions to provide policy implications for entrepreneurs' growth in Malaysia:

- RQ1. What are the challenges faced by mumpreneurs in Malaysia?
- RQ2. What factors enable the mumpreneurs-owned ventures' survival and growth?
- RQ3. What are the policy implications to enhance the existing policies?

The paper's structure is as follows. After the brief introduction, we review the pertinent literature and introduce the research context. Then, the study's research design is presented, followed by results and findings. The final section summarizes the key insights and presents future research suggestions.

LITERATURE REVIEW

An Overview of Entrepreneurship in Malaysia

Entrepreneurial development is now the country's long-term strategy for building a knowledge-driven economy and entrepreneurial culture. Aware of the importance of entrepreneurial activities towards individuals and society, the government has focused on the field of entrepreneurship through New Economic Policy (1971-1990), National Development Policy (1990-2000), National Vision Policy (2001-2010), and the New Economy Model (2011-2020) (Abdullah & Muhammad, 2008). The efforts to bridge the economic gap are an essential catalyst in building leaders with entrepreneurial ability in the future. The Malaysian government has taken several approaches to managing the national economy by creating the National Entrepreneurship Policy 2030 (NEP 2030).

The NEP 2030 is a long-term strategy to realize Malaysia as an entrepreneurial nation by 2030 (Othman et al., 2021). NEP 2030 is the first comprehensive entrepreneurship policy involving individuals (entrepreneurs), entities (enterprises), and processes (entrepreneurship). This policy is also formulated through a process that is implemented comprehensively with the involvement of all stakeholders in the field of entrepreneurship, including Malaysia's Ministry of Entrepreneur Development and Cooperatives, government agencies, academics, industry experts, non-governmental organizations (NGOs), private companies, government-related companies (GLCs), entrepreneurs as well as the public through public consultation, online feedback, dialogue, and workshop meetings, and discussions (Othman et al., 2021).

Assistance to entrepreneurs is provided in the form of the implementation of entrepreneurial development programs that are re-aligned based on current needs and developments at the global level by focusing on several areas, namely financial funding, research grants, training and capacity development, infrastructure, equipment, technology, market access, social enterprise, and internationalization (Bergman & McMullen, 2022).

Figure 1. Labor force by sex
(Department of Statistics Malaysia, January 2024)

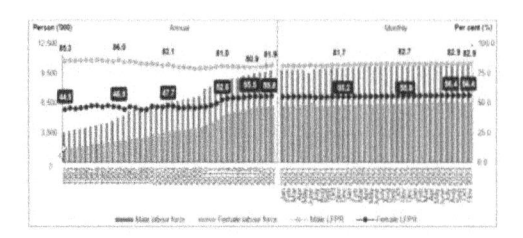

These programs aim to optimize performance and create opportunities for entrepreneurs to grow and advance their businesses through market expansion, innovation, and productivity. Among the financial support available in Malaysia are National TEKUN, Credit Guarantee Corporation (CGC), and Malaysian Industrial Development Finance Berhad (MIDF). The government also provides tax incentives to encourage the participation of local entrepreneurs in specific business areas. These include tax exemption incentives for social enterprises, tax incentives for the green technology sector, and Green Investment Tax Allowance (GITA).

The Role of Women in the Economy

Women in Malaysia are involved in the current national development, especially those who work either formally or informally. The role of women is now expanding to include various fields in all corners of the country, whether in the city, the suburbs, or the countryside. In Malaysia, women get the same opportunities and space to develop their potential. Therefore, many women can achieve outstanding success and develop their potential to the optimum level, starting from school, higher education institutes, and employment (Wells, 2021). The government's action to review the National Women's Policy in 2009 has shown the government's determination to change the position of women in the economic sector for the better. In that effort, a strategy has been adapted into the revised policy, which is the strategy of mainstreaming gender. It is a concept introduced at the international level to consider the needs of women and men in every policy that is formed. A series of various efforts have been intensified to realize the strategy.

However, the gap between the labor force participation rate of men and women is still significant. In November 2023, the male labor force registered 10.40 million persons. Meanwhile, the female labor force was 6.60 million persons. As shown in Figure 1, the labor force participation rate (LFPR) and the male and female LFPR were unchanged at 82.9% and 56.4%, respectively, as recorded in October 2023. In terms of year-on-year changes, both the male and female labor force continued an increasing trend, with a rise of 1.3% (November 2022: 10.27 million persons) and 2.5% (November 2022: 6.44 million persons) respectively (Department of Statistics Malaysia, January 2024). Based on these statistics, efforts must be made to increase women's participation in the labor market. Labor force participation for highly educated women is satisfactory. Thus, efforts and policies toward increasing participation must be directed at women with secondary and primary education. The existing data is directed only at the formal sector. Many women are involved directly in the economy. For instance, online business and part-time at home are known as informal economy.

The latest technology makes it easier for women to work part-time without interfering with their duties as housewives. Most women work to meet the workforce's needs in the labor market; however, women from low-income families work to cover the low household income. A study conducted by Tan and Yew (2023) found that women with low incomes, including single mothers, do several types of work at once to supplement their monthly income. Rodrigues et al. (2023) concluded that many women have performed dual roles in the family to survive and sustain family institutions. Therefore, the involvement of women in helping the economy of the family and the country has crossed various types of sectors regardless of areas.

According to the Minister of Entrepreneur and Cooperatives Development statistics, at least 910,000 registered Small Medium Enterprise (SME) entrepreneurs are in Malaysia. Of that number, as many as 22% or 200 200 are women entrepreneurs. The number does not include women entrepreneurs, such as stall hawkers, market sellers, and online women traders. If included, the estimated number reaches a million people. According to Iqbal et al. (2024), women entrepreneurs have been recognized as new generators of growth and economic activity in developing countries because they contribute to the well-being and prosperity of society. Love et al. (2024) explained that women's entrepreneurship concerns the community's well-being. Their involvement in community activities is to find a direct source of income, gain economic independence, and increase their status in their communities. It is appropriate that the potential of women entrepreneurs continues to be polished and highlighted. According to Abdelzaher et al. (2021), women still need to be actively involved in the business industry due to social, cultural, and traditional factors. However, if given the opportunity, women are seen to be highly committed even though they are less prominent in the public eye (Agrawal et al., 2023). Thus, women should be given protection and justification to continue to be facilitated from the aspect of training, financing, grants, and funds that need to be continued to ensure the sustainability of women's participation (Al-Fadhat, 2022; Kaciak & Welsh, 2020; Mohd Noor et al., 2024).

Challenges Faced by Mumpreneurs

Women's involvement in careers and professionals among women is increasing. This situation creates problems for women when there is pressure in the form of role conflict between the role of an entrepreneur and a housewife (Rahman et al., 2023). For example, from a time perspective, especially among mumpreneurs with young children, the level of family support received also affects the stress level faced. Family members who support women's careers can reduce stress. In addition, the level of satisfaction of mumpreneurs with work, marriage, and life also creates conflict (Love et al., 2024). First, mumprenuers face conflicts related to family structure or the time they devote to business (De Clercq & Brieger, 2022). Second, the conflict revolves around the level of business satisfaction and its response to business success. Third, if the business achieves the expected success, mumpreneurs will gain satisfaction, which can reduce conflict. Fourth, role conflict is often faced by mumpreneurs with low self-esteem (De Clercq & Brieger, 2022).

Lack of capital or financial resources is a problem continually faced by an entrepreneur who wants to start a business. Entrepreneurs must have sufficient capital or financial resources such as investment, technology, and raw materials to obtain the resources needed to run a business (Wang et al., 2020). Most entrepreneurs finance their businesses either through savings or personal loans. However, this situation is changing because business capitalists and financial institutions are changing and opening space for women entrepreneurs to get financial assistance. Furthermore, women are more disciplined in repaying the loans made. The financial gap is the difference between the amount of financial assistance women entrepreneurs require and the available assistance. This gap is narrowing as those who provide financial assistance increasingly realize that businesses managed by mumpreneurs are potential investment sites that have previously received little attention. This gap can also be reduced by increasing women's experience in the financial field.

Traditionally, mumpreneurs rarely receive formal training or education to become entrepreneurs (Noor & Isa, 2020). Most mumpreneurs become entrepreneurs and learn from their experiences. They learn the ins and outs of the business, how to negotiate with banks, make business plans, hire and fire employees, and then grow the business through real-world experience. However, the atmosphere has changed. Various training and educational opportunities related to entrepreneurship are offered to women entrepreneurs, increasing their business opportunities (Afshan et al., 2021). Next, most entrepreneurs will face the problem of competition in running a business (Lestari et al., 2020). Entrepreneurs should always ensure that the products or services produced can compete with competitors (Babina et al., 2024). In running a business, promotion is essential in beating competitors and improving the business's reputation. Therefore, entrepreneurs must always produce strategies to overcome competition and maintain sales and profits. Next, the difficulty in getting skilled and experienced workers also makes it a problem for a mumpreneur. Skilled and experienced employees can perform their duties well and may be able to meet customer satisfaction and improve the reputation of the business (Bilan et al., 2020).

One of the biggest concerns of entrepreneurs is failure. Although efforts have been made to eliminate failure, it cannot be denied that reputation can still be damaged by unfulfilled contracts and disappointment from investors (Hillson, 2023). Aside from financial problems, reputational risk is the most challenging issue for many entrepreneurs to survive. Rapid business growth is essential to running and continuing a business. Entrepreneurs need to find and ensure that their market and business can proliferate. Most women entrepreneurs need help growing their businesses to ensure the right market. Entrepreneurs should ensure customer demand for products or services in their business so that the business can grow and adapt to meet the basic needs of customers (Varadarajan, 2020).

Enablers of Mumpreneur's Success

According to Daspit et al. (2023), entrepreneurs can see, control, seize, and create new opportunities and are ready to face risks or losses. The field of entrepreneurship is a field that can generate profit, contribute to increasing per capita income, and open job opportunities. This field also has the potential to reduce the problem of poverty and empower the national economy (Sajjad et al., 2020). Successful entrepreneurs have a highly innovative nature that can reveal new ideas and products and promote competition in business (Neumann, 2021). In the business world, women have their advantages. Women are often more prepared to face a variety of customers and diligently manage the business. Entrepreneurship is a field with a high risk of failure, but the involvement of women, especially in this field, shows a positive trend. Many factors encourage a woman to engage in business as an economic activity. Most women who venture into business are already involved in other jobs, such as public or private sector. Some have been self-employed in various fields, such as agriculture, handicraft enterprises, and food. For this reason, they try to open their businesses. Some entrepreneurs enter the business field due to compelling circumstances, such as needing the appropriate qualifications. They started a business at the insistence of life, family, and people around them. They depend on the available capital, ability, experience, and support of the people around them (Jafari-Sadeghi, 2020).

Many factors affect the success of mumpreneurs in either micro or macro enterprises. Previous studies found that internal and external factors affect an entrepreneur's success. Salmony and Kanbach (2022) and Noor et al. (2023) found that the characteristics and personality of the entrepreneur are critical factors that affect the success of entrepreneurs. External factors such as networking, infrastructure, economic conditions, and government and NGO assistance also contribute to the success of entrepreneurs (Kaciak & Welsh, 2020; Mohd Noor et al., 2023). Capital is the most critical factor in business development (Al-Fadhat, 2022). If the capital is insufficient, the business will not progress and will likely face the risk of bankruptcy. Adeola et al. (2021) found that the mumpreneur development strategy must include other essential factors such as age, gender, business period, monitoring aspects, business characteristics, management efficiency, optimistic attitude, social skills, social network, and risk-taking. Hossinger et al. (2020) found that management skills, industry experience, planning and economic conditions, social relations, networking, and marketing influence the mumpreneur's success.

Belitski et al. (2020) found that skills and training are the most critical factors influencing entrepreneurs' success. According to Ubfal et al. (2022), an entrepreneur who wants to succeed must have distinctive and unique characteristics. Therefore, to be successful, entrepreneurs need to equip themselves with characteristics such as responsibility, high confidence, knowledge, and religious or spiritual characteristics (Lok et al., 2021). Previous researchers found that motivation, interest, network, and innovation are among the factors contributing to mumpreneurial success (Belitski et al. (2020; Nabi et al., 2021). In addition, technology is relevant to women's empowerment and the involvement of women entrepreneurs in the field (Kruger & Steyn, 2020).

Empowering means giving an individual the power or opportunity to participate in society. However, impoverished women often lack the resources to empower their lives. A person in poverty generally has difficulty accessing education, employment, resources, and opportunities (Banihani, 2020). Continuous support makes an entrepreneur more motivated and always strives to move forward. In Malaysia, several organizations work to uplift and support women. Ibupreneur, for example, is a social enterprise that functions as a platform for homemakers to generate income by selling food such as pastries, cakes, and others. Next, Women of Will (WOW) is an NGO that aims to change the lives of women facing economic problems through micro-credit financing and entrepreneurship programs. With this initiative, they help B40 women to get financial independence. They do this by equipping these women with the necessary entrepreneurial skills such as marketing, communication, financial management, and planning.

METHODOLOGY

This study employed a qualitative research approach under the interpretive research paradigm. Accordingly, the researchers have conducted semi-structured interviews. The purposive sampling technique is a type of non-probability sampling that is most effective when a researcher needs to study a specific cultural domain with experts. Therefore, a purposive sample consisting of 20 mumpreneurs of the food and beverage business in Kuala Lumpur, Malaysia, was used for this research. A common concept for sample size in qualitative research is data saturation. According to Malterud et al. (2016), adequate sample size depends on (a) the aim of the study, (b) the specificity of the sample, (c) the use of established theory, (d) the quality of the dialogue, and (e) the analysis strategy. Therefore, this study has selected a total of 20 respondents for interviews. These mumpreneurs who were selected as respondents have been involved in business for more than three years and have a strong business profile. A period of more than three years shows that the entrepreneur has succeeded through a critical time and has strengthened her ability as an entrepreneur. Past studies have shown that the length of time in business also contributes to entrepreneurial performance.

Based on Table 1, all key informants in this study are between 35 and 48 years old, and all had secondary-level education (i.e., the Malaysian Certificate of Education). Moreover, all informants are full-time entrepreneurs; most have been doing business for over five years. This study used personal networks, professional bodies, and communities of women entrepreneurs and social media to identify and approach study participants. Interviews were conducted face-to-face and digitally recorded with consent. On average, interviews last about an hour and a half to two hours. Interviews were transcribed word for word, and data analysis was used thematically.

FINDINGS

Challenges Involved in the Entrepreneurial Activities of Mumpreneurs

Lack of Financial Assistance

Lack of capital or financial resources is a problem continually faced by an entrepreneur who wants to start a business. Most business start-ups require a lot of financial resources and significant capital. Entrepreneurs must have sufficient capital or financial resources to obtain the resources needed to run a business (Wang et al., 2020). Most respondents admitted financial constraints are the main challenges during the start-up phase. The verbatim quote is as follows:

"Women entrepreneurs cannot run away from debt. I receive monthly Ringgit Malaysia (RM) 200 assistance from Zakat, but it is not enough to support my family life... I am not eligible for a business loan from the bank..." (R1, 45 years old).

The increasingly challenging economy makes entrepreneurs need more capital to expand their businesses. Rising raw material prices and management costs often hinder their continued growth (Al-Fadhat, 2022). The more challenging a country's economy is, the harder it is for businesses to survive. The verbatim quotes are as follows:

"I am in the cake business; a customer asked if the price has increased. Yes, the price must increase because raw materials such as planta and margarine have increased from RM4 to RM8. The price of flour has also gone up...The expenditure on kitchen items exceeded my monthly income. So, I must withdraw savings..." (R18, 36 years old).

"Previously, I sold cakes at RM2 for four grains of light flour, but now, five grains at the price of RM3 due to the increase in wheat flour. Despite raising the price by RM1, customers understand the cost of goods that are rising now" (R15, 36 years old).

Many mumprenuers in this study are not eligible for loan assistance from the bank loan due to lower credit scores. If the entrepreneurs cannot pay their debts consistently monthly, it will be difficult for the bank to allow them to make or approve a loan. Therefore, financial management needs to be more

Table 1. Profile of the mumpreneurs

No.	Informant	Age	Educational Level	Type of Product	Business Orientation	Business Duration
1	R1	45	Secondary	Cupcakes, Festive Cookies, & Pudding	Full-time	>5 years
2	R2	44	Secondary	Strawberry Shortcake, Festive Cookies, & Dessert	Full-time	>5 years
3	R3	37	Secondary	A Packed Lunch	Full-time	>5 years
4	R4	35	Secondary	Cookies & Traditional Sweet or Savoury Confectionery	Full-time	>5 years
5	R5	36	Secondary	Biscuit & Festive Cookies	Full-time	>5 years
6	R6	29	Secondary	A Packed Lunch	Full-time	≤5 years
7	R7	46	Secondary	Filled Cookies & Traditional Sweet or Savoury Confectionery	Full-time	>5 years
8	R8	37	Secondary	Sponge, Pound, & Chiffon Cakes	Full-time	≤5 years
9	R9	40	Secondary	Jelly Pudding, Chips, & Festive Cookies	Full-time	>5 years
10	R10	36	Secondary	Fruit Tarts & Festive Cookies	Full-time	≤5 years
11	R11	41	Secondary	A Packed Lunch, Festive Cookies, & Chips	Full-time	>5 years
12	R12	42	Secondary	Bread Pudding & Chips	Full-time	>5 years
13	R13	35	Secondary	Cheesecakes & Festive Cookies	Full-time	>5 years
14	R14	38	Secondary	Chocolate Chip, Festive Cookies, & Popcorn	Full-time	≤5 years
15	R15	36	Secondary	Cassava Cake & Traditional Sweet or Savoury Confectionery	Full-time	>5 years
16	R16	48	Secondary	Ice Pop, Festive Cookies, & Baby Pancakes	Full-time	>5 years
17	R17	40	Secondary	Bread Pudding, Festive Cookies, & Egg Sponge Cake	Full-time	>5 years
18	R18	36	Secondary	Banana Cake, Festive Cookies, & Puff Pastry	Full-time	>5 years
19	R19	37	Secondary	Rose Sagu Cake & Traditional Sweet or Savoury Confectionery	Full-time	>5 years
20	R20	40	Secondary	Frozen Food, Festive Cookies, & Dessert	Full-time	>5 years

organized in the future to improve credit. Some financial institutions may need to be more confident in approving high loans for first-time applicants. When the loan applicant has no credit record, the financial institution cannot check the loan payment habits. Therefore, financial institutions only dare to bear the risk if they can make repayments.

Poor Business Location

In the business world, location is critical. The scramble to get this strategic location depends on financial and political factors. Most of the mumprenuers voiced that getting the right place or a strategic location is the main reason their business performance could be more encouraging. The ideal location to start a business is an area with a large population with high purchasing power (Aladejebi, 2020). The high purchasing power of buyers shows their ability to buy a product or service. The verbatim quotes are as follows:

"When I started my business, there was a lack of raw materials (coconut) and an increase in coconut prices. Moreover, the access to shops that are less attractive because they are in remote residences" (R7, 46 years old).

"I do business on the side of the road in a residential area, and this location is indeed strategic, but there is much competition where other neighbor shops also sell the same products. The next problem is that my business area is on a busy road where cars are difficult to stop. Even if they can turn and enter the shopping area, it will be difficult to enter the busy street; at least they will have to wait a long time" (R19, 37 years old).

Therefore, the main attraction of the business industry is the potential to penetrate and dominate the market in the area. Infrastructural facilities in selected places, such as water, electricity, and telephone, make mumpreneurs' business easier. A good infrastructure makes it easier for a business to establish relationships with external parties such as customers, suppliers, research agencies, and government institutions. A suitable business site area is required for the most efficient or optimal production scale.

Poor Customer Management

Entrepreneurs must always adhere to business ethics and respect and appreciate their respective customers by being patient and tolerant. Cheating is strictly prohibited in business. The best service that touches customers' emotions and makes them purchase again (Lok et al., 2021). It is the most popular and commonly used technique by many Malaysian entrepreneurs, where a gift is necessary for every purchase. This kind of attraction always wins the behavior of Malaysian buyers. However, many entrepreneurs need to be made aware of managing customers properly. The verbatim quotes are as follows:

"I never thought nasi lemak stalls needed customer relationship management. I am confident that the sweet and spicy sambal and fragrant chicken rendang are enough to make people keep coming. When I started my business, I never knew how to promote. After knowing about this, I started to promote and give free samples to the customers, and now, more customers have come to my stall, and even many customers have ordered it for their office and personal events" (R6, 29 years old).

"I saw that many of my customers had started going to another stall at the end of the intersection. I am lurking from afar to see how the stall owner does business… There was a female customer who stopped by with a small child in a baby seat; the seller helped take the order without the female customer having to get off. The food was ready to be wrapped, and the merchant ran to deliver it to the woman's car. My friends also saw that the seller packed four free donuts for customers who bought more than three rice packs. I am surprised and disappointed because I never thought to do it" (R11, 41 years old).

Maintaining customer loyalty has become a significant challenge for businesses worldwide, including mumpreneurs in an era of increasing choice and evolving customer expectations. The ability to cultivate lasting relationships with customers is the secret ingredient that distinguishes a thriving business. Knowing the customers also involves developing personas or customer profiles that represent typical segments of the target audience. In this study, most mumprenuers do not evaluate and improve the overall customer experience. They need to change their business strategies by analyzing customer feedback, conducting usability tests, and monitoring customer satisfaction metrics to identify areas for improvement. Consistently improving the customer experience will demonstrate a commitment to meeting customer needs and preferences and strengthening loyalty.

Weak Marketing Strategy

After starting a business, an effective marketing strategy is essential to attract customers and increase revenue. There are several marketing strategies that business owners in Malaysia can use. Small business owners can use social media to promote their business. Business owners can use an effective marketing strategy to reach more customers and increase their income. Many informants admitted they use ineffective marketing strategies which affect their business performance. The verbatim quotes are as follows:

"Sometimes, I am inconsistent in managing posting, sharing, or messages regarding my products. Many of my friends have used TikTok for marketing, and their income is increasing. However, I am not good at producing creative and unique videos. Now, I have become proficient, and for me to sell goods and services online, TikTok Shop requires knowledge of how to sell wisely and effectively" (R14, 38 years old).

"When I first started doing business, I tried all kinds of marketing ways, but everything did not work out. Every day, I post a status, and people like it. Very few people ask to buy. If you can sell even one sale, feel very grateful. For me, entrepreneurs need to attend workshops, and we need to explain to customers as simply as possible, with easy-to-understand language, so that they see the value of our products" (R8, 37 years old).

Marketing needs to be data-driven. Mumpreneurs need to understand the sales funnel and make improvements to it. In today's scenario, the approach of social media is becoming a phenomenon and essential to the business. Mumpreneurs can use marketing technology through social media to ensure that marketing activities can be improved. The use of social media that is more dynamic and integrated needs to emphasize the high visibility factor during its use. The visibility factor needs attention to be competitive and gain attention from Internet users.

Product Delivery Issue

Undoubtedly, entrepreneurs and delivery service operators have a symbiotic relationship; entrepreneurs can expand their business and increase the number of customers, and delivery service operators get more users and directly contribute to the company's income. However, most informants stated that the delivery service only benefits the providers, and they suffer from the high costs. The verbatim quotes are as follows:

"With a capital of RM1, what is the lowest price that can be sold to get a gross profit above the commission given to food delivery service operators earlier if they put 30% of sales as commission? The answer is RM2.50, so 75 cents will be given to the delivery service operator as a commission, while 75 cents is the merchant's profit. Imagine food with higher capital. For example, if the commission is as much as 30%, the profit margin must be maintained at least 75%. If it is 25%, the profit margin must be maintained at least 50%. This, of course, adds to the burden. If 50 packs are sold by delivery in one day, the delivery service operator will receive as much as RM1125 in a month. That amount is close to the minimum wage of RM1200 set by the government. If the price is not increased, the profit will decrease. If the price increases, consumers will switch to cheaper options or buy from other sellers" (R4, 35 years old).

"To compete with established sellers with more followers and loyal customers, we are forced to trade with lower profit margins. The mini cake, normally RM3, must be sold for RM4.30 to maintain profit. Thus, I do not want to use food delivery services anymore…What we can do as sellers is trying to provide delivery facilities on our own and use food delivery services from outside" (R11, 41 years old).

Poor Management

Financial institutions acting as lenders focus on financial management, especially working capital management. Small businesses need to manage working capital. The receipt of cash will ensure the smoothness of the business process. Many entrepreneurs need substantial collateral, business records, questionable financial status, and an organized management system. Most entrepreneurs need to be more efficient in managing the profit and loss of their business. The verbatim quotes are as follows:

"I cannot receive a bank loan because there is no record of money going in and out. I managed my business using my account early in my business journey. I also never sent a tax form because I do not know. My record track is not pretty. I have late payment of personal loans. Thus, I borrowed money from my family members and friends" (R12, 42 years old).

"Since I am working and managing my business alone, it is hard for me to manage time between housewife and business responsibilities. I have young children, and my husband has a job. Sometimes, I am slow to respond to orders and complaints, and a few customers feel ignored and disappointed. Therefore, I always limit the order of my product due to shortage of workforce and time" (R5, 36 years old).

Mumpreneurs need to improve their business management from time to time. If they leave it static without improving, their business will remain at the same level and slow in improvement. Therefore, mumpreneurs must have a growth mindset and always look for things that can be improved.

Shift Competition

Competition in business is a natural thing and difficult to avoid. It occurs when two or more businesses sell the same product or service, or if they sell different products, they target the same group of customers. This business competition can positively and negatively impact business owners and consumers, depending on how they manage it (Lok et al., 2021). Suppose it is proven that the new competitor is much better than the existing business; slowly, the existing business will surely start to receive negative impacts (Babina et al., 2024), and most informants fear the competition. The verbatim quotes are as follows:

"The sales of the traditional confectionery made with my mother over the past nine years had declined during and after the COVID-19 pandemic. During the MCO, we got orders from regular customers; however, the number was not many. Business after the MCO is quite slow; it is hard to get sales like before. Now, it is hard to sell 200 to 300 desserts daily... To increase sales, I also do business on a cash-on-delivery (COD) basis and promote it through the social media site" (R4, 35 years old).

"This is our survival in the face of competition outside. We also market our products to corporate companies interested in placing orders. We had to work hard to expand the business since the company did not make any loans from any banking institution. If we do not work hard, recovering working capital to increase production will be difficult. This factor causes us to constantly think of ways to increase sales despite competing with other competitors" (R7, 46 years old).

Online business nowadays is increasingly gaining a place among the community in Malaysia; this is in line with the influence of the Industrial Revolution 4.0, which shows an explosion in digital technology as a new platform to work; even this digital technology is increasingly used and received during the COVID pandemic -19 which has forced part of the employment sector to work from home. Mumpreneurs also feel this. Therefore, online business is an alternative that can be explored, and it allows the long-term survival of a business. However, due to technological deficiencies, not all entrepreneurs can adapt to the changes that have left them behind. It has been found that most entrepreneurs still need help maximizing the use of digital platforms, even if they are not motivated to use digital platforms in their business dealings. This may also be because most of them need better and stronger internet facilities in the area where they live. The weakness of internet facilities in their area causes them not to switch need to switch to e-commerce usage. The use of e-commerce among entrepreneurs is still at a basic level where they only use computer operations such as basic accounting, financial data, and emailing.

Enablers for Mumpreneurs

Capital and Aid

The strength of business capital assistance from the government and relevant agencies is the main factor influencing the success of mumpreneurs. Capital obtained for free or loans are used to expand the business market. Mumpreneurs who want to expand their business and need additional capital can get information from various agencies that offer financing facilities. The interview revealed that some mumprenuers actively seek support from funding agencies such as MARA, TEKUN, SME Bank, and others. The verbatim quotes are as follows:

"After two years of operating my business, I received capital assistance from TEKUN National and TemanNita Program Funding Scheme. This scheme helps women entrepreneurs get group financing more easily, quickly, and efficiently for business needs. Using the assistance, I could buy a thermal printer, known as a barcode printer. This facilitates the courier during the pickup process. Moreover, I can buy

a photo mini studio lighting box, which helps me capture the picture of my cake with a bright LED light that can focus on the product" (R2, 44 years old).

"I have received Amanah Ikhtiar Malaysia (AIM), which provides small financing or micro-credit that is used to finance my business activities. I also received Zakat aid from the Federal Territories Islamic Religious Council (MAIWP). I also receive mobile truck financing without interest under the MAIWP program" (R6, 29 years old).

Motivation

Motivation is vital in inspiring and encouraging those who want to venture into entrepreneurship (Mohd Noor et al., 2023). A successful entrepreneur has a high spirit without knowing the meaning of despair. This group has a high self-motivation for them to dare themselves in the field of entrepreneurship that they engage in. Motivation is an internal feeling that drives an individual to form behavior to ensure perfection in achieving goals. In other words, motivation explains why people start acting to do something. Therefore, motivation from various aspects is essential for an entrepreneur to become successful. The verbatim quotes are as follows:

"Like myself, I worked for a salary while running a part-time business for two years before having the confidence to quit my job and focus on the full-time business. I believe any business is a solution to problems and needs. I always think of business as a platform for helping more people and not just a platform to make a profit" (R15, 36 years old).

"Some use dirty techniques and strategies to get a bigger market, such as cheating people, bringing other parties down, spreading bad news about other businesses, and 1001 other dirty ways and techniques. It must be very challenging. The way to win in business among competitors is to work harder. Focus efforts on branding your business and never give up. I always find positive circles" (R18, 36 years old).

Successful mumpreneurs work diligently regardless of the time. If a job needs to be completed, they will continue to work until it is completed. Mumpreneurs must have strong self-discipline to obey the rules that have been chosen and set. Attitude is a factor that will determine whether they will be successful or not. Thus, a positive attitude here will be critical to a successful mumpreneur.

Business Skills

Knowledge in business management allows managers to make better, more accurate, and faster planning and decisions, thus reducing the risk of loss (Mohd Noor et al., 2024). As a business in this digital era, entrepreneurs must rely on more than just customers to come to the physical premises. The use of technology and the presence on digital platforms, including social media, is essential to enable entrepreneurs to promote products more effectively. The results of the interviews conducted by the researchers found that every entrepreneur always strives to gain business knowledge. Making knowledge ranked at the top causes us to always follow any courses and seminars organized. These entrepreneurs always seek opportunities to gain business knowledge, especially about marketing, packaging, and branding. The right advice and training services can improve the knowledge and skills of entrepreneurs while making them more competitive and increasing creativity in challenging business environments (Belitski et al., 2020). In this study, the researchers found an informant who stated they could succeed in business because of high entrepreneurial skills. Among the verbatim quotes are the following:

"Successful entrepreneurs are those who have knowledge and experience in the business field. Mumpreneurs have many shortcomings. Therefore, they should be fully assisted and supported from a material, physical, and mental point of view. When one has extensive knowledge, the entrepreneurs can have high self-confidence because the knowledge provided is sufficient" (R2, 44 years old).

"Based on my experience, the best entrepreneurs are not the ones who think they know everything but those who are not afraid to say I am not sure, and I do not know. This makes their minds always in a state of curiosity and thinking so that they continue to learn" (R3, 37 years old).

In the fast-changing business world, it is essential to keep updating knowledge of financial management. By increasing their knowledge, entrepreneurs can make informed financial decisions for small businesses. For example, as follows:

"Financial management skills are helpful for my business. I issue a receipt each time a transaction occurs, and I record the transaction in the cash book every day after the sale. I also learned to use Microsoft Excel software, which helps in determining the selling price per product unit. By recording all these transactions accurately and promptly, I gained a better understanding of the financial health of my business" (R5, 36 years old).

It takes work to deal with customer hassles. However, suppose there is a mistake or shortage; for example, the item arrives late, needs to be faster to answer questions, or the item delivered needs to be of better quality. In that case, sellers need to apologize to the customer and professionally solve the problem quickly (Lok et al., 2021). Otherwise, they will lose customers. Managing customers is a vital element and needs to be considered by all entrepreneurs. For example, as follows:

"How much does this cake cost.. It is expensive... the cake shop in front of my house is still cheap... These words I always received when I started my business... It takes time to lock the price of the cake I produce. I produced a cake through the trial-and-error process. Not once did I get to taste the cake I wanted; it took up to 8 attempts. Also, because I make a premium cake where all the ingredients I use are carefully selected and of good quality, I must calculate the cost involved carefully. I use marketing strategies and communicate the facts with my existing and potential customers, and nowadays, I am grateful to be blessed with customers who understand. Thus, I am not afraid anymore to put value on the products produced" (R13, 35 years old).

Innovation

Continuous innovation is an internal business factor that must be addressed in the digital age. In an ever-changing world, entrepreneurs must keep innovating to adapt to technological developments. Continuous innovation involves introducing new products or services, improving business processes, or developing new business models (Belitski et al., 2020). It requires a business culture that encourages creativity, employee engagement, and investment in research and development. Innovative packaging will give the company an advantage over competitors in increasing sales (Babina et al., 2024). The verbatim quotes are as follows:

"I have changed my frozen food packaging into a retort pouches design. I like to travel and am attracted by food packs that are ready to be eaten by just putting them in hot water for a few minutes. I decided to study the technology course the Majlis Amanah Raya (MARA) conducted. The community's demand for ready-to-eat food is increasing and is now a wide-open opportunity for SMEs" (R20, 40 years old).

"Before this, I only sold Maruku, and I have expanded the flavor varieties. This includes fish, shrimp, garlic, red onion, chicken, spicy, and cheese flavors. Each of Maruku's products has been packed in a quantity of half a kilogram. I also used standing pouch packaging to attract customers. This finish is considered more unique and creative" (R7, 46 years old).

Network

In developing a business, entrepreneurs should improve the network of entrepreneurs between themselves and the people around their business. The network is a source of sustainable competitive advantage. Good guidance can help entrepreneurs to obtain information before making any investment. It gives confidence and can reduce the risk of loss, competition, and products that cannot penetrate the market (Noor et al., 2023). Networking helps build trust because much information can be shared. Through networking, many new ideas can be obtained to create new products or services (Lok et al., 2021). Most informants had agreed that networking help them to penetrate their products into the market. The verbatim quotes are as follows:

"I have attended entrepreneurship training, and thankfully, I know many coaches who can help me. For example, after the training, a trainer helped me to market my nasi lemak at a bank located in Kuala Lumpur. My nasi lemak was placed in their canteen. So, as entrepreneurs, we should not be shy. We must find a network with them in the environment. Who knows that person will help us without us thinking" (R11, 41 years old).

"I am grateful because my business is growing with strong network results. Many of my friends and customers help in promoting my products. They will inform me to get involved if there is an entrepreneurial carnival. Recently, I got an order from the ministry for the SME carnival in Putrajaya. Three hundred jars of my crackers have been ordered as door gifts" (R4, 35 years old).

Technology Absorption

In general, e-commerce is a system that enables sellers and consumers to sell and purchase goods or services on the Internet. This e-commerce application always makes business activities easier regardless of place (Tham & Atan, 2021). Furthermore, social media has become an online business medium that makes it easier for global consumers to buy. The verbatim quote is as follows:

"Since 2020, many people have started doing online business, and I started to use social media platforms. I have been doing online business for a long time, but sales are still stuck. I always receive more than 15 WhatsApp a day. Sometimes I have missed replying on WhatsApp, and finally, I decided to use an e-commerce website where customers can continue to make purchases on the website" (R15, 36 years old).

Many government agencies actively produce food and beverage processing machines and equipment, especially for products requiring unique manufacturing technology and complicated mechanization processes. The verbatim quote is as follows:

"Before this, I made donuts manually, kneaded myself, shaped myself, and fried myself. However, recently, I got the help of a machine from MARA to knead and fry donuts automatically. Today, I can prepare 500 donuts in a day. This machine can reduce costs, save time, and is not complicated" (R7, 46 years old).

Business Support

Of course, working women, especially those who are married, bear the brunt of great responsibility and role as a wife, mothers, and an entrepreneur. In addition, the workload and insufficient time to perform the task simultaneously adversely affect family institutions. Support from close family members and friends is an essential factor leading to the success of entrepreneurs. Mumpreneurs need emotional support from their social networks, especially their close relations, such as their husbands, fathers, mothers, friends, and relatives (De Clercq & Brieger, 2022). The verbatim quotes are as follows:

"I express my desire and ask for some commitment from my husband. A good husband will support you and help you facilitate online business affairs. You need to involve your husband and visualize that this online business will become a family business" (R16, 48 years old).

"I am a person who is very committed to whatever task is done. Plus, I like a challenge. That is why I am always ready to commit to the scope of my career fully. My husband's approval and support are critical to make me a successful woman. I am lucky because my husband is also a successful entrepreneur. He has been in this field longer and is familiar with the ins and outs of business" (R12, 42 years old).

DISCUSSION

Women not only play a role in the household, but they also play a significant role in uplifting the nation (Iqbal et al., 2024; Love et al., 2024). Mumpreneurs can operate enterprises dynamically. Positive thinking in business development is permanently embedded in the heart and translated through creativity and innovation in producing products and services. This study has specifically addressed knowledge gaps related to mumpreneurs in the context of developing countries. This study has answered the call for more research on the development of women entrepreneurs. Most studies on women are biased towards women's entrepreneurship in general, and there is a lack of studies on mumpreneurs. Even among the existing studies on mumpreneurs, only a few focus specifically on their challenges and enablers. Therefore, this study has added to existing knowledge about mumpreneurs by addressing this gap. The study found

Figure 2. Thematic findings summary

Challenges	Enabler
•Lack of Financial Assistance •Poor Business Location •Poor Customer Management •Weak Marketing Strategy •Weak Marketing Strategy •Product Delivery Issue •Poor Management •Shift Competition	•Capital & Aid •Motivation •Business Skills •Innovation •Network •Technology Absorption •Business Support

various entrepreneurial challenges, including lack of financial assistance, poor business location, poor customer management, weak marketing strategy, product delivery issues, poor management, and shift competition. On the other hand, the enablers identified are capital and aid, motivation, business skills, innovation, network, technology absorption, and business support. These findings have been supported by previous studies such as Al-Fadhat (2022), Afshan et al. (2021), Babina et al. (2024), Belitski et al. (2020), Lestari et al. (2020), Mohd Noor et al. (2024), Röglinger et al. (2022), and Wach et al. (2020).

From the study results, several strategies can be implemented to increase mumpreneurs' competitiveness. Among those strategies are networking and cooperation between essential stakeholders (i.e., government agencies, NGOs, universities, banks, industry, and private sector), empowering entrepreneurial skills, applying current technology, promoting gender-neutral practices, focusing on innovation and business collaboration among entrepreneurs, community-based business incubators, and establishing a social enterprise. Advances in technology, such as video blogs (Vlogs) or YouTube, need to be utilized to promote a product that wants to be commercialized. Involvement in any association can help them expand their business network further. The associations and organizations can also help mumpreneurs get more opportunities and information about entrepreneurship assistance (Kaciak & Welsh, 2020).

The government needs to review the regulatory policies related to entrepreneurship and the institutional support that can be provided to encourage more women to enter the field of entrepreneurship. The government must create and spread awareness about women's entrepreneurial business models and adopt gender-neutral practices among those who implement their initiatives. Ranwala and Surangi's (2023) study revealed that social, environmental, and individual factors are the main themes when choosing mumpreneurs as a career option, and mumpreneurs have issues satisfying family and business demands. Mumpreneurs could use coping strategies such as networking, time management, and home-based business strategies. To ensure that women's involvement in the labor market and entrepreneurship is more effective, the support system needs to be improved, especially regarding infrastructure, policies, and appropriate legislation. The Ministry of Women, Family, and Community Development needs to implement the initiative of childcare facilities not only at the workplace but also at the community center, especially in low-income group housing areas. This issue involving gender discrimination should be taken seriously and should not be taken lightly. Women should have the right to receive equal treatment and be given the space and opportunity to contribute to the country's development (Al-Fadhat, 2022).

Further, universities, associations, and NGOs must support mumpreneurs' businesses by introducing research funds, entrepreneurial activities, and moral support (Mohd Noor et al., 2024). For example, many public universities have embedded the elements of the University Social Responsibility (USR) program as part of the course assessment. Therefore, higher education institutions could play their role and share their academic expertise with the community, especially mumpreneurs. The program must be continuous and sustainable and not a one-end program. The interviews also implied that mumprenuers use traditional ways (i.e., governmental, NGOs, and banks) to get financial support. Further, the government can launch financial assistance programs by collaborating with local and regional financial institutions focusing on mumpreneurs. Al-Nuimat et al. (2023) examined motivating factors for mumpreneurs' projects and showed that education and training played significant roles in mumpreneurs' business performance. Tailored entrepreneurial education and training allow mumpreneurs to improve their knowledge and technical skills. Entrepreneurs also need to know how to record the money and expenses of their business. With sound financial management, they will avoid overspending or miscalculating costs (Llados-Masllorens & Ruiz-Dotras, 2021).

Next, community-based business incubators can also provide various facilities such as workspace, financial assistance, training, mentoring, and a vast network of business contacts (Haugh, 2021). Entrepreneurs can start their businesses more efficiently and organize with a business incubator. The business incubator has a vast network of business contacts. This network of business contacts is essential for entrepreneurs because they can obtain support from other parties, such as investors, customers, and business partners. With this support, entrepreneurs can overcome problems more effectively so that their businesses can continue to develop and grow. Currently, most business incubators are remote from the community, especially low-income group communities. These people do not have time due to family responsibilities and lack of finances, and many do not even need transportation. These limitations have caused them to be unable to participate in incubator programs.

Moreover, in a shift competition environment, the mumpreneurs need to take action to improve the quality of their products or services. Possible improvements could be in form 1) price reduction, 2) selling products in several packages, and 3) addition in terms of function, color, and design (Lestari et al., 2020). Sometimes, the competition does not necessarily need to be seen as a threat or an enemy that needs to be eliminated. The emerging competition can be advantageous for competing parties to collaborate and establish cooperation (Bills et al., 2021). For example, mumpreneurs in the food and beverage industry can collaborate to design and create an e-commerce website to sell various foods from various vendors.

Considering that the majority of these mumpreneurs lack workforce and business funds, and most of them are in the B40 group (Bottom 40%) in which household income is less than RM5,250, the researchers suggest the establishment of the entity known as a social enterprise or corporate with an existing social enterprise. Social enterprise in Malaysia has an excellent opportunity to be used as a stable job and simultaneously can unite all walks of life, including marginalized communities. Social entrepreneurs can function as small and medium-sized businesses (SMEs), billion-dollar companies, or even micro-industry business operators who can profit while positively affecting all parties (Kickul & Lyons, 2020). Ministries and government agencies have formulated policies and regulations to support women's entrepreneurship development in this country. Based on a semi-structured interview with 34 Malaysian women

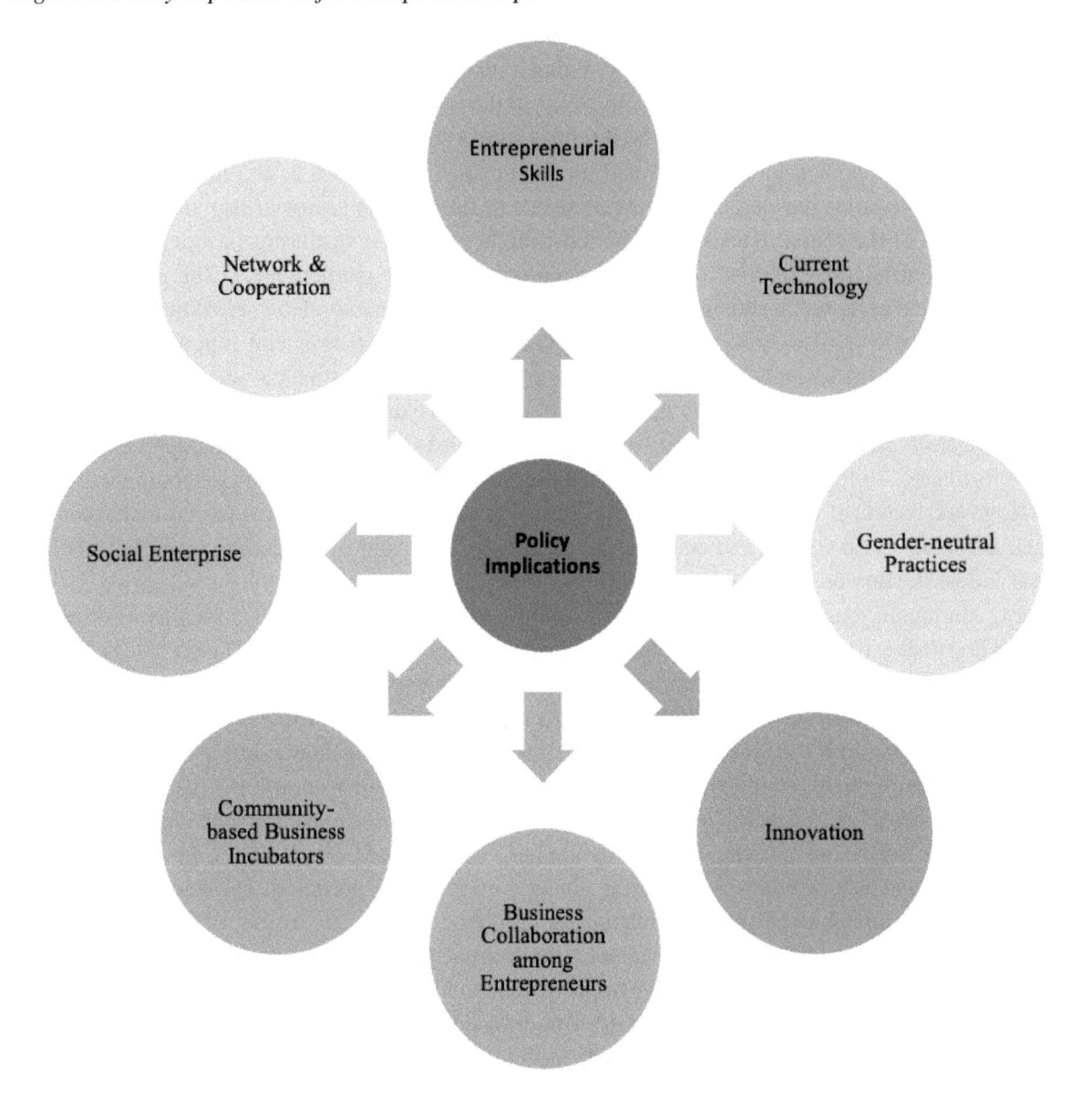

Figure 3. Policy implications for mumpreneurships

[Figure 3: A diagram with "Policy Implications" at the center, with arrows pointing to eight surrounding circles: Entrepreneurial Skills, Current Technology, Gender-neutral Practices, Innovation, Business Collaboration among Entrepreneurs, Community-based Business Incubators, Social Enterprise, Network & Cooperation.]

entrepreneurs, Au et al. (2021) findings denote that cultural practices that encourage family members to support women entrepreneurs in their career choices and actions are crucial for the growth of women's entrepreneurship. However, there are still many areas that need to be improved. Since the government has long led most entrepreneurship development efforts in Malaysia, the involvement of private parties and active communities is expected to improve the existing entrepreneurial ecosystem. It is plausible to argue that promoting women's entrepreneurship is a multidimensional process. The findings of this study are relevant at the international level as they can support the achievement of sustainable development goal 5 for gender equality worldwide. Figure 3 summarises the policy implications of the study.

CONCLUSION

The development of women entrepreneurs is a national agenda that needs to be embraced and supported. Women entrepreneurs who emerged during the COVID-19 pandemic are expected to be able to encourage the creation of gender equality in Malaysia. However, it was found that the dominance of women entrepreneurs is oriented towards fulfilling daily needs and is primarily informal, like in the home industry, rather than in long-term business development. Many still look one-eyed at businesses pioneered by women that cannot grow for a broader market. Reflecting on those challenges, women entrepreneurs need to innovate and start to be oriented towards long-term business. There must be an effort to develop innovative entrepreneurship to increase the ability to make decisions and produce a good local product. This research is one of the latest empirical studies on the challenges and enablers faced by women entrepreneurs, which emphasizes the importance of future research in a different context, namely the mumpreneurs group. Future research should focus on other groups of entrepreneurs, such as male entrepreneurs and youth entrepreneurs, to better understand the role played by each group of entrepreneurs. The most significant limitation is the small sample size, which consists of twenty mumprenuers. The sample can be insignificant to provide a clear picture of critical challenges and drivers behind women entrepreneurs. Future studies are encouraged to focus on successful entrepreneurs since these groups have validated successful business performance, and their experience can be used as a benchmark for prospective entrepreneurial programs and strategies. Future research also should answer the research questions with a more robust data collection method, including focus groups and case studies, and use further quantitative analyses that could be able to collect from extensive sample data. Another limitation is the relatively homogenous sample, which consists of mumpreneurs from urban and low-income groups. The targeted mumpreneurs may not be representative of all Malaysian mumpreneurs. Thus, in terms of research directions, it would be helpful to include more heterogeneous samples of mumpreneurs in future work to increase the generalizability of the findings of this study.

ACKNOWLEDGEMENTS

This study was funded by the Ungku Aziz Centre for Development Studies, Kuala Lumpur, Malaysia, under the Concept Paper Poverty Research Lab@UAC Grant (Grant title: Developing Inclusive Model for Small and Medium-Sized Enterprises (SMEs) Women Entrepreneurs' Capacity in the Baking Business- UM.0000694/HGA.GV) and (Grant title: Initiating Business Activity among Women Entrepreneurs in Food (Chips) Trading-UM.0000685/HGA.GV). The researchers are also thankful to the participants involved in this study.

REFERENCES

Abdelzaher, D. M., Zalila, F., & Ramadan, N. N. (2021). Stigmatized minorities: An explorative study into the challenges of Muslim women entrepreneurs. *Journal for Global Business Advancement*, *14*(6), 822–844. doi:10.1504/JGBA.2021.125015

Abdullah, S., & Muhammad, A. (2008). The development of entrepreneurship in Malaysia: State-led initiatives. *Asian Journal of Technology Innovation*, 16(1), 101–116. doi:10.1080/19761597.2008.9668649

Adeola, O., Gyimah, P., Appiah, K. O., & Lussier, R. N. (2021). Can critical success factors of small businesses in emerging markets advance UN Sustainable Development Goals? *World Journal of Entrepreneurship, Management and Sustainable Development*, 17(1), 85–105. doi:10.1108/WJEMSD-09-2019-0072

Adhikari, H. (2022). Anxiety and depression: Comparative study between working and non-working mothers. *ACADEMICIA: An International Multidisciplinary Research Journal*, 12(2), 273–282. doi:10.5958/2249-7137.2022.00152.5

Adikaram, A. S., & Razik, R. (2023). Femininity penalty: Challenges and barriers faced by STEM woman entrepreneurs in an emerging economy. *Journal of Entrepreneurship in Emerging Economies*, 15(5), 1113–1138. doi:10.1108/JEEE-07-2021-0278

Afshan, G., Shahid, S., & Tunio, M. N. (2021). Learning experiences of women entrepreneurs amidst COVID-19. *International Journal of Gender and Entrepreneurship*, 13(2), 162–186. doi:10.1108/IJGE-09-2020-0153

Agrawal, R., Bakhshi, P., Chandani, A., Birau, R., & Mendon, S. (2023). Challenges faced by women entrepreneurs in South Asian countries using interpretive structural modeling. *Cogent Business & Management*, 10(2), 2244755. doi:10.1080/23311975.2023.2244755

Al-Fadhat, F. (2022). Big business capital expansion and the shift of Indonesia's global economic policy outlook. *East Asia (Piscataway, N.J.)*, 39(4), 389–406. doi:10.1007/s12140-022-09384-3

Al-Nuimat, A. A., Alserhan, B. A., Zeqiri, J., Hasani, V. V., & Komodromos, M. (2023). The motivating pull and push factors on the performance of mompreneurs projects: Educational and training barriers as a moderating variable. International Journal of Environment. *Workplace and Employment*, 7(4), 340–367. doi:10.1504/IJEWE.2023.138013

Aladejebi, O. (2020). Managing small businesses in Nigeria during COVID-19 crisis: Impact and survival strategies. *IOSR Journal of Business and Management*, 22(8), 24–34.

Babina, T., Fedyk, A., He, A., & Hodson, J. (2024). Artificial intelligence, firm growth, and product innovation. *Journal of Financial Economics*, 151, 103745. doi:10.1016/j.jfineco.2023.103745

Banihani, M. (2020). Empowering Jordanian women through entrepreneurship. *Journal of Research in Marketing and Entrepreneurship*, 22(1), 133–144. doi:10.1108/JRME-10-2017-0047

Belitski, M., Caiazza, R., & Rodionova, Y. (2020). Investment in training and skills for innovation in entrepreneurial start-ups and incumbents: Evidence from the United Kingdom. *The International Entrepreneurship and Management Journal*, 16(2), 617–640. doi:10.1007/s11365-019-00606-4

Bergman, B. J., & McMullen, J. S. (2022). Helping entrepreneurs help themselves: A review and relational research agenda on entrepreneurial support organizations. *Entrepreneurship Theory and Practice*, 46(3), 688–728. doi:10.1177/10422587211028736

Bilan, Y., Mishchuk, H., Roshchyk, I., & Joshi, O. (2020). Hiring and retaining skilled employees in SMEs: Problems in human resource practices and links with organizational success. *Business: Theory and Practice*, *21*(2), 780–791. doi:10.3846/btp.2020.12750

Bills, K. L., Hayne, C., Stein, S. E., & Hatfield, R. C. (2021). Collaborating with competitors: How do small firm accounting associations and networks successfully manage coopetitive tensions? *Contemporary Accounting Research*, *38*(1), 545–585. doi:10.1111/1911-3846.12625

Carlsen, L., & Bruggemann, R. (2022). The 17 United Nations' sustainable development goals: A status by 2020. *International Journal of Sustainable Development and World Ecology*, *29*(3), 219–229. doi: 10.1080/13504509.2021.1948456

Castro Núñez, R. B., Bandeira, P., & Santero-Sánchez, R. (2020). Social economy, gender equality at work and the 2030 agenda: Theory and evidence from Spain. *Sustainability (Basel)*, *12*(12), 5192. doi:10.3390/su12125192

Chávez Rivera, M. E., Fuentes Fuentes, M. D. M., & Ruiz-Jiménez, J. M. (2021). Challenging the context: Mumpreneurship, copreneurship, and sustainable thinking in the entrepreneurial process of women–a case study in Ecuador. *Academia (Caracas)*, *34*(3), 368–398. doi:10.1108/ARLA-07-2020-0172

Dang, H. A. H., & Nguyen, C. V. (2021). Gender inequality during the COVID-19 pandemic: Income, expenditure, savings, and job loss. *World Development*, *140*, 105296. doi:10.1016/j.worlddev.2020.105296 PMID:34548740

Daspit, J. J., Fox, C. J., & Findley, S. K. (2023). Entrepreneurial mindset: An integrated definition, a review of current insights, and directions for future research. *Journal of Small Business Management*, *61*(1), 12–44. doi:10.1080/00472778.2021.1907583

De Clercq, D., & Brieger, S. A. (2022). When discrimination is worse, autonomy is key: How women entrepreneurs leverage job autonomy resources to find work–life balance. *Journal of Business Ethics*, *177*(3), 665–682. doi:10.1007/s10551-021-04735-1

Department of Statistics Malaysia. (November 2022). *Women at a Glance 2021 - Department of Statistics Malaysia*. Retrieved from https://www.kln.gov.my/web/chl_santiago/news-from-mission/-/blogs/women-at-a-glance-2021

Department of Statistics Malaysia. (January 2014). *Labor Force Report November 2023*. DOSM. https://storage.dosm.gov.my/labour/lfs_month_2023-11_en.pdf

Dhaliwal, A. (2022). The mompreneurship phenomenon: An examination of the antecedents and challenges of mothers in business. [IJSSMET]. *International Journal of Service Science, Management, Engineering, and Technology*, *13*(1), 1–17. doi:10.4018/IJSSMET.290334

Eden, L., & Wagstaff, M. F. (2021). Evidence-based policymaking and the wicked problem of SDG 5 Gender Equality. *Journal of International Business Policy*, *4*(1), 28–57. doi:10.1057/s42214-020-00054-w

Fisher, A. N., & Ryan, M. K. (2021). Gender inequalities during COVID-19. *Group Processes & Intergroup Relations*, *24*(2), 237–245. doi:10.1177/1368430220984248

Haugh, H. (2021). Call the midwife! Business incubators as entrepreneurial enablers in developing economies. In Business, Entrepreneurship and Innovation Towards Poverty Reduction (pp. 156–175). Routledge. doi:10.4324/9781003176107-8

Hillson, D. (Ed.). (2023). *The risk management handbook: A practical guide to managing the multiple dimensions of risk*. Kogan Page Publishers.

Hossinger, S. M., Chen, X., & Werner, A. (2020). Drivers, barriers, and success factors of academic spin-offs: A systematic literature review. *Management Review Quarterly*, *70*(1), 97–134. doi:10.1007/s11301-019-00161-w

Iqbal, S., Farrukh, M., & Bhaumik, A. (2024). A retrospective of women entrepreneurship research and future research directions. *Vision (Basel)*, 09722629231219617. doi:10.1177/09722629231219617

Jafari-Sadeghi, V. (2020). The motivational factors of business venturing: Opportunity versus necessity? A gendered perspective on European countries. *Journal of Business Research*, *113*, 279–289. doi:10.1016/j.jbusres.2019.09.058

Jephcott, P., Seear, N., & Smith, J. H. (2023). *Married women working*. Routledge. doi:10.4324/9781003317777

Kaciak, E., & Welsh, D. H. (2020). Women entrepreneurs and work–life interface: The impact of sustainable economies on success. *Journal of Business Research*, *112*, 281–290. doi:10.1016/j.jbusres.2019.11.073

Kickul, J., & Lyons, T. S. (2020). *Understanding social entrepreneurship: The relentless pursuit of mission in an ever-changing world*. Routledge. doi:10.4324/9780429270406

Kruger, S., & Steyn, A. A. (2020). Enhancing technology transfer through entrepreneurial development: Practices from innovation spaces. *The Journal of Technology Transfer*, *45*(6), 1655–1689. doi:10.1007/s10961-019-09769-2

Lestari, S. D., Leon, F. M., Widyastuti, S., Brabo, N. A., & Putra, A. H. P. K. (2020). Antecedents and consequences of innovation and business strategy on performance and competitive advantage of SMEs. *The Journal of Asian Finance. Economics and Business*, *7*(6), 365–378.

Llados-Masllorens, J., & Ruiz-Dotras, E. (2021). Are women's entrepreneurial intentions and motivations influenced by financial skills? *International Journal of Gender and Entrepreneurship*, *14*(1), 69–94. doi:10.1108/IJGE-01-2021-0017

Lok, B. L., Cheng, M. Y., & Choong, C. K. (2021). The relationship between soft skills training and development, human resource outcome, and firm performance. *International Journal of Business and Society*, *22*(1), 382–402. doi:10.33736/ijbs.3184.2021

Love, I., Nikolaev, B., & Dhakal, C. (2024). The well-being of women entrepreneurs: The role of gender inequality and gender roles. *Small Business Economics*, *62*(1), 325–352. doi:10.1007/s11187-023-00769-z

Malterud, K., Siersma, V., & Guassora, A. D. (2021). Information power: Sample content and size in qualitative studies. In P. M. Camic (Ed.), *Qualitative research in psychology: Expanding perspectives in methodology and design* (pp. 67–81). American Psychological Association.

Mohd Noor, N. H., Mohamad Fuzi, A., & El Ashfahany, A. (2023). Institutional support and self-efficacy as catalysts for new venture performance: A study of iGen entrepreneurs. *Journal of Entrepreneurship and Public Policy*, *12*(3/4), 173–196. doi:10.1108/JEPP-02-2023-0015

Mohd Noor, N. H., Yaacob, M. A., & Omar, N. (2024). Do knowledge and personality traits influence women entrepreneurs' e-commerce venture? Testing on the multiple mediation model. *Journal of Entrepreneurship in Emerging Economies*, *16*(1), 231–256. doi:10.1108/JEEE-01-2023-0023

Nabi, G., Walmsley, A., & Akhtar, I. (2021). Mentoring functions and entrepreneur development in the early years of university. *Studies in Higher Education*, *46*(6), 1159–1174. doi:10.1080/03075079.2019.1665009

Neumann, T. (2021). The impact of entrepreneurship on economic, social, and environmental welfare and its determinants: A systematic review. *Management Review Quarterly*, *71*(3), 553–584. doi:10.1007/s11301-020-00193-7

Noor, N. H. M., Kamarudin, S. M., & Shamsudin, U. N. (2023). The influence of personality traits, university green entrepreneurial support, and environmental values on green entrepreneurial intention. [IJAFB]. *International Journal of Accounting, Finance, and Business*, *8*(48), 59–71.

Noor, S., & Isa, F. M. (2020). Contributing factors of women entrepreneurs' business growth and failure in Pakistan. *International Journal of Business and Globalisation*, *25*(4), 503–518. doi:10.1504/IJBG.2020.109115

Othman, I. W., Mokhtar, S., Maidin, I., & Moharam, M. M. A. H. (2021). The relevance of the National Entrepreneurship Policy (NEP) 2030 In meeting the needs and strengthening the country's entrepreneurial ecosystem: A snapshot. *The International Journal of Accounting*, *6*(37).

Pfordten, D. (2023). Malaysia: The country's population is growing at a faster rate, here's why. *The Star*. https://www.thestar.com.my/news/nation/2023/09/07/mymalaysia-the-country039s-population-is-growing-at-a-faster-rate-here039s-why

Rahman, M. M., Dana, L. P., Moral, I. H., Anjum, N., & Rahaman, M. S. (2023). Challenges of rural women entrepreneurs in Bangladesh to survive their family entrepreneurship: A narrative inquiry through storytelling. *Journal of Family Business Management*, *13*(3), 645–664. doi:10.1108/JFBM-04-2022-0054

Ranwala, R. S., & Surangi, H. A. K. N. S. (2023). A critical analysis of the experience of mumpreneurs: A study based on tourism industry in Sri Lanka. *Middle East Journal of Management*, *10*(2), 113–132. doi:10.1504/MEJM.2023.129446

Rodrigues, M., Daniel, A. D., & Franco, M. (2023). What is important to know about mumpreneurship? A bibliometric analysis. *The International Journal of Organizational Analysis*, *31*(7), 3413–3435. doi:10.1108/IJOA-05-2022-3293

Röglinger, M., Plattfaut, R., Borghoff, V., Kerpedzhiev, G., Becker, J., Beverungen, D., vom Brocke, J., Van Looy, A., del-Río-Ortega, A., Rinderle-Ma, S., Rosemann, M., Santoro, F. M., & Trkman, P. (2022). Exogenous shocks and business process management: A scholars' perspective on challenges and opportunities. *Business & Information Systems Engineering*, *64*(5), 669–687. doi:10.1007/s12599-021-00740-w

Sajjad, M., Kaleem, N., Chani, M. I., & Ahmed, M. (2020). Worldwide role of women entrepreneurs in economic development. *Asia Pacific Journal of Innovation and Entrepreneurship*, *14*(2), 151–160. doi:10.1108/APJIE-06-2019-0041

Salmony, F. U., & Kanbach, D. K. (2022). Personality trait differences across types of entrepreneurs: A systematic literature review. *Review of Managerial Science*, *16*(3), 713–749. doi:10.1007/s11846-021-00466-9

Tan, J. D., & Yew, J. L. K. (2023). Women entrepreneurship: Mumpreneurs cruising the COVID-19 pandemic in Indonesia. *Business and Society Review*, *128*(1), 133–168. doi:10.1111/basr.12302

Ubfal, D., Arraiz, I., Beuermann, D. W., Frese, M., Maffioli, A., & Verch, D. (2022). The impact of soft-skills training for entrepreneurs in Jamaica. *World Development*, *152*, 105787. doi:10.1016/j.worlddev.2021.105787

Varadarajan, R. (2020). Customer information resources advantage, marketing strategy, and business performance: A market resources-based view. *Industrial Marketing Management*, *89*, 89–97. doi:10.1016/j.indmarman.2020.03.003

Wach, D., Stephan, U., Gorgievski, M. J., & Wegge, J. (2020). Entrepreneurs' achieved success: Developing a multi-faceted measure. *The International Entrepreneurship and Management Journal*, *16*(3), 1123–1151. doi:10.1007/s11365-018-0532-5

Wang, X., Cai, L., Zhu, X., & Deng, S. (2020). Female entrepreneurs' gender roles, social capital, and willingness to choose external financing. *Asian Business & Management*, 1–26.

Wells, S. J. (2021). *Women entrepreneurs: Developing leadership for success*. Routledge. doi:10.4324/9781003250111

KEY TERMS AND DEFINITIONS

Developing Economy: A country with a low human development index, less growth, poor per capita income, and more inclined towards agriculture-based operations rather than industrialization and business.

Entrepreneurship: The ability and readiness to develop, organize, and run a business enterprise, along with any of its uncertainties to make a profit.

Mumprenuership: Business venture by a woman who identifies as both a mother and a businesswoman.

SDG 5: Achieve gender equality and empower women and girls by ending discrimination, violence, harmful practices, and unpaid work.

Chapter 11
Harnessing Competition Law and Policy for Achieving Sustainable Development Goals:
The Chinese Experience

Mohamad Zreik
https://orcid.org/0000-0002-6812-6529
Sun Yat-sen University, China

ABSTRACT

This research focuses on China, exploring the relationship between competition law and sustainable development within the context of rapid economic growth. It specifically examines how China's competition law and policies interact with selected SDGs - SDG 8, 12, 13, and 16. The study employs a qualitative approach, incorporating a systematic review of literature, legislative actions, and empirical data. Key case studies were chosen based on their relevance to SDGs, impact on competition laws, and data availability. These cases provide insights into the successes and challenges of China's approach, highlighting the tension between fostering national industries and maintaining healthy competition. The study also examines how competition laws can contribute to societal objectives beyond economic growth. It connects China's legislative framework with real-world outcomes, identifying areas of alignment and disparity.

INTRODUCTION

On the surface, sustainable development goals (SDGs) and competition law appear to be unrelated policy domains. A closer inspection, however, uncovers an intriguing overlap and mutual impact between them. The primary goals of competition law are to provide free and open markets, curb anticompetitive behavior, and safeguard consumer interests (Dennis Jr, 2011). The goals of economic growth, responsible consumerism, climate action, and the establishment of strong institutions all fit in well with these aims.

The United Nations' sustainable development objectives are an international rallying cry for a world free of poverty, environmental degradation, and conflict by the year 2030 (Kamau, Chasek, & O'Connor,

DOI: 10.4018/979-8-3693-2758-6.ch011

2018). Many of the 17 SDGs, which span a wide range of economic, social, and environmental goals, depend on the presence of free and fair markets. The rules of competition law apply here.

In order to achieve SDG 8, which calls for increased economic growth, competition legislation prohibits anti-competitive acts and encourages fair commerce. Overexploitation of resources and the formation of wasteful monopolies are two examples of how it can indirectly promote responsible consumption and production (SDG 12). In terms of SDG 13, establishing a level playing field for firms through competition law can encourage the development and distribution of environmentally friendly technologies. In terms of SDG 16, which aims to create institutions that are effective, responsible, and inclusive, the implementation of competition law is an important factor (Coates & Middelschulte, 2019).

As a result, the overlap between competition law and SDGs is not only genuine but essential to the achievement of these global goals. Strategic application of competition law can pave the way for environmentally responsible business practices that help achieve the SDGs' lofty targets.

Due to its spectacular economic transformation and continuous efforts towards sustainable development, China's experience provides a unique case study at the junction of competition law and SDGs. China's impact on the international economy is undeniable, given its status as the world's second largest economy (Zreik, 2023a). Management of competition in its market can have far-reaching consequences on the country's economy, as well as on global trade and sustainability goals. Therefore, other nations can learn from China by studying how it employs competition legislation to promote sustainable development.

In addition, competition law has had to develop and evolve in China as the country has moved from a centrally planned economy to a market-based structure (Hitt & Xu, 2016). This interesting historical and societal setting provides a framework against which to assess the contribution of competition law to achieving the SDGs.

Even while the SDGs are focused on topics like economic growth, environmental protection, and social justice, China is currently confronting significant difficulties striking that balance. This makes the Chinese example especially instructive for other quickly growing economies that may encounter comparable difficulties in their quest for sustainable development.

The Chinese government has demonstrated its support for the SDGs by including them in the country's overall strategy for economic growth (Sharif et al., 2022). China's experience offers a wealth of practical insights into how competition law and policy can be used to achieve sustainable development goals because of the country's emphasis on sustainability and its implementation of competition law.

While considerable research has been conducted on the role of competition law in market fairness and economic efficiency, scant attention has been paid to its implications for sustainable development. This study aims to bridge this gap by posing the specific research question: 'How has China leveraged its competition law and policy to advance Sustainable Development Goals (SDGs), and what lessons can other countries draw from this experience?' The existing body of literature often treats competition law and sustainability as separate disciplines; however, their intersection is crucial for shaping business practices that are both competitive and sustainable. By focusing on China—a nation that has made significant strides in integrating competition law with sustainability aims—this research contributes a novel perspective to the current understanding of how legal frameworks can serve broader societal goals.

One might wonder why China serves as the focal point for this discussion on the interplay between competition law and sustainable development. The answer lies in China's unique position as the world's second-largest economy and its simultaneous commitment to aggressive sustainable development goals. The country offers a compelling narrative for the potential of competition law to positively influence sustainable outcomes while facing the challenges of rapid industrial growth, environmental degradation, and social inequality.

China has seen tremendous economic growth over the past few decades, yet it faces complex sustainability challenges that are both localized and global in scope. From pollution to waste management, the issues are manifold. Additionally, China has been proactive in enforcing its Anti-Monopoly Law (AML) and has high-profile cases involving major companies, offering rich case studies for examination.

The primary aim of this research is to investigate the intricate interplay between competition law and sustainable development goals (SDGs), using China as a focal case study. This endeavor seeks to: 1) Understand the historical and contemporary dynamics of China's competition law and its implications for the nation's sustainability agenda; 2) Examine specific instances where competition law has been pivotal in driving or hindering sustainable outcomes; and 3) Offer insights into the potential lessons other nations can glean from China's experience, thereby contributing to a broader discourse on the synergies and tensions between economic competitiveness and sustainability.

Given China's influence on global markets, the strategies and policies implemented here have ripple effects on sustainable development and competitive practices worldwide. Therefore, scrutinizing China's approach to integrating competition law and sustainable development can provide nuanced insights into the challenges and opportunities that come with balancing rapid economic growth and sustainability objectives.

The experiences of China in this context are not merely an academic curiosity but hold substantial relevance for other nations grappling with similar issues. Countries at different stages of economic development are struggling to reconcile growth with sustainable practices, and China's experience provides a wide array of successes and failures from which to learn.

Furthermore, as a nation that has actively used competition law to both promote economic efficiency and address broader social goals like sustainability, China serves as a useful model. Its struggles with implementing and enforcing these laws give other nations a preview of the challenges they too will face, thereby offering them an opportunity to preemptively devise strategies to navigate them.

The intricate relationship between competition law and sustainable development, particularly within the context of a rapidly developing nation like China, remains an enigma. While there's no shortage of literature on each subject in isolation, the cross-sectional analysis mapping the interplay between the two is sparse. This study specifically seeks to answer the question: "How does China's competition law and policy facilitate or hinder its pursuit of select Sustainable Development Goals (SDGs), and what lessons can be gleaned from its experience?"

Existing literature often explores the broad implications of competition laws or delves deep into sustainability goals. However, a focused examination of how the former can be instrumentally leveraged to achieve the latter, especially in the unique socio-economic landscape of China, is conspicuously absent. This research bridges this gap, positioning itself at the nexus of competition law and sustainability, thereby enriching the current body of knowledge and offering policy insights for nations grappling with similar challenges.

China offers a unique vantage point for studying the interplay between competition law and sustainable development for several reasons. As the world's second-largest economy, its economic decisions and policies reverberate on a global scale, influencing international markets and trade dynamics. China's rapid economic ascent, coupled with its substantial environmental footprint, brings to the forefront the challenges and tensions between industrial growth and sustainability. Moreover, the country has actively grappled with the harmonization of economic competitiveness and sustainability objectives, making it a rich terrain for examining how competition law and policy intersect with Sustainable Development Goals (SDGs). Its nuanced approach, characterized by the fostering of 'national champions' in juxtaposition with anti-monopoly regulations, offers a complex and enlightening case of the tightrope walk between competition and sustainability. Thus, while many nations grapple with similar issues, China's scale, global influence, and unique policy landscape make it a particularly insightful subject of study.

Adopting a qualitative methodology, this study employs a two-pronged approach. First, a systematic review of existing literature, policy documents, and legislative actions offers a macroscopic understanding. This is complemented by carefully selected case studies that offer a microscopic view into the real-world implementation of competition laws vis-à-vis specific SDGs in China. These case studies, drawn from varied industries and sectors, were chosen based on their representational significance and the richness of data they offer, providing a holistic understanding of the subject.

This study employs a doctrinal legal analysis supplemented by a case study approach to investigate the role of competition law in China's pursuit of sustainable development goals (SDGs). Primary data is sourced from legislative texts, judicial decisions, and regulatory guidelines pertaining to China's competition law. Secondary data includes scholarly articles and international reports that offer interpretive insights into these primary legal sources. This doctrinal analysis is enriched by examining concrete cases where competition law intersects with sustainability objectives. The case studies provide a real-world context, allowing to better understand the practical implications and effectiveness of legal frameworks. Through this combined methodology, the study aims to offer a comprehensive, yet nuanced, understanding of how competition law can serve as a tool to achieve sustainability goals.

This chapter is organized as follows: Section 2 provides an overview of the Sustainable Development Goals (SDGs) and their importance in the global context. Section 3 delves into the fundamentals of competition law, laying the groundwork for its intersection with sustainable development. Section 4 outlines the historical development of competition law in China. Section 5 offers several case studies to illustrate how competition law has been applied to support SDGs in China, followed by Section 6, which discusses the challenges and limitations China faces in this endeavor. Section 7 provides suggestions for the future directions of China's competition law and policy in addressing sustainability challenges, as well as implications for other nations. The chapter concludes with Section 8, summarizing the key findings and their significance in the broader context of competition law and sustainable development.

OVERVIEW OF CHINA'S COMPETITION LAW AND POLICY

Historical Background

The transition from central planning to a market economy in China provided the impetus for the development of the country's competition law. Deng Xiaoping's reforms of the late 1970s marked the first-time competition was treated seriously in China. There was little room for market dynamics because of the prevalence of state-owned firms and government central planning (Bell & Feng, 2013).

The necessity for a legal framework to manage competition became increasingly apparent as China opened to the world economy and embraced market reforms in the 1980s and 1990s. The 'Anti-Unfair Competition Law' (1993) and the 'Price Law' (1997) were two of the earliest attempts to implement competition norms (Owen, Sun, & Zheng, 2008). Despite their importance, these initiatives fell short of creating an all-encompassing framework for regulating competition since they focused on particular aspects of market behavior.

China's first comprehensive competition legislation, the 'Anti-Monopoly Law' (AML), was enacted in 2008. This was a watershed moment. The goals of the AML were to prevent and limit monopolistic behaviors, preserve free and open markets, boost economic efficiency, defend consumers' rights and the public interest, and foster the robust growth of the socialist market economy (Harris et al., 2011). This law established the bedrock of China's competition regulation, ushering in a more methodical era of competition management in the country's developing market economy.

As a result, the development of competition law in China has closely tracked the broader economic change of the country, reflecting the shifting requirements and increasingly complex dynamics of its market.

Key Legislative Measures

There are three key areas that the Anti-Monopoly Law (AML) addresses: anti-competitive agreements, misuse of a dominating market position, and merger control. The AML was passed in 2008 and serves as the foundation of competition law in China (Zhang & Wu, 2019).

The AML forbids any kind of arrangement that would eliminate or restrict competition, including horizontal agreements (between competitors) and vertical agreements (between enterprises at different stages of the supply chain). Price fixing, dividing the market, limiting production, and boycotting are all examples of collusion (Wang, 2009).

The AML prohibits companies with a dominant market position from abusing that advantage. Unfair practices include, but are not limited to, charging excessive fees, refusing to do business, bundling items and services, and engaging in discriminatory behavior.

Merger control provisions are included in the AML as well. Companies that meet specific criteria are required to inform the State Administration for Market Regulation (SAMR) of their merger plans. The proposed merger is next analyzed by the SAMR to see if it would have the impact of reducing or eliminating competition (Zhang, 2021).

The AML is just one piece of China's comprehensive framework for regulating market competition. For instance, the recently revised Anti-Unfair Competition Law (AUCL) prohibits dishonest business tactics like bribery and fraudulent advertising (Alexey & Alexander, 2018). Predatory and discriminatory pricing practices have an adverse effect on market competition, which is why the Price Law exists to curb them.

China's commitment to building a fair and competitive market environment that is in line with its sustainable development goals is demonstrated by the adoption of these legislative measures, which create a level playing field in the domestic market.

China's AML, established in 2008, marked a pivotal moment in the nation's commitment to fostering fair competition. However, to remain relevant to the changing economic landscape and the global push towards sustainability, the AML has undergone significant revisions (Marco Colino, 2022; Fox, 2019). The most recent amendments to the AML reflect a deeper integration of sustainable practices, emphasizing the dual role of competition law in promoting both economic prosperity and sustainable development (Qaqaya, 2020; Kong, Xu, & Zhang, 2022).

Some of the notable recent amendments to the AML include:

- Enhanced scrutiny on merger control, ensuring not just economic competitiveness but also considering environmental impacts.
- Strengthened regulations against monopolistic practices that harm the environment, thereby aligning competition practices with SDG objectives.
- Increased cooperation between the State Administration for Market Regulation (SAMR) and environmental agencies to ensure holistic implementation of the law.

The revised AML, under the auspices of the SAMR, plays a significant role in driving China towards its SDG targets (Soomro, Khan, & Arafa, 2021; Robertson, 2022; Takigawa, 2022). Here's how:

- SDG 8 (Decent work and economic growth): By curbing monopolistic behaviors, the AML ensures that smaller enterprises have a fair playing field, fostering innovation and job creation.
- SDG 12 (Responsible consumption and production): The AML's focus on preventing monopolies in sectors like waste management and renewable energy ensures that sustainable production methods are not stifled by dominant market players.
- SDG 13 (Climate action): With the recent amendments, practices that harm the environment can be deemed anti-competitive, thus providing an indirect mechanism to penalize environmentally detrimental actions.
- SDG 16 (Peace, justice, and strong institutions): A robust AML overseen by the SAMR is testament to China's commitment to strong institutional frameworks that drive justice and economic fairness.

The State Administration for Market Regulation (SAMR) has been pivotal in ensuring that the principles of the AML are not just restricted to promoting competition but are also aligned with China's sustainability goals (Xinning, 2023; Ng, 2019; Ng, 2020). By working in collaboration with environmental and sustainability departments, SAMR ensures that companies following the AML also indirectly contribute to China's SDG targets. Furthermore, SAMR's proactive approach in educating businesses about the dual role of AML in fostering competition and sustainability ensures greater voluntary compliance, thereby accelerating China's journey towards its SDG objectives.

Current State of Affairs

Competition law and policy in China have been developing since 2023 to accommodate the country's rapidly changing economy. High-profile cases involving both domestic and international firms have led to a dramatic increase in enforcement of the Anti-Monopoly Law (AML) over the past decade.

China's major competition authority is the State Administration for Market Regulation (SAMR), which was founded in 2018 (Petry, 2021). When it comes to enforcing the AML, SAMR has taken a more aggressive attitude, taking on difficult anti-competitive actions and instituting stronger merger control. China's dedication to maintaining market competition and the country's increasing proficiency in competition law enforcement are both reflected in this increased enforcement.

China is committed to updating its competition law to reflect changing market realities, and the 2020 amendment of the AML to fit the digital economy will do just that. As the economy becomes more and more digitized and dominated by tech behemoths, concerns about data monopolies, platform competition, and predatory pricing in the digital arena have emerged. The updated AML equips regulators with the tools they need to deal with these new threats (Pejic, 2019).

China has also demonstrated its dedication to integrating its competition policies with its sustainable development objectives. There are current initiatives to guarantee that the implementation of competition law promotes SDG goals related to environmental sustainability, responsible consumerism, and others. For instance, in order to promote environmental innovation while still maintaining market competitiveness, norms for competition in the green industry are now being created (Zreik, 2024; Ju & Lin, 2020).

APPLICATION OF CHINA'S COMPETITION LAW TOWARDS ACHIEVING SUSTAINABLE DEVELOPMENT

Although its importance to long-term growth is often overlooked, competition legislation is a cornerstone of a sustainable economy. The United Nations' idea of sustainable development, as outlined in its 17 SDGs, emphasizes the importance of striking a balance between economic, social, and environmental goals. Each of these facets is heavily influenced by competition law.

On the economic front, competition law encourages fair and efficient markets, which in turn results in better products, cheaper prices, and more innovation (Gilbert, 2022). These achievements are in line with SDG 8's mandate for inclusive, long-term economic growth. Competition legislation encourages innovation and entrepreneurship by creating a market environment free from anti-competitive actions that could lead to market dominance.

From a societal point of view, competition law safeguards consumer welfare by preventing anti-competitive economic actions that could result in higher pricing, fewer available options, or lower product quality. Sustainable consumption and production patterns are called for by SDG 12, and this is in line with that goal.

Competition law has the potential to advance environmental sustainability in a roundabout way. Markets that encourage innovation and differentiation among businesses can result in the introduction of greener goods and manufacturing techniques (Guinot, Barghouti, & Chiva, 2022). Goal 13 of the Sustainable Development Agenda addresses climate change and its effects directly. Moreover, the application of competition law aids in achieving SDG 16 (strong institutions) by fostering confidence in public institutions and displaying the rule of law.

DEEP DIVE INTO FOUR KEY SUSTAINABLE DEVELOPMENT GOALS

Decent Work and Economic Growth (SDG 8)

Goal 8 of the Sustainable Development Agenda is to ensure that all people have access to economic opportunity, gainful employment, and living wages. It places an emphasis on generating high-quality employment opportunities that benefit the economy, promote fair wages and working conditions, and ensure everyone has a fair shot at success.

In this regard, the Anti-Monopoly Law (AML) of China is crucial. Anti-competitive actions like price-fixing, market segmentation, or aggressive behavior from dominant enterprises are reduced, which makes for a more pleasant business climate (Ramesh, 2023). This competitive environment is vital for economic growth because it motivates businesses to improve, innovate, and differentiate themselves in order to stand out from the crowd (Zhang & Wu, 2019).

And because of the pressure to perform better from rivals, many businesses grow and new jobs are created as a result of increased competition. To stay ahead in a competitive market, businesses are more likely to invest in their employees, resulting in increased training opportunities and improved working conditions. This is in perfect harmony with SDG 8.

The 'inclusive' goal of SDG 8 is bolstered by the AML's enforcement. The law allows SMEs to flourish by restricting the power of large organizations to engage in anti-competitive tactics that would otherwise drive away smaller competitors (Lundqvist & Gal, 2019). Small and medium-sized enterprises (SMEs) play an important role in the economy by creating jobs for a wide range of people.

Responsible Consumption and Production (SDG 12)

The effective use of natural resources, the decrease of waste generation through waste avoidance, reduction, recycling, and reuse, and the uncoupling of economic growth and environmental degradation are all called for in Sustainable Development Goal 12. China's experience shows that competition law is crucial to accomplishing these goals.

The Anti-Monopoly Law (AML) promotes innovation and market differentiation by reducing the prevalence of monopolies. Sustainable product development and manufacturing techniques are two avenues that businesses might pursue in this direction. Therefore, in a healthy competitive market, the needs of consumers for environmentally friendly products and services might motivate businesses to take steps toward cleaner manufacturing.

More importantly for SDG 12, competition can spur the creation and spread of 'green' technologies and business models. Firms may be encouraged to innovate by the demands of a competitive market to create products and procedures that are more resourceful, waste-free, and pollution-free (Santa-Maria, Vermeulen, & Baumgartner, 2022).

Consumers are also safeguarded by competition law since they are given access to truthful data about available goods and services (Marciano, Nicita, & Ramello, 2020; Zreik, 2023b). For sustainable consumption, this is especially crucial because shoppers can't make good decisions without accurate data. The need of enforcing rules against 'greenwashing,' or the practice of making false or misleading environmental claims, cannot be overstated.

The Anti-Monopoly Law (AML) and other parts of China's competition law, such as the Anti-Unfair Competition Law, do a lot to encourage responsible consumption and production. It indirectly encourages firms to pursue sustainability in their products and operations and aids consumers in making educated purchasing decisions, both of which contribute to the achievement of SDG 12 (Huang, 2019).

Climate Action (SDG 13)

Goal 13 of the Sustainable Development Agenda is to take immediate action to reduce the effects of climate change. It emphasizes the need for enhanced institutional capacity in the areas of climate change mitigation, adaptation, impact reduction, and early warning education and awareness-raising. China's approach demonstrates the importance of competition legislation in this context, even though it is not the most obvious tool.

The fundamental purpose of competition law is to create a level playing field in the market, which in turn encourages innovation. When businesses are under intense competition, they are often pushed to the cutting edge of innovation (Verganti, 2009). In the context of SDG 13, this can result in the proliferation of environmentally friendly products and methods of doing business.

The Anti-Monopoly Law (AML), the cornerstone of China's competition law, is aiding the country's rapidly expanding market. The AML ensures fair competition between new and established businesses by outlawing monopolistic behaviors, which in turn inspires the development of novel approaches that not only benefit the economy but also have a positive effect on the natural world (Zhang & Wu, 2019).

The AML also indirectly aids climate action by helping to keep the energy market competitive. This guarantees a competitive market for renewable energy technology and limits the dominance of energy suppliers reliant on fossil fuels. A decrease in the cost of renewable energy is one way in which market forces can help reduce greenhouse gas emissions.

Peace, Justice, and Strong Institutions (SDG 16)

Goal 16 of the Sustainable Development Agenda aims to foster just, peaceful, and inclusive communities characterized by institutions that are both effective and transparent (Milton, 2021). Despite appearances, SDG 16's focus on strong institutions and the rule of law—including competition law—has a direct bearing on the pursuit of peace and justice.

Competition law enforcement is an indicator of a market governed by the rule of law. Important components of SDG 16 are demonstrated and fostered by competition authorities holding domestic and global firms accountable for anti-competitive activities.

China's dedication to sustaining robust and efficient institutions is demonstrated by the country's Anti-Monopoly Law (AML) and the SAMR's enforcement of it. China's growing institutional strength is reflected in the SAMR's rising competence and assertiveness in handling complicated competition law matters.

In addition, competition law provides a benefit to justice in the roundabout way that it promotes honest and open corporate practices. Competition authorities defend consumers and smaller firms, advancing economic justice, by preventing anti-competitive behaviors and penalizing companies that break the law (Wu, Weng, & Joseph, 2021).

A peaceful and stable society is fostered by strictly enforced competition laws. When companies know they'll have a level playing field, economic conflicts are less likely to arise, which benefits everyone. The AML in China is a prime example of how the rule of law can help build stable societies with fair legal systems and reliable government institutions. China's enforcement of competition legislation contributes to SDG 16 by maintaining a competitive market and bolstering the country's institutions.

CASE STUDIES

Several Chinese case studies provide valuable insights into the role of competition law in accomplishing sustainable development goals. These rulings highlight the various applications of competition law to promote ethical business practices, sustainable manufacturing and consumption patterns, and protection of natural resources.

The enforcement action taken against Qualcomm, a major semiconductor and telecommunications equipment manufacturer, stands out as an example. Qualcomm was fined over $1 billion in 2015 for breaking China's Anti-Monopoly Law (AML) by the National Development and Reform Commission (NDRC), then one of China's antitrust authorities (Zhang, 2019). The case sent a message to international firms and demonstrated China's dedication to fostering free and open commerce and innovation through its competition law.

The AML's use in encouraging ethical behavior in business is demonstrated by a case involving Alibaba, a major online retailer. Due to the abuse of its dominating market position, which prevented merchants from selling their wares on alternative platforms, the State Administration for Market Regulation (SAMR) penalized Alibaba a record $2.8 billion in 2021 (Cahill & Wang, 2022). Such activities, which can lead to unsustainable business practices and restrict competition, were sent a strong message that they will not be permitted by this enforcement action.

The overall framework of competition law has been helpful in promoting the development and spread of 'green' technologies and practices, which is important for environmental conservation even though there have been no specific antitrust cases in China relating to environmental issues. The AML encourages the development of eco-friendly goods and services by restricting monopolistic practices and expanding competition.

In China, for instance, fierce competition has pushed for innovation and lowered prices in the renewable energy sector, bringing wind and solar power to a wider audience (Zhang et al., 2022). Both SDG 13 (Climate Action) and SDG 12 (Responsible Consumption and Production) can benefit from this.

These decisions demonstrate how competition law can help shape corporate practices for the better. They show how China has used competition law to advance sustainable development, providing insights that other economies working toward the SDGs may find useful.

CHALLENGES AND LIMITATIONS

China has achieved great progress toward its sustainable development goals through the use of competition law and policy, but it has also encountered substantial obstacles along the way. Several problems have arisen as a result of the effort to strike a balance between rapid economic growth and sustainability goals.

First, encouraging competition and other social and economic aims often seem at odds with one another. For instance, the Chinese government has been fostering 'national champions' in important industries to compete globally while the Anti-Monopoly Law (AML) strives to avoid market dominance. The consistent application of competition law is complicated by this dual approach, which can lead to tensions (Zreik, Iqbal, & Rahman, 2022).

The specialized nature of some industries, particularly those vital to long-term growth, presents another challenge. The renewable energy and waste management industries, for example, typically have high initial investment requirements, lengthy payback periods, and erratic consumer demand (Qiu, Ruth, & Ghosh, 2015). Competition law alone may not be enough to push sustainable practices in these sectors if these inhibitors are allowed to persist.

Furthermore, competition law enforcement in China has been criticized for being opaque and inconsistent (Chang, Li, & Lu, 2015). While things have gotten better over time, there is still a need to do more to improve the openness and predictability of enforcement if it is aimed to encourage a healthy culture of competition. The use of competition law as a tool for sustainable development will be most successful if it is enforced in a fair and consistent manner.

Overproduction and overconsumption are problems for sustainability that can be exacerbated by the competitive nature of the market, which can spur innovation, particularly in 'green' technologies. China still has the challenge of figuring out how to encourage growth and innovation while minimizing their negative effects on the environment (Dou & Han, 2019).

Competition law, together with other regulatory tools and policy initiatives, must be integrated to meet these difficulties. The triumphs and failures that China has encountered on its path to sustainable development provide useful lessons for other countries facing the same challenges.

FUTURE DIRECTIONS AND IMPROVEMENTS FOR CHINA'S COMPETITION LAW AND POLICY

Suggestions for Maximizing the Role of Competition Law in Addressing Sustainability Challenges

China has a number of opportunities to improve its competition law and policy in the future, which would help it achieve its sustainable development objectives. China can make the most of competition law's potential in resolving sustainability issues by meeting the obstacles and grabbing the opportunities.

It would be helpful for competition law and policy to incorporate sustainability concerns to a greater extent. While protecting free and open markets is the primary focus of competition law, it can also take into account broader societal goals. Rules against anti-competitive activity could take into account or even assist sustainability goals, which policymakers could examine. When evaluating the impacts of mergers on competition, competition authorities could, for instance, take into account the impact of the merger on the environment.

There must be a continued focus on bolstering institutional capability. Market trust would increase, fair competition would increase, and sustainable development would be aided by a more solid, transparent, and predictable framework for enforcing competition laws. This could be accomplished through involving the public in decision-making processes, expanding opportunities for international cooperation, and maintaining high standards for professional education.

Cooperation between competition authorities and other regulators needs to be encouraged. Many of the most intractable sustainability problems are systemic in nature, spanning several industries and governments (Trump et al., 2019). It is in everyone's best interest for competition authorities, environmental regulators, and other interested parties to collaborate to maximize the effectiveness of their respective activities.

The importance of competition law in environmental sustainability can be boosted by concerted advocacy efforts. One way to accomplish this goal is to educate businesses and the public on the significance of healthy competition for environmental sustainability, and to encourage firms to voluntarily comply with competition laws and embrace environmentally friendly practices.

By continuing to use competition legislation for sustainable development, China can show other nations the potential and limitations of this strategy while also learning from their own experiences. Competition law's importance in tackling the challenges of encouraging economic development and maintaining sustainability will only increase as the globe works to meet these two imperatives.

Implications for Other Nations Striving to Balance Economic Growth and Sustainable Development

China's success in using competition law and policy to promote sustainable development has important lessons for other countries trying to strike a similar balance between economic growth and environmental protection.

First, the lessons learned from China show the need of seeing competition law as a means to achieve broader social goals, such as sustainable development, in addition to economic efficiency. Countries can influence market behaviors that are consistent with their sustainability goals if they recognize and actively use the possibilities of competition law in this regard.

Second, China's difficulties serve to emphasize the difficulty of reconciling competition law and sustainable development. The ensuing tensions can serve as an example for other countries to learn from, warning them of the dangers of poorly calibrated policies that can lead to war.

Thirdly, other nations can learn from China's extensive body of experience with applying competition legislation in practice. China's use of competition legislation in a variety of areas—from encouraging innovation and fair trade to preventing damaging business practices—can serve as a model for other countries.

The necessity of strong, transparent, and consistent enforcement in gaining market trust and guaranteeing the efficacy of competition legislation is shown by China's proactive attempts to increase its institutional capability in competition law enforcement.

Finally, the observed improvements in the Chinese context offer important suggestions that other countries should pursue, such as incorporating sustainability considerations into competition policy and enhanced cooperation between competition authorities and other regulators.

CONCLUSION

In this chapter, China was used as a case study to investigate how competition law and policy relate to sustainable development. SDG 8 (Decent work and economic growth), SDG 12 (Responsible consumption and production), SDG 13 (Climate action), and SDG 16 (Peace, justice, and strong institutions) have all been examined in detail to highlight the importance of China's competition law and policy.

China's achievements and problems in sustainable development have been evaluated against the nuanced backdrop of the country's historical development of competition law, significant legislative actions, and the current condition of affairs. Competition legislation and policy, which are typically used to guarantee market fairness and consumer protection, can be utilized to efficiently coincide with sustainability objectives, as China has shown. Positive contributions to China's SDGs have resulted from the convergence of several areas, including increased accountability in production and consumption, climate action, the promotion of decent work and economic growth, and the development of strong institutions.

A more nuanced view of the potential of competition law was obtained by analyzing concrete cases in which it was used to promote fair trade, ethical production and consumption, support innovation, and aid environmental protection. China's struggles are illustrative of the difficulty of striking a balance between rapid economic growth and sustainability goals. Among these problems are challenges faced by industries essential to sustainable development, and possible tensions between fostering 'national champions' and preventing market domination.

The suggested changes to China's competition legislation and policy in light of the country's experience show how important a comprehensive strategy is. This strategy builds institutional capacity, encourages cooperation between multiple regulators, and champions effective lobbying by combining competition law with other regulatory tools and policy initiatives such as environmental impact assessments.

The path China has taken has far-reaching consequences for other countries trying to strike a similar economic growth/sustainable development balance. The chapter highlights competition law's potential as a tool for sustainable development, issues a warning about potential conflicts, and offers concrete lessons and improvements that can be applied in a wide range of settings.

The chapter ends by highlighting the significance of China's experience for international sustainability and competition law and policy. China's policies and actions have global repercussions because of the country's status as the world's second largest economy. Its history sheds light on the potential and pitfalls of competition law and policy as instruments of sustainable development.

Countries all across the world may learn a great deal from China's successes and failures as they pursue their own distinctive paths to economic growth and sustainability. The Chinese example highlights the fundamental interdependence of competition law and sustainable development, demonstrating the importance of a comprehensive, coordinated strategy for meeting the challenges of sustainability in today's globalized world.

REFERENCES

Alexey, K., & Alexander, S. (2018). Anti-corruption in the BRICS countries. *BRICS law journal, 5*(1), 56-77.

Bell, S., & Feng, H. (2013). *The rise of the People's Bank of China: The politics of institutional change.* Harvard University Press. doi:10.4159/harvard.9780674073593

Cahill, D., & Wang, J. (2022). Addressing legitimacy concerns in antitrust private litigation involving China's state-owned enterprises. *World Competition: Law and Economic Review, 45*(1), 75–122. doi:10.54648/WOCO2022004

Chang, L., Li, W., & Lu, X. (2015). Government engagement, environmental policy, and environmental performance: Evidence from the most polluting Chinese listed firms. *Business Strategy and the Environment, 24*(1), 1–19. doi:10.1002/bse.1802

Coates, K., & Middelschulte, D. (2019). Getting Consumer Welfare Right: The competition law implications of market-driven sustainability initiatives. *European Competition Journal, 15*(2-3), 318–326. doi:10.1080/17441056.2019.1665940

Dennis, W. J. Jr. (2011). Entrepreneurship, small business and public policy levers. *Journal of Small Business Management, 49*(1), 92–106. doi:10.1111/j.1540-627X.2010.00316.x

Dou, J., & Han, X. (2019). How does the industry mobility affect pollution industry transfer in China: Empirical test on Pollution Haven Hypothesis and Porter Hypothesis. *Journal of Cleaner Production, 217*, 105–115. doi:10.1016/j.jclepro.2019.01.147

Fox, E. M. (2019). Should China's Competition Model be Exported?: A Reply to Wendy Ng. *European Journal of International Law*, *30*(4), 1431–1440. doi:10.1093/ejil/chaa010

Gilbert, R. J. (2022). *Innovation matters: competition policy for the high-technology economy*. MIT Press.

Guinot, J., Barghouti, Z., & Chiva, R. (2022). Understanding green innovation: A conceptual framework. *Sustainability (Basel)*, *14*(10), 5787. doi:10.3390/su14105787

Harris, H. S., Wang, P. J., Cohen, M. A., Zhang, Y., & Evrard, S. J. (2011). *Anti-monopoly law and practice in China*. Oxford University Press.

Hitt, M. A., & Xu, K. (2016). The transformation of China: Effects of the institutional environment on business actions. *Long Range Planning*, *49*(5), 589–593. doi:10.1016/j.lrp.2015.02.006

Huang, Y. (2019). Monopoly and anti-monopoly in china today. *American Journal of Economics and Sociology*, *78*(5), 1101–1134. doi:10.1111/ajes.12298

Ju, H., & Lin, P. (2020). China's Anti-Monopoly Law and the role of economics in its enforcement. *Russian Journal of Economics*, *6*(3), 219–238. doi:10.32609/j.ruje.6.56362

Kamau, M., Chasek, P., & O'Connor, D. (2018). *Transforming multilateral diplomacy: The inside story of the Sustainable Development Goals*. Routledge. doi:10.4324/9780429491276

Kong, X., Xu, J., & Zhang, Y. (2022). Industry competition and firm productivity: Evidence from the antitrust policy in China. *Finance Research Letters*, *47*, 103001. doi:10.1016/j.frl.2022.103001

Lundqvist, B., & Gal, M. S. (Eds.). (2019). *Competition law for the digital economy*. Edward Elgar Publishing. doi:10.4337/9781788971836

Marciano, A., Nicita, A., & Ramello, G. B. (2020). Big data and big techs: Understanding the value of information in platform capitalism. *European Journal of Law and Economics*, *50*(3), 345–358. doi:10.1007/s10657-020-09675-1

Marco Colino, S. (2022). The incursion of antitrust into China's platform economy. *Antitrust Bulletin*, *67*(2), 237–258. doi:10.1177/0003603X221084152

Milton, S. (2021). Higher education and sustainable development goal 16 in fragile and conflict-affected contexts. *Higher Education*, *81*(1), 89–108. doi:10.1007/s10734-020-00617-z

Ng, W. (2019). Changing Global Dynamics and International Competition Law: Considering China's Potential Impact. *European Journal of International Law*, *30*(4), 1409–1430. doi:10.1093/ejil/chz066

Ng, W. (2020). State Interest and the state-centered Approach to Competition Law in China. *Antitrust Bulletin*, *65*(2), 297–311. doi:10.1177/0003603X20912889

Owen, B. M., Sun, S., & Zheng, W. (2008). China's competition policy reforms: The anti-monopoly law and beyond. *Antitrust Law Journal*, *75*(1), 231–265.

Pejic, I. (2019). *Blockchain babel: The crypto craze and the challenge to business*. Kogan Page Publishers.

Petry, J. (2021). Same same, but different: Varieties of capital markets, Chinese state capitalism and the global financial order. *Competition & Change*, *25*(5), 605–630. doi:10.1177/1024529420964723

Qaqaya, H. (2020). Sustainability of ASEAN integration, competition policy, and the challenges of COVID-19. *Journal of Antitrust Enforcement, 8*(2), 305–308. doi:10.1093/jaenfo/jnaa019

Qiu, S., Ruth, M., & Ghosh, S. (2015). Evacuated tube collectors: A notable driver behind the solar water heater industry in China. *Renewable & Sustainable Energy Reviews, 47*, 580–588. doi:10.1016/j.rser.2015.03.067

Ramesh, B. N. (2023). *Cross Border Mergers and Acquisitions: A Comparative Study Between India and the USA*. Taylor & Francis.

Robertson, V. H. (2022). Antitrust, big tech, and democracy: A research agenda. *Antitrust Bulletin, 67*(2), 259–279. doi:10.1177/0003603X221082749

Santa-Maria, T., Vermeulen, W. J., & Baumgartner, R. J. (2022). How do incumbent firms innovate their business models for the circular economy? Identifying micro-foundations of dynamic capabilities. *Business Strategy and the Environment, 31*(4), 1308–1333. doi:10.1002/bse.2956

Sharif, A., Saqib, N., Dong, K., & Khan, S. A. R. (2022). Nexus between green technology innovation, green financing, and CO2 emissions in the G7 countries: The moderating role of social globalisation. *Sustainable Development (Bradford), 30*(6), 1934–1946. doi:10.1002/sd.2360

Soomro, N. E., Khan, A., & Arafa, A. (2021). Anti-monopoly law of China: A case study of coca cola's proposed merger with huiyuan. *International Journal of Business and Economics Research, 10*(1), 34–39. doi:10.11648/j.ijber.20211001.15

Takigawa, T. (2022). What Should We Do about E-Commerce Platform Giants?—The Antitrust and Regulatory Approaches in the US, EU, China, and Japan. The Antitrust and Regulatory Approaches in the US, EU, China, and Japan.

Trump, B. D., Cummings, C. L., Kuzma, J., & Linkov, I. (Eds.). (2019). *Synthetic biology 2020: Frontiers in risk analysis and governance*. Springer Nature.

Verganti, R. (2009). *Design driven innovation: changing the rules of competition by radically innovating what things mean*. Harvard Business Press.

Wang, X. (2009). The new Chinese anti-monopoly law: A survey of a work in progress. *Antitrust Bulletin, 54*(3), 579–619. doi:10.1177/0003603X0905400303

Wu, P., Weng, C. X. C., & Joseph, S. A. (2021). Crossing the Rubicon? The implications of RCEP on anti-monopoly enforcement on dominant E-commerce platforms in China. *Computer Law & Security Report, 42*, 105608. doi:10.1016/j.clsr.2021.105608

Xinning, Z. (2023). The Comparison of Securities Law and Competition Law among China, Australia and Japan. *International Journal of Frontiers in Sociology, 5*(9).

Zhang, A. (2021). *Chinese antitrust exceptionalism: How the rise of China challenges global regulation*. Oxford University Press. doi:10.1093/oso/9780198826569.001.0001

Zhang, A. H. (2019). Strategic public shaming: Evidence from Chinese antitrust investigations. *The China Quarterly, 237*, 174–195. doi:10.1017/S0305741018001340

Zhang, D., Zheng, M., Feng, G. F., & Chang, C. P. (2022). Does an environmental policy bring to green innovation in renewable energy? *Renewable Energy*, *195*, 1113–1124. doi:10.1016/j.renene.2022.06.074

Zhang, Z., & Wu, B. (2019). Governing China's administrative monopolies under the anti-monopoly law: A ten-year review (2008–2018) and beyond. *Journal of Competition Law & Economics*, *15*(1), 718–760. doi:10.1093/joclec/nhz009

Zreik, M. (2023a). Analytical study on Foreign Direct Investment Divestment Inflows and Outflows in Developing Economies: Evidence of China. *Chinese Economy*, *56*(6), 415–430. doi:10.1080/10971475.2023.2193118

Zreik, M. (2023b). Harnessing the Power of Blockchain Technology in Modern China: A Comprehensive Exploration. In L. Ferreira, M. Cruz, E. Cruz, H. Quintela, & M. Cunha (Eds.), *Supporting Technologies and the Impact of Blockchain on Organizations and Society* (pp. 94–112). IGI Global. doi:10.4018/978-1-6684-5747-4.ch007

Zreik, M. (2024). Navigating the Green Path: A Perspective on Sustainable Consumption, Business Innovation, and Customer Experience in China. In M. Machado Carvalho & M. Rodrigues (Eds.), *Sustainable Consumption Experience and Business Models in the Modern World* (pp. 70–88). IGI Global. doi:10.4018/978-1-6684-9277-2.ch003

Zreik, M., Iqbal, B. A., & Rahman, M. N. (2022). Outward FDI: determinants and flows in emerging economies: evidence from China. *China and WTO Review*, *8*(2), 385–402. doi:10.14330/cwr.2022.8.2.07

KEY TERMS AND DEFINITIONS

Anti-Monopoly Law (AML): A legal provision aimed at preventing the formation of monopolies and promoting fair competition in the marketplace.

Competition Law: A legal framework designed to promote or maintain market competition by regulating anti-competitive conduct by companies.

Economic Efficiency: The optimal distribution of resources in an economy, where it is impossible to make someone better off without making someone else worse off.

Environmental Impact Assessment: A process of evaluating the likely environmental impacts of a proposed project or development, taking into account inter-related socio-economic, cultural, and human-health impacts.

Green Technologies: Innovative tools, technologies, and approaches designed to mitigate or reverse the negative impacts of human activity on the environment.

Institutional Capability: The ability of an organization to effectively implement and enforce policies and laws.

Market Dominance: A situation where a single company or group holds substantial market power, allowing it to control pricing, supply, and other market-related factors.

National Development and Reform Commission (NDRC): A macroeconomic management agency under the Chinese State Council, which has broad administrative and planning control over the Chinese economy.

State Administration for Market Regulation (SAMR): A ministerial-level agency directly under the State Council of China that is responsible for business regulation and market supervision.

Sustainable Development Goals (SDGs): A collection of 17 global goals established by the United Nations in 2015, aimed at addressing a range of social, economic, and environmental challenges by 2030.

Compilation of References

Abate, T. G., & Elofsson, K. (2024). Environmental taxation of plastic bags and substitutes: Balancing marine pollution and climate change. *Journal of Environmental Management*, *359*, 120868. doi:10.1016/j.jenvman.2024.120868 PMID:38692024

Abbot, K. W., & Bernstein, S. (2015). The High-Level Political Forum on Sustainable Development: Orchestration by default and design. *Global Policy*, *6*(3), 222–233. doi:10.1111/1758-5899.12199

Abdelzaher, D. M., Zalila, F., & Ramadan, N. N. (2021). Stigmatized minorities: An explorative study into the challenges of Muslim women entrepreneurs. *Journal for Global Business Advancement*, *14*(6), 822–844. doi:10.1504/JGBA.2021.125015

Abdullah, S., & Muhammad, A. (2008). The development of entrepreneurship in Malaysia: State-led initiatives. *Asian Journal of Technology Innovation*, *16*(1), 101–116. doi:10.1080/19761597.2008.9668649

Abdullah, Z. T. (2024). Remanufacturing waste steel sheet from end-of-life vehicles into electrical installation wall junction boxes: Quantitative sustainability assessment. *Results in Engineering*, *21*, 101767. doi:10.1016/j.rineng.2024.101767

Acemoğlu, D., & Robinson, J. A. (2012). *Why nations fail: The origins of power, prosperity, and poverty*. Random House.

Adamowicz, M. (2022). Green deal, green growth and green economy as a means of support for attaining the sustainable development goals. *Sustainability (Basel)*, *14*(10), 5901. doi:10.3390/su14105901

Adeola, O., Gyimah, P., Appiah, K. O., & Lussier, R. N. (2021). Can critical success factors of small businesses in emerging markets advance UN Sustainable Development Goals? *World Journal of Entrepreneurship, Management and Sustainable Development*, *17*(1), 85–105. doi:10.1108/WJEMSD-09-2019-0072

Adhikari, H. (2022). Anxiety and depression: Comparative study between working and non-working mothers. *ACADEMICIA: An International Multidisciplinary Research Journal*, *12*(2), 273–282. doi:10.5958/2249-7137.2022.00152.5

Adikaram, A. S., & Razik, R. (2023). Femininity penalty: Challenges and barriers faced by STEM woman entrepreneurs in an emerging economy. *Journal of Entrepreneurship in Emerging Economies*, *15*(5), 1113–1138. doi:10.1108/JEEE-07-2021-0278

Afshan, G., Shahid, S., & Tunio, M. N. (2021). Learning experiences of women entrepreneurs amidst COVID-19. *International Journal of Gender and Entrepreneurship*, *13*(2), 162–186. doi:10.1108/IJGE-09-2020-0153

Aghahosseini, M. (2007). *Claims of dual nationals and the development of customary international law: issues before the Iran-United States Claims Tribunal*. BRILL. doi:10.1163/ej.9789004156982.i-310

Compilation of References

Agrawal, R., Bakhshi, P., Chandani, A., Birau, R., & Mendon, S. (2023). Challenges faced by women entrepreneurs in South Asian countries using interpretive structural modeling. *Cogent Business & Management*, *10*(2), 2244755. doi:10.1080/23311975.2023.2244755

Ahmad, E., Vinella, A., & Xiao, K. (2018). Contracting arrangements and public private partnerships for sustainable development. *Public Sector Economics*, *42*(2), 145–169. doi:10.3326/pse.42.2.8

Akomea-Frimpong, I., Jin, X., Osei-Kyei, R., & Tumpa, R. J. (2023). A critical review of public–private partnerships in the COVID-19 pandemic: Key themes and future research agenda. *Smart and Sustainable Built Environment*, *12*(4), 701–720. doi:10.1108/SASBE-01-2022-0009

Aladejebi, O. (2020). Managing small businesses in Nigeria during COVID-19 crisis: Impact and survival strategies. *IOSR Journal of Business and Management*, *22*(8), 24–34.

Aleksandrov, K. (2014). The role of DMO for sustainable development of a tourist destination–Bulgaria case study. *Journal of Tourism Research*, *9*(2), 198–209.

Alexey, K., & Alexander, S. (2018). Anti-corruption in the BRICS countries. *BRICS law journal*, *5*(1), 56-77.

Al-Fadhat, F. (2022). Big business capital expansion and the shift of Indonesia's global economic policy outlook. *East Asia (Piscataway, N.J.)*, *39*(4), 389–406. doi:10.1007/s12140-022-09384-3

Ali, M., & Kirikkaleli, D. (2023). Carbon taxes, resources efficiency, and environmental sustainability in a developed country. *International Journal of Sustainable Development and World Ecology*, 1–10. doi:10.1080/13504509.2023.2296492

Al-Nuimat, A. A., Alserhan, B. A., Zeqiri, J., Hasani, V. V., & Komodromos, M. (2023). The motivating pull and push factors on the performance of mompreneurs projects: Educational and training barriers as a moderating variable. International Journal of Environment. *Workplace and Employment*, *7*(4), 340–367. doi:10.1504/IJEWE.2023.138013

Amanda, T. L. (2018). Customary Law and the Domain of Federal Common Law today. *Customary Law Today*, 233-254.

Anderson, B. B., & Ratiu, C. (2019). Stakeholder considerations in public-private partnerships. *World Journal of Entrepreneurship, Management and Sustainable Development*, *15*(3), 212–221. doi:10.1108/WJEMSD-04-2018-0046

Archer, B., & Fletcher, J. (1990). Tourism: its economic importance. In *Horwath Book of Tourism* (pp. 10–25). Palgrave Macmillan UK. doi:10.1007/978-1-349-11687-4_2

Artal-Tur, A., Villena-Navarro, M., & Alamá-Sabater, L. (2020). The relationship between cultural tourist behaviour and destination sustainability. In *Culture and Cultures in Tourism* (pp. 71–85). Routledge. doi:10.4324/9780429054891-8

Asian Development Bank (ADB). (2020). *Knowledge Transfer for Successful Public-Private Partnerships: A Compendium of Case Studies*. ADB.

Atienza, M., Fleming-Muñoz, D., & Aroca, P. (2021). Territorial development and mining. Insights and challenges from the Chilean case. *Resources Policy*, *70*, 101812. doi:10.1016/j.resourpol.2020.101812 PMID:34173424

Atukunda, P., Eide, W. B., Kardel, K. R., Iversen, P. O., & Westerberg, A. C. (2021). Unlocking the potential for achievement of the UN Sustainable Development Goal 2–'Zero Hunger'–in Africa: Targets, strategies, synergies and challenges. *Food & Nutrition Research*, *65*, 65. doi:10.29219/fnr.v65.7686 PMID:34262413

Aydın, S. G., & Aydoğdu, G. (2022). Makine öğrenmesi algoritmaları kullanılarak Türkiye ve AB ülkelerinin CO2 emisyonlarının tahmini. *Avrupa Bilim ve Teknoloji Dergisi*, (37), 42–46.

Babatunde, S. O., Perera, S., & Adeniyi, O. (2019, February 22). (2028). Identification of critical risk factors in public-private partnership project phases in developing countries: A case of Nigeria. *Benchmarking*, *26*(2), 334–355. doi:10.1108/BIJ-01-2017-0008

Babina, T., Fedyk, A., He, A., & Hodson, J. (2024). Artificial intelligence, firm growth, and product innovation. *Journal of Financial Economics*, *151*, 103745. doi:10.1016/j.jfineco.2023.103745

Baghestani, A., Tayarani, M., Allahviranloo, M., & Gao, H. O. (2020). Evaluating the Traffic and Emissions Impacts of Congestion Pricing in New York City. *Sustainability (Basel)*, *12*(9), 3655. doi:10.3390/su12093655

Banihani, M. (2020). Empowering Jordanian women through entrepreneurship. *Journal of Research in Marketing and Entrepreneurship*, *22*(1), 133–144. doi:10.1108/JRME-10-2017-0047

Baranzini, A., Goldemberg, J., & Speck, S. (2000). A future for carbon taxes. *Ecological Economics*, *32*(3), 395–412. doi:10.1016/S0921-8009(99)00122-6

Barbose, G., Darghouth, N. R., Weaver, S., Feldman, D., Margolis, R., & Wiser, R. (2015). Tracking US photovoltaic system prices 1998-2012: A rapidly changing market. *Progress in Photovoltaics: Research and Applications*, *23*(6), 692–704. doi:10.1002/pip.2482

Barkat, A. (2016). *Political economy of unpeopling of indigenous peoples: The case of Bangladesh*. MuktoBuddhiProkasana.

Baxter, D. (2022, May 12). *Public-Private Partnerships and Sustainable Development Goals*. IDEES. https://revistaidees.cat/en/public-private-partnerships-and-sustainable-development-goals/

Beevers, S. D., & Carslaw, D. C. (2005). The impact of congestion charging on vehicle emissions in London. *Atmospheric Environment*, *39*(1), 1–5. doi:10.1016/j.atmosenv.2004.10.001

Begg, D. (2004). Pricing Solutions for Sustainable Transport. *Environmental Science, Economics, Engineering*. https://www.semanticscholar.org/paper/Pricing-solutions-for-sustainable-transport-Begg/8390497aab52231cc82949ea694b0025e31960a9

Belitski, M., Caiazza, R., & Rodionova, Y. (2020). Investment in training and skills for innovation in entrepreneurial start-ups and incumbents: Evidence from the United Kingdom. *The International Entrepreneurship and Management Journal*, *16*(2), 617–640. doi:10.1007/s11365-019-00606-4

Bell, S., & Feng, H. (2013). *The rise of the People's Bank of China: The politics of institutional change*. Harvard University Press. doi:10.4159/harvard.9780674073593

Benjaminsen, T. A., & Svarstad, H. (2021). *Political ecology: A critical engagement with global environmental issues*. Springer Nature. doi:10.1007/978-3-030-56036-2

Bergman, B. J., & McMullen, J. S. (2022). Helping entrepreneurs help themselves: A review and relational research agenda on entrepreneurial support organizations. *Entrepreneurship Theory and Practice*, *46*(3), 688–728. doi:10.1177/10422587211028736

Berisha, A., Kruja, A., & Hysa, E. (2022). Perspective of Critical Factors toward Successful Public–Private Partnerships for Emerging Economies. *Administrative Sciences*, *12*(4), 160. doi:10.3390/admsci12040160

Bernstein, S. (2017). The United Nations and the governance of Sustainable Development Goals. In N. Kanie & F. Biermann (Eds.), *Governing Through Goals: Sustainable Development Goals as Governance Innovation* (pp. 213–240). MIT Press. doi:10.7551/mitpress/9780262035620.003.0009

Bertrand, G., Cassard, D., Arvanitidis, N., & Stanley, G. (2016). Map of critical raw material deposits in Europe. *Energy Procedia*, *97*, 44–50. doi:10.1016/j.egypro.2016.10.016

Besra, L. (2014). *A Critical Review of Democracy and Governance Challenges in Bangladesh with special refences to a human rights-based approach for the Development of marginalized indigenous people*. [PhD Thesis, Flinders of Institute of Public Policy Management, Australia].

Bharti, M. S. (2022b). The Economic Integration of the Central and Eastern European Countries into the European Union: Special Reference to Regional Development. *Copernicus Political and Legal Studies*, *1*(2), 11–23. https://doi.org/doi.org/10.15804/CPLS.20222.01

Bharti, M. S. (2022a). China's BRI in Central and Eastern European Countries: The Role Of '17+1' Framework for Regional Economic Cooperation. *Athenaeum Polish Political Science Studies*, *76*(4), 241–262. doi:10.15804/athena.2022.76.13

Bharti, M. S. (2023a). EU's energy policy and assessing Europe's spiraling energy security crises. In M. S. Ö. Özcan (Ed.), *Analyzing Energy Crises and the Impact of Country Policies on the World* (pp. 101–118). IGI Global. doi:10.4018/979-8-3693-0440-2.ch006

Bharti, M. S. (2023b). Global Development and International Order Transition: The Role of China. In M. O. Dinçsoy & H. Can (Eds.), *Optimizing Energy Efficiency During a Global Energy Crisis* (pp. 200–212). IGI Global. doi:10.4018/979-8-3693-0400-6.ch013

Bharti, M. S. (2023c). The Sustainable Development and Economic Impact of China's Belt and Road Initiative in Ethiopia. *East Asia (Piscataway, N.J.)*, *40*(2), 175–194. doi:10.1007/s12140-023-09402-y PMID:37065271

Bharti, M. S. (2024). Impact of Industry 4.0 Technologies for Advancement of Supply Chain Management (SCM) Sustainability. In M. R. Khan, N. R. Khan, & N. Z. Jhanjhi (Eds.), *Convergence of Industry 4.0 and Supply Chain Sustainability* (1st ed., pp. 157–175). IGI Global. doi:10.4018/979-8-3693-1363-3.ch007

Bianchi, R. V., & de Man, F. (2021). Tourism, inclusive growth and decent work: A political economy critique. *Journal of Sustainable Tourism*, *29*(2-3), 353–371. doi:10.1080/09669582.2020.1730862

Biermann, F., Hickmann, T., & Sénit, C. A. (Eds.). (2022). *The Political Impact of the Sustainable Development Goals: Transforming Governance Through Global Goals?* Cambridge University Press. doi:10.1017/9781009082945

Biermann, F., & Kanie, N. (2017). Conclusion: Key Challenges for Global Governance through Goals. In N. Kanie & F. Biermann (Eds.), *Governing Through Goals: Sustainable Development Goals as Governance Innovation* (pp. 295–310). MIT Press. doi:10.7551/mitpress/9780262035620.003.0013

Biermann, F., Kanie, N., & Kim, R. (2017). Global governance by goal-setting: The novel approach of the UN Sustainable Development Goals. *Current Opinion in Environmental Sustainability*, *26-27*, 26–31. doi:10.1016/j.cosust.2017.01.010

Bilan, Y., Mishchuk, H., Roshchyk, I., & Joshi, O. (2020). Hiring and retaining skilled employees in SMEs: Problems in human resource practices and links with organizational success. *Business: Theory and Practice*, *21*(2), 780–791. doi:10.3846/btp.2020.12750

Bills, K. L., Hayne, C., Stein, S. E., & Hatfield, R. C. (2021). Collaborating with competitors: How do small firm accounting associations and networks successfully manage coopetitive tensions? *Contemporary Accounting Research*, *38*(1), 545–585. doi:10.1111/1911-3846.12625

Blosser, A. (2024). *The Concept of Sacramental Goods: Addressing Veblen's Critique of Liturgy*. Studia Liturgica.

Bluffstone, R. A. (2003). Environmental Taxes in Developing and Transition Economies. SSRN *Electronic Journal*. doi:10.2139/ssrn.461539

Borgers, M., Biermann, B., Kalfagianni, A., & Kim, R. E. (2023). The SDGs as integrating force in global governance? Challenges and opportunities. *International Environmental Agreement: Politics, Law and Economics*, *23*(2), 157–164. doi:10.1007/s10784-023-09607-9

Born, K., & Ciftci, M. M. (2024). The limitations of end-of-life copper recycling and its implications for the circular economy of metals. *Resources, Conservation and Recycling*, *200*, 107318. doi:10.1016/j.resconrec.2023.107318

Bracke, M. A. (2022). Women's rights, family planning, and population control: The emergence of reproductive rights in the united nations (1960s–70s). *The International History Review*, *44*(4), 751–771. doi:10.1080/07075332.2021.1985585

Brattberg, E. (2020, February 19). *The EU and China in 2020: More Competition Ahead*. Carnegie. https://carnegieendowment.org/2020/02/19/eu-and-china-in-2020-more-competition-ahead-pub-81096

Breuil, F. (2015a, June). BNT: High-level political forum on sustainable development: Highlights of 26 June. MediaEarth. https://www.mediaterre.org/actu,20150630095111,1.html

Bruns, E., Ohlhorst, D., Wenzel, B., & Köppel, J. (2011). *Renewable Energies in Germany's Electricity Market: A Biography of the Innovation Process*. Springer Dordrecht. doi:10.1007/978-90-481-9905-1

Buckle, D. S., & Mactavish, D. F. (2013). *Grantham Briefing Note 4: The Earth's energy budget*.

Buhalis, D., Leung, X. Y., Fan, D., Darcy, S., Chen, G., Xu, F., & Tan, W.-H. G., Nunkoo, R., & Farmaki, A. (2023). Editorial. Tourism Review (Vol. 78, Issue 2, pp. 293–313). Emerald Publishing. doi:10.1108/TR-04-2023-620

Burgers, I. J., & Weishaar, S. E. (2018). *Designing carbon taxes is not an easy task: Legal perspectives*. EconStor. https://www.econstor.eu/handle/10419/179313

Cahill, D., & Wang, J. (2022). Addressing legitimacy concerns in antitrust private litigation involving China's state-owned enterprises. *World Competition: Law and Economic Review*, *45*(1), 75–122. doi:10.54648/WOCO2022004

Carlsen, L., & Bruggemann, R. (2022). The 17 United Nations' sustainable development goals: A status by 2020. *International Journal of Sustainable Development and World Ecology*, *29*(3), 219–229. doi:10.1080/13504509.2021.1948456

Casady, C. B., Eriksson, K., Levitt, R. E., & Scott, W. R. (2020). (Re)defining public-private partnerships (PPPs) in the new public governance (NPG) paradigm: An institutional maturity perspective. *Public Management Review*, *22*(2), 161–183. doi:10.1080/14719037.2019.1577909

Castañeda, Q., & Burtner, J. (2010). Tourism as "A Force for World Peace" The Politics of Tourism, Tourism as Governmentality and the Tourism Boycott of Guatemala. *The Journal of Tourism and Peace Research*, *1*(2), 1–21.

Castro Núñez, R. B., Bandeira, P., & Santero-Sánchez, R. (2020). Social economy, gender equality at work and the 2030 agenda: Theory and evidence from Spain. *Sustainability (Basel)*, *12*(12), 5192. doi:10.3390/su12125192

CCICED. (2020, September). *Green BRI and 2030 Agenda for Sustainable Development*. BU. https://www.bu.edu/gdp/files/2020/09/SPS-4-1-Green-BRI-and-2020-Agenda-for-Sustainable-Development.pdf

Center for International Knowledge on Development. (2023, September). *China's Progress Report on Implementation of the 2030 Agenda for Sustainable Development*. MFA. https://www.mfa.gov.cn/eng/topics_665678/2030kcxfzyc/202310/P020231018367257234614.pdf

Černý, I., Vaněk, M., Maruszewska, E. W., & Beneš, F. (2021). How economic indicators impact the EU internal demand for critical raw materials. *Resources Policy*, *74*, 102417. doi:10.1016/j.resourpol.2021.102417

Chakma, N., & Maitrot, M. (2016). *How ethnic minorities became poor and stay poor in Bangladesh: A qualitative enquiry*. EEP/Shiree.

Chand, R., & Singh, J. (2023). *From green revolution to amrit kaal*. National Institution for Transforming India. GoI.

Chang, L., Li, W., & Lu, X. (2015). Government engagement, environmental policy, and environmental performance: Evidence from the most polluting Chinese listed firms. *Business Strategy and the Environment*, *24*(1), 1–19. doi:10.1002/bse.1802

Chávez Rivera, M. E., Fuentes Fuentes, M. D. M., & Ruiz-Jiménez, J. M. (2021). Challenging the context: Mumpreneurship, copreneurship, and sustainable thinking in the entrepreneurial process of women–a case study in Ecuador. *Academia (Caracas)*, *34*(3), 368–398. doi:10.1108/ARLA-07-2020-0172

Chen, C., Chaudhary, A., & Mathys, A. (2020). Nutritional and environmental losses embedded in global food waste. *Resources, Conservation and Recycling*, *160*, 104912. doi:10.1016/j.resconrec.2020.104912

Cheng, Z., Huanming, W., Xiong, W., Dajian, Z., & Cheng, L. (2021). Public–private partnership as a driver of sustainable development: Toward a conceptual framework of sustainability-oriented PPP. *Environment, Development and Sustainability*, *23*(1), 1043–1063. doi:10.1007/s10668-019-00576-1

Chen, S. J., & Hwang, C. L. (1992). Fuzzy multiple attribute decision making methods. In *Fuzzy multiple attribute decision making* (pp. 289–486). Springer. doi:10.1007/978-3-642-46768-4_5

Cherepovitsyn, A., Solovyova, V., & Dmitrieva, D. (2023). New challenges for the sustainable development of the rare-earth metals sector in Russia: Transforming industrial policies. *Resources Policy*, *81*, 103347. doi:10.1016/j.resourpol.2023.103347

China Council for International Cooperation on Environment and Development (CCICED) Secretariat. (2022). Green BRI and 2030 Agenda for Sustainable Development. In Green Consensus and High-Quality Development (pp. 375–445). Springer Singapore. doi:10.1007/978-981-16-4799-4_8

Chin, W. L., Tham, A., & Noorashid, N. (2023). Distribution of (In)Equality and Empowerment of Community-Based Tourism: The Case Study of Brunei Darussalam. *International Journal of Hospitality & Tourism Administration*, 1–32. doi:10.1080/15256480.2023.2175287

Coates, K., & Middelschulte, D. (2019). Getting Consumer Welfare Right: The competition law implications of market-driven sustainability initiatives. *European Competition Journal*, *15*(2-3), 318–326. doi:10.1080/17441056.2019.1665940

Coenen, J., Bager, S., Meyfroidt, P., Newig, J., & Challies, E. (2021). Environmental Governance of China's Belt and Road Initiative. *Environmental Policy and Governance*, *31*(1), 3–17. doi:10.1002/eet.1901

Commoner, B. (2020). *The closing circle: nature, man, and technology*. Courier Dover Publications.

Constitution of Bangladesh. (2019). Ministry of Law, Justice, and Parliamentary Affairs, GoB.

Convery, F., McDonnell, S., & Ferreira, S. (2007). The most popular tax in Europe? Lessons from the Irish plastic bags levy. *Environmental and Resource Economics*, *38*(1), 1–11. doi:10.1007/s10640-006-9059-2

Cozzi, L., Gould, T., Bouckart, S., Crow, D., Kim, T. Y., McGlade, C., & Wetzel, D. (2020). *World energy outlook 2020*. International Energy Agency.

Croes, R. (2014). *Issue 3* (Vol. 6). Tourism and poverty reduction in Latin America: Where does the region stand? Worldwide Hospitality and Tourism Themes. Emerald Group Publishing Ltd., doi:10.1108/WHATT-03-2014-0010

Damgé, M. (2017). Inequality in the world, which has been on the rise for forty years. *Le Monde*. https://www.lemonde.fr/les-decodeurs/article/2017/12/14/les-inegalites-dans-le-monde-en-hausse-depuis-quarante-ans_5229478_4355770.html

Dang, H. A. H., & Nguyen, C. V. (2021). Gender inequality during the COVID-19 pandemic: Income, expenditure, savings, and job loss. *World Development*, *140*, 105296. doi:10.1016/j.worlddev.2020.105296 PMID:34548740

Dasgupta, P. (2021). *Final Report- The Economics of Biodiversity*. UK Government. https://www.gov.uk/government/publications/final-report-the-economics-of-biodiversity-the-dasgupta-review

Daspit, J. J., Fox, C. J., & Findley, S. K. (2023). Entrepreneurial mindset: An integrated definition, a review of current insights, and directions for future research. *Journal of Small Business Management*, *61*(1), 12–44. doi:10.1080/00472778.2021.1907583

David, M., & Koch, F. (2019). "Akıllı, yeterince akıllı değil!" Akıllı şehir konseptlerinde kritik hammadde kullanımının öngörülmesi: Akıllı şebeke örneği. *Sürdürülebilirlik*, *11*(16), 4422.

De Clercq, D., & Brieger, S. A. (2022). When discrimination is worse, autonomy is key: How women entrepreneurs leverage job autonomy resources to find work–life balance. *Journal of Business Ethics*, *177*(3), 665–682. doi:10.1007/s10551-021-04735-1

Decelle, X. (2004). A conceptual and dynamic approach to innovation in tourism (pp. 1-16). Paris: OEcD.

Dede, M., Sunardi, S., Lam, K. C., & Withaningsih, S. (2023). Relationship between landscape and river ecosystem services. *Global Journal of Environmental Science and Management*, *9*(3), 637–652.

DeHart, J. L., & Soulé, P. T. (2000). Does I= PAT work in local places? *The Professional Geographer*, *52*(1), 1–10. doi:10.1111/0033-0124.00200

Delamotte, G. (2020). Dealing with China: A European Perspective. *Asia-Pacific Review*, *27*(2), 109–123. doi:10.1080/13439006.2020.1826681

Demirtaş, M., Turan, A., Car, E., & Yücel, O. (2017). Kritik Hammaddeler. *Metalurji ve Malzeme Mühendisleri Odası Dergisi*, *183*, 28–33.

Dennis, W. J. Jr. (2011). Entrepreneurship, small business and public policy levers. *Journal of Small Business Management*, *49*(1), 92–106. doi:10.1111/j.1540-627X.2010.00316.x

Department of Statistics Malaysia. (January 2014). *Labor Force Report November 2023*. DOSM. https://storage.dosm.gov.my/labour/lfs_month_2023-11_en.pdf

Department of Statistics Malaysia. (November 2022). *Women at a Glance 2021 - Department of Statistics Malaysia*. Retrieved from https://www.kln.gov.my/web/chl_santiago/news-from-mission/-/blogs/women-at-a-glance-2021

Dhaliwal, A. (2022). The mompreneurship phenomenon: An examination of the antecedents and challenges of mothers in business. [IJSSMET]. *International Journal of Service Science, Management, Engineering, and Technology*, *13*(1), 1–17. doi:10.4018/IJSSMET.290334

Dinwiddie, A. N. (2020). China's Belt and Road Initiative: An Examination of Project Financing Issues and Alternatives. *Brooklyn Journal of International Law*, *45*(2), 745–776.

Dogbe, W., & Gil, J. M. (2018). Effectiveness of a carbon tax to promote a climate-friendly food consumption. *Food Policy*, *79*, 235–246. doi:10.1016/j.foodpol.2018.08.003

Dolla, T., & Boeing, S. L. (2018). Procurement of low carbon municipal solid waste infrastructure in India through public-private partnerships. *Built Environment Project and Asset Management*, *8*(5), 449–460. doi:10.1108/BEPAM-10-2017-0087

Domaracka, L., Matuskova, S., Tausova, M., Senova, A., & Kowal, B. (2022). Efficient Use of Critical Raw Materials for Optimal Resource Management in EU Countries. *Sustainability (Basel)*, *14*(11), 6554. doi:10.3390/su14116554

Compilation of References

Dong, L., Yang, X., & Li, H. (2018). The Belt and Road Initiative and the 2030 Agenda for Sustainable Development: Seeking linkages for global environmental governance. *Zhongguo Renkou Ziyuan Yu Huanjing*, *16*(3), 203–210. doi:10.1080/10042857.2018.1487745

Dou, J., & Han, X. (2019). How does the industry mobility affect pollution industry transfer in China: Empirical test on Pollution Haven Hypothesis and Porter Hypothesis. *Journal of Cleaner Production*, *217*, 105–115. doi:10.1016/j.jclepro.2019.01.147

Dragan, G. B., Arfi, W. B., Tiberius, V., Ammari, A., & Ferasso, M. (2024). Acceptance of circular entrepreneurship: Employees' perceptions on organizations' transition to the circular economy. *Journal of Business Research*, *173*, 114461. doi:10.1016/j.jbusres.2023.114461

Du Pisani, J. A. (2006). Sustainable development–historical roots of the concept. *Environmental Sciences (Lisse)*, *3*(2), 83–96. doi:10.1080/15693430600688831

Dube, K. (2020). Touris and sustainable development goals in African context. *International journal of economics and finance studies*, *12*(1), 88-102. doi:10.34109/ijefs.202012106

Đurović-Todorović, J., Đorđević, M., & Stojanović, M. (2024). The Impact of Environmental Taxes on the Reduction of Plastic Bag Consumption in the Republic of Serbia. *TEME*, *767*, 767. doi:10.22190/TEME220529048D

ECLAC. (2015). *Uruguay Can Move Ahead on Implementing Green Taxes*. ECLAC. https://www.cepal.org/en/news/uruguay-can-move-ahead-implementing-green-taxes

Eden, L., & Wagstaff, M. F. (2021). Evidence-based policymaking and the wicked problem of SDG 5 Gender Equality. *Journal of International Business Policy*, *4*(1), 28–57. doi:10.1057/s42214-020-00054-w

EIA. (2022). *Annual Energy Outlook 2021*. EIA. https://www.eia.gov/outlooks/aeo/tables_side.php

Elahi, E., Li, G., Han, X., Zhu, W., Liu, Y., Cheng, A., & Yang, Y. (2024). Decoupling livestock and poultry pollution emissions from industrial development: A step towards reducing environmental emissions. *Journal of Environmental Management*, *350*, 119654. doi:10.1016/j.jenvman.2023.119654 PMID:38016232

Elena, P., Liesl, R., & Cummings, M. E. (2020). Diaspora investment promotion via public–private partnerships: Case-study insights and IB research implications from the Succeed in Ireland initiative. *Journal of International Business Policy*, *3*(1), 23–37. doi:10.1057/s42214-019-00044-7

Eliasson, J. (2008). Lessons from the Stockholm congestion charging trial. *Transport Policy*, *15*(6), 395–404. doi:10.1016/j.tranpol.2008.12.004

Erkara, E. (2023). Kritik Malzemeler ve Arz Riski Yaratan Faktörler. İklim değişikliği ekonomisi çalıştayı. Eskişehir.

European Commission. (2024). *Sustainable Development Goals*. EC. https://commission.europa.eu/strategy-and-policy/sustainable-development-goals_en#:~:text=Sustainable%20development%20is%20a%20core,Sustainable%20Development%20Goals%20(SDGs)

Falk, J. H., Ballantyne, R., Packer, J., & Benckendorff, P. (2012). Travel and learning: A neglected tourism research area. *Annals of Tourism Research*, *39*(2), 908–927. doi:10.1016/j.annals.2011.11.016

FAO. (2022). *Agroecology a win-win for Uruguay's farmers, environment, and economy*. FAO. https://www.fao.org/support-to-investment/news/detail/ru/c/1601307/

Farazmand, A. (2018). *The Role of Partnerships in the Implementation of the Sustainable Development Goals*. Sustainable Development Goals.

Fay, M., Martimort, D., & Straub, S. (2018). Funding and financing infrastructure: The joint-use of public and private finance. *Journal of Development Economics*, *150*, 102629. Advance online publication. doi:10.1016/j.jdeveco.2021.102629

Ferro, P., & Bonollo, F. (2019). Design for recycling in a critical raw materials perspective. *Recycling*, *4*(4), 44. doi:10.3390/recycling4040044

Feyers, S., Stein, T., & Klizentyte, K. (2020). Bridging worlds: Utilizing a multi-stakeholder framework to create extension-tourism partnerships. *Sustainability (Basel)*, *12*(1), 1–23. doi:10.3390/su12010080

Filho, W. L., Kotter, R., Özuyar, P. G., Abubakar, I. R., Eustachio, J. H. P. P., & Matandirotya, N. R. (2023). Understanding Rare Earth Elements as Critical Raw Materials. *Sustainability (Basel)*, *15*(3), 1919. doi:10.3390/su15031919

Fisher, A. N., & Ryan, M. K. (2021). Gender inequalities during COVID-19. *Group Processes & Intergroup Relations*, *24*(2), 237–245. doi:10.1177/1368430220984248

Folke, C., Carpenter, S., Elmqvist, T., Gunderson, L., & Walker, B. (2021). Resilience: Now more than ever: This article belongs to Ambio's 50th Anniversary Collection. Theme: Anthropocene. *Ambio*, *50*(10), 1774–1777. doi:10.1007/s13280-020-01487-6 PMID:33721222

Fox, E. M. (2019). Should China's Competition Model be Exported?: A Reply to Wendy Ng. *European Journal of International Law*, *30*(4), 1431–1440. doi:10.1093/ejil/chaa010

Frone, S. M., & Florin Frone, D. (2013). Sustainable Tourism and Water Supply and Sanitation Development in Romania. *Journal of Tourism and Hospitality Management, 1*(3).

Fukuda-Parr, S., Yamin, A. E., & Greenstein, J. (2013). *The Power of Numbers: A Critical Review of MDG Targets for Human Development and Human Rights*. Working Paper Series. https://www.worldbank.org/content/dam/Worldbank/document/Gender/Synthesis%20paper%20PoN_Final.pdf

FullertonD.LeicesterA.SmithS. (2008). *Environmental Taxes*. https://ssrn.com/abstract=1179867 doi:10.3386/w14197

Fullerton, D., & Stavins, R. (1998). How economists see the environment. *Nature*, *395*(6701), 433–434. doi:10.1038/26606

García-Benavente, J. M. (2016). Impact of a carbon tax on the Chilean economy: A computable general equilibrium analysis. *Energy Economics*, *57*, 106–127. doi:10.1016/j.eneco.2016.04.014

Gardner, C., & Henry, P. B. (2023). The Global Infrastructure Gap: Potential, Perils, and a Framework for Distinction. *Journal of Economic Literature*, *61*(4), 1318–1358. doi:10.1257/jel.20221530

Garidzirai, R., & Pasara, M. T. (2020). An analysis of the contribution of tourism on economic growth in South African provinces: A panel analysis. *Geo Journal of Tourism and Geosites*, *29*(2), 554–564. doi:10.30892/gtg.29214-489

Garlick, J. (2019). China's Economic Diplomacy in Central and Eastern Europe: A Case of Offensive Mercantilism? *Europe-Asia Studies*, *71*(8), 1390–1414. doi:10.1080/09668136.2019.1648764

Gaspers, J. (2018, March 2). Divide and Rule. *Berlin Policy Journal*. https://berlinpolicyjournal.com/divide-and-rule/

Ghassabian, A., Titus, A. R., Conderino, S., Azan, A., Weinberger, R., & Thorpe, L. E. (2024). Beyond traffic jam alleviation: Evaluating the health and health equity impacts of New York City's congestion pricing plan. *Journal of Epidemiology and Community Health*, *78*(5), 273–276. doi:10.1136/jech-2023-221639 PMID:38195634

Gilbert, R. J. (2022). *Innovation matters: competition policy for the high-technology economy*. MIT Press.

Global Impact Investing Network. (2023). *The Global Impact Investing Network Landscape Report 2023*. GIIN.

Göçmen, E. (2021). A maturity model for assessing sustainable project management knowledge areas: A case study within a logistics firm. *Journal of Advanced Research in Natural and Applied Sciences, 7*(4), 536–555. doi:10.28979/jarnas.958605

Göçmen, E. (2021). Smart airport: Evaluation of performance standards and technologies for a smart logistics zone. *Transportation Research Record: Journal of the Transportation Research Board, 2675*(7), 480–490. doi:10.1177/03611981211019740

Godfrey, C. M., Gurmu, A. T., & Tivendale, L. (2019). Investigation of the challenges facing public-private partnership projects in Australia. *Construction Economics and Building, 19*(1).

Gökovali, U., & Bahar, O. (2006). Contribution of tourism to economic growth: A panel data approach. *Anatolia, 17*(2), 155–167. doi:10.1080/13032917.2006.9687184

Gómez-Martín, M. B., Armesto-López, X. A., Cors-Iglesias, M., & Muñoz-Negrete, J. (2014). Adaptation strategies to climate change in the tourist sector: The case of coastal tourism in Spain. *Tourism (Zagreb), 62*(3), 293–308.

González-Aliste, P., Derpich, I., & López, M. (2023). Reducing Urban Traffic Congestion via Charging Price. *Sustainability (Basel), 15*(3), 2086. doi:10.3390/su15032086

González, J. (2020). Political economy of inequality in Chile: historical institutions, taxation, and elite power. In P. Anand, S. Fennell, & F. Comim (Eds.), *Handbook of BRICS and Emerging Economies* (pp. 746–785). Oxford University Press., doi:10.1093/oso/9780198827535.003.0028

Gopalakrishnan, V., Wadhwa, D., & Hadd, S. (2021). *A look back at 2021 in 11 graphs: The inequality pandemic.* World Bank. https://www.banquemondiale.org/fr/news/feature/2021/12/20/year-2021-in-review-the-inequality-pandemic

GoulderL. H.ParryI. W. H. (2008). *Instrument Choice in Environmental Policy.* https://ssrn.com/abstract=1117566

Government of Chile. (2020). *Chile's Nationally Determined Contribution.* UNFCCC. https://unfccc.int/sites/default/files/NDC/2022-06/Chile%27s_NDC_2020_english.pdf

Government of Chile. (2022). *A milestone in Chile's environmental history: From today, we have our first Framework Law on Climate Change.* Government of Chile. https://www.gob.cl/en/news/a-milestone-in-chiles-environmental-history-from-today-we-have-our-first-framework-law-on-climate-change/

Green, C. P., Heywood, J. S., & Navarro Paniagua, M. (2020). Did the London congestion charge reduce pollution? *Regional Science and Urban Economics, 84*, 103573. doi:10.1016/j.regsciurbeco.2020.103573

Green, D. (2012). *From poverty to power: How active citizens and effective states can change the world.* Practical Action Publishing and Oxfam International. doi:10.3362/9781780447407

Grigorieva, E., & Lukyanets, A. (2021). Combined Effect of Hot Weather and Outdoor Air Pollution on Respiratory Health: Literature Review. *Atmosphere (Basel), 12*(6), 790. doi:10.3390/atmos12060790

Grober, U. (2007). *Deep roots-a conceptual history of' sustainable development.*

Grossi, G., & Argento, D. (2022). The fate of accounting for public governance development. *Accounting, Auditing & Accountability Journal, 35*(9), 272–303. doi:10.1108/AAAJ-11-2020-5001

Gruebler, J. (2020, August). *The People's Republic of China Connecting Europe?* Asian Development Bank Institute. https://www.adb.org/sites/default/files/publication/634751/adbi-wp1178.pdf

Gruebler, J. (2021). China connecting Europe? *Asia Europe Journal, 19*(1), 77–101. doi:10.1007/s10308-021-00616-4 PMID:34248452

Gu, D., Andreev, K., & Dupre, M. E. (2021). Major trends in population growth around the world. *China CDC Weekly*, *3*(28), 604. doi:10.46234/ccdcw2021.160 PMID:34594946

Guinot, J., Barghouti, Z., & Chiva, R. (2022). Understanding green innovation: A conceptual framework. *Sustainability (Basel)*, *14*(10), 5787. doi:10.3390/su14105787

Guo, J., Del Barrio Álvarez, D., Yuan, J., & Kato, H. (n.d.). Determinants of the formation process in public-private partnership projects in developing countries: Evidence from China. *Local Government Studies*, 1–24. doi:10.1080/03003930.2023.2198221

Gu, Z., Liu, Z., Cheng, Q., & Saberi, M. (2018). Congestion pricing practices and public acceptance: A review of evidence. *Case Studies on Transport Policy*, *6*(1), 94–101. doi:10.1016/j.cstp.2018.01.004

Hache, E., Seck, G. S., Simoen, M., Bonnet, C., & Carcanague, S. (2019). Critical raw materials and transportation sector electrification: A detailed bottom-up analysis in world transport. *Applied Energy*, *240*, 6–25. doi:10.1016/j.apenergy.2019.02.057

Haites, E. (2018). Carbon taxes and greenhouse gas emissions trading systems: What have we learned? *Climate Policy*, *18*(8), 955–966. doi:10.1080/14693062.2018.1492897

Hall, S. (2023). *Uruguay is a sustainability success story-here's why*. WeForum. https://www.weforum.org/agenda/2023/01/uruguay-sustainable-energy-renewables/

Hamunyela, E., Brandt, P., Shirima, D., Do, H. T. T., Herold, M., & Roman-Cuesta, R. M. (2020). Space-time detection of deforestation, forest degradation and regeneration in montane forests of Eastern Tanzania. *International Journal of Applied Earth Observation and Geoinformation*, *88*, 102063. doi:10.1016/j.jag.2020.102063

Haque, M. N., Saroar, M., Fattah, M. A., & Morshed, S. R. (2020). Public-Private Partnership for achieving sustainable development goals: A case study of Khulna, Bangladesh. *Public Administration and Policy*, *23*(3), 283–298. doi:10.1108/PAP-04-2020-0023

Harris, H. S., Wang, P. J., Cohen, M. A., Zhang, Y., & Evrard, S. J. (2011). *Anti-monopoly law and practice in China*. Oxford University Press.

Harris, S., Weinzettel, J., Bigano, A., & Källmén, A. (2020). Low carbon cities in 2050? GHG emissions of European cities using production-based and consumption-based emission accounting methods. *Journal of Cleaner Production*, *248*, 119206. doi:10.1016/j.jclepro.2019.119206

Hasan, M. M. (2020). *Mining conflict, indigenous peoples and environmental justice: The case of Phulbari coal project in Bangladesh,* [PhD thesis, York University].

Hasegawa, T., Fujimori, S., Havlík, P., Valin, H., Bodirsky, B. L., Doelman, J. C., Fellmann, T., Kyle, P., Koopman, J. F. L., Lotze-Campen, H., Mason-D'Croz, D., Ochi, Y., Pérez Domínguez, I., Stehfest, E., Sulser, T. B., Tabeau, A., Takahashi, K., Takakura, J., van Meijl, H., & Witzke, P. (2018). Risk of increased food insecurity under stringent global climate change mitigation policy. *Nature Climate Change*, *8*(8), 699–703. doi:10.1038/s41558-018-0230-x

Haugh, H. (2021). Call the midwife! Business incubators as entrepreneurial enablers in developing economies. In Business, Entrepreneurship and Innovation Towards Poverty Reduction (pp. 156–175). Routledge. doi:10.4324/9781003176107-8

He, H. (2012). Effects of environmental policy on consumption: Lessons from the Chinese plastic bag regulation. *Environment and Development Economics*, *17*(4), 407–431. doi:10.1017/S1355770X1200006X

Helmy, R., Khourshed, N., Wahba, M., & Alaa Abd, E. B. (2020). Exploring Critical Success Factors for Public Private Partnership Case Study: The Educational Sector in Egypt. *Journal of Open Innovation*, *6*(4), 142. doi:10.3390/joitmc6040142

Herath, S. K., & Herath, L. M. (2024a). Corporate Social Responsibility (CSR) and Sustainable Development (SD) in the Digital Age. In A. Erturk, S. Colbran, E. Coşkun, F. Theofanidis, & O. Abidi (Eds.), Convergence of Digitalization, Innovation, and Sustainable Development in Business (pp. 162-184). IGI Global. doi:10.4018/979-8-3693-0798-4.ch008

Herath, S. K., & Herath, L. M. (2023). Key Success Factors for Implementing Public-Private Partnership Infrastructure Projects. In C. Popescu, P. Yu, & Y. Wei (Eds.), *Achieving the Sustainable Development Goals Through Infrastructure Development* (pp. 1–38). IGI Global. doi:10.4018/979-8-3693-0794-6.ch001

Herath, S. K., & Herath, L. M. (2024). Investigation Into the Barriers to AI Adoption in ESG Integration and Identification of Strategies to Overcome These Challenges. In A. Derbali (Ed.), *Social and Ethical Implications of AI in Finance for Sustainability* (pp. 286–311). IGI Global. doi:10.4018/979-8-3693-2881-1.ch013

Hernandez-Garcia, J. (2013). Slum tourism, city branding and social urbanism: The case of Medellin, Colombia. *Journal of Place Management and Development*, 6(1), 43–51. doi:10.1108/17538331311306122

Herrero, A. G., & Xu, J. (2017). China's Belt and Road Initiative: Can Europe Expect Trade Gains? *China & World Economy*, 25(6), 84–99. doi:10.1111/cwe.12222

Herweg, F., & Schmidt, K. M. (2022). How to Regulate Carbon Emissions with Climate-Conscious Consumers. *Economic Journal (London)*, 132(648), 2992–3019. doi:10.1093/ej/ueac045

Heydari, M., Lai, K. K., & Xiaohu, Z. (2021). *Risk management in public-private partnerships*. Routledge. doi:10.4324/9781003112051

Hiçyılmaz, B. (2022). Avrupa Birliği Kritik Hammaddeler Yasası. İklim değişikliği ekonomisi çalıştayı. Eskişehir.

Hillson, D. (Ed.). (2023). *The risk management handbook: A practical guide to managing the multiple dimensions of risk*. Kogan Page Publishers.

Hirsch, F. (1976). *Social limits to growth*. Harvard University Press. doi:10.4159/harvard.9780674497900

Hitt, M. A., & Xu, K. (2016). The transformation of China: Effects of the institutional environment on business actions. *Long Range Planning*, 49(5), 589–593. doi:10.1016/j.lrp.2015.02.006

HLPF. (2024). *High-Level Political Forum*. HLPF. https://hlpf.un.org/

Hodge, G. A., & Greve, C. (2007). Public–Private Partnerships: An International Performance Review. *Public Administration Review*, 67(3), 545–558. doi:10.1111/j.1540-6210.2007.00736.x

Hong, P. (2016). Jointly Building the 'Belt and Road' towards the Sustainable Development Goals. Department of Economic and Social Affairs, United Nations. https:// ssrn.com/abstract =2812893

Hoque, M. A., Lovelock, B., & Carr, A. (2022). Alleviating Indigenous poverty through tourism: The role of NGOs. *Journal of Sustainable Tourism*, 30(10), 2333–2351. doi:10.1080/09669582.2020.1860070

Horochowski, K., & Moisey, R. N. (1999). The role of environmental NGOs in sustainable tourism development: A case study in northern Honduras. *Tourism Recreation Research*, 24(2), 19–30. doi:10.1080/02508281.1999.11014872

Horvath, B. (2016). *Identifying Development Dividends along the Belt and Road Initiative*. UNDP. https://www.undp.org/sites/g/files/zskgke326/files/migration/cn/139e87df8c74c6731e5da60079ce6c88d59e7fe6e5282c3a8f4c472955315493.pdf

Hossain, M. S., Sharifuzzaman, S. M., Nobi, M. N., Chowdhury, M. S. N., Sarker, S., Alamgir, M., Uddin, S. A., Chowdhury, S. R., Rahman, M. M., Rahman, M. S., Sobhan, F., & Chowdhury, S. (2021). Seaweeds farming for sustainable development goals and blue economy in Bangladesh. *Marine Policy*, 128, 104469. doi:10.1016/j.marpol.2021.104469

Hossinger, S. M., Chen, X., & Werner, A. (2020). Drivers, barriers, and success factors of academic spin-offs: A systematic literature review. *Management Review Quarterly*, *70*(1), 97–134. doi:10.1007/s11301-019-00161-w

Huang, Y. (2019). Monopoly and anti-monopoly in china today. *American Journal of Economics and Sociology*, *78*(5), 1101–1134. doi:10.1111/ajes.12298

Hussain, A., Javed, Z., Kishwa, F., Bangash, M. K., Raza, H. M. Z., & Farooq, M. (2020). Impact of single use polyethylene shopping bags on environmental pollution, a comprehensive review. *Pure and Applied Biology*, *9*(3). Advance online publication. doi:10.19045/bspab.2020.90209

IDRC. (2019). *Leaving no one behind: Principles of research in fragile contexts*. IDRC. https://www.idrc.ca/fr/perspectives/ne-laisser-personne-de-cote-principes-de-la-recherche-dans-les-contextes-fragiles

IEA. (2023), *World Energy Outlook 2023*. IEA, Paris https://www.iea.org/reports/world-energy-outlook-2023, License: CC BY 4.0 (report); CC BY NC SA 4.0 (Annex A)

IISD. (2022, July 18). Summary of the 2022 session of the high-level political Forum on sustainable development: 5-15 July 2022. *Earth Negotiations Bulletin*. IISD. enb.iisd.org/high-level-political-forum-hlpf-2022

International Monetary Fund. (2024, April 12). *World Economic Outlook: April 2024*. IMF. https://www.imf.org/en/Publications/WEO

IPCC. (2022). *Climate Change 2022: Impacts, Adaptation and Vulnerability*. IPCC. https://www.ipcc.ch/report/ar6/wg2/

Iqbal, S., Farrukh, M., & Bhaumik, A. (2024). A retrospective of women entrepreneurship research and future research directions. *Vision (Basel)*, 09722629231219617. doi:10.1177/09722629231219617

Işik, C., Dogan, E., & Ongan, S. (2017). Analyzing the tourism–energy–growth nexus for the top 10 most-visited countries. *Economies*, *5*(4), 40. doi:10.3390/economies5040040

Islam, M. A., Rashed, C. A. A., & Hasan, J. (2019). Raw Materials Shortage and Their Impact on the Manufacturing Business-an Empirical Study in the Pharmaceutical Sector of Bangladesh. *Review of General Management*, *29*(2).

Ivanov, M. O., Pinskaya, M. R., & Bogachov, S. V. (2024). Ecological tax as a tool for leveling the negative impact on the environment. *BIO Web of Conferences, 83*, 04003. 10.1051/bioconf/20248304003

Jackson, P. (1983). A World Charter for Nature. *Ambio*, *12*(2), 133–134.

Jafari-Sadeghi, V. (2020). The motivational factors of business venturing: Opportunity versus necessity? A gendered perspective on European countries. *Journal of Business Research*, *113*, 279–289. doi:10.1016/j.jbusres.2019.09.058

Jahromi, F. S., & Jahromi, F. S. (2023). Policy and legal frameworks for underground natural gas storage in Iran. *Utilities Policy*, *80*(C), 101471. doi:10.1016/j.jup.2022.101471

Jeje, Y. (2006). *Southern Alberta Landscapes: Meeting the Challenges Ahead: Export Coefficients for Total Phosphorus, Total Nitrogen and Total Suspended Solids in the Southern Alberta Region: A Review of Literature*. Alberta Environment.

Jensen, N. M., & Malesky, E. J. (2018). Incentives to Pander: How politicians Use Corporate Welfare for Political Gain. In N. M. Jensen & E. J. Malesky (Eds.), *Incentives to Pander: How Politicians Use Corporate Welfare for Political Gain* (pp. v–v). Cambridge University Press. https://www.cambridge.org/core/product/8AF81E7336F02EA245DFC3684F20E98F doi:10.1017/9781108292337

Jephcott, P., Seear, N., & Smith, J. H. (2023). *Married women working*. Routledge. doi:10.4324/9781003317777

Compilation of References

Jesenský, M., & Jesenský, M. (2019). Development for All: We Still Can. *The United Nations under Ban Ki-moon: Give Diplomacy a Chance*, 11-20.

Jin, L. (2018). Synergies between the Belt and Road Initiative and the 2030 SDGs: From the perspective of development. *Economic and Political Studies*, *6*(3), 278–292. doi:10.1080/20954816.2018.1498990

Johansson, C., Burman, L., & Forsberg, B. (2009). The effects of congestions tax on air quality and health. *Atmospheric Environment*, *43*(31), 4843–4854. doi:10.1016/j.atmosenv.2008.09.015

Joncoux, F. (2020). *Focus on inequalities in Italy*. Major-Prep. https://major-prepa.com/langues/italien/inegalites-italie/#Les%20In%C3%A9galit%C3%A9s%20Hommes/Femmes%20en%20Italie

Jones, P., Hillier, D., & Comfort, D. (2015). 'Sustainability in the Hospitality Industry: Some Personal Reflections on Corporate Challenges and Research Agendas'. *International Journal of Contemporary Hospitality Management*, *28*(1), 36–67. doi:10.1108/IJCHM-11-2014-0572

Jones, P., Hillier, D., & Comfort, D. (2017). The sustainable development goals and the tourism and hospitality industry. *Athens Journal of Tourism*, *4*(1), 7–18. doi:10.30958/ajt.4.1.1

Joseph Gerald, T. N., Kwame, A. D., Buabeng, T., & Maloreh-Nyamekye, T. (2022). Governance and effectiveness of public–private partnership in Ghana's rural-water sector. *International Journal of Public Sector Management*, *35*(7), 709–732. doi:10.1108/IJPSM-05-2021-0129

Joshi, D. K., Hughes, B. B., & Sisk, T. D. (2015). Improving governance for the post-2015 Sustainable Development Goals: Scenario forecasting the next 50 years. *World Development*, *70*, 286–302. doi:10.1016/j.worlddev.2015.01.013

Joudyian, N., Doshmangir, L., Mahdavi, M., Jafar, S. T., & Gordeev, V. S. (2021). Public-private partnerships in primary health care: A scoping review. *BMC Health Services Research*, *21*(1), 1–18. doi:10.1186/s12913-020-05979-9 PMID:33397388

Ju, H., & Lin, P. (2020). China's Anti-Monopoly Law and the role of economics in its enforcement. *Russian Journal of Economics*, *6*(3), 219–238. doi:10.32609/j.ruje.6.56362

Jung, S. H., & Feng, T. (2020). Government subsidies for green technology development under uncertainty. *European Journal of Operational Research*, *286*(2), 726–739. doi:10.1016/j.ejor.2020.03.047

Kaciak, E., & Welsh, D. H. (2020). Women entrepreneurs and work–life interface: The impact of sustainable economies on success. *Journal of Business Research*, *112*, 281–290. doi:10.1016/j.jbusres.2019.11.073

Kaffashi, S., Radam, A., Shamsudin, M. N., Yacob, M. R., & Nordin, N. H. (2015). Ecological conservation, ecotourism, and sustainable management: The case of Penang National Park. *Forests*, *6*(7), 2345–2370. doi:10.3390/f6072345

Kamau, M., Chasek, P., & O'Connor, D. (2018). *Transforming multilateral diplomacy: The inside story of the Sustainable Development Goals*. Routledge. doi:10.4324/9780429491276

Kanie, N. (2016). Governance through goal-setting: A new governance challenge for navigating sustainability in the 21st century. In N. Kanie (Ed.), *The WSPC reference on natural resources and environmental policy in the era of global change* (pp. 61–76). World Scientific. doi:10.1142/9789813208162_0003

Karademir, Ö. Ü. N., & Bilinir, A. G. Ş. (2020). *Mazidaği (Mardin)'daki Fosfat Madeninin Sosyo-Ekonomik Etkileri*.

Karaman, M. (2021). Grafit Cevherleşmelerinin Sentinel-2 Uydu Görüntülerinden Belirlenmesinde En Uygun Bant Kombinasyonları. *Avrupa Bilim ve Teknoloji Dergisi*, (25), 749–757. doi:10.31590/ejosat.945779

Katharina, S., & Thaler, J. (2020). Partnering for good? An analysis of how to achieve sustainability-related outcomes in public–private partnerships. *Business Research*, *13*(2), 485–5. doi:10.1007/s40685-019-0097-3

Katircioğlu, S. T. (2010). International tourism, higher education and economic growth: The case of North Cyprus. *World Economy*, *33*(12), 1955–1972. doi:10.1111/j.1467-9701.2010.01304.x

Kaval, A. (2023). Pensions: In Italy persistent inequalities between women and men. *Le Monde*. https://www.lemonde.fr/economie/article/2023/01/18/retraites-en-italie-des-inegalites-persistantes-entre-les-femmes-et-les-hommes_6158374_3234.html

Kavishe, N., & Chileshe, N. (2019). Critical success factors in public-private partnerships (PPPs) on affordable housing schemes delivery in Tanzania: A qualitative study. *Journal of Facilities Management*, *17*(2), 188–207. doi:10.1108/JFM-05-2018-0033

Kawwass, J. F., Penzias, A. S., & Adashi, E. Y. (2021). Fertility—a human right worthy of mandated insurance coverage: The evolution, limitations, and future of access to care. *Fertility and Sterility*, *115*(1), 29–42. doi:10.1016/j.fertnstert.2020.09.155 PMID:33342534

Kelly, J., & Williams, P. W. (2007). Modelling tourism destination energy consumption and greenhouse gas emissions: Whistler, British Columbia, Canada. *Journal of Sustainable Tourism*, *15*(1), 67–90. doi:10.2167/jost609.0

Kenya U. N. (2024). *Sustainable Development Goal 4 Quality Education*. UN. https://kenya.un.org/en/sdgs/4/key-activities

Khadaroo, J., & Seetanah, B. (2007). Transport infrastructure and tourism development. *Annals of Tourism Research*, *34*(4), 1021–1032. doi:10.1016/j.annals.2007.05.010

Kickul, J., & Lyons, T. S. (2020). *Understanding social entrepreneurship: The relentless pursuit of mission in an ever-changing world*. Routledge. doi:10.4324/9780429270406

Kimbu, A. N., & Tichaawa, T. M. (2018). Sustainable development goals and socio-economic development through tourism in central Africa: Myth or reality? *Geo Journal of Tourism and Geosites*, *23*(3), 780–796. doi:10.30892/gtg.23314-328

Knox, J. H. (2018). *Report of the Special Rapporteur on the Issue of Human Rights Obligations Relating to the Enjoyment of a Safe, Clean, Healthy and Sustainable Environment on his mission to Uruguay*. Digital Library. https://digitallibrary.un.org/record/1475218?ln=en&v=pdf

Koncul, N. (2012). Wellness: A new mode of tourism. Ekonomska Istrazivanja (Vol. 25, Issue 2, pp. 525–534). doi:10.1080/1331677X.2012.11517521

Kong, X., Xu, J., & Zhang, Y. (2022). Industry competition and firm productivity: Evidence from the antitrust policy in China. *Finance Research Letters*, *47*, 103001. doi:10.1016/j.frl.2022.103001

Konuk, A., Gürsoy, Y. H., & Hakan, A. K. (2021). Doğal Grafit İhracatı Yoğunlaşmasının Ekonomik Büyüme Üzerindeki Etkisi. *Eskişehir Osmangazi Üniversitesi Mühendislik ve Mimarlık Fakültesi Dergisi*, *29*(3), 316–327. doi:10.31796/ogummf.964124

Korinek, J. (2013). *Mineral Resource Trade in Chile: Contribution to Development and Policy Implications*. https://doi.org/10.1787/5k4bw6twpf24-en

Kort, I., Verweij, S., & Klijn, E.-H. (2015). In search for effective public-private partnerships: An assessment of the impact of organizational form and managerial strategies in urban regeneration partnerships using fsQCA. *Environment and Planning. C, Government & Policy*, *34*(5), 777–794. doi:10.1177/0263774X15614674

Kreager, P. (2022). Smith or Malthus? A Sea-Change in the Concept of a Population. *Population and Development Review*, *48*(3), 645–688. doi:10.1111/padr.12488

Kruger, S., & Steyn, A. A. (2020). Enhancing technology transfer through entrepreneurial development: Practices from innovation spaces. *The Journal of Technology Transfer*, *45*(6), 1655–1689. doi:10.1007/s10961-019-09769-2

Kuldoshev, A. T. (2024). THE NECESSITY OF DEVELOPING A" GREEN ECONOMY". Best Journal of Innovation in Science. *Research for Development*, *3*(2), 611–615.

Kumar, S., Kumar, N., & Vivekadhish, S. (2016). Millennium Development Goals (MDGs) to Sustainable Development Goals (SDGs): Addressing unfinished agenda and strengthening sustainable development and partnership. *Indian Journal of Community Medicine*, *41*(1), 1–4. doi:10.4103/0970-0218.170955 PMID:26917865

Kumcu, S., & Özyörük, B. (2023). Sürdürülebilir yeşil bir kalkınma için salınan karbonun yakalanması, depolanması ve kullanımına yönelik bir araştırma. *Niğde Ömer Halisdemir Üniversitesi Mühendislik Bilimleri Dergisi*, *12*(2), 386–394.

Kundu, T., & Sheu, J.-B. (2019). Analyzing the effect of government subsidy on shippers' mode switching behavior in the Belt and Road strategic context. *Transportation Research Part E, Logistics and Transportation Review*, *129*, 175–202. doi:10.1016/j.tre.2019.08.007

Labeaga, J. M., & Labandeira, X. (2020). Economics of Environmental Taxes and Green Tax Reforms. *Sustainability (Basel)*, *12*(1), 350. doi:10.3390/su12010350

Lestari, S. D., Leon, F. M., Widyastuti, S., Brabo, N. A., & Putra, A. H. P. K. (2020). Antecedents and consequences of innovation and business strategy on performance and competitive advantage of SMEs. *The Journal of Asian Finance. Economics and Business*, *7*(6), 365–378.

Levy, S. E., & Hawkins, D. E. (2009). Peace through tourism: Commerce based principles and practices. *Journal of Business Ethics*, *89*(S4, SUPPL. 4), 569–585. doi:10.1007/s10551-010-0408-2

Lewicka, E., Guzik, K., & Galos, K. (2021). On the possibilities of critical raw materials production from the EU's primary sources. *Resources*, *10*(5), 50. doi:10.3390/resources10050050

Lianos, G., & Sloev, I. (2024). Investment and Innovation in Emerging Versus Advanced Market Economies: A Schumpeterian Approach. *Journal of the Knowledge Economy*, 1–24. doi:10.1007/s13132-023-01681-3

Lisha, L. (2021). The relationship between tourism development and sustainable development goals in Vietnam. *Caudemos de Economia*, *44*, 42–49. doi:10.32826/cude.v1i124.504

Litman, T. (2009). Evaluating Carbon Taxes as an Energy Conservation and Emission Reduction Strategy. *Transportation Research Record: Journal of the Transportation Research Board*, *2139*(1), 125–132. doi:10.3141/2139-15

Liu, H., Xu, Y., & Fan, X. (2020, June 29). *Development finance with Chinese characteristics: financing the Belt and Road Initiative*. RBPI. https://www.redalyc.org/journal/358/35863121008/html/#B6

Llados-Masllorens, J., & Ruiz-Dotras, E. (2021). Are women's entrepreneurial intentions and motivations influenced by financial skills? *International Journal of Gender and Entrepreneurship*, *14*(1), 69–94. doi:10.1108/IJGE-01-2021-0017

Lok, B. L., Cheng, M. Y., & Choong, C. K. (2021). The relationship between soft skills training and development, human resource outcome, and firm performance. *International Journal of Business and Society*, *22*(1), 382–402. doi:10.33736/ijbs.3184.2021

Love, I., Nikolaev, B., & Dhakal, C. (2024). The well-being of women entrepreneurs: The role of gender inequality and gender roles. *Small Business Economics*, *62*(1), 325–352. doi:10.1007/s11187-023-00769-z

Luís, I. P., & Spínola, H. (2010). The influence of a voluntary fee in the consumption of plastic bags on supermarkets from Madeira Island (Portugal). *Journal of Environmental Planning and Management*, *53*(7), 883–889. doi:10.1080/09640568.2010.490054

Lundqvist, B., & Gal, M. S. (Eds.). (2019). *Competition law for the digital economy*. Edward Elgar Publishing. doi:10.4337/9781788971836

M., H. & Margot, H. (2022). Reflecting on twenty years of international agreements concerning water governance: insights and key learning. *International Environmental Agreements: Politics, Law and Economics*, *22*(2), 317-332.

Mahapatra, S. (1986). *Modernization and ritual: Identity and Change in Santal society*. Oxford University Press.

Malik, S., & Kaur, S. (2021). Multi-dimensional public–private partnership readiness index: a sub-national analysis of India. Transforming Government: People. *Process and Policy*, *15*(4), 483–511.

Malterud, K., Siersma, V., & Guassora, A. D. (2021). Information power: Sample content and size in qualitative studies. In P. M. Camic (Ed.), *Qualitative research in psychology: Expanding perspectives in methodology and design* (pp. 67–81). American Psychological Association.

Ma, M., Wang, N., Mu, W., & Zhang, L. (2022). The Instrumentality of Public-Private Partnerships for Achieving Sustainable Development Goals. *Sustainability (Basel)*, *14*(21), 13756. doi:10.3390/su142113756

Mamun, M. (Ed.). (2021). *Subaltern, Revolt and Armed Resistance in Bangladesh (1763-1950)*. Kothaprokash.

Manberger, A. (2023). Critical Raw Material Supply Matters and the Potential of the Circular Economy to Contribute to Security. *Inter Economics*, *58*(2), 74–78. doi:10.2478/ie-2023-0016

Mancini, L., Eynard, U., Eisfeldt, F., Ciroth, A., Blengini, G., & Pennington, D. (2018). Social assessment of raw materials supply chains. *A life-cycle-based analysis*. Luxemburg.

Mancini, L., & Sala, S. (2018). Social impact assessment in the mining sector: Review and comparison of indicators frameworks. *Resources Policy*, *57*, 98–111. doi:10.1016/j.resourpol.2018.02.002

Mandic, A., Mrnjavac, Ž., & Kordic, L. (2018). Tourism infrastructure, recreational facilities and tourism development. *Tourism and Hospitality Management*, *24*(1), 41–62. doi:10.20867/thm.24.1.12

Marciano, A., Nicita, A., & Ramello, G. B. (2020). Big data and big techs: Understanding the value of information in platform capitalism. *European Journal of Law and Economics*, *50*(3), 345–358. doi:10.1007/s10657-020-09675-1

Marco Colino, S. (2022). The incursion of antitrust into China's platform economy. *Antitrust Bulletin*, *67*(2), 237–258. doi:10.1177/0003603X221084152

Marina., S. & Astina, I., K. (2020). Sustainable marine ecotourism management: A case of marine resource conservation based on local wisdom of Bojo Mola community in Wakatobi national park. *GeoJournal of Tourism and Geosites*, *32*(4), 1317–1323. https://doi.org/ doi:10.30892/gtg.3

Market, S. (2024). *The Uruguay Way: Achieving Energy Sovereignty in the Developing World*. Earth.org. https://earth.org/the-uruguay-way-achieving-energy-sovereignty-in-the-developing-world/

Martin, L. A., & Thornton, S. (2017). Can Road Charges Alleviate Congestion? SSRN *Electronic Journal*. doi:10.2139/ssrn.3055522

Martínez, S. (2020). Environmental Taxation in Chile: A Critical Analysis. *Latin American Legal Studies*, *6*, 119–158. doi:10.15691/0719-9112Vol6a7

Martinho, G., Balaia, N., & Pires, A. (2017). The Portuguese plastic carrier bag tax: The effects on consumers' behavior. *Waste Management (New York, N.Y.)*, *61*, 3–12. doi:10.1016/j.wasman.2017.01.023 PMID:28131637

McCann, P. (2019). *Perceptions of regional inequality and the geography of discontent: insights from the UK*. Regional Studies.

McKinley, J. (2007). San Francisco Board Votes to Ban Some Plastic Bags. *The New York Times*. https://www.nytimes.com/2007/03/28/us/28plastic.html

Meadows, D. H., Meadows, D. L., Randers, J., & Behrens, W. (1972). *Club of Rome. The limits to growth.*

Meadows, D. H., Meadows, D. L., Randers, J., & Behrens, W. W. (2018). The limits to growth. In *Green Planet Blues*. Routledge. doi:10.4324/9780429493744-3

Mebratu, D. (2017). Systems concept of sustainability and sustainable development. In *Sustainable development policy and administration* (pp. 85–112). Routledge. doi:10.4324/9781315087535-4

Medina-Muñoz, D. R., Medina-Muñoz, R. D., & Gutiérrez-Pérez, F. J. (2016). The impacts of tourism on poverty alleviation: An integrated research framework. *Journal of Sustainable Tourism*, *24*(2), 270–298. doi:10.1080/09669582.2015.1049611

Mehmetoglu, M. (2009). Predictors of sustainable consumption in a tourism context: A CHAID approach. *Advances in Hospitality and Leisure*, *5*, 3–23. doi:10.1108/S1745-3542(2009)0000005005

Meng, S., Siriwardana, M., & McNeill, J. (2013). The Environmental and Economic Impact of the Carbon Tax in Australia. *Environmental and Resource Economics*, *54*(3), 313–332. doi:10.1007/s10640-012-9600-4

Mentis, C., Maroulis, G., Latinopoulos, D., & Bithas, K. (2022). The effects of environmental information provision on plastic bag use and marine environment status in the context of the environmental levy in Greece. *Environment, Development and Sustainability*. doi:10.1007/s10668-022-02465-6 PMID:35729922

Meza, L. E., & Rodriguez, A. G. (2022). *Nature-Based Solution and the Bioeconomy*. ECLAC-Natural Resources and Development Series No. 210.

Mhlanga, D. (2023). The Role of FinTech and AI in Agriculture, Towards Eradicating Hunger and Ensuring Food Security. In *FinTech and Artificial Intelligence for Sustainable Development: The Role of Smart Technologies in Achieving Development Goals* (pp. 119–143). Springer Nature Switzerland. doi:10.1007/978-3-031-37776-1_6

Michal, C., & Zuzana, Š. (2021). Critical raw materials as a part of sustainable development. *Multidiszciplináris Tudományok*, *11*(5), 12–23. doi:10.35925/j.multi.2021.5.2

MIEM. (2022). *Green Hydrogen Roadmap in Uruguay*. GUB. https://www.gub.uy/ministerio-industria-energia-mineria/sites/ministerio-industria-energia-mineria/files/documentos/noticias/Green Hydrogen Roadmap in Uruguay.pdf

Milton, S. (2021). Higher education and sustainable development goal 16 in fragile and conflict-affected contexts. *Higher Education*, *81*(1), 89–108. doi:10.1007/s10734-020-00617-z

Mingyang, T., & Yeping, Y. (2024, January 31). China-Europe freight trains under BRI stabilize transport amid Red Sea tensions. *Global Times*. https://www.globaltimes.cn/page/202401/1306453.shtml#:~:text=China%2DEurope%20freight%20trains%20under%20the%20Belt%20and%20Road%20Initiative,cargo%20space%20on%20the%20trains

Ministerio de Energia. (2021). *Planning Together the Future of Energy in Chile*. https://energia.gob.cl/sites/default/files/documentos/pelp2023-2027_informe_preliminar_ingles.pdf

Ministry for Europe and Foreign Affairs. (2019). *2030 Agenda for sustainable development: Where is France?* Diplomatie. https://www.diplomatie.gouv.fr/fr/politique-etrangere-de-la-france/developpement/l-agenda-2030-du-developpement/article/l-agenda-2030-et-les-objectifs-de-developpement-durable-odd

Ministry of Education Republic of Kenya. (2017). *Education for Sustainable Development Policy for the Education Sector*. Ministry of Education Republic of Kenya. https://www.education.go.ke/sites/default/files/2022-05/Education-for-Sustainable-Development-Policy-for-the-Education-Sector.pdf

Mintrom, M. (2019). *Public Policy: Investing for a Better World*. Oxford University Press.

Mishenina, H., & Dvorak, J. (2022). Public–Private Partnership as a Form of Ensuring Sustainable Development of the Forest Management Sphere. *Administrative Sciences*, *12*(4), 156. doi:10.3390/admsci12040156

Mohd Noor, N. H., Mohamad Fuzi, A., & El Ashfahany, A. (2023). Institutional support and self-efficacy as catalysts for new venture performance: A study of iGen entrepreneurs. *Journal of Entrepreneurship and Public Policy*, *12*(3/4), 173–196. doi:10.1108/JEPP-02-2023-0015

Mohd Noor, N. H., Yaacob, M. A., & Omar, N. (2024). Do knowledge and personality traits influence women entrepreneurs' e-commerce venture? Testing on the multiple mediation model. *Journal of Entrepreneurship in Emerging Economies*, *16*(1), 231–256. doi:10.1108/JEEE-01-2023-0023

Mohsin, A. (2022). The Chittagong Hill Tracts, Bangladesh. In The Emergence of Bangladesh (pp. 251-258). Palgrave Macmillan

Mohsin, A. (2002). *The Politics of Nationalism: The Case of the Chittagong Hill Tracts Bangladesh* (2nd ed.). The University Press Limited.

Morales-Olmos, V., & Siry, J. P. (2009). Economic Impact Evaluation of Uruguay Forest Sector Development Policy. *Journal of Forestry*, *107*(2), 63–68. doi:10.1093/jof/107.2.63

Moresi, M., & Cimini, A. (2024). A Comprehensive Study from Cradle-to-Grave on the Environmental Profile of Malted Legumes. *Foods*, *13*(5), 655. doi:10.3390/foods13050655 PMID:38472768

Mulley, S. (2008). From *Poverty to Power: How Active Citizens and Effective States Can Change the World*. Oxfam International. https://oxfamilibrary.openrepository.com/bitstream/handle/10546/112422/fp2p-bp-global-governance-_1;jsessionid=28E506FF03D9E298EA44D2D56DA52435?sequence=1

Munnich, W. L. (2010). Enhancing Livability and Sustainability by Linking Congestion Pricing with Transit. *Environmental Science, Engineering, Economics*. https://www.semanticscholar.org/paper/Enhancing-Livability-and-Sustainability-by-Linking-Munnich-Lee/5a93cf156f932fda9d93e9f1ea8899742c783838

Mycoo, M. (2014). Sustainable tourism, climate change and sea level rise adaptation policies in Barbados. *Natural Resources Forum*, *38*(1), 47–57. doi:10.1111/1477-8947.12033

Nabi, G., Walmsley, A., & Akhtar, I. (2021). Mentoring functions and entrepreneur development in the early years of university. *Studies in Higher Education*, *46*(6), 1159–1174. doi:10.1080/03075079.2019.1665009

Narbaev, T. (2022). A meta-analysis of the public-private partnership literature reviews: Exploring the identity of the field. *International Journal of Strategic Property Management*, *26*(4), 318–331. doi:10.3846/ijspm.2022.17860

Ncube, T., Murray, U., & Dennehy, D. (2023). Digitalising Social Protection Systems for Achieving the Sustainable Development Goals: Insights from Zimbabwe. *Communications of the Association for Information Systems*, *53*, 53. doi:10.17705/1CAIS.05306

Neumann, T. (2021). The impact of entrepreneurship on economic, social, and environmental welfare and its determinants: A systematic review. *Management Review Quarterly*, *71*(3), 553–584. doi:10.1007/s11301-020-00193-7

Ng, W. (2019). Changing Global Dynamics and International Competition Law: Considering China's Potential Impact. *European Journal of International Law*, *30*(4), 1409–1430. doi:10.1093/ejil/chz066

Ng, W. (2020). State Interest and the state-centered Approach to Competition Law in China. *Antitrust Bulletin*, *65*(2), 297–311. doi:10.1177/0003603X20912889

Nielsen, T. D., Holmberg, K., & Stripple, J. (2019). Need a bag? A review of public policies on plastic carrier bags – Where, how and to what effect? *Waste Management (New York, N.Y.)*, *87*, 428–440. doi:10.1016/j.wasman.2019.02.025 PMID:31109543

Njoroge, J. M. (2015). Climate change and tourism adaptation: Literature Review. *Tourism and hospitality management*, *21*(1), 95-108.

Noor, N. H. M., Kamarudin, S. M., & Shamsudin, U. N. (2023). The influence of personality traits, university green entrepreneurial support, and environmental values on green entrepreneurial intention. [IJAFB]. *International Journal of Accounting, Finance, and Business*, *8*(48), 59–71.

Noor, S., & Isa, F. M. (2020). Contributing factors of women entrepreneurs' business growth and failure in Pakistan. *International Journal of Business and Globalisation*, *25*(4), 503–518. doi:10.1504/IJBG.2020.109115

Nordhaus, W. D. (1993). Rolling the 'DICE': An optimal transition path for controlling greenhouse gases. *Resource and Energy Economics*, *15*(1), 27–50. doi:10.1016/0928-7655(93)90017-O

Norman, E. S., & Carr, D. (2009). Rio Summit. In R. Kitchen & N. Thrift (Eds.), *International encyclopedia of human geography* (pp. 406–411). Elsevier Science. doi:10.1016/B978-008044910-4.00119-X

Obrien, P. W. (2011). Business, Management and Poverty Reduction: A Role for Slum Tourism? *Journal of Business Diversity*, *11*(1), 33–46.

Odén, B. (2002). Implications for International Governance and Development Cooperation. In B. Hettne & B. Odén (Eds.), *Global Governance in the 21st Century: Alternative Perspectives on World Order* (pp. 184–202). Almkvist & Wiksell International.

OECD (Organisation for Economic Co-operation and Development). (2022). *Public-Private Partnerships: A Toolkit for Decision-makers*. OECD.

OECD. (2007). *Subsidy Reform and Sustainable Development: Political Economy Aspects*. OECD. https://www.oecd-ilibrary.org/environment/subsidy-reform-and-sustainable-development_9789264019379-en

OECD. (2015). *Chile: Policy Priorities for Stronger and More Equitable Growth*. OECD. https://www.oecd.org/chile/chile-policy-priorities-for-stronger-and-more-equitable-growth.pdf

OECD. (2016). *Regional inequalities are worsening in many countries*. OECD. https://www.oecd.org/fr/social/les-inegalites-regionales-saggravent-dans-de-nombreux-pays.htm

OECD. (2024). *OECD and the Sustainable Development Goals*. OECD. https://www.oecd.org/sdgs/

Oosterhuis, F., Papyrakis, E., & Boteler, B. (2014). Economic instruments and marine litter control. *Ocean and Coastal Management*, *102*, 47–54. doi:10.1016/j.ocecoaman.2014.08.005

Opricovic, S., & Tzeng, G. H. (2004). Compromise solution by MCDM methods: A comparative analysis of VIKOR and TOPSIS. *European Journal of Operational Research*, *156*(2), 445–455. doi:10.1016/S0377-2217(03)00020-1

Österblom, H., Jouffray, J. B., Folke, C., & Rockström, J. (2017). Emergence of a global science–business initiative for ocean stewardship. *Proceedings of the National Academy of Sciences of the United States of America*, *114*(34), 9038–9043. doi:10.1073/pnas.1704453114 PMID:28784792

Othman, I. W., Mokhtar, S., Maidin, I., & Moharam, M. M. A. H. (2021). The relevance of the National Entrepreneurship Policy (NEP) 2030 In meeting the needs and strengthening the country's entrepreneurial ecosystem: A snapshot. *The International Journal of Accounting*, *6*(37).

Owen, B. M., Sun, S., & Zheng, W. (2008). China's competition policy reforms: The anti-monopoly law and beyond. *Antitrust Law Journal*, *75*(1), 231–265.

Page, S., & Connell, J. (2014). Transport and tourism. *The Wiley Blackwell Companion to Tourism*, 155-167. Wiley.

Parente, S. A. (2023). The New Horizons of Tax Law between Energy Policies and Ecological Transition: The Case of Energy Communities. *Teka Komisji Prawniczej PAN Oddział w Lublinie*, *16*(2), 267–278. doi:10.32084/tkp.8029

Parris, T. M., & Kates, R. W. (2003). Characterizing and measuring sustainable development. *Annual Review of Environment and Resources*, *28*(1), 559–586. doi:10.1146/annurev.energy.28.050302.105551

Partnership, N. D. C. (2019). *Chile's Carbon Tax: An Ambitious Step towards Environmentally Friendly Policies and Significant Greenhouse Gas Emission Reductions*. NDC. https://ndcpartnership.org/knowledge-portal/good-practice-database/chiles-carbon-tax-ambitious-step-towards-environmentally-friendly-policies-and

Paul, B. D. (2008). A history of the concept of sustainable development: Literature review. The Annals of the University of Oradea. *Economic Sciences Series*, *17*(2), 576–580.

Pawłowski, A., & Cao, Y. (2014). The role of CO_2 in the Earth's ecosystem and the possibility of controlling flows between subsystems. *Gospodarka Surowcami Mineralnymi*, *30*(4), 5–19. doi:10.2478/gospo-2014-0037

Pejic, I. (2019). *Blockchain babel: The crypto craze and the challenge to business*. Kogan Page Publishers.

Peña-Sánchez, A. R., Ruiz-Chico, J., Jiménez-García, M., & López-Sánchez, J. A. (2020). Tourism and the SDGs: An analysis of economic growth, decent employment, and gender equality in the European Union (2009-2018). *Sustainability (Basel)*, *12*(13), 5480. doi:10.3390/su12135480

Petry, J. (2021). Same same, but different: Varieties of capital markets, Chinese state capitalism and the global financial order. *Competition & Change*, *25*(5), 605–630. doi:10.1177/1024529420964723

Pfordten, D. (2023). Malaysia: The country's population is growing at a faster rate, here's why. *The Star*. https://www.thestar.com.my/news/nation/2023/09/07/mymalaysia-the-country039s-population-is-growing-at-a-faster-rate-here039s-why

Phang, S.-Y., & Toh, R. S. (2004). Road Congestion Pricing in Singapore: 1975 to 2003. *Transportation*, *43*(2), 16–25. https://www.jstor.org/stable/20713563

Pigou, A. C. (1932). *The Economics of Welfare*. Macmillan.

Piketty, T. (2020). Global inequality: Where do we stand? *Le Monde*. https://www.lemonde.fr/blog/piketty/2020/11/17/inegalites-mondiales-ou-en-sommes-nous/

Piketty, T. (2014). *Capital in the Twenty-First Century*. Harvard University Press. doi:10.4159/9780674369542

Ping, H., & Zuokui, L. (2017). *How the 16+1 Cooperation promotes the Belt and Road Initiative*. SHA. https://sha.static.vipsite.cn/media/thinktank/attachments/0127811c10d2e4b9c9090b6240f73362.pdf

Compilation of References

Pino, P., Iglesias, V., Garreaud, R., Cortés, S., Canals, M., Folch, W., Burgos, S., Levy, K. P., Naeher, L., & Steenland, K. (2015). Chile Confronts its Environmental Health Future After 25 Years of Accelerated Growth. *Annals of Global Health*, *81*(3), 354. doi:10.1016/j.aogh.2015.06.008 PMID:26615070

Polat, E. G., Yücesan, M., & Gül, M. (2023). A comparative framework for criticality assessment of strategic raw materials in Turkey. *Resources Policy*, *82*, 103511. doi:10.1016/j.resourpol.2023.103511

Pommeret, A., Ricci, F., & Schubert, K. (2022). Critical raw materials for the energy transition. *European Economic Review*, *141*, 103991. doi:10.1016/j.euroecorev.2021.103991

Pouresmaieli, M., Ataei, M., & Qarahasanlou, A. N. (2023). A scientometrics view on sustainable development in surface mining: Everything from the beginning. *Resources Policy*, *82*, 103410. doi:10.1016/j.resourpol.2023.103410

Pozo-Gonzalo, C. (2023). UN Sustainable Development Goals 7 and 13. How sustainable are the metals in our journey to clean energy storage? *RSC Sustainability*, *1*(4), 662–664. doi:10.1039/D3SU90020G

Pratt, S., & Liu, A. (2016). Does Tourism Really Lead to Peace? A Global View. *International Journal of Tourism Research*, *18*(1), 82–90. doi:10.1002/jtr.2035

Prip, C. (2022). Arctic Ocean governance in light of an of an international legally binding instrument on the conservation and sustainable use of marine biodiversity of areas beyond national jurisdiction. *Marine Policy*, *142*, 103768. doi:10.1016/j.marpol.2019.103768

Provan, K. G., & Milward, H. B. (1995). A Preliminary Theory of Interorganizational Network Effectiveness: A Comparative Study of Four Community Mental Health Systems. *Administrative Science Quarterly*, *40*(1), 1–33. doi:10.2307/2393698

Pulea, M. (1993). *An Overview of Constitutional and Legal Provisions Relevant to Customary Marine Tenure and Management Systems in the South Pacific*. USP.

Qamar, M. Z., Ali, W., Qamar, M. O., & Noor, M. (2021). Green technology and its implications worldwide. *The Inquisitive Meridian*, *3*, 1–11.

Qaqaya, H. (2020). Sustainability of ASEAN integration, competition policy, and the challenges of COVID-19. *Journal of Antitrust Enforcement*, *8*(2), 305–308. doi:10.1093/jaenfo/jnaa019

Qiu, R., Xu, J., Xie, H., Zeng, Z., & Lv, C. (2020). Carbon tax incentive policy towards air passenger transport carbon emissions reduction. *Transportation Research Part D, Transport and Environment*, *85*, 102441. doi:10.1016/j.trd.2020.102441

Qiu, S., Ruth, M., & Ghosh, S. (2015). Evacuated tube collectors: A notable driver behind the solar water heater industry in China. *Renewable & Sustainable Energy Reviews*, *47*, 580–588. doi:10.1016/j.rser.2015.03.067

Rahman, M. M., Dana, L. P., Moral, I. H., Anjum, N., & Rahaman, M. S. (2023). Challenges of rural women entrepreneurs in Bangladesh to survive their family entrepreneurship: A narrative inquiry through storytelling. *Journal of Family Business Management*, *13*(3), 645–664. doi:10.1108/JFBM-04-2022-0054

Ramesh, B. N. (2023). *Cross Border Mergers and Acquisitions: A Comparative Study Between India and the USA*. Taylor & Francis.

Ramey V. A. (2021, April). The Macroeconomic Consequences of Infrastructure Investment. CEPR Discussion Paper No. DP15998. SSRN. https://ssrn.com/abstract=3846053

Ranwala, R. S., & Surangi, H. A. K. N. S. (2023). A critical analysis of the experience of mumpreneurs: A study based on tourism industry in Sri Lanka. *Middle East Journal of Management*, *10*(2), 113–132. doi:10.1504/MEJM.2023.129446

Renwick, N., Gu, J., & Gong, S. (2018, September). *The impact of BRI investment in infrastructure on achieving the Sustainable Development Goals*. Assets Publishing. https://assets.publishing.service.gov.uk/media/5be9560ced915d6a166edb35/K4D_Helpdesk_BRI_REPORT_2018_final.pdf

Reuveny, R. (2007). Climate change-induced migration and violent conflict. *Political Geography*, 26(6), 656–673. doi:10.1016/j.polgeo.2007.05.001

Rietveld, E., Bastein, T., van Leeuwen, T., Wieclawska, S., Bonenkamp, N., Peck, D., & Poitiers, N. (2022). *Strengthening the security of supply of products containing Critical Raw Materials for the green transition and decarbonisation*. European Parliament.

Rist, G. (2014). *The history of development: from Western origins to global faith*. Bloomsbury Publishing.

Ritch, E., Brennan, C., & MacLeod, C. (2009). Plastic bag politics: Modifying consumer behaviour for sustainable development. *International Journal of Consumer Studies*, 33(2), 168–174. doi:10.1111/j.1470-6431.2009.00749.x

Ritchie, H., Rosado, P., & Roser, M. (2023). *CO2 and Greenhouse Gas Emissions*. https://ourworldindata.org/co2-and-greenhouse-gas-emissions

Ritchie, H., & Roser, M. (2024). *How many people does synthetic fertilizer feed?* Our World in Data.

Rizzo, A., Goel, S., Luisa Grilli, M., Iglesias, R., Jaworska, L., Lapkovskis, V., Novak, P., Postolnyi, B. O., & Valerini, D. (2020). The critical raw materials in cutting tools for machining applications: A review. *Materials (Basel)*, 13(6), 1377. doi:10.3390/ma13061377 PMID:32197537

Robertson, V. H. (2022). Antitrust, big tech, and democracy: A research agenda. *Antitrust Bulletin*, 67(2), 259–279. doi:10.1177/0003603X221082749

Robinson, R. N., Martins, A., Solnet, D., & Baum, T. (2019). Sustaining precarity: Critically examining tourism and employment. *Journal of Sustainable Tourism*, 27(7), 1008–1025. doi:10.1080/09669582.2018.1538230

Rockström, J., Gupta, J., Qin, D., Lade, S. J., Abrams, J. F., Andersen, L. S., Armstrong McKay, D. I., Bai, X., Bala, G., Bunn, S. E., Ciobanu, D., DeClerck, F., Ebi, K., Gifford, L., Gordon, C., Hasan, S., Kanie, N., Lenton, T. M., Loriani, S., & Zhang, X. (2023). Safe and just Earth system boundaries. *Nature*, 619(7968), 102–111. doi:10.1038/s41586-023-06083-8 PMID:37258676

Rockström, J., Steffen, W., Noone, K., Persson, Å., Chapin, F. S. III, Lambin, E. F., Lenton, T. M., Scheffer, M., Folke, C., Schellnhuber, H. J., Nykvist, B., de Wit, C. A., Hughes, T., van der Leeuw, S., Rodhe, H., Sörlin, S., Snyder, P. K., Costanza, R., Svedin, U., & Foley, J. A. (2009). A safe operating space for humanity. *Nature*, 461(7263), 472–475. doi:10.1038/461472a PMID:19779433

Rockström, J., Steffen, W., Noone, K., Persson, Å., Chapin, F. S. III, Lambin, E., Lenton, T. M., Scheffer, M., Folke, C., Schellnhuber, H. J., Nykvist, B., de Wit, C. A., Hughes, T., van der Leeuw, S., Rodhe, H., Sörlin, S., Snyder, P. K., Costanza, R., Svedin, U., & Foley, J. (2009). Planetary boundaries: Exploring the safe operating space for humanity. *Ecology and Society*, 14(2), art32. doi:10.5751/ES-03180-140232

Rodrigues, M., Daniel, A. D., & Franco, M. (2023). What is important to know about mumpreneurship? A bibliometric analysis. *The International Journal of Organizational Analysis*, 31(7), 3413–3435. doi:10.1108/IJOA-05-2022-3293

Röglinger, M., Plattfaut, R., Borghoff, V., Kerpedzhiev, G., Becker, J., Beverungen, D., vom Brocke, J., Van Looy, A., del-Río-Ortega, A., Rinderle-Ma, S., Rosemann, M., Santoro, F. M., & Trkman, P. (2022). Exogenous shocks and business process management: A scholars' perspective on challenges and opportunities. *Business & Information Systems Engineering*, 64(5), 669–687. doi:10.1007/s12599-021-00740-w

Compilation of References

Rosell, J., & Saz-Carranza, A. (2020). Determinants of public–private partnership policies. *Public Management Review*, *22*(8), 1171–1190. doi:10.1080/14719037.2019.1619816

Rothstein, B. (2011). *The quality of government: Corruption, social trust, and inequality in international perspective*. University of Chicago. doi:10.7208/chicago/9780226729589.001.0001

Roy, P. K. (2024). *Customary Law and Sustainable Community Development: A Study of the Santals of Bangladesh*, [PhD Thesis, Universiti Malaya].

Roy, P. K., Abd Wahab, H., & Hamidi, M. (2023). A Philosophical Discussion of Sustainable Development: A Case From the Bangladeshi Santal Community. Handbook of Research on Implications of Sustainable Development in Higher Education, (pp. 97-114). IGI Global. doi:10.4018/978-1-6684-6172-3.ch005

Roy, P., Chowdhury, J. S., Abd Wahab, H., & Saad, R. B. M. (2022). Ethnic Tension of the Bangladeshi Santal: A CDA of the Constitutional Provision. In Handbook of Research on Ethnic, Racial, and Religious Conflicts and Their Impact on State and Social Security (pp. 208-226). IGI Global. doi:10.4018/978-1-7998-8911-3.ch013

Roy, R. D., & Chakma, P. (2010). The Chittagong Hill Tracts Accord & Provisions on Lands, Territories, Resources and Customary Law. *Hope and Despair: Indigenous Jumma Peoples Speak on the Chittagong Hill Tracts Peace Accord*. Tetebba. http://tebtebba. org/index. php/all-resources/category/8-books

Sabina, J. M., & Nicolae, J. C. (2013). Gender Trends in Tourism Destination. *Procedia: Social and Behavioral Sciences*, *92*, 437–444. doi:10.1016/j.sbspro.2013.08.698

Sachs, J. D. (2012). From millennium development goals to sustainable development goals. *Lancet*, *379*(9832), 2206–2211. doi:10.1016/S0140-6736(12)60685-0 PMID:22682467

SachsJ. D.LafortuneG.FullerG.DrummE. (2023). Implementing the SDG Stimulus. Sustainable Development Report 2023. Paris: SDSN, Dublin: Dublin University Press, 2023. doi:10.25546/102924

Sachs, J. D., Schmidt-Traub, G., Mazzucato, M., Messner, D., Nakicenovic, N., & Rockström, J. (2019). Six transformations to achieve the sustainable development goals. *Nature Sustainability*, *2*(9), 805–814. doi:10.1038/s41893-019-0352-9

Sajjad, M., Kaleem, N., Chani, M. I., & Ahmed, M. (2020). Worldwide role of women entrepreneurs in economic development. *Asia Pacific Journal of Innovation and Entrepreneurship*, *14*(2), 151–160. doi:10.1108/APJIE-06-2019-0041

Salmony, F. U., & Kanbach, D. K. (2022). Personality trait differences across types of entrepreneurs: A systematic literature review. *Review of Managerial Science*, *16*(3), 713–749. doi:10.1007/s11846-021-00466-9

Salvi, A., Arosio, V., Compagnoni, L. M., Cubiña, I., Scaccabarozzi, G., & Dotelli, G. (2023). Considering the environmental impact of circular strategies: A dynamic combination of material efficiency and LCA. *Journal of Cleaner Production*, *387*, 135850. doi:10.1016/j.jclepro.2023.135850

Sánchez-Lozano, J. M., Teruel-Solano, J., Soto-Elvira, P. L., & García-Cascales, M. S. (2013). Geographical Information Systems (GIS) and Multi-Criteria Decision Making (MCDM) methods for the evaluation of solar farms locations: Case study in south-eastern Spain. *Renewable & Sustainable Energy Reviews*, *24*, 544–556. doi:10.1016/j.rser.2013.03.019

Sandmo, A. (2004). Environmental Taxation and Revenue for Development. In A. B. Atkinson (Ed.), *New Sources of Development Finance* (pp. 33–57). Oxford University Press Oxford. doi:10.1093/0199278555.003.0003

Santa-Maria, T., Vermeulen, W. J., & Baumgartner, R. J. (2022). How do incumbent firms innovate their business models for the circular economy? Identifying micro-foundations of dynamic capabilities. *Business Strategy and the Environment*, *31*(4), 1308–1333. doi:10.1002/bse.2956

Sarker, M. A. R., Khan, N. A., & Musarrat, K. M. (2016). Livelihood and vulnerability of the Santals community in Bangladesh. *The Malaysian Journal of Social Administration*, *12*(1), 38–55. doi:10.22452/mjsa.vol12no1.2

Sarma, V. V. S. S., Krishna, M. S., Paul, Y. S., & Murty, V. S. N. (2015). Observed changes in ocean acidity and carbon dioxide exchange in the coastal Bay of Bengal–a link to air pollution. Tellus B. *Tellus. Series B, Chemical and Physical Meteorology*, *67*(1), 24638. doi:10.3402/tellusb.v67.24638

Saussine, A. P., & Murphy, J. B. (Eds.). (2007). *The nature of Customary Law*. Cambridge University Press. doi:10.1017/CBO9780511493744

Scheiner, S. M. (Ed.). (2024). *Encyclopedia of Biodiversity*. Elsevier, Academic Press.

Scheyvens, R. (2018). Linking tourism to the sustainable development goals: A geographical perspective. *Tourism Geographies*, *20*(2), 341–342. doi:10.1080/14616688.2018.1434818

Seetanah, B., Juwaheer, T. D., Lamport, M. J., Rojid, S., Sannassee, R. V., & Subadar, A. U. (2011). Does infrastructure matter in tourism development? *University of Mauritius research journal*, *17*, 89-108.

Selin, S. (1999). Developing a Typology of Sustainable Tourism Partnerships. *Journal of Sustainable Tourism*, *7*(3&4), 260–273. doi:10.1080/09669589908667339

Sen, A. (2009). *The Idea of Justice*. Allan lane Penguin Books.

Sen, A. (2017). Elements of a theory of human rights. In *Justice and the capabilities approach* (pp. 221–262). Routledge. doi:10.4324/9781315251240-6

Seo, Y., & Kudo, F. (2022). Charging plastic bags: Perceptions from Japan. *PLOS Sustainability and Transformation*, *1*(5), e0000011. doi:10.1371/journal.pstr.0000011

Setyaningsih, W., Nuryanti, W., Prayitno, B., & Sarwadi, A. (2016). Urban Heritage Towards Creative-based Tourism in the Urban Settlement of Kauman - Surakarta. *Procedia: Social and Behavioral Sciences*, *227*, 642–649. doi:10.1016/j.sbspro.2016.06.127

Shaikh, N. U. R. (2020). *Tool to assess raw material social supply risks* [Master's thesis, University of Waterloo].

Shannon, N. G. (2022). What Does Sustainable Living Look Like? Maybe Like Uruguay. *New York Times*. https://www.nytimes.com/2022/11/20/podcasts/the-daily/uruguay-sustainable-living.html

Sharif, A., Saqib, N., Dong, K., & Khan, S. A. R. (2022). Nexus between green technology innovation, green financing, and CO2 emissions in the G7 countries: The moderating role of social globalisation. *Sustainable Development (Bradford)*, *30*(6), 1934–1946. doi:10.1002/sd.2360

Sharpley, R. (2021). On the need for sustainable tourism consumption. *Tourist Studies*, *21*(1), 96–107. doi:10.1177/1468797620986087

Shawon, I. H., Haider, M. Z., & Oni, F. A. (2023). Effectiveness of banning plastic bag in Bangladesh for environmental protection. *Khulna University Studies*, 112–118. doi:10.53808/KUS.SI.2023.ICES.A40-ss

Shin, Y. J., Midgley, G. F., Archer, E. R., Arneth, A., Barnes, D. K., Chan, L., Hashimoto, S., Hoegh-Guldberg, O., Insarov, G., Leadley, P., Levin, L. A., Ngo, H. T., Pandit, R., Pires, A. P. F., Pörtner, H.-O., Rogers, A. D., Scholes, R. J., Settele, J., & Smith, P. (2022). Actions to halt biodiversity loss generally benefit the climate. *Global Change Biology*, *28*(9), 2846–2874. doi:10.1111/gcb.16109 PMID:35098619

Simeonova, E., Currie, J., Nilsson, P., & Walker, R. (2021). Congestion Pricing, Air Pollution, and Children's Health. *The Journal of Human Resources*, *56*(4), 971–996. doi:10.3368/jhr.56.4.0218-9363R2

Compilation of References

Smotrytska, M. (2020, October 1). *Belt and Road in Central and East Europe: Roads of opportunities.* Modern Diplomacy. https://moderndiplomacy.eu/2020/10/01/belt-and-road-in-central-and-east-europe-roads-of-opportunities/

Sneddon, C., Howarth, R. B., & Norgaard, R. B. (2006). Sustainable development in a post-Brundtland world. *Ecological Economics*, *57*(2), 253–268. doi:10.1016/j.ecolecon.2005.04.013

Solomon, B. D. (2023). Millennium Ecosystem Assessment. In Dictionary of Ecological Economics (pp. 352-353). Edward Elgar Publishing. doi:10.4337/9781788974912.M.48

Soomro, N. E., Khan, A., & Arafa, A. (2021). Anti-monopoly law of China: A case study of coca cola's proposed merger with huiyuan. *International Journal of Business and Economics Research*, *10*(1), 34–39. doi:10.11648/j.ijber.20211001.15

Stavins, R. N. (2003). Experience with Market-Based Environmental Policy Instruments. In K.-G. Mäler & J. R. Vincent (Eds.), *Handbook of Environmental Economics* (Vol. 1, pp. 355–435). North-Holland. doi:10.1016/S1574-0099(03)01014-3

Steenge, A. E. (1997). On background principles for environmental policy: "polluter pays", "user pays" or "victim pays"? In *Public priority setting: Rules and costs* (pp. 121–137). Springer Netherlands. doi:10.1007/978-94-009-1487-2_7

Steenwegen, C. (2000). Can Ecological Taxes Play a Role in Diminishing the Health Impacts of Waste Management? In P. Nicolopoulou-Stamati, L. Hens, & C. V. Howard (Eds.), *Health Impacts of Waste Management Policies* (pp. 199–213). Springer. doi:10.1007/978-94-015-9550-6_13

Steijn, B., Klijn, E.-H., & Edelenbos, J. (2011). Public Private Partnerships: Added Value by Organizational from OR Management? *Public Administration*, *89*(4), 1235–1252. doi:10.1111/j.1467-9299.2010.01877.x

Steiner, A. (2018). The Extraordinary Opportunity of the 2030 Agenda for Sustainable Development. *European Journal of Development Research*, *30*(2), 163–165. doi:10.1057/s41287-018-0131-x

Strasser, S., Stauber, C., Shrivastava, R., Riley, P., & O'Quin, K. (2021). Collective insights of public-private partnership impacts and sustainability: A qualitative analysis. *PLoS One*, *7*(16), e0254495. doi:10.1371/journal.pone.0254495 PMID:34283847

Sumner, J., Bird, L., & Dobos, H. (2011). Carbon taxes: A review of experience and policy design considerations. *Climate Policy*, *11*(2), 922–943. doi:10.3763/cpol.2010.0093

Tafuro, A., Dammacco, G., & Costa, A. (2023). A Conceptual Study on the Role of Blockchain in Sustainable Development of Public–Private Partnership. *Administrative Sciences*, *13*(8), 175. doi:10.3390/admsci13080175

Takigawa, T. (2022). What Should We Do about E-Commerce Platform Giants?—The Antitrust and Regulatory Approaches in the US, EU, China, and Japan. The Antitrust and Regulatory Approaches in the US, EU, China, and Japan.

Tan, J. D., & Yew, J. L. K. (2023). Women entrepreneurship: Mumpreneurs cruising the COVID-19 pandemic in Indonesia. *Business and Society Review*, *128*(1), 133–168. doi:10.1111/basr.12302

Tercero, L. A., (2019). *Report on the future use of critical raw materials.* SCRREEN project, Deliverable D, 2.

The World Bank. (2018). *Procuring Infrastructure Public-Private Partnerships: A Guide for Public Authorities.* The World Bank. https://ppp.worldbank.org/public-private-partnership/sites/ppp.worldbank.org/files/documents/Procuring_Infrastructure_PPPs_2018_EN.pdf

Theodosopoulos, V. (2020). *The Geopolitics of Supply: towards a new EU approach to the security of supply of critical raw materials?* Institute for European Studies Policy Brief.

Thomas, G. O., Sautkina, E., Poortinga, W., Wolstenholme, E., & Whitmarsh, L. (2019). The English Plastic Bag Charge Changed Behavior and Increased Support for Other Charges to Reduce Plastic Waste. *Frontiers in Psychology*, *10*, 266. doi:10.3389/fpsyg.2019.00266 PMID:30863332

Thuraiswamy, R., & Rogan, J. M. (2018). Public-private partnerships for delivering social infrastructure in developing countries. *International Journal of Public Sector Management*, *31*(7), 867–889.

Timilsina, G. R. (2009). Carbon tax under the Clean Development Mechanism: A unique approach for reducing greenhouse gas emissions in developing countries. *Climate Policy*, *9*(2), 139–154. doi:10.3763/cpol.2008.0546

Tisdell, C. (2003). Economic Aspects of Ecotourism: Wildlife-based Tourism and its Contribution to Nature. *Sri Lankan journal of agricultural economics*, *5*(1), 83-95. http://ageconsearch.umn.edu

Tiwari, A., & Pandey, C. M. (2020). Public–private partnerships: A way forward for sustainable infrastructure development in India. *International Journal of Sustainable Development and Planning*, *15*(7), 835–846.

Tobin, B. (2014). *Indigenous peoples, customary law and human rights-why living law matters*. Routledge. doi:10.4324/9781315778792

Torres, R. (2003). Linkages between tourism and agriculture in Mexico. *Annals of Tourism Research*, *30*(3), 546–566. doi:10.1016/S0160-7383(02)00103-2

Torrubia, J., Valero, A., Valero, A., & Lejuez, A. (2023). Challenges and Opportunities for the Recovery of Critical Raw Materials from Electronic Waste: The Spanish Perspective. *Sustainability (Basel)*, *15*(2), 1393. doi:10.3390/su15021393

Trave, C., Brunnschweiler, J., Sheaves, M., Diedrich, A., & Barnett, A. (2017). *Are we killing them with kindness? Evaluation of sustainable marine wildlife tourism. Biological Conservation* (Vol. 209). Elsevier Ltd., doi:10.1016/j.biocon.2017.02.020

Triantafyllos, D., Illera, C., Djukic, T., & Casas, J. (2019). Dynamic congestion toll pricing strategies to evaluate the potential of route-demand diversion on toll facilities. *Transportation Research Procedia*, *41*, 731–740. doi:10.1016/j.trpro.2019.09.121

Trump, B. D., Cummings, C. L., Kuzma, J., & Linkov, I. (Eds.). (2019). *Synthetic biology 2020: Frontiers in risk analysis and governance*. Springer Nature.

Trupp, A., & Dolezal, C. (2020). Tourism and the Sustainable Development Goals in Southeast Asia. ASEAS - Austrian. *Journal of Southeast Asian Studies*, *13*(1), 1–16. doi:10.14764/10.ASEAS-0026

Ubfal, D., Arraiz, I., Beuermann, D. W., Frese, M., Maffioli, A., & Verch, D. (2022). The impact of soft-skills training for entrepreneurs in Jamaica. *World Development*, *152*, 105787. doi:10.1016/j.worlddev.2021.105787

Uddin, S. A., & Zaman, S. (2022). Assessing value for money in public–private partnership projects: A conceptual framework. *International Journal of Construction Project Management*, *17*(2), 242–257.

Ujaczki, É., Feigl, V., Molnár, M., Cusack, P., Curtin, T., Courtney, R., O'Donoghue, L., Davris, P., Hugi, C., Evangelou, M. W. H., Balomenos, E., & Lenz, M. (2018). Re-using bauxite residues: Benefits beyond (critical raw) material recovery. *Journal of Chemical Technology and Biotechnology*, *93*(9), 2498–2510. doi:10.1002/jctb.5687 PMID:30158737

UN Department of Economic and Social Affairs (UN DESA). (2023). *The Sustainable Development Goals Report 2023*. UNDDESA. https://unstats.un.org/sdgs/report/2023/.

Compilation of References

UN Office for Partnerships. (2021). *Public-Private Partnerships and the 2030 Agenda for Sustainable Development: Fit for Purpose?* UN. https://www.un.org/en/desa/public-private-partnerships-and-2030-agenda-sustainable-development-fit-purpose

UN System Task Team. (2012). *Realizing the Future We Want for All. Report to the Secretary-General*. UN.

UN. (1992). Earth Summit: Agenda 21. Rio de Janerio, Brazil: United Nations (UN).

UN. (1992a). *United Nations Conference on Environment and Development*. UN. https://www.un.org/en/conferences/environment/rio1992

UN. (1992b). *United Nations Conference on Environment & Development*. UN. https://sdgs.un.org/sites/default/files/publications/Agenda21.pdf

UN. (1995). *Copenhagen Declaration on Social Development*. World Summit for Social Development, Copenhagen.

UN. (2002). *Report of the world summit on sustainable development*. Johannesburg, South Africa, UN.

UN. (2012). *The Future We Want: Outcome document of the United Nations Conference on Sustainable Development, RIO+20*. UN. https://sustainabledevelopment.un.org/content/documents/733FutureWeWant.pdf

UN. (2015). *We can end poverty: Millennium Development Goals and beyond 2015*. UN. https://www.un.org/millenniumgoals/bkgd.shtml

UN. (2019). *The sustainable development agenda*. UN. https://www.un.org/sustainabledevelopment/fr/development-agenda/

UN. (2024). *Times of crisis, times of change: Science for accelerating transformations to sustainable development*. Global Sustainable Development Report. https://sdgs.un.org/sites/default/files/2023-09/FINAL%20GSDR%202023-Digital%20-110923_1.pdf

UNDDG. (2019). *Leaving no one behind*. UNDDG. https://unsdg.un.org/fr/2030-agenda/universal-values/leave-no-one-behind

UNDDG. (2022). T*he high-level political forum on sustainable development calls for a renewed global commitment to save the SDGs and get the world back on track*. UNSDG. https://unsdg.un.org/fr/latest/stories/le-forum-politique-de-haut-niveau-pour-le-developpement-durable-appelle-un

Underdal, A., & Kim, R. E. (2017). The Sustainable Development Goals and multilateral agreements. In N. Kanie & F. Biermann (Eds.), *Governing Through Goals: Sustainable Development Goals as Governance Innovation* (pp. 241–258). MIT Press. doi:10.7551/mitpress/9780262035620.003.0010

UNDESA. (2020). *The SDG partnership guidebook: A practical guide to building high impact multi-stakeholder partnerships for the Sustainable Development Goals*. UNDESA. https://sdgs.un.org/sites/default/files/2022-02/SDG%20Partnership%20Guidebook%201.11.pdf

UNDESA. (2024a). *Multi-stakeholder partnerships*. UNDESA. https://sdgs.un.org/topics/multi-stakeholder-partnerships

UNDESA. (2024b). *Transforming our world: the 2030 Agenda for Sustainable Development*. UNDESA. https://sdgs.un.org/2030agenda

UNDESA. (2024c). *About the SDG accelerations*. UNDESA. https://sdgs.un.org/partnerships/action-networks/acceleration-actions/about

UNDESA. (2024d). *Sustainable Development*. UNDESA. https://sdgs.un.org/goals

UNDP. (2024). *Climate Promise: Uruguay*. UNDP. https://climatepromise.undp.org/what-we-do/where-we-work/uruguay

UNEP. (2018). *Single-use plastics: A roadmap for sustainability*. UNEP. https://www.unep.org/resources/report/single-use-plastics-roadmap-sustainability

UNEP. (2022). *State of Finance for Nature. Time to act: Doubling investment by 2025 and eliminating nature-negative finance flows*. UNEP. https://www.unep.org/resources/state-finance-nature-2022

UNFCCC. (1998). *Kyoto Protocol to the United Nations Framework Convention on Climate Change*. UNFCCC. https://unfccc.int/resource/docs/convkp/kpeng.pdf

UNFCCC. (2024). *The Paris Agreement: What is the Paris Agreement?* UNFCC. https://unfccc.int/process-and-meetings/the-paris-agreement

United Nations Development Programme. (2013). *Humanity divided: Tackling inequality in developing countries. UNDP, Bureau for Development Policy (BDP)*. UNDP. https://www.undp.org/sites/g/files/zskgke326/files/publications/French_web_low.pdf

United Nations Sustainable Development Group. (2023). *Six Transitions: Investment Pathways to Deliver the SDGs*. UN.

United Nations World Tourism Organisation. (2015). *Tourism and the Sustainable Development Goals*. UN. http://cf.cdn.unwto.org/sites/all/files/pdf/sustainable_deve lopment_goals_brochure.pdf

United Nations World Tourism Organisation/ Pacific Asia Travel Association. (2015). Global Trends Shaping Tourism in Asia Pacific. UN. http://www.hotelsandtravel ler.com/review/unwtopata-report-

United Nations. (2015). *Transforming our world: The 2030 Agenda for Sustainable Development*. UN. https://sdgs.un.org/2030agenda

United Nations. (2016). *Public-Private Partnerships and the 2030 Agenda for Sustainable Development: Fit for purpose?* UN. https://sdgs.un.org/publications/public-private-partnerships-and-2030-agenda-sustainable-development-fit-purpose-18018

United Nations. (2018). *Sustainable Development Goal 11: Make cities and human settlements inclusive, safe, resilient and sustainable*. UN. https://sustainabledevelopment.un.org/sdg11

United Nations. (2021). *SDG7 Energy Compact of Germany; A next Decade Action Agenda to advance SDG7 on sustainable energy for all, in line with the goals of the Paris Agreement on Climate Change*. UN. https://un.org/sites/un2.un.org/files/germany.pdf

United Nations. (2022, December). *High level political forum on sustainable development*. UN. https://sustainabledevelopment.un.org/hlpf

UNOPS. (2024). *Projects and locations*. UNOPS. https://www.unops.org/project-locations

Unterhalter, E. (2017). Measuring education for the Millennium Development Goals: reflections on targets, indicators, and a post-2015 framework. In The MDGs, Capabilities and Human Rights (pp. 80-91). Routledge.

UNWater. (2022). *Country Acceleration Case Study - Senegal*. UNWater. https://www.unwater.org/publications/country-acceleration-case-study-senegal

UNWTO. (n.d.). *Tourism and the sustainable development goals*. UNWTO. publication/tourism-and-sustainable-development-goal

van den Hurk, M., Brogaard, L., Lember, V., Helby Petersen, O., & Witz, P. (2016). National Varieties of Public–Private Partnerships (PPPs): A Comparative Analysis of PPP-Supporting Units in 19 European Countries. *Journal of Comparative Policy Analysis*, *18*(1), 1–20. doi:10.1080/13876988.2015.1006814

Compilation of References

Varadarajan, R. (2020). Customer information resources advantage, marketing strategy, and business performance: A market resources-based view. *Industrial Marketing Management*, *89*, 89–97. doi:10.1016/j.indmarman.2020.03.003

Vargas, G., & De La Vega- Navarro, A. (2021). Public-Private Partnerships for a Sustainable Urban Development: A Literature Review. *Sustainability*, *13*(24), 14222.

Var, T., & Ap, J. (2013). Tourism and world peace. In *Global tourism* (pp. 63–76). Routledge.

Väyrynen, R. (2002). Reforming the World Order: Multi- and Plurilateral Approaches. In B. Hettne & B. Odén (Eds.), *Global Governance in the 21st Century: Alternative Perspectives on World Order* (pp. 106–146). Almkvist & Wiksell International.

Verganti, R. (2009). *Design driven innovation: changing the rules of competition by radically innovating what things mean*. Harvard Business Press.

Verhun, A. M. & Bondarchuk, J. A. (2022). Role of tourism industry growth in attaining sustainable development goals in a modern globalized world. *Journal of strategic economics of research*, *1*(6), 8-16. doi:10.30857/2786-5398.2022.1.1

Vortiguez, T., Giordano, T., Bakkour, N., & Boussichas, M. (2014). Financing the post-2015 sustainable development agenda. In R. K. Pachauri, A. Paugam, T. Ribera, L. Tubiana, P. G. D. Chakrabarti, R. Jozan, D. Kamelgarn & T. Voituriez (Eds.), Building the future we want (179-190). UNDESA.

Vujko, A., & Gajić, T. (2014). The government policy impact on economic development of tourism. *Ekonomika Poljoprivrede*, *61*(3), 789–804. doi:10.5937/ekoPolj1403789V

Wach, D., Stephan, U., Gorgievski, M. J., & Wegge, J. (2020). Entrepreneurs' achieved success: Developing a multi-faceted measure. *The International Entrepreneurship and Management Journal*, *16*(3), 1123–1151. doi:10.1007/s11365-018-0532-5

Wachira, J. M., Karimi, N., & Mberia, D. K. (2022). Critical success factors influencing the effectiveness of public-private partnerships (PPPs) in infrastructure development projects: A case study of Kenya. *Journal of Public Procurement*, *22*(3), 399–422.

Wang, C. N., Nguyen, V. T., Duong, D. H., & Thai, H. T. N. (2018). A hybrid fuzzy analysis network process (FANP) and the technique for order of preference by similarity to ideal solution (TOPSIS) approaches for solid waste to energy plant location selection in Vietnam. *Applied Sciences (Basel, Switzerland)*, *8*(7), 1100. doi:10.3390/app8071100

Wang, H., Sun, X., & Shi, Y. (2024). Commercial investment in public–private partnerships: The impact of government characteristics. *Local Government Studies*, *50*(1), 230–260. doi:10.1080/03003930.2023.2198217

Wang, H., Xiong, W., Wu, G., & Zhu, D. (2018). Public–private partnership in Public Administration discipline: A literature review. *Public Management Review*, *20*(2), 293–316. doi:10.1080/14719037.2017.1313445

Wang, X. (2009). The new Chinese anti-monopoly law: A survey of a work in progress. *Antitrust Bulletin*, *54*(3), 579–619. doi:10.1177/0003603X0905400303

Wang, X., Cai, L., Zhu, X., & Deng, S. (2020). Female entrepreneurs' gender roles, social capital, and willingness to choose external financing. *Asian Business & Management*, 1–26.

Wapner, P. (2021). Thresholds of injustice: challenging the politics of environmental postponement. In *Our Extractive Age* (pp. 48–67). Routledge. doi:10.4324/9781003127611-5

Waylen, K. A., Blackstock, K. L., van Hulst, F. J., Damian, C., Horváth, F., Johnson, R. K., Kanka, R., Külvik, M., Macleod, C. J. A., Meissner, K., Oprina-Pavelescu, M. M., Pino, J., Primmer, E., Rîşnoveanu, G., Šatalová, B., Silander, J., Špulerová, J., Suškevičs, M., & Van Uytvanck, J. (2019). Policy-driven monitoring and evaluation: Does it support adaptive management of socio-ecological systems? *The Science of the Total Environment, 662*, 373–384. doi:10.1016/j.scitotenv.2018.12.462 PMID:30690371

Weisbach D. Metcalf G. E. (2009). *The Design of a Carbon Tax*. https://ssrn.com/abstract=1327260 doi:10.2139/ssrn.1327260

Weiss, T. G. (2000). Governance, good governance and global governance: Conceptual and actual challenges. *Third World Quarterly, 21*(5), 795–814. doi:10.1080/713701075

Wells, S. J. (2021). *Women entrepreneurs: Developing leadership for success*. Routledge. doi:10.4324/9781003250111

Werners, S. E., Sparkes, E., Totin, E., Abel, N., Bhadwal, S., Butler, J. R., Douxchamps, S., James, H., Methner, N., Siebeneck, J., Stringer, L. C., Vincent, K., Wise, R. M., & Tebboth, M. G. (2021). Advancing climate resilient development pathways since the IPCC's fifth assessment report. *Environmental Science & Policy, 126*, 168–176. doi:10.1016/j.envsci.2021.09.017

WHO. (2022). *Ambient (outdoor) air pollution*. WHO. https://www.who.int/news-room/fact-sheets/detail/ambient-(outdoor)-air-quality-and-health

Willis, K. (2023). Development as modernisation: Rostow's the stages of economic growth. *Geography (Sheffield, England), 108*(1), 33–37. doi:10.1080/00167487.2023.2170073

Wirna-Putri, N., Pristi-Rahmah, S., Djafri, D., Sandra-Olivia, I., & Winanda-Putri, U. (2021). The effectiveness of the non-free plastic bag policy to reduce plastic waste in the community of Padang. *E3S Web of Conferences, 331*, 02022. doi:10.1051/e3sconf/202133102022

Wissema, W., & Dellink, R. (2007). AGE analysis of the impact of a carbon energy tax on the Irish economy. *Ecological Economics, 61*(4), 671–683. doi:10.1016/j.ecolecon.2006.07.034

World Bank. (2024). *World Bank Group and The 2030 Agenda*. World Bank. https://www.worldbank.org/en/programs/sdgs-2030-agenda

Wright, S., & Mallia, C. (2003). The Potential of Eco-Taxes as Instruments for Sustainability: An Analysis of the Critical Design Elements. *The Journal of Transdisciplinary Environmental Studies, 2*(2), 1 14. https://journal-tes.ruc.dk/wp-content/uploads/2021/05/Stuart-og-Christina_lav-1.pdf

Wu, P., Weng, C. X. C., & Joseph, S. A. (2021). Crossing the Rubicon? The implications of RCEP on anti-monopoly enforcement on dominant E-commerce platforms in China. *Computer Law & Security Report, 42*, 105608. doi:10.1016/j.clsr.2021.105608

Xie, J., Xia, Z., Tian, X., & Liu, Y. (2023). Nexus and synergy between the low-carbon economy and circular economy: A systematic and critical review. *Environmental Impact Assessment Review, 100*, 107077. doi:10.1016/j.eiar.2023.107077

Xinning, Z. (2023). The Comparison of Securities Law and Competition Law among China, Australia and Japan. *International Journal of Frontiers in Sociology, 5*(9).

Yalçın, A. Z. (2010). Sürdürülebilir kalkınma için düşük karbon ekonomisinin önemi ve Türkiye için bir değerlendirme. *Balıkesir Üniversitesi Sosyal Bilimler Enstitüsü Dergisi, 13*(24), 186–203.

Ye, S. (2012). Research on Urban Road Traffic Congestion Charging Based on Sustainable Development. *Physics Procedia, 24*, 1567–1572. doi:10.1016/j.phpro.2012.02.231

Compilation of References

Yin, J., Li, H., & Wang, Y. (2023). Public-private partnership and responsible innovation: A framework based on a systematic literature review. *Technological Forecasting and Social Change*, *192*, 120452.

Yin, W. (2019). Integrating Sustainable Development Goals into the Belt and Road Initiative: Would It Be a New Model for Green and Sustainable Investment? *Sustainability (Basel)*, *11*(24), 69–91. doi:10.3390/su11246991

Young, O., Arild, U., Kanie, N., Andresen, S., Bernstein, S., Biermann, F., Gupta, J., Haas, P. M., Iguchi, M., Kok, M., Levy, M., Nilsson, M., Pintér, L., & Stevens, C. (2014). Earth System Challenges and a Multi-Layered Approach for the Sustainable Development Goals. *POST2015/UNU-IAS Policy Brief. United Nations University Institute for the Advanced Study of Sustainability*. UNU. https://i.unu.edu/media/ias.unu.edu-en/project/2218/Post2015_UNU-IAS_PolicyBrief1.pdf

Zeng, J. (2017). Does Europe Matter? The Role of Europe in Chinese Narratives of 'One Belt One Road' and 'New Type of Great Power Relations.'. *Journal of Common Market Studies*, *55*(5), 1162–1176. doi:10.1111/jcms.12535

Zeng, Y. (2024). Riding the Trojan Horse? EU Accession and Chinese Investment in CEE Countries. *Journal of Contemporary China*, *33*(147), 486–501. doi:10.1080/10670564.2023.2196507

Zhang, A. (2021). *Chinese antitrust exceptionalism: How the rise of China challenges global regulation*. Oxford University Press. doi:10.1093/oso/9780198826569.001.0001

Zhang, A. H. (2019). Strategic public shaming: Evidence from Chinese antitrust investigations. *The China Quarterly*, *237*, 174–195. doi:10.1017/S0305741018001340

Zhang, D., Zheng, M., Feng, G. F., & Chang, C. P. (2022). Does an environmental policy bring to green innovation in renewable energy? *Renewable Energy*, *195*, 1113–1124. doi:10.1016/j.renene.2022.06.074

Zhang, J., & Zhang, Y. (2020). Tourism and gender equality: An Asian perspective. *Annals of Tourism Research*, *85*, 103067. doi:10.1016/j.annals.2020.103067

Zhang, J., & Zhang, Y. (2021). A qualitative comparative analysis of tourism and gender equality in emerging economies. *Journal of Hospitality and Tourism Management*, *46*, 284–292. doi:10.1016/j.jhtm.2021.01.009

Zhang, Z., & Wu, B. (2019). Governing China's administrative monopolies under the anti-monopoly law: A ten-year review (2008–2018) and beyond. *Journal of Competition Law & Economics*, *15*(1), 718–760. doi:10.1093/joclec/nhz009

Zhao, A., Song, X., Li, J., Yuan, Q., Pei, Y., Li, R., & Hitch, M. (2023). Effects of Carbon Tax on Urban Carbon Emission Reduction: Evidence in China Environmental Governance. *International Journal of Environmental Research and Public Health*, *20*(3), 2289. doi:10.3390/ijerph20032289 PMID:36767655

Zhou, L. (2023). Towards sustainability in mineral resources. *Ore Geology Reviews*, *160*, 105600. doi:10.1016/j.oregeorev.2023.105600

Zimmer, C. (2014). The Oldest Rocks on Earth. *Scientific American*, *310*(3), 58–63. doi:10.1038/scientificamerican0314-58 PMID:24660329

Zreik, M. (2023a). Analytical study on Foreign Direct Investment Divestment Inflows and Outflows in Developing Economies: Evidence of China. *Chinese Economy*, *56*(6), 415–430. doi:10.1080/10971475.2023.2193118

Zreik, M. (2023b). Harnessing the Power of Blockchain Technology in Modern China: A Comprehensive Exploration. In L. Ferreira, M. Cruz, E. Cruz, H. Quintela, & M. Cunha (Eds.), *Supporting Technologies and the Impact of Blockchain on Organizations and Society* (pp. 94–112). IGI Global. doi:10.4018/978-1-6684-5747-4.ch007

Zreik, M. (2024). Navigating the Green Path: A Perspective on Sustainable Consumption, Business Innovation, and Customer Experience in China. In M. Machado Carvalho & M. Rodrigues (Eds.), *Sustainable Consumption Experience and Business Models in the Modern World* (pp. 70–88). IGI Global. doi:10.4018/978-1-6684-9277-2.ch003

Zreik, M., Iqbal, B. A., & Rahman, M. N. (2022). Outward FDI: determinants and flows in emerging economies: evidence from China. *China and WTO Review*, 8(2), 385–402. doi:10.14330/cwr.2022.8.2.07

Zürn, M. (2013). Globalization and global governance. In *Handbook of International Relations* (pp. 401–425). SAGE Publications. doi:10.4135/9781446247587.n16

About the Contributors

Ali Gökhan Gölçek is a Ph.D. Research Assistant of Department of Public Finance at Niğde Ömer Halisdemir University, Turkey. His scholarly interests span poverty, energy policy, public finance policy, health economics, and international political economy. He completed his PhD in Public Finance at Pamukkale University in 2022. Gölçek has published numerous articles and book chapters.

Şeyda Güdek-Gölçek is a Ph.D. Research Assistant at Niğde Ömer Halisdemir University's Department of Political Science and International Relations. She completed her PhD in International Relations at Ege University in 2022. Her research focuses on women's poverty, International Relations theory, and international political economics. Güdek-Gölçek has published numerous articles exploring the socio-economic status of women in Turkey, contributing significant insights into gender disparities and their policy implications within the Turkish context.

***

Mukesh Shankar Bharti is an assistant professor and research scholar with a research background in foreign policy analysis and social science research. The author holds a PhD degree in International Relations with a specialization in Central and Eastern Europe. His research area includes democracy, political institutions, geopolitics, European Union, East and Southeast Asia.

Laksitha M. Herath (BA in accounting, MSc in Accounting) Laksitha M. Herath earned her Master of Science in Accounting degree at New York University's Stern School of Business and works at Pricewaterhouse Coopers (PwC). Prior to her current endeavor, she gained valuable experience as a program accountant at Enstar Group Limited, a well-known global insurance company, and at Deloitte, a Big Four accounting firm, in Atlanta and New York. Laksitha holds a Bachelor of Arts degree in Accounting from Clark Atlanta University, where she held executive positions in its Toastmasters Club and she and a team of selected classmates won the Deloitte Regional Case Study Competition. She also published 4 book chapters and an article in a reputable journal. In her leisure time, she enjoys photography, cooking, and quality time with her family and friends.

Siriyama Kanthi Herath (BCOM Hons), MBA, MCOM (Hons, ACCY), PhD Dr. Siriyama Kanthi Herath is an Associate Professor of Accounting at Clark Atlanta University's School of Business (CAU) and was a Renwick Faculty Fellow at New York University's Stern School of Business in 2022. She earned a Bachelor of Commerce Honors and an MBA from the University of Colombo in Sri Lanka, as well as a Ph.D. and a Master of Commerce Honors in Accounting from the University of Wollongong in Australia. She worked at the University of Lynchburg, Georgia State University and Georgia Institute of Technology before joining CAU. Prior to relocating to the United States, Dr. Herath worked in Australia at the University of Wollongong and Western Sydney University and in Sri Lanka at the University of Ruhuna and the University of Colombo. She holds positions on the editorial boards of multiple academic journals and has contributed over 70 publications to a diverse range of journals. She has published 6 book chapters. Her research areas include Accounting Education, Management Control and Outsourcing, Cost Management, Corporate Governance, Data Analytics, and Sustainability Accounting. She is a Distinguished Toastmaster and served as the President and Treasurer of the Georgia Institute of Technology Toastmasters International Club from 2019 to 2020, the Treasurer of the Emory University Toastmasters International Club from 2019 to 2020, and as an Area Director from 2020 to 2021 in Georgia, United States. Additionally, she possesses the TESOL Professional Certificate from Arizona State University and the Professional Certificate in Google Data Analytics. In her leisure time, she enjoys traveling and gardening.

Nurul Hidayana Mohd Noor, Ph.D. is Senior Lecturer in Faculty of Administrative Science and Policy Studies, Universiti Teknologi MARA (UiTM), Seremban, Negeri Sembilan, Malaysia (ORCID:). Her main research activity is entrepreneurship, environmental, nonprofit, organizational management, and youth studies. She has published widely on these subjects in publications such as the Journal of Entrepreneurship in Emerging Economies, Journal of Entrepreneurship and Public Policy, and Human Service Organizations: Management, Leadership & Governance.

Noralina Omar, Ph.D. is a Senior Lecturer in the Department of Social Justice and Administration, Faculty of Arts and Social Sciences, Universiti Malaya, Kuala Lumpur, Malaysia (ORCID:). Her main research activity is family well-being, children's development and welfare, social work studies, and youth studies. She has published widely on these subjects in publications such as The Malaysian Journal of Social Administration, Sarjana, and Pertanika Journal of Social Sciences & Humanities.

Marlissa J Phillips, DBA, MBA, CPA, CFE Assistant Accounting Professor at Clark Atlanta University in Atlanta, Georgia. Marlissa has been training and encouraging accounting students for over 10 years at Clark Atlanta. She is an advocate of minority students pursing CPA designation. Her research area deals primarily with addressing the needs of accounting programs and elevating the accounting profession.

Parimal Roy had his career was triggered in January 2006, and had worked in the project management sector for ten years (2006-2015). Then, paced in academia from 2015; before that, he started a career in 2006 in the Development sector, collaborating with international development partners like ADB, DFID, UNFPA, SIDA, PKSF, and Orbis International. Nevertheless, he is immensely inquisitive about the affinity between theory, policy, and development practice among ethnic groups; to this end, he dissected several policies and international frameworks that have been published. He is an undergraduate and post-graduated in Anthropology and another Master's in Business Administration and is now pursuing a PhD (expected in 2024) on customary law and Community[Indigenous-Santals] Development at Universiti Malaya, Malaysia. Furthermore, satisfied the "FinTech & Regulator Innovation" and "Digital Assets for Regulator" at the University of Cambridge, UK, by getting ADBI scholarship. Studied Social justice for resilience, inclusive and productive rural economics at ITCILO by getting its scholarship.

About the Contributors

UNHCR also awarded him to study International refugee law. He also obtained two PGDs in Project Management and Criminology.

Manisha Seal is an academician and a keen researcher presented research papers in many national and international level conferences and published numerous research articles in UGC care, Scopus indexed and peer reviewed journals. She has recently been honored with Indian Women Talent Award (IWTA) in Educators- Category on 19th March 2022 for her contribution in guiding, teaching, empowering and developing research aptitude among young Women and also been awarded with Certificate of Honor - Teacher's Day 2021 by Chairman BOE (2020-21) BCom (Vocational), Bangalore University & Principal, Bengaluru Amrita Degree College on 5th September 2021 for being the guiding force and strength to students' community. Dr Manisha holds 19 plus Years of teaching experience to impart knowledge to PG and UG students at reputed colleges. Presently designated as Assistant Professor in Department of Tourism and Travel Management, Jyoti Nivas College Autonomous.

Yogendra Singh is an acting head of the Amity Institute of Public Policy at Amity University, Noida, Uttar Pradesh, India. He is a professor of public policy and governance with expertise in public administration.

Sureyya Yigit is a Professor of Politics and International Relations at the School of Politics and Diplomacy at New Vision University in Tbilisi, Georgia. His current research interests focus on the Ukraine crisis, Globalisation, African development and post-communist transition. He is an Editorial Board member of the IGI Book Series Conflict Management - 3 Volumes, an International Academic Board member of RIPEA - Journal of Argentine Foreign Policy Research, an Associate Editor on the Editorial Board of the International Journal of Green Business. He is also the senior consultant to ZDS – Women's Democracy Network Public Fund, a non-governmental organisation based in Bishkek, Kyrgyz Republic, and a consultant to Aeropodium, a London-based business. Professor Yigit has recently published books entitled India-Mongolia Relations: Beyond Greater Central Asia in 2023 and Africa at Crossroads; Society, Security and Geopolitics, published in April 2024.

Mohamad Zreik, a Postdoctoral Fellow at Sun Yat-sen University, is a recognized scholar in International Relations. His recent work in soft power diplomacy compares China's methods in the Middle East and East Asia. His extensive knowledge spans Middle Eastern Studies, China-Arab relations, East Asian and Asian Affairs, Eurasian geopolitics, and Political Economy, providing him a unique viewpoint in his field. Dr. Zreik is a proud recipient of a PhD from Central China Normal University (Wuhan). He's written numerous acclaimed papers, many focusing on China's Belt and Road Initiative and its Arab-region impact. His groundbreaking research has established him as a leading expert in his field. Presently, he furthers his research on China's soft power diplomacy tactics at Sun Yat-sen University. His significant contributions make him a crucial figure in understanding contemporary international relations.

Index

A

Academic Contribution 136, 144
Agriculture 21-22, 25, 27, 29-30, 35, 87, 102-104, 107, 109, 166, 186-187, 194, 202
Anti-Monopoly Law (AML) 225, 227-232, 238

B

Belt and Road Initiative (BRI) 146-149, 151-159, 161-163
Biodiversity 2, 17, 19-20, 22-25, 27, 31, 35-36, 41, 95, 103-104, 107, 112, 153-154, 163, 166, 169, 186
Biosphere 19-20, 23-24, 26, 37

C

Carbon Footprint 37, 94, 104, 118, 169
Carbon Neutral 37
Carbon Tax 94, 96-98, 104-107, 109-110, 112, 114-118
Carbon taxation 97
Case Studies 94, 103, 108, 113, 120, 126, 128, 133, 135, 140, 144, 217, 223, 225-226, 231
Central and Eastern Europe (CEE) 158, 163
Challenges 1-2, 9, 11-13, 15-17, 28, 33-34, 37, 40-43, 59, 88-89, 92-94, 96-98, 100-101, 103, 105-106, 108-111, 120-121, 123-125, 129-131, 134-135, 137-138, 141, 144, 147-148, 150, 152-158, 162-163, 168, 177-178, 181, 183, 186-187, 190, 192, 196-199, 201, 204, 213-214, 217-219, 221, 223, 225-226, 232-235, 237, 239
China 34, 98, 117, 146-149, 151-162, 170-171, 197, 223-239
Circular Economy 19, 32-34, 37, 106, 166-167, 171, 177, 180-181, 237
Climate Action 6-7, 11, 93, 96, 106, 165-166, 190, 223, 228, 230-232, 234
Climate Change 6-7, 19, 21-22, 24-25, 27, 31, 37-38, 50, 92, 94-98, 100, 102, 104-106, 108-109, 111-113, 117-118, 120, 124, 133-134, 137, 143, 163, 165-167, 169, 184, 186, 189, 192-193, 229-230
Commitment 19, 39-41, 43-45, 47-50, 62-63, 98-99, 104-106, 108, 110, 149, 155, 158, 207, 213, 224, 227-228
Community 2, 4, 6, 11, 13, 40-41, 43, 45, 48-49, 60-61, 68-69, 75-76, 78-88, 90-91, 94, 110, 112, 117, 122-123, 125, 127-128, 133, 161, 184, 186-187, 189, 193, 201, 209, 212, 214-215
Competition Law 223-238
Competition Law and Policy 223-226, 228, 232-235
Consumption 17, 19, 21-22, 26, 28-33, 37, 93, 95, 98-100, 112-114, 165, 167, 169, 177, 187, 192-194, 224, 228-232, 234, 238
Corporate Social Responsibility 38, 141
Critical raw materials 164, 167-168, 170-172, 177-181
Customary law 75-76, 79, 84, 87-88, 90-91

D

decision-making 4, 60, 79, 84, 86, 100, 125, 130-132, 135, 138, 144, 148, 150, 155, 164, 167, 173, 177, 191, 233
Developing Economy 196, 222
Development 1-17, 21-23, 25-45, 47, 50, 54, 59-63, 75-86, 88-95, 98-99, 101-102, 105-111, 113-149, 151-167, 170-172, 175-176, 178, 180, 182-184, 186-197, 199-201, 203, 212-227, 229-239
Discontent 39, 42, 44, 53-64, 71-73

E

Eco-fiscal policies 92-94, 109-110, 118
Eco-Fiscal Policy 94, 103, 107, 110, 118
Ecology 17, 32, 36, 88, 111, 219
Economic Efficiency 100, 224-225, 227, 234, 238
Economic Growth 4, 26, 33, 36, 76, 94-95, 97, 105-106, 110, 129-130, 137, 147-148, 151, 153-154, 156, 158, 163-165, 169, 171, 175, 177-178, 182, 184,

186, 188-190, 192-193, 196, 223-225, 228-230, 232, 234-235
Enablers 196, 198, 202, 209, 213-214, 217, 220
Entrepreneurship 34, 134-135, 140, 172, 196-199, 201-203, 210, 212-218, 220-222, 229, 235
Environment 2-4, 10-11, 14, 17-19, 26-29, 32-33, 38, 45, 81-82, 89, 91, 95, 104, 107, 111-115, 117, 123-125, 132-134, 138, 140, 144, 147-149, 159-160, 167, 169-170, 186-187, 198, 212, 215, 218, 227-229, 233, 235-238
environmental concerns 164, 178, 183, 187
Environmental Conservation 136, 147, 223, 232
Environmental externalities 92-94, 118
Environmental Impact Assessment 181, 238
Ethical Considerations 144
ethical standards 119
Ethnic Groups 75, 77-78, 80-81, 85, 87, 91

F

Fair Trade 223, 234
Fiscal sustainability 92
fuzzy approach 164

G

Global Governance 1-7, 9, 11-16
Global Partnership 1, 4, 15-16
Goal-setting Governance 16
Governance and Accountability 144
Governance Theory 125, 144, 150
Green Technologies 102, 165, 167, 169, 175, 177, 238
Greenwashing 38, 230

H

HLPF 6, 11, 13, 39-40, 43-44, 60-62

I

Impact Investing 134-135, 141, 144
Inclusivity 10, 137, 144, 153
Informed Consent 144
Infrastructure Development 121, 124, 127, 129-130, 141, 143-144, 147-149, 151-156, 163
Innovation 4, 6, 8, 13-14, 35, 41, 50, 95, 97, 103, 110-111, 127, 129-130, 134, 137, 139, 141, 144, 148, 156, 158, 163, 165, 172, 175, 186-187, 189, 191, 196, 200, 203, 211, 213-214, 218, 220, 222, 228-234, 236-238
Innovation and Learning Culture 144

Institutional Capability 233-234, 238
Institutional Theory 125, 144, 150
Interdisciplinary Approach 144
International Cooperation 4, 15-16, 147-148, 159, 233
International Development 2, 4, 16, 127, 158

L

Leaves No One Behind (LNOB) 63
literature review 89, 113, 119-123, 143-144, 161, 166, 182, 193, 199, 220, 222

M

Market Dominance 229, 232, 238
Member States 4-7, 11, 39-40, 63, 120, 149, 152-153
Mumprenuers 196, 198, 201, 204-205, 207, 209, 215, 217
Mumprenuership 222

N

National Development and Reform Commission (NDRC) 232, 238
Nationally Determined Contributions (NDC) 118

O

Oceans 17, 19-21, 25, 29, 100

P

Policy Fortification 144
Policy Implications 113, 144, 196, 199, 216
Pollution 18, 21-22, 24, 29, 31-32, 34, 36-38, 41, 93-97, 99-101, 103, 105, 107, 111, 113, 116-117, 122, 165-166, 169, 186-187, 225, 235
Population 17, 19, 21-22, 26-31, 33-35, 54, 57, 64, 84-85, 87, 95, 100, 127, 131, 156, 169, 172, 175, 177, 197, 206, 221
Practical Guidance for Practitioners 144
Public-Private Partnership (PPP) 126-127, 145-148, 150-151, 163

R

regional development 42, 149, 155, 159, 164, 184
Responsible Consumption and Production 93, 165, 187, 224, 228, 230, 232, 234
Risk Management 8, 129-130, 133-135, 137, 141, 145, 220

S

Santals 75-78, 86-88, 90-91
Social Inequalities 39, 47, 60, 63
State Administration for Market Regulation (SAMR) 227-228, 232, 239
supply risks 167, 178, 181
Sustainable 1-8, 10-17, 23, 25-26, 28-31, 33-35, 37-45, 47, 50, 59-63, 75-104, 106-107, 109-111, 113, 115-130, 132, 134-147, 151-156, 158-161, 163-167, 169-171, 173, 176-184, 186-197, 212, 215-216, 218-220, 223-239
Sustainable Development 1-4, 6-8, 10-17, 23, 25-26, 28-31, 33-35, 37-45, 47, 50, 59-63, 75-79, 81-82, 84-86, 89-95, 98-99, 102, 106, 110-111, 115-130, 134-147, 152-156, 158-161, 163-167, 176, 178, 180, 182-184, 186-197, 216, 218-219, 223-227, 229-237, 239
Sustainable Development Goals (SDGs) 2-3, 11, 13, 39-40, 63, 79, 84, 92, 94, 110, 119-122, 124-126, 137-138, 144-145, 152, 154-155, 164, 182-183, 186, 190, 197, 223-226, 239
Sustainable Tourism 182, 190-194
Systems Thinking 125, 145

T

Technology 3-4, 6, 8, 10, 12, 19, 26, 29-31, 34, 37, 81, 87, 98, 102, 113, 120, 122, 124, 128, 133-135, 153, 157, 164-165, 167, 169-172, 180-181, 196, 199-201, 203, 207, 209-210, 212-214, 218-220, 231, 237-238
The Geography of Discontent 54-56, 62, 64
TOPSIS 164, 167, 173-174, 176, 180-181
Tourism and SDG 182

V

VNRs 39, 43, 45

Publishing Tomorrow's Research Today

Uncover Current Insights and Future Trends in Scientific, Technical, & Medical (STM)
with IGI Global's Cutting-Edge Recommended Books

IGI Global
www.igi-global.com

Print Only, E-Book Only, or Print + E-Book.
Order direct through IGI Global's Online Bookstore at **www.igi-global.com** or through your preferred provider.

Artificial Intelligence in the Age of Nanotechnology
ISBN: 9798369303689
© 2024; 299 pp.
List Price: US$ **300**

Quantum Innovations at the Nexus of Biomedical Intelligence
ISBN: 9798369314791
© 2024; 287 pp.
List Price: US$ **330**

Intelligent Engineering Applications and Applied Sciences for Sustainability
ISBN: 9798369300442
© 2023; 542 pp.
List Price: US$ **270**

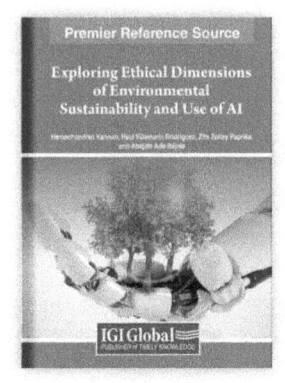

Exploring Ethical Dimensions of Environmental Sustainability and Use of AI
ISBN: 9798369308929
© 2024; 426 pp.
List Price: US$ **265**

AI-Based Digital Health Communication for Securing Assistive Systems
ISBN: 9781668489383
© 2023; 299 pp.
List Price: US$ **325**

Applications of Synthetic Biology in Health, Energy, and Environment
ISBN: 9781668465776
© 2023; 454 pp.
List Price: US$ **325**

Do you want to stay current on the latest research trends, product announcements, news, and special offers?
Join IGI Global's mailing list to receive customized recommendations, exclusive discounts, and more.
Sign up at: **www.igi-global.com/newsletters**.

Scan the QR Code here to view more related titles in STM.

www.igi-global.com | Sign up at www.igi-global.com/newsletters | facebook.com/igiglobal | twitter.com/igiglobal | linkedin.com/igiglobal

Ensure Quality Research is Introduced to the Academic Community

Become a Reviewer for IGI Global Authored Book Projects

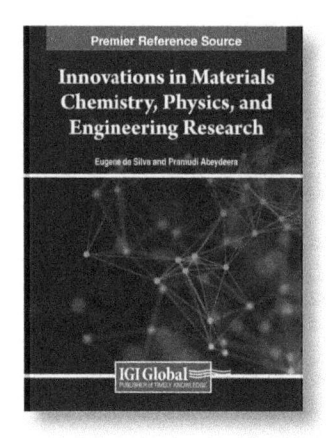

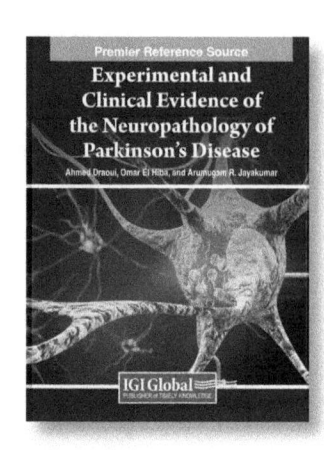

The overall success of an authored book project is dependent on quality and timely manuscript evaluations.

Applications and Inquiries may be sent to:
development@igi-global.com

Applicants must have a doctorate (or equivalent degree) as well as publishing, research, and reviewing experience. Authored Book Evaluators are appointed for one-year terms and are expected to complete at least three evaluations per term. Upon successful completion of this term, evaluators can be considered for an additional term.

If you have a colleague that may be interested in this opportunity, we encourage you to share this information with them.

IGI Global
Publishing Tomorrow's Research Today
www.igi-global.com

IGI Global Open Access Journal Program

Publishing Tomorrow's Research Today
IGI Global's Open Access Journal Program

Including Nearly 200 Peer-Reviewed, Gold (Full) Open Access Journals across IGI Global's Three Academic Subject Areas: Business & Management; Scientific, Technical, and Medical (STM); and Education

Consider Submitting Your Manuscript to One of These Nearly 200 Open Access Journals for to Increase Their Discoverability & Citation Impact

Web of Science Impact Factor **6.5**	Web of Science Impact Factor **4.7**	Web of Science Impact Factor **3.2**	Web of Science Impact Factor **2.6**
 JOURNAL OF **Organizational and End User Computing**	JOURNAL OF **Global Information Management**	INTERNATIONAL JOURNAL ON **Semantic Web and Information Systems**	JOURNAL OF **Database Management**

Choosing IGI Global's Open Access Journal Program Can Greatly Increase the Reach of Your Research

Higher Usage
Open access papers are 2-3 times more likely to be read than non-open access papers.

Higher Download Rates
Open access papers benefit from 89% higher download rates than non-open access papers.

Higher Citation Rates
Open access papers are 47% more likely to be cited than non-open access papers.

Submitting an article to a journal offers an invaluable opportunity for you to share your work with the broader academic community, fostering knowledge dissemination and constructive feedback.

Submit an Article and Browse the IGI Global Call for Papers Pages

We can work with you to find the journal most well-suited for your next research manuscript.
For open access publishing support, contact: journaleditor@igi-global.com

Publishing Tomorrow's Research Today
IGI Global
e-Book Collection

Including Essential Reference Books Within Three Fundamental Academic Areas

Business & Management
Scientific, Technical, & Medical (STM)
Education

- Acquisition options include Perpetual, Subscription, and Read & Publish
- No Additional Charge for Multi-User Licensing
- No Maintenance, Hosting, or Archiving Fees
- Continually Enhanced Accessibility Compliance Features (WCAG)

| Over **150,000+** Chapters | Contributions From **200,000+** Scholars Worldwide | More Than **1,000,000+** Citations | Majority of e-Books Indexed in Web of Science & Scopus | Consists of Tomorrow's Research Available Today! |

Recommended Titles from our e-Book Collection

Innovation Capabilities and Entrepreneurial Opportunities of Smart Working
ISBN: 9781799887973

Advanced Applications of Generative AI and Natural Language Processing Models
ISBN: 9798369305027

Using Influencer Marketing as a Digital Business Strategy
ISBN: 9798369305515

Human-Centered Approaches in Industry 5.0
ISBN: 9798369326473

Modeling and Monitoring Extreme Hydrometeorological Events
ISBN: 9781668487716

Data-Driven Intelligent Business Sustainability
ISBN: 9798369300497

Information Logistics for Organizational Empowerment and Effective Supply Chain Management
ISBN: 9798369301593

Data Envelopment Analysis (DEA) Methods for Maximizing Efficiency
ISBN: 9798369302552

Request More Information, or Recommend the IGI Global e-Book Collection to Your Institution's Librarian

For More Information or to Request a Free Trial, Contact IGI Global's e-Collections Team: eresources@igi-global.com | 1-866-342-6657 ext. 100 | 717-533-8845 ext. 100

Are You Ready to Publish Your Research?

IGI Global
Publishing Tomorrow's Research Today

IGI Global offers book authorship and editorship opportunities across three major subject areas, including Business, STM, and Education.

Benefits of Publishing with IGI Global:

- Free one-on-one editorial and promotional support.
- Expedited publishing timelines that can take your book from start to finish in less than one (1) year.
- Choose from a variety of formats, including Edited and Authored References, Handbooks of Research, Encyclopedias, and Research Insights.
- Utilize IGI Global's eEditorial Discovery® submission system in support of conducting the submission and double-blind peer review process.
- IGI Global maintains a strict adherence to ethical practices due in part to our full membership with the Committee on Publication Ethics (COPE).
- Indexing potential in prestigious indices such as Scopus®, Web of Science™, PsycINFO®, and ERIC – Education Resources Information Center.
- Ability to connect your ORCID iD to your IGI Global publications.
- Earn honorariums and royalties on your full book publications as well as complimentary content and exclusive discounts.

Join Your Colleagues from Prestigious Institutions, Including:

- Australian National University
- Massachusetts Institute of Technology
- Johns Hopkins University
- Tsinghua University
- Harvard University
- Columbia University in the City of New York

Learn More at: www.igi-global.com/publish
or Contact IGI Global's Aquisitions Team at: acquisition@igi-global.com

Milton Keynes UK
Ingram Content Group UK Ltd.
UKHW020126150624
444031UK00007B/135